CO 1 02 44286 E1

STANLEY

28. APR. 1973

-6 DEC. 1973
DC

27. NOV. 2003

CW01215456

1 - 496.   Form L 31.

BOOKSTORE LOAN

A557398

COUNTY COUNCIL OF DURHAM
COUNTY LIBRARY

The last date entered is the date by which the book must be returned, and fines will be charged if the book is kept after this date.

WAR, POLITICS AND FINANCE
UNDER EDWARD I

WAR, POLITICS AND FINANCE
UNDER EDWARD I

MICHAEL PRESTWICH

FABER AND FABER LIMITED
3 Queen Square, London

*First published in 1972
by Faber and Faber Limited
3 Queen Square London WC1
Printed in Great Britain by
Western Printing Services Limited
All rights reserved*

ISBN 0 571 09042 7

© *1972, M. C. Prestwich*

TO M.P. AND J.O.P.

PREFACE

The reign of Edward I is notable for its many and varied achievements, the most familiar being the conquest of Wales and the series of campaigns in Scotland, the clarification and development of the law, and the growth of parliament. To the historian who wishes to go behind these achievements to discover the methods employed, the resources available, the difficulties encountered and the costs incurred, the period is also notable for the profusion of evidence which has survived. The chronicles are weaker than for the twelfth century, but the government records are far richer and fuller than for any previous period. Most striking is the volume of exchequer and household material, including writs, correspondence and accounts, and ranging from the most formal pipe rolls to the scrappiest of memoranda. There is a great deal to be learnt from such evidence about the detailed workings of Edward I's administration and the society he sought to control.

It is not the purpose of this book to do equal justice to all aspects of the period. Much of the surviving evidence was produced for the purpose of organizing and conducting war, and the aim is to consider how Edward I mobilized and directed his resources for the many campaigns in Wales, Gascony, Flanders and Scotland, how these campaigns were financed, and what the political and social consequences were of these expensive endeavours.

The book has developed out of a more limited study submitted as a doctoral thesis to the University of Oxford in 1968, on 'Edward I's Wars and Their Financing, 1294–1307'. My thanks are due to Dr. G. A. Holmes of St. Catherine's College who

PREFACE

supervised that study, and to Mr. J. Campbell of Worcester College who read and criticized much of it, and also made very helpful suggestions about the present work. I am also very grateful to Dr. E. B. Fryde of the University of Aberystwyth for his kind help in the early stages of my research. The staff of the Public Record Office showed much kindness and patience towards me. I am deeply indebted to the Governing Body of Christ Church, Oxford, for electing me to a Research Lectureship and thus making me a member of a highly stimulating and exceptionally agreeable society. I am equally grateful to the members of the Department of Mediaeval History at St. Andrews for their help and encouragement, and I apologize to those of them who may feel affronted by my refusal to bow to the Caledonian insistence on the use of the word 'Scottish'. In particular, I am extremely grateful to Professor Lionel Butler and to Miss Ann Kettle for reading the book in typescript, and for helpful advice and criticism. My thanks are also due to Douglas and Ann Johnson for their help with the proofs. By far my largest debt of gratitude is to my parents, especially to my father, for invaluable help, criticism and encouragement.

CONTENTS

	LIST OF ABBREVIATIONS	page 11
I	INTRODUCTION	13
II	HOUSEHOLDS AND RETINUES	41
III	CAVALRY SERVICE	67
IV	THE INFANTRY	92
V	VICTUALLING	114
VI	THE NAVY	137
VII	THE ADMINISTRATION AND COSTS OF WAR	151
VIII	THE CROWN REVENUE	177
IX	CREDIT FINANCE	204
X	THE CROWN AND THE MAGNATES	224
XI	THE CRISIS OF 1297 AND ITS ORIGINS	247
XII	POLITICS AND THE KING, 1298–1307	262
XIII	THE SOCIAL CONSEQUENCES OF WAR	282
	LIST OF SOURCES	291
	INDEX	299

Maps

1	Wales in the Time of Edward I	16
2	Scotland in the Time of Edward I	34

Figures

1	The Infantry Forces in 1300	96
2	The Infantry Forces in the Royal Army in 1301	97
3	The Infantry Forces in 1303	98

ABBREVIATIONS

B.I.H.R.	Bulletin of the Institute of Historical Research
B.M.	British Museum
Cal. Docs. Scot.	Calendar of Documents relating to Scotland, ed. J. Bain (Edinburgh, 1881–8)
C.C.R.	Calendar of Close Rolls
C.Ch.R.	Calendar of Charter Rolls
C.F.R.	Calendar of Fine Rolls
C.I.P.M.	Calendar of Inquisitions Post Mortem
C.P.R.	Calendar of Patent Rolls
C.V.C.R.	Calendar of Various Chancery Rolls
Ec.H.R.	Economic History Review
E.H.R.	English Historical Review
M.I.Ö.G.	Mitteilungen des Instituts für Österreichischen Geschichtsforschung
Parl. Writs	Parliamentary Writs and Writs of Military Summons, ed. F. Palgrave (London, 1827)
Rot. Parl.	Rotuli Parliamentorum
T.R.H.S.	Transactions of the Royal Historical Society

Unless otherwise specified, all manuscripts cited are in the Public Record Office, London.

I
INTRODUCTION

The historical importance of war extends far beyond the realms of tactics and strategy, victories and defeats. Edward I fought against the Welsh, the French and the Scots: today the great castles of Harlech, Conway, Caernarvon and Beaumaris still stand as a permanent reminder of his conquest of Wales, while the presence of the Stone of Scone in Westminster Abbey symbolizes the humiliation of Scotland at his hands. But the importance and interest of the king's wars do not lie only in such achievements. The country had to be organized on a massive scale to provide the armies, materials and money that were required for the many campaigns, and in this way war had a very powerful impact upon government, politics and society.

The period is of course remembered for much more than its wars. It was under Edward I that parliament was established as a normal feature of English political life. Important administrative developments took place under the guidance of Edward's civil servants, and in the history of English law his reign is of the greatest significance. The series of statutes that were enacted marked a new stage in the maturing of the legal system and provided an essential element if the common law was not to become hopelessly inflexible and antiquated. One major crisis and a series of subsequent disputes make the reign one of considerable constitutional interest. But this was above all a militaristic age, and war had its influence on all these developments. One of the major functions of parliament was the granting of war taxation, while the composition of the assembly was profoundly influenced by the king's methods of summoning magnates to serve on campaigns.

INTRODUCTION

The administrative changes that took place were a response to the needs of wartime. The issue of military service was central to the constitutional disputes of the later years of the reign, along with the royal right to purvey foodstuffs for the army. War also affected legal developments, for the most part adversely, since the government's single-minded concentration on war in the latter part of the reign brought to a virtual end the ambitious programme of the earlier years.

Edward I succeeded to the throne in 1272. What was there at that date to suggest that the resources of England could be successfully mobilized for wars of conquest, or that Edward was the man to do it? The English military record so far during the century had been a dismal one. Under John, Normandy had been lost, and despite immense and exhausting efforts he had failed to recover anything of what Philip Augustus had taken from him. John was not assisted in his attempt to maintain the English position on the continent by the lack of enthusiasm displayed by the English baronage for his policy. Opposition to military service abroad was a very important element in the crisis of the last years of his reign, and English dislike of foreign adventures continued throughout the century. No effective riposte was made to the loss of Poitou to the French in 1224. An elaborate and expensive military demonstration in Brittany in 1230 achieved virtually nothing, and Henry III's next attempt to use force in France in 1242 ended in complete failure. His Poitevin allies deserted him at Taillebourg; a defeat at Saintes followed. The hostility of the English nobility to the expedition proved to be justified by events, but it was their refusal to co-operate that had paved the way for the failure. In 1259, under baronial pressure, Henry made peace with Louis IX, and the changing of the royal seal at about that time was considered significant. Whereas the king had been depicted on the old one bearing a sword, on the new he carried a sceptre.[1]

Failure abroad was not matched by any triumphs nearer home. There was certainly no baronial hostility towards the wars in Wales, and lack of success here can be attributed to the leadership of Llywelyn the Great who provided Wales with a new unity,

[1] *Chronica Johannis de Oxenedes*, ed. H. Ellis (Rolls Series, 1859), p. 219.

INTRODUCTION

and was able to exploit to the full the weaknesses of John and Henry III. Both the Marcher lords and the crown suffered a series of defeats at Llywelyn's hands, while the territory regained at considerable expense in the campaigns of 1223 and 1231 was hardly commensurate with the efforts that the government put into the war. After Llywelyn's death in 1240 Welsh unity crumbled and the English did rather better. Henry III's most successful campaign took place in 1245, but even then, in spite of massive preparations, the army went no further than Deganwy. At the peace of Montgomery in 1247 the Four Cantrefs, the region between Chester and the Conway, were ceded to the English.

The crown lands in Wales, including those gained in 1247, were granted to the Lord Edward, the future Edward I, in 1254.[1] Two years later the men of the Four Cantrefs revolted and appealed to Llywelyn's grandson, Llywelyn ap Gruffydd. The rising became general, and the English government failed to make any effective moves against Llywelyn. According to one account, Edward so despaired of the whole position that he suggested abandoning Wales altogether.[2] In the following years the Welsh leader was able to strengthen his position very considerably by taking full advantage of the political crises and civil wars of the period 1258–1267. With the re-establishment of royal authority in England after the battle of Evesham the extent of Llywelyn's gains could be seen. The Four Cantrefs were recognized to be Welsh. Robert de Mohaut had to agree not to construct a castle at Harwarden for thirty years. In the south Llywelyn was allowed to keep his conquest of Brecon. The Welsh ruler's main gain was not territorial, however, but lay in the recognition by the English of his title of prince of Wales, a title which carried with it the overlordship of all the chieftains of that country. It seemed that the whole series of English campaigns during the reign of Henry III had been in vain: in 1272 Llywelyn ap Gruffydd held a position of strength and dominance in the principality equivalent to that of Llywelyn the Great in 1216.

[1] *C.P.R., 1247–1258*, p. 270.
[2] *Matthaei Parisiensis, Chronica Majora*, ed. H. R. Luard (Rolls Series, 1872–83), v, p. 639.

Map 1. Wales in the time of Edward I

The evidence does not suggest that the English armies under Henry III were militarily formidable. During the Barons' Wars it was to the continent that Henry III and his son Edward looked for the men whom they hoped would win the war for them. Simon de Montfort, trained in the schools of continental warfare, had no great opinion of English troops, and when he saw the disciplined and regular advance of the royalist forces at Evesham is said to have remarked arrogantly that it was from him that they had learnt such techniques.[1] One chronicler noted that the methods of fortification and siege warfare used by de Montfort were far superior to anything that had been seen in England before.[2] The most successful operation of Henry III's wars in Wales, a march in 1246 led by Nicholas de Molis from South Wales into Meirionydd, skirting Snowdonia, and up to Deganwy, was the achievement of a force largely composed of Welsh troops.[3]

A far more important reason for the military failures of Henry III than the inadequacies of his armies was the political instability of England. In 1233 the opposition of the Earl Marshal led to a brief civil war, and the succeeding years witnessed a series of crises, which culminated in the setting up a committee of twenty-four to reform the state of the realm in 1258. The situation degenerated into civil war once more; Simon de Montfort's victory at Lewes in 1264 was followed by the triumph of the royalist forces a year later. The grievances that led to this crisis were many. There were the excesses of the king's foreign favourites, his Poitevin half-brothers and his wife's Savoyard relations. The irresponsible plan to install Henry's second son, Edmund, on the Sicilian throne, which involved the English in obligations to pay some 135,000 marks to the papacy, did much to discredit the government. Discontent was increased by the inadequacies and failings of local administration. After 1258 the political struggle between the royalists and the baronial partisans became increasingly bitter and complex as the issues of principle were confused by personal rivalries and jealousies which the arrogant and intolerant attitude of the self-appointed baronial leader, Simon de Montfort, did much to exacerbate.

The political situation made it hard for the government to raise troops. A successful campaign required both the support of the

[1] F. M. Powicke, *Henry III and the Lord Edward* (Oxford, 1947), ii, p. 502.
[2] *Flores Historiarum*, ed. H. R. Luard (Rolls Series, 1890), ii, pp. 489–90.
[3] R. F. Walker, 'The Anglo-Welsh Wars, 1217–67' (Oxford Univ. D.Phil. thesis, 1953), pp. 555–60.

magnates and adequate financial backing. Henry III was not in a strong position financially.[1] The traditional revenues of the crown, from royal lands, escheats, wardships, profits of justice and similar sources, were quite inadequate for his needs. The prerogative right to levy the tax known as tallage on the royal demesnes and the towns was less profitable than might have been expected. The fines and scutages paid as an alternative to performing military service did not come near to raising the funds needed to pay troops. Some national taxes, collected on a valuation of people's personal property, were levied, but the grant of such aids might be refused, as in 1254. On occasion the clergy might assist the king with grants. But no regular and reliable system of taxation had been established: there was, for example, no national levy of customs duties. Nor did the king have an effective way of obtaining funds on credit. He survived by means of a series of temporary and often unsatisfactory expedients.

If the English military record between 1200 and 1272 was not a good one, nor was the career of the future king Edward in the years before his accession particularly inspiring.[2] Matthew Paris has some unappetizing stories of his behaviour as a youth. When the Welsh revolted in 1257, the young man's first reaction was to flee to his uncle Richard of Cornwall to ask for money. When he and his household came to Wallingford his followers installed themselves in the priory without asking for permission. Food was seized, furniture and windows broken.[3] On another occasion, Edward is said to have met a young man going peaceably along a road, whom he ordered without provocation to be mutilated, entirely contrary to all justice.[4] This second story is without

[1] F. M. Powicke, *The Thirteenth Century, 1216-1307* (Oxford, 2nd ed., 1962), pp. 31-6, has a good summary of the finances of Henry III.
[2] For Edward's career before he came to the throne, and for the events of this period, see in particular Powicke, *Henry III and the Lord Edward* and *The Thirteenth Century*; R. F. Treharne, *The Baronial Plan of Reform, 1258-63* (Manchester, 1932); C. Bémont, *Simon de Montfort* (Paris, 1884, translated by E. F. Jacob, Oxford, 1930); T. F. Tout, 'Wales and the March during the Barons' Wars', in *Collected Papers*, ii (Manchester, 1934), pp. 47-100.
[3] Matthew Paris, *Chron. Maj.*, v, pp. 593-4.
[4] *Ibid.*, p. 598.

corroboration, but similar behaviour to that alleged at Wallingford was reported by the men of Southwark in 1258, when they complained that Edward had unjustly installed his men in Southwark and had taken food supplies contrary to all precedent and custom.[1] Matthew Paris felt that the prospects for the future were gloomy: if Edward was like this as a young man, how much worse would he be in maturity?[2]

The causes of the crisis of 1258 were many and complex. Edward's personal contribution resulted from his position as the lord of great estates in the Welsh Marches. While Henry III's policy had been to rule the Welsh according to their own customs, his son's officials did not take this attitude. Edward's steward was Geoffrey of Langley, a former justice of the Forest, and a man who deserved all the odium that traditionally went with that office. In July 1256 Edward himself visited his lands in North Wales, reaching Dyserth and Deganwy on a brief tour from Chester. No attention was paid to such complaints against his officials as may have reached him, with the result that the men of the Four Cantrefs revolted in November of that year. It was pointed out at the time that the rising was specifically directed against the Lord Edward, rather than the English as a whole.[3] Edward was greatly hampered in his campaign by lack of funds and by his father's failure to back him adequately until it was too late. He was conspicuously unsuccessful in dealing with the Welsh rebels, who derided the efforts that he made. The failure of English policy in Wales was one of the grievances that caused the barons to act as they did at the Oxford parliament in 1258.

The author of the *Song of Lewes*, that famous panegyric of the baronial cause, condemned Edward for his inconstancy and changeableness, for the way in which he was prepared to break promises, and for his refusal to regard himself as bound by the law.[4] The young heir to the throne was certainly fickle in his

[1] Assize Roll, J.I. 1/873, m. 8d.
[2] Matthew Paris, *Chron. Maj.*, v, pp. 594, 598.
[3] 'Chron. Wykes', in *Annales Monastici*, ed. H. R. Luard, iv (Rolls series, 1869), p. 111.
[4] *The Song of Lewes*, ed. C. L. Kingsford (Oxford, 1890), pp. 14-15.

INTRODUCTION

political career between 1258 and 1265. Like his father, Edward was forced to issue letters patent agreeing to accept the decisions of the committee of twenty-four set up early in 1258. But when at the close of the Oxford parliament the king's detested Poitevin half-brothers decided to resist, Edward followed their example in refusing to swear to the Provisions of Oxford. Provocatively, he appointed one of the alien group, Geoffrey de Lusignan, as Seneschal of his duchy of Gascony. However, the Poitevin stand failed dismally, and Edward was forced to swear to the Provisions and accept four barons as his councillors.

The young Edward was not at this stage of his career a man of single-minded purpose. In the spring of 1259 he quarrelled with the earl of Gloucester, one of the baronial leaders, not about national politics, but over rival claims to land. By the autumn Edward's initial hostility towards the reforms had turned into enthusiasm, as it became clear that the movement was a genuinely constructive political enterprise, not simply a vendetta against Henry III's foreign favourites. The first indication of a change in attitude was his response to the much discussed protest of the Bachelors in October. A body of uncertain composition calling themselves the Community of the Bachelors of England presented to Edward, the earl of Gloucester and the others sworn as members of the council at Oxford a demand that they implement the reforms that had been promised. They threatened that if nothing was done, they would take matters into their own hands. Edward replied that although he had taken the oath unwillingly he was fully prepared to stand by it, and was ready to expose himself to death on behalf of the community of England. If the barons did not carry out their promises, Edward clearly stated that he was ready to join with the Bachelors in their threatened rebellion.[1]

Edward's answer to the Bachelors might be taken as a political move intended to embarrass the baronial leaders, whose intention of reaching a final peace with France threatened his position as duke of Gascony, a title first granted to him in 1249 and made effective in 1254. But Edward's objections to the plan that Henry

[1] 'Burton Annals', in *Annales Monastici*, ed. H. R. Luard, i (Rolls series, 1864), p. 471.

III should do homage to Louis IX for Gascony were evidently assuaged, and at the parliament of Westminster in October 1259, when important measures of reform were promulgated, he swore an oath to support Simon de Montfort against all men, and promised to uphold the baronial enterprise. By this time Simon had not emerged decisively as the leader of the baronial opposition to Henry III, though it must have been clear that he was one of the most extreme of the great barons. Edward's adherence to him is not easy to explain save in terms of the impact of the earl's powerful personality on an impressionable youth. It may also have seemed to Edward that the royalist cause was lost, and that the best chance of securing his inheritance was to attach himself to his father's enemies.

Henry III, in Paris, heard disquieting reports about his son, notably that he was plotting with de Montfort to seize power by force and usurp the throne. A special envoy was sent to check on the veracity of the letters that the young man was sending to his father, and it does not seem that his report was reassuring. Early in April 1260 Henry sent orders to prevent Edward from entering London, where the king had heard that he was intending to stay in the bishop of London's palace at St. Paul's while a parliament was held contrary to royal instructions. Some of Edward's retinue who did occupy the palace behaved there with their customary callousness and brutality. Trouble between them and the followers of the earl of Gloucester was feared, but Edward and the earl were refused entry to the city, and the crisis was averted. When his father returned to England Edward publicly denied that he had ever participated in hostilities against Henry. He refused to submit to the judgement of the magnates on the grounds that they were not his peers, but agreed to accept the decision of his father and his uncle, Richard of Cornwall. A reconciliation duly took place.

So ended Edward's first independent political venture: one which can have done nothing to enhance what little reputation he possessed at this stage of his career. He had overestimated the power of Simon de Montfort, and had failed to appreciate the authority that Henry III still possessed. His persistent quarrels with Gloucester contributed to the decline of the reform movement to a state in which personal ambitions and rivalries were more important than questions of principle. His denials that he was involved in opposition to his father, and his refusal to stand trial before the magnates, must have thrown doubt upon his honesty. After his reconciliation with Henry III he was wisely allowed no further opportunity that year to meddle in politics, and was sent abroad to engage in what was at this period of his life his favourite sport, the tournament. According to one account he did not distinguish himself, but suffered a series of defeats, losing almost all the horses and armour that he had set out with. He also incurred a substantial debt to the king of France.[1]

In 1261 Henry III made a systematic effort to reverse all that had been achieved by the reformers. Edward, who was in England during the early summer, did not support him in this. He refused to accept papal absolution from the oath he had sworn in 1259 to observe the Provisions of Oxford, and once again allied himself with de Montfort. But his determination was no greater than in 1260, and the persuasions of his mother soon brought him back to the royalist cause. He speedily returned to Gascony and indulged in no more flirtations with the baronial party.

Events in Wales necessitated Edward's return from the continent early in 1263. He brought with him a band of foreign mercenaries to assist in the defence of his lands against Llywelyn, an act which hardly enhanced his popularity. Even with their aid his campaign was not a success, and before Whitsun he was recalled to England. In June he went to London, where his parents had taken refuge in the Tower. With typical impetuosity he and his men broke into the New Temple and seized money and jewels. These may have helped to finance the struggle against de Montfort, but the incident had the unfortunate effect of turning the Londoners firmly against the king and his supporters. The queen, going up river by boat, was pelted with refuse by the citizens: a deed for which her son never forgave them.

After this, Edward marched rapidly to Bristol, presumably hoping to make a stand in his castle there, but the townspeople

[1] 'Annales Prioratus de Dunstaplia', in *Annales Monastici*, ed. H. R. Luard, iii (Rolls Series, 1866), pp. 216–17; *Close Rolls, 1259–61*, p. 448.

INTRODUCTION

rose against him and his foreign troops. On the intervention of the bishop of Worcester Edward surrendered. As the bishop was conducting him towards London he escaped to Windsor, although he had agreed to a truce. Superior baronial strength, however, compelled him to surrender and disband his mercenaries. Nevertheless, de Montfort's apparent success did not last long. Personal quarrels and rivalries split the baronial movement in the autumn, at the October parliament in particular, and Edward profited, most significantly by winning over the majority of the Marchers who suspected that de Montfort had come to an amicable agreement with Llywelyn. The most notable of Edward's new allies was Roger Mortimer, and by the end of the year the only major Marcher lords not supporting him were Humphrey de Bohun and Peter de Montfort. Edward now reconciled himself with Roger Clifford, his former bailiff of the Three Castles, and with Roger Leyburn, who had been his steward until Edward, on a brief visit to England in the previous year, 1262, had accused him of misappropriating £1,820.[1] De Montfort's position was drastically weakened by the defection of the Marchers, and he was forced to agree to Henry III's plan of submitting the whole dispute to Louis IX for arbitration. Edward had contributed more than any other single person to this new turn of events. When early in the next year Louis' verdict was predictably pronounced firmly in Henry's favour, the earl of Leicester was left with no alternative save a full-scale recourse to arms if he wished to maintain his position of predominance in England.

Edward's early moves in the civil war that resulted from Louis' arbitration in the Mise of Amiens did him little credit. He seized the castle at Gloucester, but was soon threatened by a large baronial force, and agreed to a truce. Once his opponents had withdrawn, Edward ignored the promises he had made, and punished the citizens of Gloucester viciously for the support they had given his enemies. He then joined his father in Oxford, and the royal forces moved on Northampton where de Montfort's son Simon and many important baronial leaders were captured. This victory was followed up by Edward with great energy if

[1] E. 159/36, mm. 8d., 17.

INTRODUCTION

little prudence: the excesses of the royalist troops lost them popularity, and the speed of his advance, combined with the absence of proper victualling arrangements, exhausted the army by the time of the crucial engagement with Simon de Montfort at Lewes. At that battle Edward commanded the right wing and routed the Londoners who opposed him. With headlong impetuosity he drove them from the field, but returning to the battlefield at the end of the day, he found that his father's cause was lost.

Reckless and over-confident as he had shown himself to be, Edward learnt from his mistakes. In March 1265 he was released from close custody on harsh conditions: remaining under restraint, he had to swear to maintain the form of government established by de Montfort, and to grant his castle, town and lands of Chester to the baronial leader. Edward was not a man to be bound by such an agreement; at the end of May he made a dramatic escape and, with the aid of the young Gloucester, son of his old enemy, soon built up a powerful force in the Welsh Marches. The renewal of war culminated in Edward's victory at Evesham, a battle won as much by the exercise of low cunning as by military skill, for the baronial banners recently captured when the young Simon de Montfort was surprised at Kenilworth were used to disguise his advance.

Although de Montfort was killed at Evesham, and the royalist victory had plainly been decisive, resistance continued for the next two years. The leading part in the pacification of England was taken by the Lord Edward, while a significant contribution was made by Roger Leyburn. The settlement of England after Evesham called for the exercise of considerable statesmanship, and Edward was in the strongest position to control the course of events. It cannot be said, however, that he used that position to the best advantage. The bitter resistance of men like John d'Eyville was provoked by the royal policy of taking all rebel lands into the king's hands, and de Montfort's supporters found little satisfaction in the modification of this policy in the Dictum of Kenilworth of 1266 which allowed redemption of their lands at seven times, five times or twice their annual value, according to the extent of their involvement in the rebellion. Even the earl of Gloucester, who

INTRODUCTION

had done so much to ensure Edward's triumph in 1265, marched to London in April 1267 and joined forces with d'Eyville in opposing the government's policies. His action did something to compel moderation, but the process of redemption was a complex one. Many of the Disinherited did not have the funds to buy back their lands, and the processes of law involved were often bitter and protracted.[1]

There is little evidence to suggest that Edward exercised his influence in the direction of moderation. Before Evesham he had allowed some rebels to make their peace, and shortly afterwards he offered the garrison of Kenilworth the opportunity of surrendering themselves. But once it was clear that the royalists were in a position of overwhelming strength his attitude changed. Edward was not one of those responsible for the Dictum of Kenilworth, and harsh as that settlement was, he seems to have desired a harsher one. Certainly his active connivance in the treatment of Robert Ferrers, earl of Derby, indicated scant respect for the Dictum. This unfortunate young man was compelled under duress to enter into an obligation to pay the impossible sum of £50,000 to Edmund of Cornwall for the redemption of his lands, as a result of which he lost most of his estates and his title.[2] Considerable vindictiveness was shown towards London, fined 20,000 marks. The citizens were refused the right of redeeming their lands according to the Dictum, and it was the friends and dependants of the Lord Edward who profited most from the confiscation of London property. Leading London rebels were handed over to Edward, and it was to him that they paid their fines to obtain their freedom. In 1269 the whole city was handed over to Edward, and only because he needed to raise money for his crusade were the citizens allowed to buy back their liberties in 1270.[3] It is ironical that in 1239 the Londoners had greeted the

---

[1] E. F. Jacob, *Studies in the Period of Baronial Reform and Rebellion, 1258–67* (Oxford, 1925), pp. 147 *seqq.*
[2] K. B. McFarlane, 'Had Edward I a "policy" towards the earls?', *History*, l (1965), pp. 149–50.
[3] G. A. Williams, *Medieval London from Commune to Capital* (London, 1963), pp. 232–42; W. H. Blaauw, *The Barons' War* (London, 1843), pp. 276–7.

INTRODUCTION

news of Edward's birth with special delight, since it took place at Westminster.[1]

It has been said that 'in a sense' Edward 'began to reign in the summer of 1265',[2] but the extent of his influence on the government should not be exaggerated. The policy adopted towards the important question of Wales was contrary to his interests. The Peace of Montgomery, which accepted most of the gains made by Llywelyn, was largely the work of the papal legate Ottobuono. Edward had begun to abdicate his position in Wales late in 1265, when Carmarthen and Cardigan were transferred to his younger brother Edmund. By the time of the peace treaty of 1267 he retained only Montgomery of his once vast estates in the Marches.[3] Edward's policy in the Marches in the late 1260s was directed not so much against the Welsh as against Gilbert de Clare, earl of Gloucester. The earl revived his family claim to Edward's town of Bristol, while Edward gave support to the Welsh in an attempt to limit the earl's power in South Wales. There was a strong personal element in the quarrel: one rumour had it that Edward was taking too much interest in Gilbert's wife. Arbitration by Richard of Cornwall did something to ease matters, though it was probably only Edward's departure on crusade that prevented the quarrel from developing into armed conflict.[4]

The auspices for the future at the time of Henry III's death in 1272 were not very encouraging. Edward was abroad, winning himself a considerable reputation for chivalry, determination and energy in what was becoming recognized as a futile cause. He had served an extremely arduous apprenticeship in politics and war before setting out on crusade. By the late 1260s it was becoming clear that he had learnt much from his earlier impetuous mistakes, but his behaviour during the crisis that began in 1258 had given him a reputation for deceit and trickery that he had not overcome. He had made an enemy of the most important lay magnate

[1] Matthew Paris, *Chron. Maj.*, iii, p. 539.
[2] Powicke, *Henry III and the Lord Edward*, ii, p. 503.
[3] Walker, 'The Anglo-Welsh Wars, 1217-67', pp. 710-15.
[4] Michael Altschul, *A Baronial Family in Medieval England: the Clares, 1217-1314* (Baltimore, 1965), pp. 126-9.

INTRODUCTION

in the country, Gilbert de Clare, and the citizens of London had no cause to love him. The country as a whole had barely recovered from the civil wars by 1272; the conflicts had left a legacy of bitterness which it would take long to obliterate. However, one great advantage Edward did have. He returned from crusade to begin his effective rule in 1274: his long absence from the country had temporarily isolated him from the political scene, and he was in a position to make a fresh start.

Edward I proved to be a king of great ambition. His experiences before his accession had made him aware of the necessity of establishing the crown in a position of clear and undisputed authority. This can be seen in many facets of his domestic policies —in his relations with the magnates, with the church, and with the towns—but the most striking expression of the king's determination and aggressiveness was of course in his wars. The requirements of war, the need for men, money and materials, increasingly dominated the actions of the government, and exercised an immense influence over the political events of the reign. The aim of this book is to provide an analytical study of the way in which the country was mobilized for war, the means used to recruit men, the size of the armies, the methods used to supply them with victuals, and the consequences, both financial and political, of the measures adopted. As the arrangement is not chronological, it is necessary to provide a brief account of the wars, so as to indicate the sequence and scale of Edward's campaigns in Wales, Gascony, Flanders and Scotland.

The first part of the reign, following the king's return from crusade, was dominated by affairs in Wales.[1] The Lord Edward may have been prepared to abandon his Welsh estates, and to accept the Peace of Montgomery, but King Edward was not the man to assent to the continued disorder in the Marches, the projected marriage of Llywelyn with Eleanor, Simon de Montfort's daughter, and above all the refusal of the Welsh prince to perform homage. Nor was Llywelyn willing to stand aside while Edward sheltered his brother Dafydd who had revolted against him in 1274.

[1] The best account of the Welsh wars is J. E. Morris, *The Welsh Wars of Edward I* (Oxford, 1901).

INTRODUCTION

War was inevitable, and Edward conducted his first campaign in Wales as king in 1277. In July he advanced from Chester, employing large numbers of woodcutters to prepare a road for the army. By the end of August forces had reached Deganwy, and from there troops were sent by sea to Anglesey, where they reaped the harvest, thus threatening the Welsh in Snowdonia with starvation. This was enough for Llywelyn, and negotiations began. By the end of September, the first Welsh war was effectively over.

The peace terms were surprisingly reasonable. A massive war indemnity of £50,000 was imposed, and two of the Four Cantrefs were acquired by Edward, together with Cardigan and Carmarthen. Dafydd was reinstated in his lands, and Llywelyn allowed to marry Eleanor. But problems soon arose once more. Edward was determined to force an interpretation of the treaty as favourable as possible to himself, one which would allow him the widest possible scope for intervention in Welsh affairs. Arguments centred on the question of jurisdiction, and the king was in no way deterred by the fact that precedents carefully collected from the records of Henry III's reign and inquests held by his own officials did not justify the position he adopted. As in the 1250s, Edward and his officials displayed an intolerance of Welsh traditions and Welsh law. Only in one case was a definite instruction given that it should be heard by Welsh law, and only one case was referred to Llywelyn's court. The prince was himself involved in a dispute with Gruffydd ap Gwenwynwyn over the cantref of Arwystli in Powys; the one claiming by Welsh law, the other by Marcher custom. Adjournments were innumerable and frustrating, even insulting, to Llywelyn, and—despite the precedents—Edward ruled, for obvious political reasons, that the case should be heard according to the customs of the March.[1] Before the case was completed, however, the Welsh were in revolt once more.

The war of 1282 was sparked off by Dafydd, Edward I's former ally. Probably he felt that he had been insufficiently rewarded, and, like Llywelyn, he had become involved in the tangled complexities of English law, being summoned to appear before the Justiciar of Chester to prove his rights to some of his lands. The revolt

[1] *The Welsh Assize Roll, 1277–1284*, ed. J. Conway Davies (Cardiff, 1940).

INTRODUCTION

spread rapidly. Llywelyn could hardly stand by while his brother championed the Welsh cause against the English oppressors, and with Dafydd's success in enlisting the aid of the rulers of South Wales, the rising became general.

The campaign took longer and was more expensive than that of 1277. The main royal army again advanced from Chester round the coast of North Wales, while Gloucester commanded a separate army in the south, and Roger Mortimer and Roger l'Estrange were active at Montgomery and Builth respectively. Once more it was intended to cross to Anglesey, and a bridge of boats was constructed for the purpose. But before arrangements for the crossing had been completed, an English force under Luke de Tany was ambushed and routed, many of the soldiers being drowned. A winter campaign seemed necessary. However, while the king had not yet made any decisive move, news came of a striking success at Orewin Bridge early in December. A small English force, probably commanded by John Giffard, made a surprise attack on the Welsh, and in the engagement Llywelyn was killed. The campaign of the new year, 1283, went smoothly. In April the last important Welsh castle, Bere, surrendered and in June Dafydd was captured. The war was over.

The victory of 1283 was consolidated by a massive programme of castle building; Snowdonia was ringed round on the coast by Conway, Caernarvon, Criccieth and Harlech. Edward continued his policy of extending the English system of justice and administration into Wales by issuing the Statute of Wales of 1284. The counties of Flint, Merioneth, Caernarvon and Anglesey were created, and the criminal law was anglicized as far as possible. The king's son Edward, born at Caernarvon, was made prince of Wales. Welsh independence was at an end.

But if the settlement of 1284 marked the conquest of Wales by Edward, it did not end Welsh resistance. In 1287, seizing the opportunity of the king's absence in Gascony, Rhys ap Maredudd revolted. He had formerly been a consistent ally of the English, and clearly felt aggrieved that he had not been shown greater favours by Edward. The rising appeared serious, but the regent, Edmund of Cornwall, swiftly raised an army and defeated the rebels. Far more dangerous was the last rising that Edward had to face, which took place in 1294. Once again the Welsh took advantage of the fact that the English were preparing a lavish expedition to Gascony, and although the leaders were not members of the former princely family and do not appear to have been men of great standing, the rising spread with great rapidity throughout Wales.

The troops intended for Gascony were diverted to Wales, and a major expedition was organized. The king advanced from Chester, while the earl of Warwick commanded an army based at Montgomery. The earl of Pembroke had forces at Carmarthen, and the earl of Hereford in the south-east. The Welsh won one success, capturing the royal baggage train, and so leaving the king and his troops in Conway with insufficient food and drink. But while Edward was at Conway, Warwick defeated a Welsh force on 5 March 1295 at Maes Moydog. Edward himself soon moved into Anglesey, and the Welsh abandoned the struggle.

The determination and obstinacy which helped Edward to succeed in Wales could lead him into extraordinary miscalculations. Nowhere is this clearer than in the case of the French war.[1] Trouble between Norman sailors and those of the Cinque Ports developed in 1293 into a full-scale naval war, in which the men of Bayonne were involved. This provided Philip IV with an opportunity to cite Edward as duke of Aquitaine before the *parlement* of Paris; he was anxious to define his rights and authority over Edward in much the same way as the English king had been doing in Wales and Scotland. However, what Edward wanted from Philip was not war but a wife, for Eleanor of Castile had died in 1290. Edmund of Lancaster was put in charge of the negotiations, which culminated in the drafting of a formal marriage treaty. Arrangements were made for much of the duchy of Aquitaine to be handed over to Philip for a nominal period, at the end of which Edward was to receive it back in full sovereignty. The English kept their part of the bargain in 1294, but the French did not. Philip failed to withdraw the summons requesting Edward

---

[1] Powicke, *The Thirteenth Century*, pp. 644–50, 658–69, describes the events of the French war.

INTRODUCTION

to appear before the *parlement* and, instead of granting Aquitaine to the English king in accordance with the agreed terms, he declared the duchy confiscate. It was widely believed in England that Edward's passion for the French princess, of whom he had seen no more than a full-length portrait, led to this situation. This seems unlikely, though, particularly since the chroniclers name Philip's sister Blanche as the object of Edward's desires, rather than Margaret, who was specified in the marriage treaty, and who eventually married the English king in 1299. But it is very understandable that contemporaries should have interpreted the remarkable scheme for the temporary surrender of Gascony to Philip as the result of lust rather than of a carefully calculated policy.[1]

Edward I's strategy in Wales had been very similar to that employed by Henry III in his Welsh campaigns. His strategy in the war with Philip IV was no more original, resembling as it did that employed by John after the loss of Normandy. Edward's plan was to fight a largely defensive war in Gascony, while attacking Philip in the north with the aid of a massive coalition of rulers from the Low Countries, Germany and the eastern borders of France, who were paid substantial subsidies. Like John's schemes, Edward's did not work out as intended.

The first expeditionary force to Gascony sailed in October 1294, under the command of John of Brittany. Some reinforcements were sent in 1295, but the next substantial expedition, headed by Edmund of Lancaster and the earl of Lincoln, did not set out until early in 1296. Although these forces, combined with local Gascon levies, did not distinguish themselves against the French, being defeated at Rioms in 1295 and Bellegarde in 1297, the English retained a foothold in Gascony. Edward's main hopes of success in the war lay in operations in the north, rather than in Gascony, but his plans to take an army to the Low Countries were thwarted by the Welsh situation in 1295, and by his Scotch war in 1296. It was not until 1297 that the campaign took place. The lengthy

---

[1] *Foedera*, I, ii, pp. 795-6; *The Chronicle of Walter of Guisborough*, ed. H. Rothwell (Camden Soc., 3rd ser., lxxxix, 1957), pp. 241-2; *Bartholomaei de Cotton, Historia Anglicana*, ed. H. R. Luard (Rolls Series, 1859), p. 232; *The Chronicle of Pierre de Langtoft*, ed. T. Wright, ii (Rolls Series, 1868), pp. 196-8.

INTRODUCTION

delay made it hard to maintain the alliance, and the king was faced by increasingly bitter domestic opposition to his plans. Even so, Edward was too proud and stubborn to admit failure, and landed in Flanders with totally inadequate forces shortly after the defeat of some of his allies at the battle of Veurne. The only fighting that the English troops were involved in was rioting with their Flemish allies; no attempt was made to join battle with the French. The English chroniclers tried to explain the failure of the campaign in terms of the timidity of the count of Flanders and the fear felt by the French, but it seems clear that it was the English, with no desire to fight, who were glad to seize any chance of ending hostilities. Edward accordingly negotiated a truce with Philip in October 1297, shamefully deserting his Flemish allies and so exposing the fraudulence of his own propaganda in which he had stressed his obligations towards his allies. It has been argued that the German king Adolf of Nassau had been bribed by French agents to desert Edward, which weakened the allied cause further, though the evidence for this is highly dubious. Six days after Edward agreed to a truce Adolf was still expressing his willingness to fight, and it is most probable that it was the German ruler's domestic difficulties, rather than French gold, that prevented his intervention.[1]

With the truce of 1297 Edward I achieved the fundamental aim of his war with Philip—the retention of Gascony. Even if none of the points at issue were properly settled in the truce negotiations, neither country was prepared for a resumption of hostilities. War was succeeded by a lengthy series of negotiations, culminating in a peace treaty in 1303. That Philip IV was prepared to agree to this was largely due to the Flemings who, although deserted by Edward I, won a striking victory over the French at Courtrai in 1302.

Just as the French difficulties in Flanders prevented Philip IV from reopening his conflict with the English, so his problems in Scotland prevented Edward I from engaging in any further continental wars, or in the crusade he hoped to conduct. Edward's original intention had been to acquire Scotland by means of a marriage alliance between his son Edward and the heiress to the

---
[1] See *infra*, p. 174.

INTRODUCTION

Scotch crown, Margaret of Norway.[1] Her death in 1290 put an end to this plan, and Edward determined to achieve his object in a different way. The succession dispute that took place on Margaret's death provided him with a splendid opportunity of extending his influence, as he had in Wales, by deliberately misinterpreting treaties and manipulating legal processes. It is hard to dismiss, as Powicke does, the account of Edward's explanation to his magnates that he intended to subdue Scotland just as he had brought Wales under control.[2] A feudal summons to the northern magnates was issued, so that in the discussion held at Norham, the Scots were threatened by force. Edward, invited to arbitrate, reserved any claims that he might have on the Scotch throne, attempted to obtain a full recognition of his suzerainty over Scotland from the Guardians, and instead received recognition of his standing as 'superior lord' of the northern kingdom from the contenders to the throne. The outcome of the hearings in the court set up under Edward's authority was the coronation of John Balliol. While he does appear to have had the better claim, it was also plainly to Edward's advantage that he should succeed and Robert Bruce fail. With Balliol king, Edward made his position clear. He had not obtained all that he wanted in the negotiations leading up to the hearing of the Great Cause, and he now calmly stated that he did not regard himself as bound by any promises he had made. Balliol was forced to free Edward from any such obligations, and the English king began to hear appeals from Scotch courts, and even to summon Balliol and his magnates to perform military service. No English king had made such extensive claims in the past, and Balliol's attempts to co-operate with Edward led to very natural baronial resentment, which culmin-

[1] The best account of Edward's Scotch wars is that of G. W. S. Barrow, *Robert Bruce and the Community of the Realm of Scotland* (London, 1965). A useful brief account, differing in interpretation, is by A. A. M. Duncan, *The Nation of Scots and the Declaration of Arbroath (1320)* (Historical Association Pamphlet, 1970).

[2] 'Waverley Annals', in *Annales Monastici*, ii, p. 409; Powicke, *Thirteenth Century*, p. 603, n. 1. Powicke does not explain why he regards this passage as 'misplaced': presumably he did so because it did not accord with his view of Edward's character.

Map 2. Scotland in the time of Edward I

ated in 1295 with the appointment of a council of twelve to take charge of the government. Allies were needed against the English. When agreement with Philip IV of France was reached, it was clear that war was inevitable.

Edward I's first campaign in Scotland took place in 1296, and was a triumph for the English. Berwick was captured, and the

INTRODUCTION

inhabitants put to the sword. Earl Warenne then won a decisive victory over the Scotch feudal host at Dunbar. Resistance was now virtually at an end, and the campaign turned into a progress through the conquered kingdom. Balliol was forced to abdicate; oaths of fealty were exacted from a substantial number of landholders and clergy. Edward set up a new form of government, ruling the country as direct lord and keeping the kingship in abeyance. His appropriation of the Stone of Destiny makes it difficult to imagine that he intended to revive the office. But the triumph of 1296 proved short-lived.

In 1297 the Scots revolted. Not only was there a natural hostility towards the English king, but it was also believed that Edward was intending to introduce into Scotland some of the measures he was employing in England to raise men, money and materials for his war with Philip IV. The most successful and picturesque Scotch leader was William Wallace, who, with Andrew Murray, won a striking and startling victory at Stirling Bridge over Earl Warenne, the king's lieutenant in Scotland. The achievement of 1296 was most forcibly shown to have been superficial: Scotland could not be conquered in a single campaign.

Despite the absence of the king and much of the administrative staff in Flanders, a limited counter offensive was mounted in the winter following the disaster of Stirling Bridge. When Edward I returned from abroad in the spring of 1298 to a country exhausted by the demands he had made on it for the French war, he immediately began to plan a major campaign in Scotland. The army he assembled was one of the largest of the reign, and the administrative efforts that went into its creation were rewarded with success. At Falkirk the Scots under Wallace were so soundly defeated that it was not until Bannockburn in 1314 that they willingly risked a large army in battle with the English host once again.

Notable as the victory of Falkirk was, it did not win the war for Edward. The English only had effective control of the areas where they held castles, and had no foothold north of Stirling. Even that castle was lost to the enemy in 1299. The next major English campaign took place in 1300. An impressive army mustered at Carlisle and marched into Galloway. But, because of the enemy's

INTRODUCTION

tactics of withdrawing and refusing battle, little more was achieved than the capture of Caerlaverock castle. The following year Edward adopted a more ambitious plan. One army, under the king himself, mustered at Berwick and advanced across Scotland towards the Clyde, while another army, nominally commanded by the prince of Wales, advanced from Carlisle round the coast of Galloway. The aim was clearly to effect a pincer movement, but the two forces failed to meet and again the enemy refused battle. The chief English achievement was the capture of Bothwell castle, with the aid of an elaborate wooden tower, which took almost two months to construct, and was carried on thirty carts on the two-day journey from Glasgow.[1]

In spite of a comparative lack of success on these campaigns of 1300 and 1301, the English hold on southern Scotland was increasing through the possession of important groups of castles. Jedburgh, Selkirk and Roxburgh commanded an important Border region; the southern shore of the Firth of Forth could be dominated from the castles of Dirleton, Edinburgh and Linlithgow. Stirling was held by the English until 1299. In the south-west the crown held two important castles, Dumfries and Lochmaben, which commanded the entry into Scotland from Carlisle and in addition served as centres to control Nithsdale and Annandale. The increased security of the English position in Scotland at the end of the 1301 campaign was demonstrated by the fact that the king remained in the north for the winter, staying at Linlithgow. Lack of unity among the Scotch leaders assisted the English cause, and in 1302 the patriotic side was deserted by the important figure of Robert Bruce, earl of Carrick and future king of Scotland. Victory for Edward seemed to be in sight.

The year 1303 began with two successes for the Scots. Selkirk castle was captured, and in a skirmish at Roslin Ralph Manton, an important royal official, was killed. In the summer a large English army marched north. Once more the Scots refused to give battle, but their delaying tactics were not as successful as in earlier years, and Edward was able, for the first time since 1298, to take the step he regarded as essential for the conquest of Scotland of

[1] B.M. Add. MS, 7966a, ff. 39v., 115; *Cal. Docs. Scot.*, iv, pp. 451–2.

INTRODUCTION

moving his army across the Firth of Forth. He went as far north as Elgin. For the second time he wintered in Scotland, and in May 1304 the task of besieging Stirling was begun. This was the last really important castle held by the Scots, and once the garrison yielded, Scotland was unable to offer serious resistance. The capture of William Wallace in 1305 was the culmination of the English triumph.

The settlement reached in 1305 created effective English rule in southern Scotland, while the north was left in the hands of apparently obedient Scotch magnates. As in the case of Wales, Edward found the legal system of the conquered country unacceptable, and a commission was set up under the royal lieutenant, John of Brittany, to reform the laws and customs of Scotland. Though surprisingly conciliatory in some ways, this settlement did not last long. The story of the murder of John Comyn by Robert Bruce in the church at Dumfries, and of Bruce's subsequent seizure of the throne in 1306, is well known. The English were completely unprepared for such a move, and the castle garrisons that formed the occupation force were wholly inadequate for dealing with the situation. But forces were quickly raised, and before the main English army under the king's eldest son had mustered, Aymer de Valence defeated Bruce at the battle of Methven near Perth. Less than three months after his coronation the king of Scotland became a hunted fugitive.

The response of the English king to the news of Bruce's revolt was, not surprisingly, vindictive. Edward's merciless attitude may well have assisted in the rapid growth of enthusiasm for the cause that Bruce represented. The Scotch king spent the winter of 1306–1307 in hiding. However, when he re-emerged early in the year it became clear that the tide was turning against the English. Methven was avenged at Loudoun Hill, where Valence was defeated. The earl of Gloucester was defeated three days later. In July Edward I himself advanced from Lanercost priory, where he had spent the winter in ill-health, but before he had even reached the border he died at Burgh-by-Sands. Deprived of his forceful personality the English were incapable of continuing the struggle with the same determination that they had shown up to

INTRODUCTION

1307. If seven years were to pass before the Scotch triumph at Bannockburn, the English cause was doomed long before that disastrous engagement. The events of the wars of Edward's reign are familiar to historians, but while a narrative account demonstrates the extent of the king's military concerns, it can do little more than hint at many of the problems which faced a government involved in campaigns of such frequency and magnitude. The methods used to mobilize the resources of the country for war on the scale that was required have not been fully examined, nor have the political consequences of the decisions that were taken been fully investigated.

The first problem that needs to be examined is that of the composition of the armies. The knights of the royal household played a very important part in Edward I's armies, and it is also necessary to look at the way in which the magnates with their retinues were summoned to perform cavalry service. The infantry forces were organized on a quite different system from the cavalry, and the method by which local communities met the demands of the government for men needs scrutiny as well as the pay rolls of the armies that were kept once the men had mustered. Examination of the composition of the military forces leads to the question of wages and victualling. The country had to bear far more than the burden of supplying the manpower for the campaigns, for in most cases the government had the responsibility of paying the men's wages, and had to ensure that they were provided with sufficient food. The armies could not simply live off the land, so supplies had to be collected in England and sent to the campaigning areas. This task was one of the most considerable of those facing the administration in this period, involving as it did the central government, the sheriffs and their officials, together with special victuallers appointed to take charge of the supplies when they reached their destination. The navy had an important part to play in transporting men and supplies as well as assisting in the defence of the realm when there was a threat of invasion from France.

The costs of war were very considerable, and perhaps the most difficult problem the government had to face was that of finding

INTRODUCTION

sufficient money to meet them. There was no chance of increasing the ordinary revenue of the crown to meet the demand for funds. Taxation was the obvious answer. The laity could be taxed by means of grants of subsidies assessed on the basis of valuations of moveable property. The crown also had a right to the traditional feudal aids. Customs duties provided a means by which the considerable profits of English trade could be tapped by the government. Taxation of the clergy could be achieved either by approaching the English church for grants, or by reaching agreement with the papacy for a division of the spoils of papal taxes. But taxation alone was not enough. The main government department responsible for financing the wars, the Wardrobe, was constantly incurring expenditure far in excess of its receipts, particularly in the later stages of the reign. In order to meet its obligations the government was forced to borrow money, notably from Italian merchants. But even with the aid of such expedients, the crown's debts by the end of the reign were substantial.

The political repercussions of Edward I's wars were extremely wide-ranging. The backing of the magnates was essential if military success was to be achieved, and the techniques of persuasion and compulsion that were employed by the crown to obtain this must be examined. The needs of war had a considerable influence on Edward's attitude to the legal franchises of the baronial class, and they had their effect on some of the legal reforms of the reign. It was not until the period of the French war that the demands made by the king on the country aroused really extensive criticism, but by 1297 the calls for military service, the succession of direct taxes, the heavy customs duties and the seizures of wool and food supplies led to a major constitutional crisis with the opposition being led by the Marshal and Constable. The solution of the crisis, the reissue of Magna Carta and the Forest Charter, together with some additional concessions, was not adequate, and subsequent years saw continuing political argument. The connection of the French war with the crisis of 1297 is very evident, though the political effects of the campaigns in Scotland are less so. Did the policies of Edward I help to stave off the crisis that broke out so

INTRODUCTION

swiftly on the accession of Edward II by diverting the attention of the magnates towards a popular war, or did the measures needed to keep the war going create an intolerable situation in England? Did the single-minded concentration of Edward I's government on war in the last years of the reign mean that Edward II received an impossible legacy from his father?

Warfare on Edward I's scale had many effects on society. The methods used to summon men to fight did not merely reflect the social structure but influenced it. The burden of the demand for men, money and goods in support of the war effort was economically significant. The breakdown in law and order, which became marked in the later stages of the reign, was clearly linked to the king's concentration on his military objectives. The intention of this book is to examine the way in which the problems of raising armies and financing war were dealt with, and to investigate the relationship of Edward I's wars to administration, politics and society.

II

HOUSEHOLDS AND RETINUES

The cavalry troops formed the elite of the Edwardian army. There was a clear distinction between these men, many of whom were knights, prominent as landowners and officials in their counties, and the levies of footsoldiers. The king never tried to enforce cavalry service from men below the rank of those holding land worth twenty pounds a year. The cavalry were heavily armoured and fought with sword and lance. They were mounted on horses which were 'barded', or protected with armour and padding, and which might equal in value a year's revenue from their lands. A knight would receive 2s. a day in pay, a sergeant-at-arms, whose equipment was similar, 1s., whereas the wage of an ordinary infantryman was only 2d. In the field the cavalry were organised and paid on a different system from the infantry, and it was rare for the two to be combined into a fully integrated force.

The most important cavalry troops were those of the royal household. Tout, who did much to explain and elucidate the very important rôle played by the household—in particular the department of the Wardrobe—in the wars of Edward I, considered that the reign saw the process of 'a little company of peace-time guards' being enlarged 'into the dimensions of a small army'.[1] But Tout, whose concern was mainly with the clerical element of the household, underestimated the military rôle of royal knights whose functions he considered to be chiefly administrative. It has been pointed out that the household of Henry I was far more like the

[1] T. F. Tout, *Chapters in the Administrative History of Mediaeval England*, ii (Manchester, 1937), p. 31.

developed military household of Edward I than he would have allowed. Just as Edward's household knights provided one of the four battalions of the army which won the battle of Falkirk in 1298, so did those of Henry I form one of the divisions of the army at Brémule in 1119. The career of Robert Tiptoft in the household of Edward I can be paralleled by that of Brian Fitz-Count under Henry.[1] Later, even so unwarlike a king as Henry III could usually put at least 100 household knights into the field in an emergency, and there was a permanent core of thirty or more knights in receipt of annual fees at the Exchequer.[2]

There was therefore nothing novel in the fact that Edward I's household was more of a small army than a domestic establishment. In addition to the sergeants-at-arms who received £2 6s. 8d. a year in robes, the military element consisted of bannerets, paid £24 a year in fees and robes, knights who were given half as much, and squires who had only £2 a year in robes.[3] Edward had of course a substantial household before he came to the throne. According to Matthew Paris, he increased its size to two hundred horse after his first quarrel with his father, in 1256.[4] In 1261 he was expected to be able to put fifty knights into the field.[5] Naturally, many of the members of Edward's household after his accession had served him during his father's reign, and an important group of men were those who went on crusade with him. Roger Clifford was one of the Marcher lords whose adherence to Edward in the autumn of 1263 had done much to advance the royalist cause—he had already served as one of Edward's bailiffs,[6] and had in the past been a household knight of Henry III. He went on crusade with the Lord Edward, taking with him nine knights, and was paid a fee of 1,000 marks.[7] Clifford served Edward in his Welsh wars,

---

[1] J. O. Prestwich, 'Anglo-Norman Feudalism and the Problem of Continuity', *Past and Present*, 26 (1963), pp. 50–2.

[2] Walker, 'The Anglo-Welsh Wars, 1217–67', pp. 66–7.

[3] *Liber Quotidianus Contrarotulatoris Garderobiae* (London, 1787), pp. 188–95, 310–31.

[4] *Chron. Maj.*, v. p. 539.   [5] Walker, *op. cit.*, p. 665.

[6] *Supra*, p. 23.

[7] T. H. Turner, 'Unpublished Notices of the Times of Edward I', *The Archaeological Journal*, viii (1851), p. 46.

being entrusted with Hawarden castle in 1277. He was captured there by Prince Dafydd in 1282, and his career ended with his death in 1286.[1]

Robert Tiptoft, an Essex man, was associated with Edward as early as 1260, and was in 1264 one of the knights garrisoning Bristol castle. A man of no great means initially, he profited considerably from the wave of confiscations of rebel property that followed Evesham. He took a retinue of five knights with him on crusade, and was rewarded on his return for his good service by appointment to the keepership of Nottingham castle. His importance is indicated by the recurrence of his name in lists of councillors in the early stages of Edward's reign, but it was not until 1280 that he was given an office of great importance in the form of the Justiciarship of West Wales, also receiving the custody of the royal lands in those parts. Tiptoft served loyally in the Welsh wars, and fought in Gascony in the 1290s. He died in 1298, after a lifetime spent in Edward's service.[2] Another who served Edward long and loyally was William Latimer. He went on crusade with him, fought for him in Wales, Gascony and Scotland, investigated the malpractices of his justices and officials, and was still retained as a banneret of the household in 1300, as was his son.[3] A more exotic figure was Otto de Grandson, a Savoyard brought to England in 1258 when he entered Edward's service. He is found witnessing charters for Edward before his accession,[4] and the high regard the king had for him is indicated by his appointment as an executor when Edward made his will the day after he was wounded by an assassin in Syria. According to one account it was Grandson, not the queen, who sucked the poison from the wound. Otto served in Wales, and in 1284 was made Justicier of North Wales, an office he largely exercised by deputy, for his main functions were diplomatic. As a Savoyard he was an obvious choice to negotiate on Edward's behalf abroad. These activities

---

[1] Morris, *Welsh Wars*, pp. 144, 153. There is an account of Clifford's career in W. Dugdale, *The Baronage of England* (London, 1675-6), i, pp. 337-8.

[2] *C.C.R., 1272-76*, pp. 338, 342. His career is adequately summarized by C. Moor, *Knights of Edward I*, v (Harleian Soc., lxxxiv, 1932), pp. 20-3.

[3] *Ibid.*, iii (1930), pp. 22-3.   [4] *C.Ch.R., 1267-1300*, p. 177.

took him away from the household, and after the early stages of his career he was never so closely associated with the household as were men like Latimer.[1] Important as the group of men who accompanied Edward on crusade were, including as it did Luke de Tany, Geoffrey de Geneville, Thomas de Clare and Hugh FitzOtto, in addition to those already mentioned,[2] they were but a small section of the household knights. How were men recruited for the household, how long did they serve, and what were their rewards? Unfortunately no actual agreements for service in the household survive, although there are two ordinances for the diet, robes, and allowances for horses and servants of two magnates' sons, John de Warenne and Roger Mortimer, both of whom were squires in the household at the end of the reign of Edward I.[3] These do not suggest that the way by which the king retained men differed greatly from the methods of the major magnates. They received liveries of robes and fees twice a year, and were fed in the royal hall, though there was no question of their remaining permanently at court.

There was a family tradition of service among the men who became household knights. John l'Estrange had been a household knight under Henry III, and two members of the family, Roger and his nephew John, were knights of Edward's household. Among the familiar names in Edward's household which are also found in his father's are Rivers, Tregoz, Beauchamp, Grey, Oddingseles, Turberville and Gorges.[4] In 1300 Walter Beauchamp as steward of the household was in command of his son Walter; and William Charles, an earlier steward, was followed in the royal service by his son Edward. Three members of the Gascon family of Ferre were household knights: Guy senior, Guy junior, and Reginald. In addition to the family partnerships of the Beau-

[1] C. L. Kingsford, 'Sir Otho de Grandison, 1238?–1328', *T.R.H.S.*, 3rd ser., iii (1909), pp. 125 *seqq.*
[2] A list of those who received protections to go on the crusade is given by R. Röhricht, 'Etudes sur les derniers temps du royaume de Jerusalem. A. La croisade du Prince Edouard d'Angleterre (1270–1274)', *Archives de l'orient latin*, i (Paris, 1881), pp. 630–2.
[3] E. 101/371/8/97; E. 101/370/19.   [4] Walker, *op. cit.*, pp. 74–6.

champs and the Latimers, John Russel, a veteran Montfortian, and William Russel were also serving in the household in 1300. Examples could be multiplied, with the families of Badlesmere, Bikenore, le Brun, Cantilupe, Felton, Hausted, Knoville, Leyburn, Maulay, Morham, Segrave, Sulleye and Welles each providing two household knights during this period from 1297 to 1306.[1]

Often, men were brought straight into the household as knights, especially when military needs made it necessary to augment the household strength, as in 1297 when twenty-two knights were enrolled to meet the demands of the expedition to Flanders for additional household troops.[2] But many entered the household at a lower rank. John l'Estrange, Alexander Freville, Thomas de Bikenore, Robert de Bures and William Felton, to name only a few, all began their careers as squires.[3] Eustace de l'Hacche first appears in the household records as a sergeant-at-arms in 1276. He was a knight by 1285, a banneret by 1300, and was still in receipt of fees within two years of his death in 1306. His devotion to Edward's service brought him honour and promotion, but—according to his executors—no riches. They were forced to petition for payment of what was due to him for robes, wages and loss of horses in royal service; unless this was made the many legacies left by Eustace to the Holy Land and to his dependants could not be paid.[4]

The majority of this tightly-knit body of knights were English, but Edward also employed Gascons and Spaniards. Naturally during his stay in Gascony from 1286 to 1289 many local men were brought into the household,[5] and in 1297 four Gascons and one Aragonese were admitted.[6] Arnold de Gaveston, father of the notorious Piers, was a household knight in the late 1280s, and

---

[1] The wardrobe accounts provide lists of the household knights under Edward I. See in particular E. 101/351/17; E. 101/4/24; C. 47/4/3; E. 101/369/11; and B.M. Add. MSS, 7965; 7966a; 8835; *Liber Quotidianus*.
[2] B.M. Add. MS, 7965, f. 60.
[3] These men were all squires in 1285: E. 101/351/17.
[4] Morris, *Welsh Wars*, p. 51; E. 101/351/17; *Liber Quotidianus*, p. 188; B.M. Add. MS, 8835, f. 54; *Rot. Parl.*, i, p. 199.
[5] E. 101/4/24.
[6] B.M. Add. MS, 7965, f. 60.

again in 1301.[1] The Gascon Arnold de Cavapenna's household career lasted from at least 1285, when he was a squire, unil 1301.[2] Aragon provided Jaime, señor de Gerica, and Pascual of Valencia, known as the *adalid*.[3] These men were full members of the household, in a different category from the handful of foreigners who appear in the wardrobe accounts of the years up to 1297 as receiving annual pensions, but did not attend the royal court regularly.[4] A further class of foreigner present in Edward's household during the first half of the reign was that of the sons of foreign rulers, sent to England to receive an education at the court of a king who, following his crusade, had an extremely high reputation on the continent. Both John II, duke of Brabant, who married Edward's daughter Margaret in 1290, and John, count of Holland, who married another daughter, Elizabeth, in 1297, spent much of their childhood in Edward's household.[5]

The earliest list of Edward I's reign showing the establishment of the household knights dates from 1284–5, and reveals that fourteen bannerets and eighty-seven knights were in receipt of robes.[6] Eight men are named as *commiltones*, a term which Denholm-Young tentatively suggested meant that they were 'more equal' than their fellows: he felt that use of the word might 'point to the intention of founding some confraternity or military order'.[7] But the account makes it clear that this word was simply used of knights serving with a companion, so that although only eight men are named, payments to sixteen knights were made. These men had presumably made agreements of mutual assistance with their partners; they were 'brothers-in-arms'.[8] An account of

---

[1] E. 101/4/24; B.M. Add. MS, 7966a, f. 78v.

[2] E. 101/351/17; B.M. Add. MS, 7966a, f. 79.

[3] B.M. Add. MSS, 7965, f. 60; 7966a, f. 79; 8835, f. 52. I am very grateful to Professor P. E. Russell for his advice on the names of these Spaniards, given in the sources as Pascasius Valentinus dictus Ladalil and Jacobus de la Ryke.

[4] See the enrolled wardrobe accounts in E. 372/144.

[5] F. Bock, 'Englands Beziehungen zum Reich unter Adolf von Nassau', *M.I.Ö.G.*, erg. bd, xii (1932–3), pp. 214, 216, 219.

[6] E. 101/351/17.

[7] N. Denholm-Young, *History and Heraldry* (Oxford, 1965), pp. 31–2.

[8] One such agreement, not between household members, is printed by

fees for the next year makes no mention of this category of *commiltones*. It shows that at Michaelmas 1285 twenty bannerets and fifty-six knights were paid fees, and that by the following Easter numbers had fallen to thirteen bannerets and thirty-nine knights.[1] A wardrobe book of the next two years shows that fees were paid to some eighty bannerets and knights,[2] but in 1289, when the household was in Gascony, the strength stood at about fifty knights and ten bannerets.[3]

The period of almost continuous warfare after 1294 did not see the expansion of the force of household knights that might have been expected. In 1297 only ten bannerets and twenty-six knights were listed as being in receipt of fees, but of the twenty-two new recruits to the household only two appear in the fees section of the account.[4] By 1300, although the number of bannerets had risen to thirty, there were only fifty knights,[5] and despite a campaign in Scotland in the following year, the size of the military establishment was cut sharply, to eighteen bannerets and thirty-six knights. As a result, expenditure on fees was reduced from £590 to £350.[6] For the rest of the reign numbers continued at much the same level. In 1303 there were twenty-three bannerets and thirty-one knights,[7] and in 1306 seventeen bannerets and twenty-eight knights.[8] Besides changes in personnel, the documents also reveal that in the 1280s the class of *commiltones* disappeared, and that at the end of the reign the proportion of bannerets to knights rose.[9]

The class of squires retained by the household included many who never attained knighthood, while it also comprised sons of nobles like John de Warenne and Roger Mortimer. In the winter of 1296–7 there were almost 100 squires in receipt of robes, but by the following summer the figure was nearer seventy. In 1300

K. B. McFarlane, 'An Indenture of Agreement between two English Knights of Mutual Aid and Counsel in Peace and War, 5 December 1298', *B.I.H.R.*, xxxviii (1965), pp. 200–10.

[1] E. 101/4/14. [2] C. 47/4/3. [3] E. 101/4/24.
[4] B.M. Add. MS, 7965, ff. 60–2. [5] *Liber Quotidianus*, pp. 188–95.
[6] B.M. Add. MS, 7966a, ff. 78–9. [7] B.M. Add. MS, 8835, ff. 52–5.
[8] E. 101/369/11, ff. 102, 106–7.
[9] B.M. Add. MS, 7965, ff. 126–7, 131–2.

there were about sixty in all,[1] and the same number in 1304,[2] but by 1306 numbers had fallen to fifty. In the 1280s there had been over thirty sergeants-at-arms, and in 1306 they numbered only fifteen.[3] All the indications are that, far from increasing the military establishment of the household, towards the end of the reign financial stringency forced an appreciable reduction in its size. Regrettably there are no lists of the household for the Welsh wars of 1277 and 1282 that can be compared with those of the Scotch campaigns, but in 1277 Edward had a corps of some forty household knights and seventy sergeants immediately available to fight for him in Wales, which suggests that the total number retained must have been appreciably higher.[4]

The lists of the household knights show a higher degree of continuity of personnel in royal service than was usual in the retinues of the great magnates. Almost 150 men are named in the entries in these lists for the period from 1297 to 1306. About 100 of these occur more than once, while of the other fifty, some were men whose service in the household ended in 1297, and eleven were knights newly admitted in 1306. A few men, however, departed from the service of the crown after a very brief period. Of the twenty-two admitted in 1297, seven never appear in later lists, but of these, four were Gascons, which makes their disappearance very explicable. Nonetheless, there is a striking lack of continuity between the lists of royal knights in the 1280s and those of the later years of the reign. Only twenty-one of the eighty men in the household in 1285–6[5] feature in the later lists, and only ten of those in receipt of fees in 1288–9 appear again.[6] The reason for this changeover of personnel is simple. Moor has worked out the biographies of fifty-three of the eighty household knights of the 1280s.[7] Fourteen were still in the household in 1297 or later. One man, Simon de Grey, abjured the realm for felony,[8] eight had retired from royal service, including Roger l'Estrange, a loyal veteran of the Welsh wars who from 1298 was too ill to

[1] *Liber Quotidianus*, pp. 320–6.
[2] B.M. Add. MS, 8835, f. 114.
[3] E. 101/369/11, ff. 157, 159.
[4] Morris, *Welsh Wars*, p. 115.
[5] C. 47/4/3.
[6] E. 101/4/24.
[7] Moor, *Knights of Edward I, passim*.
[8] *Ibid.*, ii, p. 55.

take any part in public affairs.[1] But no less than thirty were dead by 1297, and this is why the corps of household knights changed in composition.

The household knights of the early years of Edward I's reign were very much of one generation. In the Welsh wars the king was able to rely on the service of men of roughly his own age and sympathies. The majority had been royalists in the Barons' Wars, though there were exceptions, of whom the most striking was the leader of the Disinherited, John d'Eyville.[2] A typical figure was Hugh Turberville, whose connection with Edward went back to 1263, when he had been made constable of Carmarthen and Cardigan castles. He was one of the obstinate Marcher lords who refused to accept the defeat of Lewes and continued the war, even attempting to rescue Edward from custody at Wallingford. For a time he served in Gascony, but resigned the Seneschalship in 1272 and returned to England. He fought in Wales in 1277 and 1282, was engaged in recruiting infantrymen on the latter occasion, became constable of Bere castle and acted as Otto de Grandson's deputy in North Wales. He was also a member of an embassy to Germany late in 1283. He died in 1293. His son Thomas was also a household knight, but—in great contrast to his father—turned traitor in 1295.[3]

During the Scotch wars of the latter part of the reign the king was served by a younger body of men, who must have lacked the sense of being the king's companions in arms that the men who fought in Wales possessed. Many of them were the sons of those who had served Edward in his youth and prime. One of the most notable knights of the later years was Robert Clifford, the grandson of the Roger Clifford who had served the king so well and loyally earlier.[4]

The main activity of the military establishment of the household

---

[1] H. Le Strange, *Le Strange Records, 1100–1310* (1916), p. 243.
[2] E. 101/351/17.
[3] Moor, *op. cit.*, v, pp. 56–7; Morris, *Welsh Wars*, p. 85; N. Denholm-Young, *The Country Gentry in the Fourteenth Century* (Oxford, 1969), pp. 74–5; *infra*, p. 59.
[4] Denholm-Young, *History and Heraldry*, pp. 98–100, 113–16.

was, of course, fighting. Each of the household bannerets and knights would have a small troop of his own retainers, so that the total number of men that the household could put into the field was very considerable. In addition, men might be paid wages by the household simply for the duration of a campaign, so increasing its military strength further. In fact, almost all the paid troops employed by Edward I received their wages from the household, so that it has been suggested that 'the king's army was essentially the household in arms'.[1]

The accounts for the Welsh wars do not distinguish as clearly as do some later documents between the permanent household troops and other paid cavalry forces. Some squadrons composed solely of household men can be identified in the war of 1277, but many household bannerets and knights were divided up between different commands, serving alongside men who were being paid for the duration of the war only and were not permanently retained. For instance, Grandson with a retinue of fifteen and Leyburn with one of ten were both serving on the middle March in a squadron commanded by Henry de Lacy, the earl of Lincoln. Other household bannerets, among them Ralph Daubeny and Alan Plukenet, were serving for pay in South Wales under Payn de Chaworth, who as a Marcher lord was not accepting wages from the king. In this first Welsh war there were probably at least 300 paid cavalrymen, and possibly more: the incomplete nature of the records makes exact calculation impossible.[2]

Documentation is fuller for the second Welsh war, but the main cavalry pay roll is not organized in a way which facilitates calculations,[3] and detailed accounts for the subsidiary armies engaged in the campaign do not survive. Morris calculated that the headquarters army at Chester was composed of almost 300 paid troops in June 1282, while a paid squadron of about 100 cavalrymen was sent to fight in the south.[4] It was customary for the king to recompense any of those in royal pay whose horses were lost on campaign, and to prevent fraudulent claims a brief description and valuation of each man's horse was enrolled. The list of horses for

[1] Tout, *Chapters*, ii, p. 133.
[2] Morris, *Welsh Wars*, pp. 115–43.
[3] E. 101/4/1.
[4] Morris, *op. cit.*, pp. 159, 163.

HOUSEHOLDS AND RETINUES

this campaign gives the names of some 600 men, but not all of these were serving at the same time: the document includes men who joined the army as late as December 1282.[1] Similar horse valuation lists give details of the contribution made by the household to the army. On 5 April 1282 a council was held at Devizes, where plans for the war were discussed and household troops, numbering 116 in all, mustered.[2] Later, as the campaign proceeded, the number of household troops was very considerably increased: one document lists thirty-six bannerets and knights, who with their retinues provided a force of 173 heavy cavalrymen. In addition, there were seventy-two squires separately organized in seven constabularies, bringing the total to 245, which probably represents the total of the household forces engaged in the war.[3] It therefore seems probable that the household contributed roughly one-third of the paid cavalry engaged by Edward I.

There was a brief campaign in Wales in 1287, when the revolt of Rhys ap Maredudd was put down. The king, with the household, was abroad in Gascony at the time, so the knights of the household were not employed in Wales. But an important rôle was played by men who had considerable household experience, such as William Leyburn, John l'Estrange and John de Mohaut.[4] The one pay roll that survives in full for the war of 1294 is that of the subsidiary army commanded by Warwick, which won the battle of Maes Moydog.[5] There is no complete record of the household contribution to the campaigns of this war. Likewise, there are no accounts for the first of Edward's campaigns in Scotland, the highly successful one of 1296. But for the years from 1297 until the end of the reign the evidence is both fuller and easier to analyse.

[1] C. 47/2/7.   [2] *Parl. Writs*, i, p. 222; C. 47/2/5.
[3] C. 47/2/6. Of the troop leaders listed by Morris, *op. cit.*, p. 159, Tateshale, Audley, FitzWalter, Butler, St. Amand, Bruce and Leyburn appear on this horse list.
[4] See the account of the Riccardi for Wales in E. 372/132.
[5] J. G. Edwards, 'The Battle of Maes Madog and the Welsh campaign of 1294-5', *E.H.R.*, xxxix (1924), pp. 1-12, analyses the pay roll. *Book of Prests*, ed. E. B. Fryde (Oxford, 1962), contains much information about the activities of various members of the household, but it is not a comprehensive account.

For the remarkably futile campaign in Flanders in 1297, which saw no action with the French enemy, but some with the Flemish allies, Edward set sail on 22 August with 670 cavalry. By the end of September reinforcements had brought numbers up to a maximum of 895. But of this total, only 527 were strictly speaking household troops, the others being termed 'forinsec' troops, men not permanently retained by the crown, but paid wages by the household for the duration of the campaign only.[1] Numbers on the Falkirk campaign of 1298 were more impressive. The horse valuation rolls show a household strength of just under 800, with non-household contingents numbering 564.[2] Two years later, on the expedition glorified by the *Song of Caerlaverock*, a splendid heraldic poem, 522 men had their horses valued and enrolled on the household horse list, while there were in all about 850 cavalrymen paid by the Wardrobe.[3] The account book for the year makes no emphatic distinction between the true household troops and the 'forinsec' element: for practical purposes there was no difference, and by the end of the reign the differentiation had been virtually abandoned in the accounts.

During the first years of the fourteenth century the household continued to put appreciable forces into the field, though never again on quite the scale of 1298. In 1301 there was an ambitious double campaign, a pincer movement with the king advancing from Berwick and his son from Carlisle. At one time there were nearly 1,000 cavalrymen in household pay in the two armies. Unfortunately there is no full account for the year 1303, which saw the next expedition to Scotland. But the wardrobe account for the next year begins on 20 November 1303, at which date there were 588 heavily armed cavalry in pay, ninety of them bannerets and knights.[4] Numbers had been higher in the summer,

[1] N. B. Lewis, 'The English Forces in Flanders', in *Studies in Medieval History presented to F. M. Powicke* (Oxford, 1948), pp. 313–14.

[2] Tout, *Chapters*, ii, p. 142, nn. 2, 3.

[3] *Ibid.*, pp. 139–41. This estimate of 750 cavalry given by Tout should be increased by 100, as he omits the garrison troops from Berwick, Lochmaben, Jedburgh and Edinburgh. *Liber Quotidianus*, pp. 220–1, makes it quite clear that these men joined the main army.

[4] B.M. Add. MS, 8835, ff. 55–8.

for the horse list for 1303 shows 542 men in the royal household and 182 in that of the prince of Wales,[1] who, following his failure as a military leader in 1301, had not again been given an independent command.[2] During 1304 the cavalry was maintained at roughly the same strength as it had been in the autumn of the previous year: in June there were 570 cavalrymen in royal pay.[3] The main military operation of 1304 was the siege of Stirling castle, which lasted some three months. At the end of this time, Edward cruelly refused to accept the unconditional surrender of the garrison until the castle had been bombarded by a newly completed engine, the *Warwolf*, for one day:[4] an incident which displayed a lack of chivalry and a degree of viciousness reminiscent of Matthew Paris's stories of the king's youth. The capture of Stirling marked the end of concerted and serious resistance in Scotland, and when William Wallace was caught and executed in the following year it must have seemed to Edward that success had been achieved at last.

News of the murder of John Comyn by Robert Bruce, the move which restarted war in Scotland, reached Edward by 24 February 1306, but not until the beginning of March were there any signs of the government taking any action, and then all that was done was to issue orders for the purveyance of supplies.[5] In the campaigns against Bruce in the last two years of the reign Edward I abandoned his earlier strategy of sending huge armies north to subdue the Scots by a show of strength. The hosts of 1300, 1301 and 1303 had been hard to manoeuvre, expensive, and above all, unsuccessful in engaging the enemy in battle. Faced by Bruce's guerilla tactics, the English forces were split up into smaller, more mobile units, much as had been done in Wales in 1294–5. This, combined with the fact that full accounts were never properly drawn up, makes it hard to work out how large

---

[1] E. 101/612/11.
[2] H. Johnstone, *Edward of Caernarvon, 1284–1307* (Manchester, 1946), pp. 72–95, provides a narrative of the prince's activities on these campaigns.
[3] B.M. Add. MS, 8835, ff. 55–68.
[4] Barrow, *Robert Bruce*, p. 181.
[5] *Cal. Docs. Scot.*, ii, no. 1747; *C.P.R.*, 1301–7, pp. 417–19.

the forces put into the field by the household were in these campaigns.

On 5 April 1306 Aymer de Valence, Henry Percy and Robert Clifford were commissioned to levy troops in the north of England to lead against Bruce.[1] All that is known of Percy and Clifford's men is that the former had a troop of thirty cavalry with him,[2] and that both commanders received prests as an advance on wages.[3] Valence's men can hardly be described as household troops. Numbering by July almost 300 horse and 1,500 foot, they were paid wages by the Chamberlain of Scotland, John Sandale. Of the eight bannerets in the force, only two, Gilbert Pecche and Matthew de Mont Martin, were retained by the household.[4] On 3 March Clifford recaptured Dumfries castle from the Scots, while Valence's force was strikingly successful, winning what appeared to be a decisive battle against Bruce at Methven, outside Perth. A new element of brutality seems to have been introduced into the war, with the killing of prisoners and the burning of the lands and houses of traitors, as the Scotch patriots were termed.[5]

The king's original intention had been to lead an army in person against the Scots. However, by 24 May he had decided to send his son with the main force, and follow on later himself.[6] True to his oath made at the Feast of the Swans which followed his knighting, when he swore not to sleep two nights in one place until he reached Scotland,[7] the prince set out. No account rolls survive for his army, but it cannot have been large, for Walter Reynolds, Keeper of the prince's Wardrobe, paid out only £629 2s. 0d. to the knights and bannerets, and £296 2s. 4d. to the squires and sergeants.[8] A list of liveries of food made at Perth and Aberdeen includes the names of only about twenty bannerets and knights, of whom three were members of the royal household.[9] Those of the household knights not already engaged in the war came north

---

[1] *Ibid.*, p. 426. [2] E. 101/369/11, f. 89.
[3] *Cal. Docs. Scot.*, ii, no. 1762. [4] Sandale's account, E. 101/13/16.
[5] Barrow, *Robert Bruce*, pp. 215–16; *Cal. Docs. Scot.*, ii, nos. 1782, 1790.
[6] *Ibid.*, no. 1773. [7] H. Johnstone, *op. cit.*, p. 108.
[8] E. 101/369/11, ff. 109, 113.
[9] Accounts of the prince's household, E. 101/369/10.

with Edward I later in the year, though this was no large army either: a horse list shows a total strength of eighty-eight cavalry.[1]

In the military operations of the next year, 1307, the household knights did not serve in one unit; they were divided between the various forces sent against the Scots. Valence was serving under contract with 100 horse until Easter, but he had additional men serving under him for pay, bringing the total strength up to 160 in mid-March.[2] In February John Botetourt, a very important household banneret, led a small force of some fifty-five horse against Bruce, and towards the end of March he made a raid, lasting a month, up the Nith valley with seventy-seven cavalry. Another small force was sent into Glentrool in mid-April.[3] No accounts survive for the armies commanded by Gloucester and Percy, although the latter was almost certainly paid wages, as he had been in the previous year. Late in May a new force was organized under John St. John with William de Rue as paymaster. It was intended that it should consist of forty men-at-arms in pay, along with 1,000 infantry,[4] but the account shows that it was in fact composed of forty hobelars, or light cavalry, eight constables of foot and 826 infantrymen, the number of these rising to roughly 1,700 in mid-June.[5] Clearly the heavy cavalry were all fully engaged in the other armies. The earl of Hereford was also on campaign, but only one payment, of about £70 in June,[6] to men under his command is recorded. It seems likely that he was serving at his own expense with a mounted retinue, only accepting wages for the infantry accompanying him.

Although the royal household was present in Scotland during the campaigns of the last two years of the reign, and its knights took a prominent part in much of the fighting, it was no longer the impressive body that had been capable of forming a whole battalion at Falkirk and at Caerlaverock. Reduced in size, split up under separate commands, the army at the end of the reign could

---

[1] E. 101/612/19.
[2] E. 101/13/16.
[3] *Cal. Docs. Scot.*, ii, no. 1923; there is a horse list for Botetourt's men in E. 101/612/21.
[4] E. 101/370/16, f. 13v.   [5] E. 101/531/11.   [6] E. 101/370/16, f. 15v.

not be described as virtually 'the household in arms'. The obvious explanation for the small size of the English forces in Scotland during these years is financial stringency, combined with a failure to realize the scale of the opposition to English rule. The result was that the English simply did not have enough troops to contain Bruce. The Glentrool raid was ambushed and driven back with heavy losses. Only three days after Valence was defeated at Loudoun Hill, Gloucester was also vanquished.[1] It is hardly surprising that on 15 May 1307 an ally of the English wrote from Forfar a well-known letter informing the administration of the general support that Bruce was receiving, and stating that 'Men say openly that ... victory will go to Bruce.'[2]

The way the household was organized to fight, in those campaigns when it did serve as one body, should be examined. One interesting document, probably dating from 1301, lists the household cavalry divided into *constabularia*, each of which consisted as far as was possible of ten men. Over sixty men, headed by John Botetourt, are designated as being of the king's Chamber. This does not mean that they were paid their wages by the Chamber: the very fact of their inclusion in what is obviously a wardrobe document shows this. But it does suggest that these men had some special status in the household, and were probably more closely associated with the king than the other household knights and squires. They do not appear to have been under the control of the steward of the household, Walter Beauchamp, for his is the first name of the 280 men that the document proceeds to list. Where a retinue numbered more than ten men, such as that of William de Cantilupe with fourteen, it was not split up but served as one unit. The sergeants-at-arms were not divided up between the various *constabularia*; they formed distinct sections of their own. They were not even given knights to command their units.[3]

But although the household knights generally served together, forming a coherent military unit, some of them might be detached

---

[1] Barrow, *Robert Bruce*, p. 244.   [2] *Cal. Docs. Scot.*, ii, no. 1926.
[3] E. 101/13/35/11. This document cannot be later than 1303, as it mentions Ralph Manton, killed at Roslin in that year, and it lists several men who first appeared as household knights in 1301.

from the main body and be given individual responsibilities. Several were made constables of castles, both in Wales and in Scotland. The raids or *chevauchées* used to harry the Scots were very frequently commanded by household knights. In addition to his raid up the Nith in 1307, John Botetourt led a force of about 130 horse and 1,770 foot from Annandale into Nithsdale early in 1304,[1] and at about the same time John Segrave was joined by two household bannerets, Clifford and Latimer, in a similar expedition into Selkirk Forest. The composition of this force was strictly laid down by indenture, and instructions given that no one not included in the document was to be allowed to accompany the raid, as a precaution against infiltration by enemy spies.[2]

Naval command often went to household knights. In 1294 William Leyburn was captain of the fleet, and in 1297 he was titled admiral. Edward Charles, who held this office in 1306, had been a household knight until 1300, and Simon de Montague, captain and governor of the whole fleet in 1307, had also served in the household.[3] Another household man who served at sea was John Botetourt, Leyburn's second in command in 1294, and commander of a fleet of ninety-four vessels with a total complement of 3,578 men drawn from the ports between Harwich and Lynn, in 1296.[4] Botetourt was one of the most important of the household bannerets in the later years of the reign, being the only one to become a member of the council on a reasonably permanent basis, and summoned to parliament in that capacity in 1305.[5] A curious genealogical table in a chronicle suggests that he was an illegitimate son of Edward I. However, this evidence is suspect

[1] Dalilegh's account, E. 101/11/19, ff. 2-3. *Cal. Docs. Scot.*, ii, no. 1437, gives a higher figure for the infantry strength, which was probably depleted by desertion.

[2] *Ibid.*, ii, no. 1432. This technique was used on at least one other occasion, as is shown by E. 101/371/8/56.

[3] *C.P.R., 1292-1301*, p. 126; Denholm-Young, *History and Heraldry*, pp. 36-7.

[4] C. 47/2/11. This document is undated, but as the payments it records start on 7 March, and preparations in 1296 began early in the year, it seems that it must date from that year.

[5] *Parl. Writs*, i, p. 160.

and there is nothing to support it in any other source.[1] He first appears as a squire of the household in the course of the second Welsh war, and by Christmas 1284 had been knighted. In 1298 he was promoted to the rank of a banneret.[2] Besides his loyal service in Edward's wars, he was employed as a justice, being on a commission of gaol delivery in 1293 and serving on the Trailbaston enquiry of 1305.[3] Not a rich man in his own right, probably a younger son, he became lord of Mendlesham in Suffolk by marriage,[4] but plainly owed his prestige and power to the appointments he received from the crown. His loyalty was to Edward I, and not to the crown: his hostility to Edward II was indicated as early as 1308, and he was one of those involved in the capture and death of the unsavoury Piers Gaveston.[5]

During the Welsh wars the household knights were often used to assist in the task of recruiting troops and organizing the preparatory stages of campaigns. Richard du Bois, Hugh Turberville and Grimbald Pauncefoot were employed in this way in 1282, as were Roger l'Estrange and Bogo de Knoville.[6] In the closing stages of the second Welsh war Philip d'Arcy and Gilbert de Briddeshale each commanded small contingents convoying food supplies being brought from Chester and Flint to Rhuddlan castle.[7] In 1300 William Felton bought the lances from which five banners of the army were to be flown: two with the arms of England, one with the cross of St. George, one with the arms of St. Edmund and one with those of St. Edward. Before the campaign began that year, Thomas de Bikenore was sent to Berwick in advance of the main army to make preparations for the arrival of the household.[8] Both in 1304 and in 1306 household knights were employed in escorting Scotch prisoners to England.[9]

[1] This problem is discussed by N. Denholm-Young, *op. cit.*, pp. 38–9. Botetourt's name in the table in the Hailes chronicle, B.M. Cotton. MS, Cleop. D. iii, f. 51, is written over an erasure.
[2] E. 101/4/1; E. 101/351/17; Denholm-Young, *op. cit.*, p. 38, n. 6.
[3] N. H. Nicolas, *The Siege of Carlaverock* (London, 1828), pp. 202–4.
[4] I. J. Sanders, *English Baronies* (Oxford, 1960), p. 11.
[5] Denholm-Young, *op. cit.*, pp. 39, 130.   [6] *Parl. Writs*, i, p. 247.
[7] E. 101/351/9.   [8] *Liber Quotidianus*, pp. 64, 74.
[9] B.M. Add. MS, 8835, f. 12; E. 101/370/16, f. 5.

Household knights might be used on matters of state quite unconnected with the business of campaigning. When the king returned from his extended stay in Gascony in the summer of 1289 loud complaints of the corruption and incompetence of the judicial administration reached him. The commission appointed to enquire into them included among its members John St. John and William Latimer, both household knights,[1] and in October John de Mold was employed in arresting the sheriff of Surrey and Sussex together with various other malefactors, and then in holding inquisitions into administrative failures. Elias de Hauville was sent to Norfolk to inquire into a murder committed by the servants of the most notorious of the evil judges, Thomas de Weyland.[2] The conduct of negotiations with foreign powers was usually the preserve of such experts as Amadeus of Savoy, Otto de Grandson, or John of Berwick, though late in 1300 Arnold de Cavapenna was sent to his native Gascony to discuss various matters with members of Philip IV's council,[3] and in 1304 another household knight, John de Bokland, was sent to negotiate with Philip.[4] But such tasks as these, examples of which could be multiplied, were not part of the normal rôle of the household knights, and appointments of this type owed at least as much to the qualities and abilities of the individuals as to their status in the household.

The military household provided Edward I with a solid and generally reliable corps of men, whose main duties were military, but who could be useful in other ways. Thomas Turberville, who went over to the French following his capture in Gascony was a notable exception to the general loyalty of the group;[5] more excusable was the behaviour of the Scot Simon Fraser, who rejoined his own countrymen in 1300 or early 1301.[6] But such cases were exceptional. The loyalty of the household knights

---

[1] Powicke, *The Thirteenth Century*, pp. 361-2.
[2] E. 101/352/14.   [3] B.M. Add. MS, 7966a, f. 49v.
[4] B.M. Add. MS, 8835, f. 19v.
[5] J. G. Edwards, 'The Treason of Thomas Turberville', in *Studies in Medieval History presented to F. M. Powicke*, pp. 269-309.
[6] Barrow, *Robert Bruce*, p. 171, n. 2.

perhaps provided an element of political stability in the régime of Edward I. One former member, John Lovel, was involved in the opposition during the crisis of 1297; however, he was alone in this.

The household knights did not take any large part in the affairs of state conducted in parliament. The only ones to sit as county members were Bartholomew Badlesmere and Thomas Chaucecombe for Kent and Hampshire respectively in the Carlisle parliament of 1307.[1] Some of the more important and wealthy of the bannerets of the household received summonses to the upper house, but Walter Beauchamp, who attained the position of steward of the household, never had one. Nevertheless, it is probably true that it was only through the royal household that a man such as Eustace de l'Hacche could rise from the rank of a *serviens* to that of a lord of parliament. Few household knights were members of the royal council: in the later years of the reign the only one was John Botetourt, summoned to parliament as a councillor in 1305,[2] and it seems likely that this distinction was more a result of his services as a judge than of those on the field of battle. A list of councillors in 1276 suggests that the lay councillors were in general men of a wealth and standing that made it unlikely that they would seek paid employment in Edward's household, even though they might be closely associated with the king.[3]

Important as they were in war, even here the rôle of the household knights should not be exaggerated. The major military commands were rarely entrusted to them. In 1282 Edward's intention was that Tiptoft should be commander-in-chief in South Wales, but after protests the position was given to the earl of Gloucester, whose status rendered him more suitable for the task.[4] During the last campaigns of the reign Valence, Gloucester and Percy all led more important forces than did John Botetourt. The household provided the armies of 1298 and 1300 with one battalion, but played no real part in the leadership or organization of the others.

[1] *Parl. Writs*, i, pp. 188–9. [2] *Ibid.*, i, p. 160.
[3] *C.C.R.*, *1272–79*, p. 360. [4] *Infra*, pp. 71–2.

Just as the king had his permanent following of knights, which might be expanded for the needs of war, so the magnates maintained their own households and retinues. The volume of material available to show how the forces brought by the magnates to fight in Edward's wars were organized is of course very limited in extent when compared with the evidence that survives for the royal household. Private records are scanty, while the royal sources only provide some incidental information.

Although many of the agreements made between lords and their followers were probably never put down in writing, some formal contracts have survived. The earliest dates from the end of Henry III's reign, and was made between the Lord Edward and Adam of Jesmond in 1270, Adam promising to accompany the future king on his crusade with four knights in return for 600 marks.[1] One indenture survives from the Welsh wars, and it provides for Peter Maulay to serve with ten men-at-arms under Edmund Stafford.[2] The earliest agreement for life service dates from 1297, and in it John Segrave promised to provide a force of sixteen or on occasion twenty horse in the service of Roger Bigod when required.[3] A few other indentures, some temporary and some for life, survive from the later years of the reign.[4] These documents are sufficiently uniform in phraseology and content to suggest that there was nothing particularly novel or abnormal in the system of magnate retinues during the reign of Edward I. It has been remarked that 'most aspects of bastard feudalism, in both temporary and permanent forms, were already developed in the reign of Edward II, and any appearance that they were very much more developed at the end of the century is largely a documentary

[1] H. G. Richardson and G. O. Sayles, *The Governance of Mediaeval England from the Conquest to the Great Charter* (Edinburgh, 1963), pp. 463–5.
[2] N. B. Lewis, 'An Early Indenture of Military Service, 27 July 1287', *B.I.H.R.*, xiii (1935), pp. 85–9.
[3] N. Denholm-Young, *Seignorial Administration in England* (Oxford, 1937), pp. 167–8.
[4] *The Red Book of Ormond*, ed. N. B. White (Irish Hist. MSS Comm., 1932), p. 103, no. 53; G. Barraclough, *The Earldom and County Palatinate of Chester* (Oxford, 1953), p. 36; *Cal. Docs. Scot.*, ii, nos. 905, 981, 1004, 1407, 1899; Altschul, *A Baronial Family*, pp. 279–80.

illusion.'[1] The statement applies equally well to the reign of Edward I.

The indentures illustrate the normal conditions under which men were taken into the service of a magnate. They and their servants would be provided with food. Aymer de Valence, Roger Bigod and Humphrey de Bohun all provided robes for their men, and the latter gave them saddles as well. Permanent retainers were usually granted land. John Segrave received the manor and advowson of Lodden in Norfolk from Bigod, while Bartholomew de Enfield obtained land worth forty marks a year in Annandale from Bohun. Temporary retainers were rewarded with money fees. Thomas de Berkeley was to receive £50 a year from Valence if he served in England, and 100 marks if abroad. In time of war he was to be paid wages at the normal rates. Like the king, Valence promised to recompense those in his retinue for any horses they lost while on campaign. Indentures might provide for service in tournaments and at parliament as well as in war.

A valuable source for the composition of the magnates' contingents in Edward's wars is the record of the protections issued to those going on campaign, guaranteeing the security of their lands during their absence.[2] Many of the applications for such writs, sent in by magnates and listing their retinues, also survive. But not all of those on campaign would have protections enrolled. Morris pointed out that often only a third of the men in a given retinue would have this done.[3] However, this evidence from protections gives valuable indications of the extent of continuity in retinues from year to year. A good example is the following of Henry de Lacy, earl of Lincoln. Taking the fifty-two men who received protections to go to Scotland with him in 1307, only eighteen appear in other years as being with him. Of these, only two men, William Stopham and Nicholas Leyburn, had been given protections to go with the earl to Gascony in 1294. Of the twenty-four men who had protections to accompany Lincoln on the Caerlaverock campaign, no less than fourteen were with him

[1] G. A. Holmes, *The Estates of the Higher Nobility in XIV Century England* (Cambridge, 1957), p. 80.
[2] *Infra*, p. 237.
[3] Morris, *Welsh Wars*, p. 246.

at some other date. Eight had protections for Gascony, and the same number for Scotland in 1307.[1]

The surviving account rolls for Lincoln's estates provide further information on his household and retinue. Fees and robes for his steward and constable came out of the proceeds of the manor of Accrington: twenty marks in the first case, £7 10s. in the second.[2] The household account shows that seven sumpter horses and eight hackneys, lost in the earl's service, were paid for. Four of the men recompensed in this way appear on the protection lists. John Stapleton was clearly retained on a short-term basis, for he was paid £20, and appears in 1306 and 1307 with protections to follow Lincoln. Richard of Arundel appears in the same lists, but as a member of another comital family, received special favours—his tunics were bought for him, and his expenses in going to tournaments paid for.[3] Those permanently retained by the earl were paid fees charged on the estates: Nicholas Leyburn and his brother Robert each received £10 a year from the manor of Halton.[4] The total size of Lincoln's regular standing retinue is suggested by the amount spent on robes. In 1305 seventeen cloths were bought for the earl and his knights at Whitsun, and a further eighteen for his men-at-arms. The robes of the bannerets of the royal household cost eight marks each, and those of the knights four marks. If Lincoln issued robes of equal value to his men, then the £79 spent on them would indicate he was responsible for clothing about two bannerets and twenty-five knights. The robes of the men-at-arms cost £60, suggesting a force of between forty-five and sixty men.[5] Obviously, such calculations must be treated extremely cautiously, but the size of retinue they point to is not implausible. Issues of hay and oats to the army awaiting embarkation at Portsmouth in 1294 show that Lincoln had with him no less than 228 horses, which must mean at least 100 cavalrymen,[6]

---

[1] *Rôles Gascons*, ed. Bémont, iii, pp. 96 seqq.; C. 67/14, 15, 16; *Scotland in 1298*, ed. H. Gough (Paisley, 1888), pp. 14–15; C. 81/1731/48.

[2] *Two 'Compoti' of the Lancashire and Cheshire manors of Henry de Lacy, Earl of Lincoln*, ed. P. A. Lyons (Chetham Soc., cxii, 1884), p. 15.

[3] D.L. 29/1/2, m. 16.   [4] Lyons, *op. cit.*, p. 67.

[5] D.L. 29/1/2, m. 16.   [6] E. 101/4/30.

although when he actually reached Gascony in 1296 he had only contracted to provide a force of sixty men-at-arms.[1] The paid squadron Lincoln commanded in the first Welsh war was 100 lances strong.[2]

Unfortunately no other household accounts like those of the earl of Lincoln survive. But the size of retinues can be determined from other sources. A contract between the government and five earls, together with Henry Percy, for service in Scotland in the winter of 1297-8 shows that Norfolk was to have no less than 130 men-at-arms with him. The smallest retinue was that of Warwick, with only thirty.[3] A list of those with Roger Bigod in 1295, presumably in Wales, indicates that he was accompanied by Hugh le Despenser with ten knights, presumably on a short-term contract, and by Thomas de Berkeley with his son Maurice and six men. The list continues with the names of fourteen knights, twenty-three men-at-arms, and five valets. There were seven clerks in the household, the total strength of which was about sixty cavalry.[4]

Aymer de Valence was the most important magnate who was prepared to accept royal pay in the later years of the reign. In 1298 he had forty-nine cavalry with him, according to the horse lists,[5] of whom twenty-five had protections.[6] In 1306-7 no less than forty-six men had protections to go to Scotland with Valence.[7] He was then the commander of a small army, and as such it was natural that he should attract many men to his banner who did not usually serve under him. The account book for the campaign shows that from May to July 1306 he had a squadron of two bannerets, fifteen knights and thirty-seven men-at-arms. During the winter he served under contract with 100 horse for £1,000.[8] The fact that Valence always served for pay suggests that he was not rich enough to afford a large permanent retinue. The evidence of the protection lists certainly supports this hypothesis. Only Roger Inkpen and his son appear regularly in his following.

[1] E. 101/353/2, f. 1.   [2] Morris, *Welsh Wars*, p. 121.
[3] H. Gough, *Scotland in 1298*, pp. 64-5.   [4] C. 47/2/10/8.
[5] Morris, *Welsh Wars*, p. 288.   [6] Gough, *op. cit.*, pp. 14-51.
[7] C. 67/15, 16.   [8] E. 101/13/16, f. 4.

Inkpen's association with the Valence family went back to 1294, when he had acted as royal counsel in an important case between William de Valence and the bishop of Worcester.[1] He was almost certainly Aymer's steward, for he had been previously employed in this capacity to look after the Cornish estates of Edmund of Cornwall. A Berkshire man, this post had led to his becoming sheriff of Cornwall. His financial expertise is demonstrated by his appointment, along with Hugh Cressingham, to audit the accounts of Amesbury priory. In 1297 he is found going to the Exchequer to draw the annual fee due to Valence, his lord. Inkpen was more violent than might be expected of such a professional administrator. He was indicted for a series of crimes for which he received a pardon in 1303, at Valence's request. His most notable victim was an even more criminal fellow steward, Adam Stratton.[2]

The rolls of protection reveal that a lack of continuity in personnel was common in the retinues of most magnates. The tendency for men to serve under different lords in several campaigns is well illustrated by Baldwin Manners, who appeared in 1300 with John Botetourt, in 1306 with Lincoln, and in the last year of the reign with the prince of Wales.[3] No names appear in the retinue of Henry Percy more than once, but that other great figure of the northern marches, Robert Clifford, obviously had the power of inspiring loyalty. The author of the *Song of Caerlaverock* stated that had he been a girl, he would have given himself, heart and body, to Clifford.[4] Of the men who had protections to accompany him in 1301, all but one served with him at some other time.[5] The most outstanding of Clifford's knights was Bartholomew Badlesmere, who served with him in 1303 and again at the end of the reign. When Clifford died in 1314

---

[1] *Select Cases before the King's Council 1243-1482*, ed. I. S. Leadam and J. F. Baldwin (Selden Soc., xxxv, 1918), pp. 5-8.

[2] E. 405/1/11, 1 August; *C.C.R., 1296-1302*, p. 560; *C.C.R., 1302-7*, p. 381; *C.P.R., 1292-1301*, p. 82; *C.P.R., 1301-7*, pp. 122, 212; *Parl. Writs*, i, p. 290. For Stratton's career, see N. Denholm-Young, *Seignorial Administration*, pp. 77-85.

[3] C. 67/14, 15, 16.

[4] Denholm-Young, *History and Heraldry*, pp. 114-15.

[5] C. 67/14-16; C. 81/1722/74.

Badlesmere, along with Warwick and Percy, became an administrator of his property.[1]

The average size of the retinues provided by the ordinary bannerets is indicated by the household records. The horse rolls of the Caerlaverock campaign show that thirteen was the normal number, and this average is confirmed by the details of wages.[2] The Falkirk horse lists provide the similar figure of fifteen.[3] But these of course were the retinues of bannerets accepting wages from the crown; it is probable that men who served at their own expense were wealthier, and so would have had larger followings.

The way in which the cavalry was organized in retinues shows that the so-called 'bastard feudalism' of the later middle ages was already well established in the reign of Edward I. The crown did not, however, make much use of the possibilities such a system offered as a means of recruitment; it was not until the reign of Edward III that the normal method of raising a cavalry force was to negotiate with the leaders of retinues. To provide a complete picture of the cavalry in Edward I's armies it is necessary to investigate the methods used to summon men for service.

[1] Denholm-Young, *History and Heraldry*, p. 142, n. 1.
[2] Morris, *Welsh Wars*, p. 299; *Liber Quotidianus*, pp. 195 *seqq*.
[3] Gough, *Scotland in 1298*, pp. 161–205.

III

CAVALRY SERVICE

The reign of Edward I is generally believed to have seen the transformation of the army from an ill-disciplined, badly-organized body into an efficient and almost professional force. J. E. Morris saw the systematic use of pay as the means by which the king converted the incoherent feudal host into the kind of army which was to prove so successful in the Hundred Years War.[1] Following Morris, Sir Maurice Powicke wrote that 'in Edward's time, the feudal levy became subsidiary to the paid forces, or was not summoned at all'.[2] Only Miss Chew produced a different verdict, writing of Edward that 'the feudal levy formed the nucleus of every army he led into Wales or Scotland'.[3] The prevailing view is summarized by Michael Powicke, who regards the reign as having witnessed 'the triumph of the paid retinues over the feudal quota'.[4] The argument is that Edward found the cavalry forces raised by the summons for the traditional forty days of unpaid service inadequate, and that he developed a system of paying his troops as a more attractive alternative.

There are considerable difficulties in this theory. One problem is to explain why, if feudal service was so inadequate, Edward continued to issue feudal summonses right up to the end of his reign, the last being in 1306. The investigation of the paid troops of the household does not suggest that the crown was turning

[1] Morris, *Welsh Wars*, p. 68.
[2] Powicke, *Thirteenth Century*, p. 554.
[3] H. M. Chew, *The English Ecclesiastical Tenants in Chief and Knight Service* (Oxford, 1932), p. 71.
[4] M. Powicke, *Military Obligation in Medieval England* (Oxford, 1962), p. 103.

more and more to the use of paid troops as the reign proceeded. One way of testing the conventional view is to examine the composition of the cavalry forces for the years when the evidence is fullest, 1298, 1300 and 1304.

For the 1298 campaign, the climax of which was the great English triumph of Falkirk, there is a source entirely independent of the royal administration. The *Falkirk Roll of Arms* is a heraldic document, probably drawn up for Henry Percy, which lists all the most important men present in the army.[1] The army is shown to have been divided into four battalions, and the roll lists 110 bannerets who commanded the retinues that made them up. This can be compared with the horse lists which provide details of the contingents paid wages by the crown, totalling over 1,300 men.[2] Morris noticed that only forty-eight of the men mentioned in the roll of arms also appear in the horse lists, and he drew the obvious conclusion, that the other sixty-two bannerets in the roll were not paid wages by the crown.[3] Examination of the composition of individual battalions shows, as would be expected, that most of the bannerets in the battalion commanded by the king himself were paid: of the forty-six serving in it, only eight are not named in the horse inventories. This was of course the household battalion.

Morris assumed that the majority of the cavalry, those who do not appear on the horse lists, were unpaid feudal troops, but Denholm-Young, aware that there was no feudal summons in 1298, produced a different theory. Unjustly accusing Morris of having left out of account 'about a quarter or even a third of the heavy cavalry', he suggested that the troops in question were serving under contract agreements made with the king. He stated that where such a contract was made, the horses were not registered, though it is hard to see why this should be the case.[4] In support of his contention Denholm-Young cited a contract made

[1] N. Denholm-Young, *History and Heraldry*, p. 105. The roll is printed by H. Gough, *Scotland in 1298*, pp. 139–57.
[2] *Supra*, p. 52. These horse lists are printed by Gough, *op. cit.*, pp. 161–237.
[3] Morris, *Welsh Wars*, p. 314.
[4] Denholm-Young, *op. cit.*, p. 104.

by Henry Percy and five earls for an entirely different campaign, the winter expedition mounted in retaliation for the defeat of Stirling Bridge, which began in December 1297 and ended early in March 1298. This contract was clearly stated to be for a period of three months only, and was not renewed for the summer campaign.[1] It was a highly exceptional arrangement, entered into for a winter campaign at a time when the normal army pay office, the Wardrobe, was out of the country on the Flanders expedition.

The most plausible explanation of the evidence about the cavalry forces at Falkirk is that while many paid troops were present, nearly all in the household battalion, the majority of the cavalry, although not serving under a strict feudal obligation, were not paid by the crown. Their commanders must have been fighting at their own expense. It may be objected that the horse inventories are not the most reliable evidence of the number of paid troops: not everyone may have taken the trouble to have their horses enrolled, and the lists may be incomplete. But a study of the documents dealing with the Caerlaverock campaign, with better evidence of the cavalry who were paid wages by the crown, confirms that much of the army was neither paid nor feudal.

The famous *Song of Caerlaverock*, composed by a herald, provides a list of the most important men present on the 1300 campaign in much the same way as the *Falkirk Roll of Arms* gives such a list for 1298. In it eighty-seven bannerets are named, and it can be shown that of these only twenty-three served for pay. The wardrobe account for the year provides an absolutely reliable list of all those in receipt of wages on the campaign, and shows that four bannerets were omitted by the author of the *Song*, which is hardly surprising, for he excuses himself for his inability to remember the names of all those with the earl of Lincoln.[2] It is not possible to argue that the records of the paid troops are incomplete,

---

[1] The contract is printed by Gough, *op. cit.*, pp. 64–5. Tout, *Chapters in Mediaeval Administrative History*, ii, p. 139 and n. 1, suggested that it was for the winter campaign of 1299–1300, but the hesitation he indicated about this was wholly justified: the document is clearly dated, and can only apply to the winter campaign of 1297–98.

[2] *The Siege of Carlaverock*, ed. N. H. Nicolas (London, 1828), p.12.

and that the sixty-four apparently unpaid bannerets named in the *Song* were in fact receiving wages from some department of the government other than the Wardrobe. For the liberate rolls, and the exchequer issue and receipt rolls make it quite plain that there was no other department being issued with funds to pay for the war in Scotland.[1] There is no record of the appointment of any paymasters for the campaign who were not responsible to the Wardrobe, nor any references to contracts of the type entered into by Percy and the earls in the winter of 1297-8.

However, the situation in 1300 was not quite the same as in 1298, for there was a formal feudal summons issued for the Caerlaverock campaign.[2] Did this mean that the unpaid men were all doing feudal service? The roll of the Constable, which records details of the performance of service in 1300, shows that in fact only about 400 men were doing strict feudal service. Of the men named in the *Song of Caerlaverock*, only the earl of Gloucester, Hugh le Despenser and John Hastings served in person. The other bannerets on the campaign who owed service as tenants-in-chief merely detached members of their retinues to go through the formalities of feudal service, and it is these men who made up the quotas recorded on the roll.[3]

For most of the campaigns of Edward I's reign there are full details only of those men serving for pay, or performing strict feudal service. The heraldic documents available for 1298 and 1300 are exceptional. But for 1304 there are lists of the men present in the army which can be compared with the pay records of the Wardrobe.[4] These indicate that, as in 1298 and 1300, many magnates evidently served at their own expense. One document lists the bannerets and knights who were in the army in the early months of the year, when Edward was in his winter quarters in Dunfermline abbey. About 140 men were named, and at least 100 of them do not appear in the wardrobe account as being in

---

[1] E. 403/106, 107; C. 62/67.   [2] *Parl. Writs*, i, p. 327.
[3] *Documents and Records Illustrative of the History of Scotland*, ed. F. Palgrave (London, 1837), pp. 208-31. The question of feudal service is discussed more fully *infra*, pp. 78-82.
[4] Palgrave, *Documents*, pp. 262-74; B.M. Add. MS, 8835, ff. 55v-68v.

receipt of wages. The other list splits up the cavalry into twenty-eight companies; out of all the company leaders named, only Robert FitzPayn, William de Rithre, William Latimer the younger and Hugh Bardolf appear on the pay lists of the household. Richard de Burgh, earl of Ulster, alone accepted wages among the seven earls on the campaign, and as an Irishman he was in a rather special position.

How usual was it for large numbers of cavalry to serve neither for pay, nor under a strict feudal obligation? Is it likely that 1298, 1300 and 1304 were exceptional years, and that the armies raised for all the other campaigns of the reign fitted the conventional picture drawn by historians? For the first Welsh war there is evidence of unpaid, non-feudal service. The men of Cheshire were thanked for doing the service they owed, and for doing more than they were obliged to.[1] The knights and others of the counties of Shropshire and Hereford were thanked by the king for fighting 'not by reason of any service owed to us at present, but graciously and of their own accord'. They were promised that no precedent would be made of this.[2] Such letters were not normal, and it seems that they must refer to unpaid voluntary service. Although the earls of Warwick and Lincoln commanded paid squadrons, the earl of Hereford fought what was virtually a private war with his own resources. Payn de Chaworth, in command of paid troops, was fighting near his own estates, and took no pay for himself or his personal retinue. Furthermore, it is most improbable that the magnates when performing their feudal service of forty days, would have been content to appear with the very small retinues of the formal quotas. They must have brought with them many more knights and squires than they actually registered with the Marshal and Constable, just as had been the case earlier, in 1245. It is also probable that after the end of the forty days some of the unpaid contingents remained on campaign without accepting the king's wages.[3]

The second Welsh war saw Edward attempt to conduct a campaign with an army entirely paid royal wages. In April 1282

[1] Morris, *Welsh Wars*, p. 119.   [2] *Parl. Writs*, i, p. 196.
[3] Morris, *op. cit.*, pp. 69, 118–23, 132.

the king invited six earls and 152 others to serve for pay.[1] But his plans provoked opposition. At the council at Devizes early in April 1282 the household knight Robert Tiptoft was replaced in the command of the forces in South Wales by the earl of Gloucester. The earl of Hereford, seeing a threat to his position, insisted on his rights as Constable. Then, in mid-May, the original summonses were replaced by new ones. In these no mention was made of pay, but the tenants-in-chief were instead requested in formal feudal terms to provide their forty days service.[2] The chroniclers make no mention of what was evidently a considerable crisis, and the baronial objections to paid service can only be guessed at. Probably, if the whole army was paid wages, the king would have complete rights over all lands and castles captured, whereas if they were taken by a feudal army, they would be allocated to the man with the best claim.[3] In a paid army, the king may have had rights to booty that he would not have had were he employing unpaid feudal troops.[4] The explanation, however, may be simpler: that men of the stature of the earls of Hereford and Gloucester resented the degree of subordination implied in accepting royal pay. An earl could not with dignity accept orders from such a man as Tiptoft.

The results of this opposition to Edward's plans were clear enough. The earl of Lincoln who had twice accepted pay before 1282 never did so again, except on his campaigns in Gascony.[5] In 1287 various magnates, including the earls of Warwick, Surrey and Norfolk accepted prests, or advances of cash, from the government; these may have been advances on wages, but more probably were simply loans to assist them in their preparations for war.

[1] *Parl. Writs*, i, pp. 222-4.

[2] *Ibid.*, i, pp. 224-7; Morris, *Welsh Wars*, pp. 155-7.

[3] For a discussion of this in a later period, with rather different circumstances, see M. H. Keen, *The Laws of War in the Late Middle Ages* (London, 1965), pp. 148-9.

[4] There was some trouble in 1277 when Dafydd ap Gruffydd, who was demanding pay for his troops, withheld booty that was claimed by the crown, *Calendar of Ancient Correspondence concerning Wales*, ed. J. G. Edwards (Cardiff, 1936), p. 55.

[5] Morris, *Welsh Wars*, p. 158.

There is no evidence at all to suggest that Cornwall, Hereford or Gloucester were paid for this campaign.[1] In the final Welsh war, that of 1294–5, none of the earls can be proved to have taken pay. Warwick's army which, when based on Oswestry,[2] won the battle of Maes Moydog, was a paid force, but the name of the earl does not appear on the pay roll. Nor does that of the earl of Arundel, who later joined Warwick.[3] No pay rolls survive for the rest of the campaign, but a wardrobe account of prests contains no mention of wages being paid to any of the earls.[4]

The evidence already discussed has shown that none of the English earls received pay for the campaigns in Scotland in 1298, 1300 or 1304. Nor is there evidence for their accepting wages for any other of Edward's summer campaigns in the north.[5] But pay was taken for the expedition which set out late in 1297. The contract arranged for the earls of Surrey, Norfolk, Hereford, Gloucester and Warwick, with Henry Percy, to serve for three months with a total of 500 horse, in return for £7,691 16s. 8d.[6] In addition the earl of Arundel with thirty-nine horse served for wages.[7] A similar contract scheme was envisaged in the autumn of 1301, but there is no evidence that it was put into effect.[8] It may be that the earls were prepared to serve under contract when the king was not present on campaign, but that they resented the subordinate position that they were put in by taking pay when Edward was at

[1] *Ibid.*, p. 210; account of the Riccardi for Wales in E. 372/132.

[2] The Hagnaby chronicle, B.M. Cotton MS, Vesp. B. xi, f. 37. This chronicle contains a hitherto unnoted newsletter about the battle of Maes Moydog, which confirms the suggestion made in the *Book of Prests*, ed. Fryde, p. xxxvi, that the English army marched on the Welsh from Oswestry.

[3] J. G. Edwards, 'The Battle of Maes Madog and the Welsh campaign of 1294–5', *E.H.R.*, xxxix (1924), pp. 1–12.

[4] *Book of Prests*, ed. Fryde, p. 81, shows that, like Warwick, Pembroke and Lancaster commanded troops in royal pay, but there is no evidence that the earls themselves were paid.

[5] A possible exception is Thomas of Lancaster, who was paid wages in 1298, and did homage for his lands on 8 September of that year. He may well have been paid up to, and not after, that date.

[6] Gough, *Scotland in 1298*, pp. 64–5; *supra*, pp. 68–9.

[7] E. 101/7/8.

[8] E. 159/75, mm. 5d–6.

the head of the army. Furthermore, feudal service could not be performed in the absence of the king, according to the argument advanced in 1297 by Bigod and Bohun, and this shows that a distinction between campaigns when the king was present, and those when he was not, was made at this period. Edward did not go to fight in Gascony, and the earls who served there were prepared to accept wages. A further exception to the general rule that the earls were unwilling to accept royal pay must be made in the case of the Scots and Irish: the earls of Dunbar and Ulster in particular had no hesitation in serving for wages. In 1296 the earl of Ulster provided Edward with some 300 men-at-arms, 260 hobelars and 2,500 foot, and appreciable numbers of Irish troops served in Scotland in 1301 and 1303.[1]

It was only in the case of garrison service that it was common to make contracts. Castle constables would often agree to remain at their posts with a specified number of men in return for a lump sum rather than receive daily wages. For example, on 18 October 1297 an indenture was drawn up with Robert Hastang for the custody of Roxburgh castle with a force of eighteen men-at-arms, twenty crossbowmen and ninety-two archers until the following Whitsun in return for £130.[2] Interestingly, English constables on occasion received better terms than the Scots employed by Edward. In 1302 John de Kingston contracted to keep Edinburgh castle with ten men-at-arms from September until Christmas for £40, while Archibald Livingstone received only £30 for the custody of Linlithgow with a force of identical strength for the same period.[3] Often the contract system was only used to supply the cavalry forces for the castles, the infantry being paid daily wages, while there were periods, notably in the summer, when the whole garrison would be paid on a daily basis.[4] Of course, not all of the castles held by the English in Scotland were in the hands of the crown. Caerlaverock was granted to Robert Clifford

[1] J. F. Lydon, 'An Irish Army in Scotland in 1296', *The Irish Sword*, v (1962), pp. 184-90; 'Irish Levies in the Scottish Wars, 1296-1302', *ibid.*, pp. 207-17.
[2] E. 101/7/10. [3] E. 101/369/11, f. 90.
[4] There are many examples of these contracts with castle constables, as in *Cal. Docs. Scot.*, ii, nos. 1170-74, 1286, 1287, 1321; E. 101/9/15, 16; E. 101/10/15; E. 101/13/34/25.

in 1298,[1] and Bothwell was held by Aymer de Valence after its capture in 1301 and Inverkip by the earl of Lincoln.[2] In addition, Edward I naturally left many castles, especially in the north, in the hands of those Scotch magnates he regarded as trustworthy. Just as the field armies were composed of both paid and unpaid soldiers, therefore, so were the forces garrisoning the castles.

The armies that were sent to fight in Gascony and Flanders do not fit into the same pattern as those that campaigned in Wales and Scotland. Men who were prepared to serve at their own expense against the Welsh or the Scots in a cause they approved of had no desire to join in unpopular campaigns abroad. Opposition to service on the continent had been frequent and vociferous since the reign of Richard I. It had been an element in the struggle of the baronage against King John, and one of the grievances of the Marshal and Constable in 1297 was that Edward I wanted them to serve overseas. In 1294 Edward issued a strictly feudal summons to raise an army to defend Gascony against the designs of Philip IV.[3] The inclusion of the king of Scotland and several Scotch magnates in this summons did much to provoke the revolt against English suzerainty in the following year, but surprisingly there is no direct evidence of the English baronage resenting the summons. Morris assumed that, although they were couched in feudal terms, the writs 'cannot but have been mere invitations to professional soldiers to raise cavalry for the king's pay'.[4] This seems highly unlikely. Certainly the abbot of Ramsey did not interpret his summons in this way, for he actually sent men to the muster to perform his service for him.[5] The Treasurer was appointed to accept fines from those ecclesiastics and women who preferred to commute their service.[6] There clearly were difficulties in enforcing the demand for service, for on 17 August the muster which had been ordered for 1 September was postponed until the end of the month.[7] It looks very much as if it never actually took place. Miss

---

[1] Bodleian Library MS, Dodsworth 70, f. 64.
[2] *Cal. Docs. Scot.*, ii, nos. 1214, 1519.
[3] *Parl. Writs*, i, pp. 259–63.   [4] Morris, *Welsh Wars*, p. 276.
[5] Chew, *English Ecclesiastical Tenants in Chief*, p. 45.
[6] *Rôles Gascons*, iii, pp. 213–14.   [7] *Ibid.*, pp. 262–3.

Chew assumed that it was cancelled because of the news of the Welsh revolt,[1] but as it was not until 15 October that the seriousness of the situation in Wales became apparent to the government,[2] this argument is not convincing. It is much more likely that opposition to a feudal levy involving service abroad had compelled Edward to abandon his plans before the news of the Welsh revolt came through.

The army that was sent to Gascony in October 1294 was composed entirely of paid men. Fourteen magnates, headed by the king's brother Edmund of Lancaster, were granted on 10 October a liberate writ of £1,983 6s. 8d., as a loan with which to prepare themselves and their men for the expedition.[3] Such advances were not normally accepted by men not serving for pay, and this case was no exception. Edmund contracted to serve for a year with 140 men-at-arms in return for 4,000 marks. The earl of Lincoln was to receive 2,000 marks.[4] Later in the war, different rates were in force. By 1298 Lincoln was being paid £1,000 a year for sixty men-at-arms, or twenty-five marks per man, while Edmund of Cornwall with 150 men was contracted at a rate of £2,000 a year, which works out at twenty marks per man.[5] Other troops in Gascony were paid wages on a daily basis, and it appears that even the Gascons recruited locally were paid wages. Not all the English baronage welcomed paid service in Gascony. In 1295 nineteen barons were ordered to set out there, but several of them proved unco-operative. Edward accordingly sent a vicious letter to the Exchequer, asking that their lands be harshly distrained, and that they be persecuted in every conceivable way. The debts that these men owed to the crown were impressive; the earl of Arundel, for example, owed £5,232, and William de Vescy £1,019. In the normal way, such debts were allowed to run on for years: the threat of collecting them was sufficient to force the dissident barons to abandon their stand, and they dutifully set off for Gascony.[6]

[1] Chew, op. cit., p. 99.
[2] Morris, op. cit., p. 242.
[3] C. 62/71.
[4] E. 101/353/2, f. 1.
[5] E. 101/377/20, f. 1. This is part of an account of the Keeper of the Wardrobe for 1319–20, and its date provides a good example of the length of time it took to settle many of the accounts of Edward I's reign.
[6] Book of Prests, ed. Fryde, p. xlviii; E. 159/68, mm. 65–6; Parl. Writs, i, p. 269.

The opposition to service, both paid and feudal, in Gascony seems slight in comparison with the resentment aroused by the king's plan of fighting on two fronts in 1297, with one army in Flanders and one in south-western France. At the Salisbury parliament early in the year the king proposed a feudal summons, and that the Marshal and Constable should lead one army in Gascony, while Edward himself launched the attack in the Low Countries. The plan was opposed on two grounds. Firstly it was claimed that the Marshal and Constable should accompany the king on campaign. Secondly, the old argument that there was no obligation to serve overseas was revived. The climax was the famous scene between Edward and Roger Bigod the Marshal when, to the king's saying, 'By God, sir Earl, either you go or you hang', Bigod retorted, 'By the self-same oath, sir King, I shall neither go nor hang'. In the subsequent struggle the king was forced to withdraw the idea of a feudal summons, and an alternative form of summons invented by the government met with little success.[1] Although the council felt that Edward was putting himself in considerable danger by going abroad without sufficient funds,[2] he set sail from Winchelsea on 22 August. The constitutional crisis had deprived him of a feudal host; he was accompanied merely by a small army composed of paid troops, mostly loyal members of his household. Even if promotions made on the campaign are included, there were fewer bannerets in the whole army in 1297 than were in the household battalion alone in 1298. But, rather surprisingly, there were some unpaid cavalry on the Flanders campaign. Antony Bek, one of Edward's staunchest supporters at this time, had about thirty men-at-arms with him. William Hotham, archbishop-elect of Dublin, the earl of Athol, Hugh le Despenser, Bartholomew Badlesmere, Robert de Mohaut and John de Hastings all served voluntarily with smaller retinues. The Treasurer, Walter Langton, does not appear to have been paid for the followers he brought with him.[3]

[1] *Chron. Guisborough*, pp. 289–90; *infra*, pp. 84–6.
[2] *Rôles Gascons*, iii, no. 4392.
[3] N. B. Lewis, 'The English Forces in Flanders', *Studies in Medieval History presented to F. M. Powicke*, p. 312, n. 4.

CAVALRY SERVICE

In 1277, 1282, 1300, 1303 and 1306 the tenants-in-chief of the crown provided their due quotas of feudal service in response to a royal summons. If this picture of armies composed partly of paid troops and, notably in the case of Wales and Scotland, partly of magnates serving voluntarily at their own expense, is correct, where do these strict feudal quotas fit in, and why did Edward summon them?

A radical reduction in the number of troops obliged to muster in response to a feudal summons had taken place in the course of the thirteenth century. The old structure of knights' fees, created in the Conqueror's reign and brought up to date by Henry II in 1166, had been intended to provide the crown with the service of over 5,000 knights. It is unlikely that there ever were enough knights in England to perform this full feudal service: Henry II and his sons on several occasions demanded only a fraction of the total owed by the tenants-in-chief. As the equipment of knights became more elaborate, and better horses were required to carry the increased weight of armour, so the cost of knighthood rose sharply and fewer men were able to afford it. The duties and obligations of a knight were, of course, by no means confined to the field of battle. In the thirteenth century these men carried a vast burden of local administrative work, sitting on juries, acting as commissioners of all sorts, and serving as sheriffs, coroners and escheators. The onerousness of such duties meant that many men were anxious to avoid becoming knights. The result was that the number of men of this class was small. In Essex in 1295 there were only twenty-four fit for active service, and it has been estimated that about this time there were only some 1,250 in the whole of England. Although it was decided, probably in 1230, that for the purpose of a feudal muster the formally dubbed knight could be equated with two sergeants-at-arms, who would be heavily armed and mounted, it was impossible in the thirteenth century for a full-scale feudal muster on the twelfth-century assessment of knights' fees to take place. A further difficulty was that in many cases the tenants-in-chief were finding it hard to get their own sub-tenants to provide service.[1]

[1] Sally Harvey, 'The Knight and the Knight's Fee in England', *Past and*

The solution to these problems was a radical reduction in the size of the feudal quotas. The process by which this was achieved is a mysterious one, but seems to have been a gradual one of negotiation with individual tenants-in-chief. There was no standard formula adopted to reduce the old quotas: the new were rather established on the basis of a reasonable, if low, assessment of the number of men a lord could be expected to provide. For the most part the new levels of service were established by the time of the Welsh campaign of 1245, although it was possible for the abbot of Abingdon to produce his full service of thirty knights as late as 1266.[1] In some cases the new quotas were so small that magnates actually provided larger contingents than they were legally obliged to. The earl of Winchester appeared with ten knights for the Welsh campaign of 1245, although only bound to attend with three and a half.[1] On the old assessment he had owed sixty-six.[2] The reductions might be very startling. Hugh de Courtenay was due to provide ninety-two knights on the old system, but by Edward I's reign his quota of service was only three.[3]

As a result of the establishment of these new quotas of service, the numbers of troops performing formal feudal military service under Edward I was not considerable. The first summons of the reign, in 1277, produced a total service of 228 knights and 294 sergeants, two of the latter being considered as equivalent to one knight. For the second Welsh war the Marshal's roll lists only 123 knights and 190 sergeants, but there may well have been other musters not recorded in the main roll.[4] By the time of the Caerlaverock campaign of 1300 many more were sending sergeants

---

Present, 49 (1970), pp. 30-43; N. Denholm-Young, 'Feudal Society in the Thirteenth Century: the Knights', *History*, xxix (1944), p. 61; M. Powicke, *Military Obligation in Medieval England*, pp. 77-8; I. J. Sanders, *Feudal Service in England* (Oxford, 1956), pp. 50-5; S. K. Mitchell, *Studies in Taxation under John and Henry III* (New Haven, 1914), pp. 307-9.

[1] *C.P.R., 1258-66*, p. 592. The process of the reduction of the old quotas of service is described and analysed by Sanders, *Feudal Military Service in England*, pp. 59-90 and by Walker, 'The Anglo-Welsh Wars, 1217-1267', pp. 40-60.
[2] Mitchell, *Studies in Taxation under John and Henry III*, p. 246, n. 86.
[3] Morris, *Welsh Wars*, p. 64.   [4] *Ibid.*, p. 45.

rather than knights to do service, and most of the tenants-in-chief preferred to have their service done by deputies even if they themselves were present on the campaign. The roll of service records forty knights and 366 sergeants.[1] The rolls for 1303 show a much smaller service, composed of fifteen knights and 267 sergeants, along with about twenty lightly armed horsemen.[2] But, as in 1282, it is very likely that records of subsidiary musters have not survived. For the next campaign for which there was a feudal summons, that of 1306, two small muster rolls show service done by about twelve knights and eighty sergeants.[3] There was more commutation that year than before, but writs issued between 1314 and 1316 allowing those who had served in 1306 to levy scutage on their own lands show that almost a hundred tenants-in-chief either served in person, or made arrangements for others to do their service for them.[4] Late in 1306 accusations of non-performance of service were brought by the government against fifteen men. Five of them stated that they had appeared,[5] and it seems very likely that full and correct records of the feudal service done in 1306 were never properly drawn up. The fact that in some cases evidence that men had served in the army was given to Edward II by the Chancellor, rather than by the Constable or Marshal, whose duty it was to keep records of the performance of military service, reinforces this suggestion.

Although Edward I went on issuing formal feudal summonses almost up to the very end of the reign, it does not seem that the forces yielded by the strict quotas were of any great importance. The problem was that the quotas were quite unrealistic, being unrelated to the wealth of the men who produced them. An important royal knight like Adam de Welles owed service for only one half of a sergeanty.[6] In 1300 William de Cantilupe, banneret, was on campaign with three knights and eight sergeants for sixty days, for which he was paid. His feudal service was for

[1] Palgrave, *Documents*, pp. 208–31.
[2] E. 101/612/29 and C. 47/5/6 are copies of the main roll. E. 101/612/10 is a record of a subsidiary muster.
[3] C. 47/5/7.
[4] *C.V.C.R. 1277–1326*, pp. 384–92.
[5] *Rot. Parl.*, i, p. 216.
[6] Palgrave, op. cit., p. 229.

one tenth of a knight's fee, so he detached one of his sergeants for eight days to perform it.[1] Different tenants found different ways of meeting their obligations. For the war of 1282 the abbot of St. Augustine's, Canterbury, simply paid Henry de Cobham £20 to do his service for him.[2] In 1300 the bishop of Hereford arranged that William de Grandson should perform his feudal service for the sum of 120 marks. When the forty days of service came to an end, the leader of the contingent representing the bishop, Thomas de Birmingham, joined Grandson's paid retinue.[3] In some cases the connection between the tenants-in-chief and the soldiers performing their service is clear. In 1300 one of the knights sent by Walter Langton to the muster was his brother, Robert Peverel. Of the four men doing service for Robert Chandos, two bore his surname.[4] But usually there was no way of telling whether the soldiers were the tenants of the men they were representing, or were simply hired to do the job.

Feudal levies always produced their comedy turns. In 1282 one man came to the muster carrying a side of bacon, which he ate and then promptly departed.[5] In 1300 there was an archer who came with a bow and one arrow, which he shot off on first seeing the enemy and immediately left for home. John de Langford, whose tenure committed him to serve on a horse worth five shillings, carrying a wooden stick with a sack for holding armour, cannot have been much use to the army. In 1300 he was ordered to pay a fine, but in 1303 he appeared in person.[6] Such men were hardly the normal type of those doing feudal service, and were probably regarded with amusement just as they would be now. But even if the musters did for the most part produce reasonably competent soldiers, the system of feudal service hardly created an

[1] *Ibid.*, p. 223; *Liber Quotidianus*, p. 198.
[2] *Historiae Anglicanae Scriptores Decem*, ed. R. Twysden (London, 1652), p. 1939.
[3] *Registrum Ricardi de Swinfield*, ed. W. W. Capes (Canterbury and York Soc., 1909), pp. 375-6; Palgrave, *Documents*, p. 214; *Liber Quotidianus*, p. 192.
[4] Palgrave, *Documents*, pp. 210, 214.   [5] *Parl. Writs*, i, p. 208.
[6] Palgrave, *op. cit.*, pp. 218-20; E. 101/612/29. Other examples of this type of service are cited in *Calendar of the County Court, City Court and Eyre Rolls of Chester, 1259-1297*, ed. R. Stewart Brown (Chetham Soc., n.s. lxxxiv, 1925), p. lix.

army. It has been estimated that the cavalry was 2,000 strong in 1300;[1] less than a quarter of these were feudal, and the campaign lasted much longer than the forty days of the traditional service. The men performing their feudal service probably did not serve as a separate brigade, but were assimilated into the normal structure of the army. In 1300 Hugh of St. Philibert even managed to have himself registered as performing feudal service at the same time as he was in receipt of household pay, which was wholly improper.[2] The incident shows that he was not made to leave the household battalion during the time that he was performing his service.

Although the crown had a definite and well-established right to feudal service for forty days, the troops raised under the system were not particularly impressive or important. Nor was the use of the feudal summons of any considerable financial benefit to the crown. At this time the Exchequer was fighting a losing battle to collect scutage on the old assessment of fees, rather than on the new reduced quotas. No appreciable sums were raised, and it was more trouble than it was worth to try to collect scutage. Fines might be paid on the basis of the new quotas in lieu of service, and in 1300 these were collected at the high rate of £40 for each knight. The total revenue from fines in that year came to almost £2,000.[3] A feudal summons might be of substantial financial benefit to the tenants-in-chief, for they were entitled to collect a scutage on their own lands. Though they refused to pay scutage levied on the old assessment to the Exchequer, it was on this obsolete basis that they collected it for their own benefit. So the earl of Lincoln received from the honour of Pontefract, assessed at nearly sixty-three fees, £125 18s. 2½d. for the scutage of the Caerlaverock campaign.[4] It seems that the magnates had a greater interest than did the crown in seeing that armies were recruited by means of a feudal summons, for the military burden was slight and the financial benefits worthwhile.

[1] Morris, *Welsh Wars*, p. 300.
[2] Palgrave, *Documents*, p. 224; *Liber Quotidianus*, p. 202.
[3] H. M. Chew, 'Scutage under Edward I', *E.H.R.*, xxxvii (1922), pp. 321–6.
[4] D.L. 29/1/2.

The obligation of all tenants-in-chief to produce knight service was consequent upon the act of homage. But the right of the crown to expect the rest of the cavalry, the paid troops of the household and the unpaid men who are revealed by the *Falkirk Roll of Arms* and the *Song of Caerlaverock*, to serve in the wars, and the means used to summon them should also be examined. Edward I could appeal to the general obligation to bear arms in defence of the realm, part of the fealty all his subject owed him. The duty of all free men to possess the arms and military equipment appropriate to their status and wealth had been set out by Henry II in the Assize of Arms. This legislation was brought up to date in 1242, when the unfree were included in the scheme, and it was re-enacted by Edward I in the Statute of Winchester.[1] Quite early in the reign Edward began to extend this principle, and to try to enforce an obligation to do military service on all those with sufficient wealth to afford the equipment needed. It made no difference whether or not they had taken up knighthood, nor whether they held their land in chief or as subtenants. In November 1282 all with at least twenty librates of land who were not serving in the Welsh war were summoned to appear at Northampton early in the next year, along with shire and borough representatives. The object was probably to make them pay monetary compensation in lieu of the service they were not doing, but it is doubtful that they would have accepted any claim that they did owe service. Certainly no such grant was forthcoming.[2] In 1285 Edward rewarded the class of twenty-librate men for their part in the Welsh wars by raising the qualification for compulsory knighthood to £100, and in the writ he conceded that their service had been freely bestowed. But the king's benevolence did not last long, and in 1292 the level was brought down to forty librates.[3]

The period of almost constant war after 1294 naturally saw the

---

[1] W. Stubbs, *Select Charters* (9th ed., Oxford, reprinted 1962), pp. 183, 363, 466.
[2] *Parl. Writs*, i, p. 10.
[3] Morris, *Welsh Wars*, p. 76; M. Powicke, *Military Obligation in Medieval England*, p. 109.

crown attempting to take advantage of such precedents to persuade and even compel men to serve in the campaigns. In February 1295 the king ordered the Treasurer to make the sheriffs hold inquests into the number of men who held more than forty librates of land. Such men should be ready to set out on campaign at royal wages, equipped with horses and arms, at only three weeks' notice. The inquisition was duly carried out in March, and seems to have been successful in providing Edward with much needed reinforcements in Wales.[1] That the magnates did not approve of this type of appeal is perhaps suggested by the method used later in the same year by the bishop of Durham and Earl Warenne for raising troops to defend the north of England. They were given power to compel all men to assist them, but chose not to use the forty-librate qualification for service, instead simply requesting the sheriffs of the northern counties to send all knights, together with two men from each vill, to a muster at York on 2 November 1295.[2]

But the crown stuck to the new system. In 1296 the forty-librate landholders were still requested to be prepared to set out at three weeks' notice, and in January the earl of Arundel was appointed to check on the organization of the scheme in Shropshire and Staffordshire. Presumably many of the troops who served in Scotland for pay in 1296 came as a result of this obligation though unfortunately no writ of summons to these men has survived. That sent to the magnates, however, was enrolled. It was not feudal in form, but politely requested them to come on account of the fealty and esteem they owed to the king, with as many horses as they felt was honourable and proper. Although the formula was very like that used in the demand for paid service in 1282, this time no promise of pay was made.[3]

As already shown, Edward I's initial plan in 1297 was to demand feudal service for the campaign against Philip IV, but the strong opposition at the Salisbury parliament, led by Roger Bigod, forced him to abandon this idea.[4] Even so, the king persisted in his

[1] *Ibid.*, p. 110; Morris, *op. cit.*, p. 77; *Parl. Writs*, i, pp. 267-8.
[2] *Parl. Writs*, i, p. 270.   [3] *Ibid.*, pp. 222, 275, 278.
[4] *Supra*, p. 77.

intention of taking an English army to Flanders, and after ordering the sheriffs on 5 May to draw up lists of all those holding twenty librates or more, he issued a summons ten days later ordering all such men to muster at London on 7 July. Ecclesiastics and women were to send their feudal quotas, while some 130 magnates received individual summonses. These writs did not take the usual form. Instead of making reference to the fealty and esteem the magnates owed to the king, as was normal in a non-feudal summons, they were 'affectionately required and requested' to attend the muster for the 'salvation and general advantage of the realm'.[1] It looks as if the writ was deliberately vague, as there was no well-established obligation, based on either fealty or homage, that Edward could appeal to for service overseas.

The summonses to the muster at London naturally aroused suspicion. According to the chronicler Langtoft, many barons were inclined to refuse to come as they suspected that the king was trying to create a new form of military service, and 'to do new service without condition would be disinheritance by custom'.[2] In the petition presented to the king known as the *Monstraunces*, the opposition put their case over the summons cautiously, pointing out that it was not stated where the service was to be done, and that if it was to be Flanders, as was rumoured, there was no precedent for it.[3] Edward then conceded that no one was bound to go to Flanders with him, save at royal wages. But the earls of Norfolk and Hereford and their followers were not content with this, and refused to have anything to do with the campaign. The two earls were asked by the king to draw up lists of the horses of those who attended the muster at London, in accordance with their duties as Marshal and Constable. They refused, and were accordingly replaced in their offices by Geoffrey de Geneville and Thomas de Berkeley.[4] On 28 July writs were sent out under the privy seal requesting the sheriffs to ask all those who had agreed to go to Flanders to prepare themselves and make their

[1] *Parl. Writs*, i, p. 282.   [2] *Chron. Langtoft*, ii, pp. 286–8.
[3] J. G. Edwards, '*Confirmatio Cartarum* and Baronial Grievances in 1297', *E.H.R.*, lviii (1943), pp. 153, 170.
[4] *Chron. Cotton*, pp. 327, 331. *Infra*, p. 251.

way to Winchelsea as soon as they could. The sheriff of Lancashire reported that he could find none who agreed to go with Edward, and his Devonshire colleague could only produce one name, that of Miles Pychard. Other returns do not survive, but these two are indicative of the mood of the country in the summer of 1297.[1] Edward was able to persuade very few men who were not of his own household to cross the Channel with him.

The quarrel over service was a very important element in the crisis of 1297, but it was an issue over which the opposition were not very sure of their rights. The final settlement, the *Confirmatio Cartarum*, made no mention of the question, but simply dealt with such matters as prises and customs duties.[2] The pardon granted on 5 November, guaranteed in advance by letters of the king's son Edward and his council on 10 October, forgave the members of the opposition their failure to answer the summons, but there was no statement won from the crown that the demand for service had been unconstitutional. And very little attention seems to have been paid to the question of the twenty-librate landholders. The only document that mentions them is the *De Tallagio non Concedendo*, of questionable authenticity, but most probably representing the baronial demands as they stood in the autumn of 1297. Even this makes no challenge to the royal claim to the service of this class of men, but simply promises them pardon for not responding to the summons.[3] That few of them had done so is shown by the fact that of the 713 men named in the surviving returns, which cover thirteen counties, only seventy-six appear in the roll of those who received protections to go on the Flanders campaign.[4]

The threat of civil war in the autumn of 1297 saw a new expedient adopted to recruit cavalry, with commissions being set up to select loyal knights and squires to come to a muster at London.[5] but for the Scotch wars Edward reverted to more normal methods.

[1] C. 47/2/16/2, 3.   [2] Stubbs, *Select Charters*, pp. 490–1.
[3] Edwards, *op. cit.*, p. 166; H. Rothwell, 'The Confirmation of the Charters, 1297', *E.H.R.*, lx (1945), pp. 311–13.
[4] M. Powicke, *Military Obligation in Medieval England*, p. 111.
[5] *Parl. Writs*, i, pp. 299–300.

Writs issued on 21 October to 180 individuals to serve in Scotland used a formula akin to that used to ask the magnates to come to the London muster on 7 July, without the usual appeal to fealty.[1] However, the next summons, sent out on 26 October, asking for reinforcements for the army in Flanders, went back to the old formula, with an appeal to fealty and the esteem owed to the king.[2] Variations in the phraseology of military summonses cannot be regarded as insignificant. The writs sent out on 15 May 1297 demanding attendance at London on 7 July had been hotly resented, and it was not the royal concession that wages would be paid in Flanders, but the full reversion to the old style of summons at the end of October that marked the baronial victory on the question of military service.

Edward I made no attempt to introduce innovations in the method of summoning the cavalry for the Falkirk campaign of 1298. The formula used was almost identical to that of a non-feudal summons issued in 1287, stressing fealty and esteem.[3] There was no demand for the service of the twenty- or forty-librate class, and no mention was made of whether the troops were to be paid royal wages. For this campaign the horse lists and the *Falkirk Roll of Arms* provide a means of discovering whether all those who were summoned did in fact appear, and also whether all the more important men in the army were sent individual writs. Of the 110 bannerets in the heraldic roll, only twenty-nine had received direct summonses for the expedition, while a further twelve had been asked to muster for the winter campaign that immediately preceded the Falkirk one, which made any further summons unnecessary. Taking a list of sixty-eight men summoned on 30 March 1298, there is no evidence in thirty-two cases to show that they appeared at the muster on 25 May. Seventeen men appear on the horse lists, and eleven on the roll of arms, while eight more obtained protections to go on the campaign, though this cannot be taken as definite evidence that they in fact went.[4]

[1] *Ibid.*, pp. 302–4.
[2] *Ibid.*, p. 304.
[3] *Ibid.*, pp. 250, 309–12.
[4] Gough, *Scotland in 1298, passim; Parl. Writs*, i, pp. 310–11.

A new list of magnates was used for summonses sent out at the end of September 1298, requesting service in Scotland the following year: a campaign which never took place.[1] But although this army never mustered, the list was not abandoned. It provided an authoritative record of the hundred or so most important and reliable military leaders, whose status also entitled them to a leading part in the deliberations of the nation, and it was accordingly the basis of all the military and parliamentary summonses of the rest of the reign of Edward I.[2] For the Caerlaverock campaign the summons took strict feudal form, the tenants-in-chief being asked to provide their quotas. But in addition they were asked to bring with them as many men-at-arms as they felt they could provide.[3] It was this second half of the writ of summons that produced the non-feudal unpaid troops who formed the majority of the cavalry present on the campaign. The response to the summonses was better in 1300 than it had been in 1298: sixty out of the eighty-seven bannerets named in the *Song of Caerlaverock* received individual demands for their service.

Alongside the feudal summons in 1300, Edward I revived the conception of a wealth qualification for service. He established commissions to draw up lists of all men holding at least forty librates of land, and to summon them to serve at royal wages in Scotland.[4] This was reminiscent of 1297, and naturally provoked opposition. In a statement of grievances it was requested that the summons be withdrawn on the grounds that most of these men were not tenants-in-chief and so did not owe service, while those who were tenants-in-chief were already obliged to provide men in response to the demand for feudal service. In other words, the only form of service that the opposition was prepared to recognize was the strictly feudal one. They did not accept any more general obligation to serve.[5] The king was unwilling to accede to these

---

[1] *Ibid.*, pp. 317–18.
[2] J. E. A. Jolliffe, *The Constitutional History of Medieval England* (2nd edn., 1948), p. 348.
[3] *Parl. Writs*, i, p. 327.   [4] *Ibid.*, p. 330.
[5] *Sixth Report of the Royal Commission on Historical Manuscripts* (London, 1877), Appendix, p. 344.

arguments, and the opposition was not strong enough to force him to revoke his claims in the *Articuli super Cartas* issued on 6 March 1300.[1] The lists of forty-librate landholders were drawn up, but there is no evidence to show that pressure was brought on those named in the lists to force them to go on the campaign. The absence of complete lists of all those present in Scotland makes it impossible to estimate the efficacy of the measure; however, the success of the opposition is amply demonstrated by the fact that Edward did not dare repeat the summons of men of specified landed wealth. The next similar summons was in 1316, when the qualification was set at fifty librates.[2]

But Edward did not admit complete defeat. In 1301 the magnates were asked to muster for the new campaign in Scotland with a style of writ similar to that used in 1297, making no reference to fealty and allegiance.[3] In place of a summons of forty-librate landholders, inexpedient in view of the previous year's row, some 935 men were sent individual summonses. Unlike the writs to the magnates, these promised pay, but like them made no reference to fealty.[4] Once again, there is no way of finding out how many of the men who were summoned actually came to Scotland.

The precedents of 1301 were not followed up in the rest of the reign. The summonses issued for 1303 and 1306 were feudal in form, that for 1306 not even including the clause that had featured in 1298, asking for more men-at-arms than the strict quotas provided for.[5] In 1304 and 1307 there was no need for general summonses, as in both cases the army was already in Scotland, having wintered there. These last years of the reign saw only one request for non-feudal service, with the formula of fealty and esteem being used once more. This was in January 1303, and the summons was only sent to twenty-seven northern magnates.[6] An unusual arrangement was negotiated with the men of Northumberland by the Treasurer, Walter Langton, late in 1302, by which they were to serve for eight days at their own expense. This was

---

[1] *Statutes of the Realm*, i, pp. 137–9.
[2] M. Powicke, *Military Obligation in Medieval England*, pp. 143–4.
[3] *Parl. Writs*, i, p. 347.   [4] *Ibid.*, pp. 349–56.
[5] *Ibid.*, pp. 366, 377.   [6] *Ibid.*, pp. 369–70.

an entirely exceptional case, though, resulting from the particular responsibilities of the northern counties to protect the Border.[1]

By the end of his reign, therefore, Edward I had virtually given up non-feudal summonses and requests for the service of the twenty- or forty-librate class. The evidence for the composition of the armies that fought in the Scotch wars suggests that the army in the field was much the same, no matter how it was summoned, and it may be that the king had found that there was little point in experimenting with novel methods of recruiting. But it seems much more probable that political opposition forced Edward to abandon the methods he had been developing and to revert to straightforward feudal summonses. Innovations in the forms of the summonses were objected to for fear that acceptance might establish a precedent, enabling the crown to demand additional service as of right in the future. The final baronial victory on this point must have been won at some time between the 1301 campaign and the issue of the feudal summons for 1303, and it is tempting to assume that the king abandoned his claim to non-feudal service at the October parliament in 1302. According to a little-known chronicle, that of Hagnaby in Lincolnshire, there was then a major crisis, with a committee of thirty-five being set up under the leadership of Archbishop Winchelsey to discuss the affairs of the church and of the realm.[2] No other chronicler records anything of the sort, but the story is given plausibility by the fact that there was a precedent for the setting up of such a committee; at the Lincoln parliament in the previous year the complaints of the opposition were placed before a commission of twenty-six.[3] Although it has been argued by Rothwell that during the latter years of his reign Edward I was generally successful in going back on the concessions formally granted in 1297,[4] and although the opposition never obtained a written condemnation of the attempt to enforce a wider, more general military obligation from the king, yet on this issue they won a clear

[1] *Ibid.*, p. 369; M. Powicke, *op. cit.*, p. 115.
[2] B.M. Cotton. MS, Vesp. B. xi, f. 53.   [3] *Chron. Langtoft*, ii, pp. 330-2.
[4] H. Rothwell, 'Edward I and the Struggle for the Charters, 1297-1305', *Studies in Medieval History presented to F. M. Powicke*, pp. 319-32.

victory. No later medieval monarch was able to enforce any general obligation to cavalry service in England. There were some abortive attempts under Edward II, and in the early years of Edward III; in general, however, reliance was placed on a limited number of magnates to provide adequate cavalry forces under a contract system.

There is no simple way of describing the cavalry forces in the armies of Edward I's reign: they cannot with justice be termed either mercenary, feudal or contractual. As many men served at their own expense, it is not possible to produce accurate estimates of numbers, though it is probable that there were some 3,000 heavily armed cavalrymen on the Falkirk campaign, perhaps the largest concentration that Edward ever assembled. The royal household provided a very substantial and important paid element in the armies, but in the major campaigns this was outnumbered by the contingents of the magnates who refused to accept pay for themselves or their men. Whether novel techniques of summons, based on wealth rather than on traditional obligations, or obsolete feudal methods forced on the crown by the opposition, were used, the armies as they assembled in the field were similar. The majority of the cavalry were organized in retinues, built up by means of formal agreements and indentures, yet in general the crown scarcely recognized the existence of this system in its methods of recruiting. In none of the summer campaigns in Scotland did the crown enter into contracts with the army captains. Although it would be false to state that Edward I created a national army to fight national wars, he succeeded in welding together the miscellaneous cavalry forces available to him into a coherent and well-organized military weapon.

IV

THE INFANTRY

Much of the credit for the successes of Edward I's armies is conventionally accorded to the infantry. In order to assess the rôle of the footsoldiers it is necessary to discover how many were employed in the wars. Is it true that the numbers of infantry were very substantial, as high, it has been suggested, as 60,000 for the campaign of 1296 against the Scots?[1] The methods of recruitment need to be examined. Were there any changes in the techniques used which suggest that the crown was developing new policies in the course of the reign? Then the way in which the infantry forces were used in war must be investigated. It has been argued that this reign saw for the first time the use of mounted men-at-arms and archers in one line of battle, and that in this way the foundations of later victories such as Halidon Hill and the triumphs of the Hundred Years War were laid by Edward I.[2] But the evidence for such assumptions needs to be examined.

The many accounts which survive give a clear idea of the size of the armies that Edward I put into the field. At one time during the first Welsh war there were some 15,000 foot in royal pay, of whom 9,000 were Welsh. The accounts for this campaign are hard to disentangle; contingents melted away rapidly and the remnants were combined into new units. Similar numbers were employed in the war of 1282, but not all in one force; it was rare to find more than 3,000 or 4,000 in one army. In 1287 an army of almost 11,000 foot was assembled, of whom only just over a third were English,

---

[1] Barrow, *Robert Bruce*, p. 294.
[2] Morris, *Welsh Wars*, pp. 99-104; M. Powicke, *Military Obligation in Medieval England*, pp. 118-22.

the remainder being recruited in Wales.[1] In November 1294 there were probably over 31,000 infantry in pay in various armies in Wales, and 16,000 assembled at Chester early in December. Such a large concentration was not maintained for long. Warwick's army reached a maximum strength of some 14,500 early in January 1295, yet by the time of the battle of Maes Moydog it numbered a mere 2,489.[2]

Detailed accounts of the infantry involved in the Gascon campaigns have not survived. Some English and Welsh were sent, but probably not in large numbers. The enrolled account for the war reveals that they, together with Spanish footsoldiers, were paid only £17,928 over the four years of the war,[3] which compares with a total cost of £26,388 for sergeants-at-arms and infantry in Wales in 1294-5.[4] It is not known how much the locally-recruited infantry were paid: Gascon cavalry and infantry together received £137,595. These Gascon footsoldiers were crossbowmen, superior to the ordinary Welsh or English infantry, and they were paid proportionately more; one shilling a day in local money as against the eight shillings of a knight, whereas the English infantry received only one-twelfth of a knight's wages.[5] In Flanders for the campaign of 1297-8 Edward had with him in the middle of October roughly 7,800 infantry, of whom almost 5,300 were Welsh. Numbers declined only slightly during the rest of the king's stay abroad: by late February the army was some 7,300 strong.[6]

Edward's intention in Scotland in all but the last campaigns of the reign appears to have been to try to crush the enemy by sheer weight of numbers. According to Walter of Guisborough, he

---

[1] Morris, *Welsh Wars*, pp. 95-6, 207-9; E. 101/3/11, 30.

[2] *Book of Prests*, ed. Fryde, pp. xxix-xxxi, xxxvi-xxxvii; J. G. Edwards, 'The Battle of Maes Madog and the Welsh Campaign of 1294-5', *E.H.R.*, xxxix (1924), p. 3.

[3] Account of John Sandale and Thomas of Cambridge, paymasters in Gascony, E. 372/160.

[4] Wardrobe account, 1294-5, E. 372/144.

[5] Sandale and Cambridge's account, E. 372/160.

[6] N. B. Lewis, 'The English Forces in Flanders', *Studies presented to Powicke*, p. 311; C. 47/2/20.

assembled a huge army for his campaign of 1296: 4,000 horse and 30,000 foot from England, to which were later added 400 cavalry and a further 30,000 foot from Ireland.[1] But chroniclers' figures are notoriously inaccurate, and it can be shown that there were only about 2,500 Irish infantry present.[2] Guisborough's figures are, however, no more extraordinary than the total of 60,000 which comes from an official source, a demand made by Edward that the Exchequer should supply him with £5,000 a week for the wages of 1,000 men-at-arms and 60,000 footsoldiers, together with the expenses of the household. This is, however, better evidence of the ambitious nature of Edward's plans than of the size of the army in 1296.[3] Only £21,443 was spent on the infantry for the campaign—nothing like enough to pay for the force originally envisaged.[4] A reasonable estimate would be that the army was some 25,000 strong in infantry, but no pay rolls survive to confirm this.

The evidence is fuller for the later campaigns in Scotland. During the winter of 1297-8, when the king was in Flanders, an expedition was sent north under the command of Warenne. The writs of summons requested some 29,000 foot from Wales, Chester and nine English counties to muster at Newcastle on 6 December. The date was as optimistic as the number. By the middle of February roughly 9,700 men had arrived, with numbers building up to 18,500 in the middle of the month, though they then declined in late February and in March as a result of many desertions.[5] For the campaign which culminated in the victory of Falkirk in 1298 the records detail orders to recruit 10,500 Welsh

[1] *Chron. Guisborough*, pp. 272, 279.
[2] J. F. Lydon, 'An Irish Army in Scotland, 1296', *The Irish Sword*, v (1962), pp. 184-90.
[3] E. 159/69, m. 11d. This is transcribed by Stevenson, *Documents*, ii, pp. 20-1, but regrettably the sum is given as £1,000 a week, which led J. H. Ramsay to point out in 'The Strength of English Armies in the Middle Ages', *E.H.R.*, xxix (1914), p. 222, that the amount was inadequate for the force specified. £5,000 was in fact quite sufficient.
[4] Wardrobe account in E. 372/144.
[5] *Parl. Writs*, i, pp. 304-5; E. 101/7/8. I have preferred my own addition to that of Morris, *Welsh Wars*, p. 285. His total is 21,500.

THE INFANTRY

troops and 2,000 men from Lancashire.[1] The number of Welsh who served actually exceeded the demand, for at the start of the expedition they numbered 10,900. After over two months in the field, desertion and death had thinned their ranks by only 400. Not all the writs of summons asking for English infantry were enrolled. Large numbers were recruited: on 20 July there were 14,800 in pay, including some Irish, but a week later numbers had fallen to 12,600. The battle of Falkirk was fought on 22 July, so this is an interesting and rare indication of the number of casualties. Unfortunately there are no accounts for the English foot during the rest of the campaign, and it is impossible to say how far numbers were depleted by desertion as the summer proceeded. However, the rolls do show that at the time of Falkirk Edward had some 25,700 infantry with him, an impressive number.[2]

Although the value of huge concentrations of what must have been largely ill-armed and inexperienced troops seems questionable, it was not until the very end of the reign that the English government ceased summoning large numbers of troops to go to Scotland. For a winter expedition in 1299–1300, 16,000 were called but it proved abortive as only 2,500 appeared and promptly deserted *en masse*.[3] The summer campaign was taken more seriously. In accordance with a decision taken about the expedition planned for the previous year, no Welsh were summoned: they were granted respite in recognition of their service in previous years.[4] A total of 16,000 English foot was demanded from Nottinghamshire, Derbyshire and the four most northerly counties.[5] But far fewer actually mustered; the maximum strength of the army being no more than 9,000. As figure 1 shows, this level was not maintained, numbers falling away rapidly after the siege of Caerlaverock. By early September Edward had only about 500 infantrymen with him.[6]

Edward was very displeased by the desertions of the infantry in 1300. On 15 July he wrote to the Keeper of the Wardrobe

[1] *Parl. Writs*, i, pp. 312–16.　　[2] E. 101/12/17.
[3] Morris, *Welsh Wars*, p. 298; *Liber Quotidianus*, pp. 241–3.
[4] E. 159/73, m. 16.　　[5] *Parl. Writs*, i, pp. 342–3.
[6] *Liber Quotidianus*, pp. 243–70.

complaining of the behaviour of the Yorkshire levies, saying that as they had maliciously deceived and treacherously failed him, they were to be immediately imprisoned and their lands and chattels seized. Local officials were not to be entrusted with this task, as the king had gathered that on occasion sheriffs and bailiffs had aided and abetted miscreants. Trustworthy men were to be given special commissions to do as the king wished, and to make an example of the deserters.[1] But this did not solve the problem, as was clear in the following year.

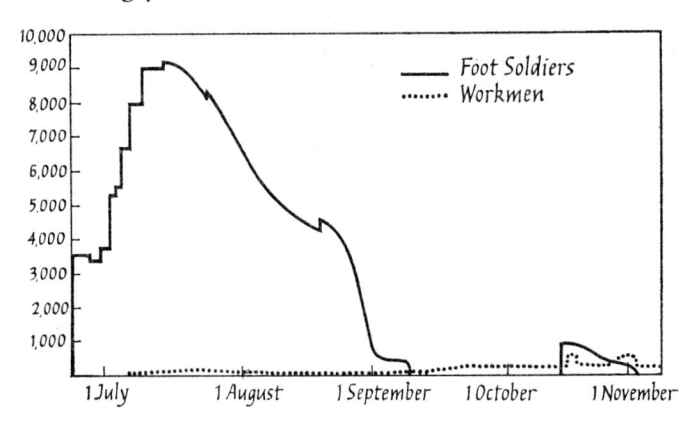

Figure 1. The Infantry Forces in 1300

The king's patience was wearing thin by the autumn of 1300. After conversation with the Scotch envoys, with whom a truce was arranged, he swore that he would lay waste the whole of Scotland and force its people into submission.[2] With this intent, large numbers of infantry were summoned for the ambitious double campaign of the following year, in which the king was to advance from Berwick and his son from Carlisle in a pincer movement. For the royal army 12,000 troops were summoned,[3] of whom just over 7,500 appeared.[4] Again the ranks were thinned by desertion. The royal officials estimated that numbers had

[1] S.C. 1/61/63.
[2] *Willelmi Rishanger, Chronica et Annales*, ed. H. T. Riley (Rolls series, 1865), p. 447.
[3] *Parl. Writs*, i, pp. 358–9.   [4] B.M. Add. MS, 7966a, ff. 116–28.

fallen to 3,500 in the first week of September,[1] but the accounts show that in fact there were only 2,500. By mid-November, as Figure 2 shows, there were less than 400. The cost of this force was roughly £4,500. In contrast, £11,273 was spent on the infantry in the Carlisle army.[2] This suggests that, since 100 men cost roughly £1 a day in wages, the total strength must have been at least 12,500. As most of the men were Welsh, who were less prone to desert than the English, it is probable that the strength of this force was better maintained than that of the royal army, which was drawn from the north of England and the counties bordering on Wales.[3]

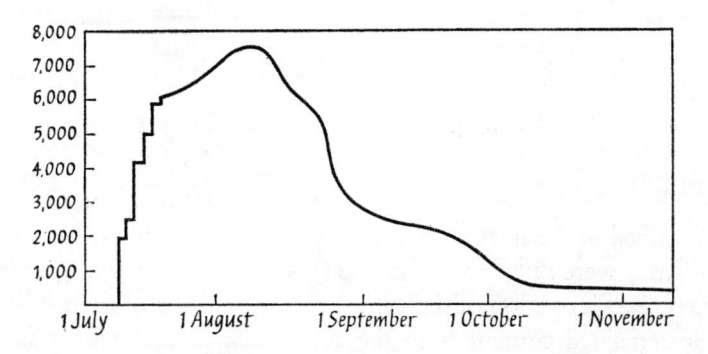

Figure 2. The Infantry Forces in the Royal Army in 1301

The number of men requested for the expedition of 1303 was less than in the past: only 9,500, all from the north of England. For once, they mostly appeared at the date for which they were summoned, and at one time numbered almost 7,500. Inevitably desertion thinned the ranks, though, as Figure 3 shows, more slowly than in previous years. A harsh new ordinance for the punishment of deserters was drawn up. Those suspected of leaving the army without permission were to be imprisoned, and the wages paid them recovered by distraint. If found guilty, they were to find guarantors to ensure that they served on some future occasion at their own cost. Severe measures were to be taken

[1] E. 159/75, m. 6.   [2] B.M. Add. MS, 7966a, ff. 116–28.
[3] *Parl. Writs*, i, pp. 370–1; B.M. Add. MS, 8835, ff. 72–90.

against any bailiffs found to have accepted bribes to let men selected for service stay at home.[1] Such threats may have deterred some, but there is little evidence that many legal actions were brought.

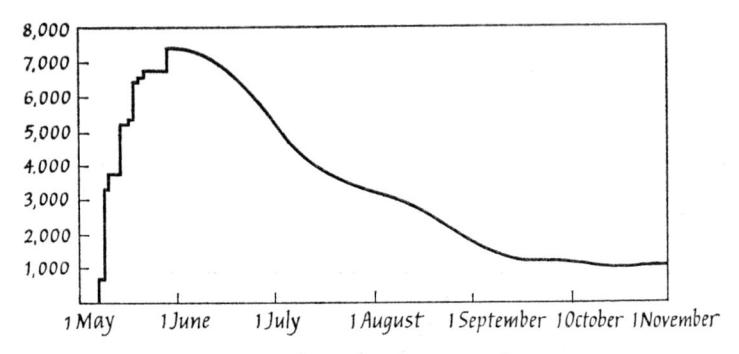

Figure 3. The Infantry Forces in 1303

The military operations of 1303 were inconclusive, so Edward remained in the north with his troops over the winter. No extra infantry were called for, which suggests that the king was coming to revise his opinion of the value of large numbers of footsoldiers. He remained content with the 1,000 men he had with him at Dunfermline in January. For the siege of Stirling he had in addition the service of a number of workmen: at one time as many as 445. The largest corps was engaged on the construction of an elaborate siege engine, known as the *Warwolf*,[2] but just as this was ready for use against the castle, the Scots offered to surrender. Callously and unchivalrously Edward refused to accept their submission until the machine had been brought to bear on the walls.[3]

Experience was proving that large numbers of infantry were of little use in a war where the greatest problem was becoming that of achieving sufficient mobility to catch an elusive enemy. Small as the cavalry forces put into the field against Bruce were, the infantry were even more strikingly reduced in numbers. In 1306

[1] Palgrave, *Documents*, pp. 204–5.   [2] E. 101/11/15.
[3] Barrow, *Robert Bruce*, pp. 181–2.

THE INFANTRY

Valence had some 1,500 with him during July,[1] but his victory at Methven owed little to them, being won by a cavalry charge. The number of foot who came north with the prince of Wales is not known, but as wages only totalled £1,142 there cannot have been many.[2] Orders for the recruitment of infantry were issued early in 1307, but desertions rendered an attempt to raise troops in February futile. No further efforts were made until mid-March, when writs were issued for 1,000 men to be selected in Lancashire. They were needed to pursue Bruce in the moors and marshes where he was thought to be hiding, which could not be penetrated by cavalry. Eight days later a further 1,200 footsoldiers from various northern liberties were requested. In June 1,500 Welsh were summoned.[3] From these writs it is clear that nothing on the scale of the earlier campaigns was envisaged, and the accounts confirm this. In June, John St. John had 1,700 foot with him,[4] and at the beginning of the next month Valence was sent 200 marks to pay the wages of 2,000 infantry in Argyll.[5] For the period after 23 July a full account of the infantry survives. There were exactly 500 men from North Wales, and 848 from the rest of the country. There were also contingents from the lands of the Marcher lords. Arundel's provided 150, Warenne's 200, and those of Lancaster, Lincoln and Hereford roughly 100 each. From the Grey estates came 265. The total number of infantry thus came to just over 2,900 men. By the beginning of September numbers had dropped to 2,660.[6] As might be expected with a small army, easy to organize and discipline, there was less desertion than in the past. Even so, in June a letter was sent to Walter Langton complaining of the desertion of footsoldiers from Lancashire, Northumberland, Cumberland and Westmorland.[7]

The normal method of recruiting infantry for the wars was to set up special commissions, known as commissions of array, for the selection of men in the counties. In 1277 the sheriffs had been used to raise troops, but from 1282, when household knights were

---

[1] E. 101/13/16.   [2] E. 101/369/11, f. 136.
[3] *Parl. Writs*, i, pp. 379-80; C.P.R., *1301-7*, p. 529.
[4] E. 101/531/11.   [5] E. 101/370/16, f. 17v.
[6] E. 101/373/15.   [7] S.C. 1/61/68.

used,[1] it was usual to appoint men especially for this task. For the Welsh war of 1294–5 important councillors and justices were entrusted with the task: Hugh Cressingham, Roger Brabazon and Peter Malory, for example, were to select troops in six northern counties.[2] For the arraying of infantry to be sent to Gascony in the following year Cressingham was again employed, as was John of Berwick, one of the most important of the king's clerks, and this time they were given the assistance of laymen with military experience, such as Robert FitzPayn and William Mortimer. One group of commissioners was given four counties to deal with, though none had so considerable a task as that of Cressingham and his colleagues in the previous year.[3] To collect the Welsh troops needed for the Flanders campaign Edward relied on the services of local magnates and their officials, but for the Falkirk campaign of the following year, along with such men, a prominent rôle was given to royal officials, notably John de Havering, justice of North Wales, Reginald de Grey, justice of Cheshire, and William Felton, constable of Beaumaris castle.[4]

This technique of making full use of the local knowledge of important laymen, initiated in Wales, was followed up in the rest of the reign. For the abortive winter campaign of 1299–1300 local men were combined with royal clerks, with a separate commission for each county. But clerks were not used again, and the commissions were increasingly dominated by professional soldiers: for example, in 1303 Richard le Brun and John de Hudlestone were appointed in Cumberland, and Robert FitzRoger and Walter de Huntercombe in Northumberland. As time went on, the area allocated to each commission was reduced. In 1300 and 1301 three men were appointed for the whole of Yorkshire, but in 1303 three were commissioned for each riding. In 1307 even more specialised commissions were set up for raising troops in the north of England, with a separate one for each liberty. By now, four men were appointed to choose 140 foot in Eskdale and Gillesland, a considerable contrast to the commission of two men in 1295 to levy 4,000 to go to Gascony.[5]

[1] *Supra*, p. 58. [2] *Parl. Writs*, i, p. 266. [3] *Ibid.*, p. 270.
[4] *Ibid.*, pp. 294, 312–15. [5] *Ibid.*, pp. 270, 325, 342, 358, 370, 371, 379.

THE INFANTRY

Evidence for the activities of these commissions is not as full for this period as it is later, perhaps because, as the system became better established and more familiar in its operation, so opportunties for abuse multiplied. The abuses leave more trace in the records than do the regular workings of the system. The one chronicle account of the operation of a commission of array refers to the collection of infantry from the southern counties for service in Gascony in 1295. According to Bartholomew Cotton, Hugh Cressingham and William Mortimer came into Norfolk and assembled from towns and villages a large number of foot-soldiers at Newmarket. The men were inspected there, and those not up to standard sent back, but shortly afterwards the whole muster was abandoned, and all returned to their homes. Equipment consisting of white tunics, knives and swords was provided at the expense of the localities.[1] This was a considerable burden. The hundred of Launditch produced 187 men for the array, their equipment and expenses costing £52 10s. 8½d. This compares with tax assessments of £241 19s. 6d. for the tenth of 1294, and £97 5s. 7d. for the ninth of 1297.[2] Cancellation of the plan to send the men to Gascony provided the opportunity for some profiteers at Newmarket to make off with the tunics, popularly known as *blaunchecotes*, and worth three shillings each, but legal action was successful in recovering at least some of them for the villagers who had paid for them.[3]

The commissioners of array generally seem to have left the task of selecting a specified number of men to the hundred and village communities. On occasion, the men of the localities even selected their own army officers. For the Welsh war of 1294–5 the Nottinghamshire hundred of Bassetlaw made John de Veer their 'centenar', or man in charge of a unit of 100 men.[4] There were ample opportunities for corruption. In the East Riding village of South Cave

---

[1] *Chron. Cotton*, p. 307.
[2] E. 401/1656. Although catalogued as an exchequer receipt roll, this document is in fact a record of the financial burdens placed on the hundred between 1294 and 1297.
[3] Norfolk plea roll of 1298, J.I. 1/587, mm. 6d, 7.
[4] Notts. plea roll, J.I. 1/672, m. 7d.

a man chosen for service by the villagers was offered protection by the bailiff and two other men, in return for ten shillings.[1] In the Yorkshire village of Etton the local constable was assigned, presumably by the arrayers, the task of raising money to pay the expenses of a centenar going to Scotland. But the community of the village appointed one Adam of Boulton to collect the money, which he then paid over to the constable. The latter appropriated three shillings of it to his own use, for which he was imprisoned and fined 3*s.* 4*d*.[2] It was possible for those chosen to serve to hire substitutes, and one ingenious rogue was found in the court at Halesowen to have gone round to each of the men selected to go to Wales and taken payment from each to go as his substitute. He then vanished.[3] The whole community of a village might decide to hire soldiers from elsewhere to go to the muster on their behalf. This is illustrated by a court case in which it was claimed that Nicholas de Stillingfleet had agreed to find twenty men to go with him to Scotland as the contingent from a group of Yorkshire villages. He took over £3 from them, and failed to provide any soldiers.[4]

In the Welsh wars the responsibility of the county to pay the men continued until they had reached the point from which the whole army was to set out,[5] but in the Scotch wars it was normal practice for the crown to take over financial liability from the time of the county muster. In 1298 three royal clerks were appointed to pay the troops on their way north,[6] and this precedent was followed in the rest of the reign. Even in the case of the grant of military service negotiated by the Treasurer with the community of the county of Northumberland late in 1302 the infantry were to be paid by the crown once they crossed the county boundary.[7]

[1] *Select Cases in the Exchequer of Pleas*, ed. H. Jenkinson and B. E. R. Formoy (Selden Soc., xlviii, 1932), pp. 196–8.   [2] Yorks. plea roll, J.I. 1/1105, m. 3.
[3] G. C. Homans, *The English Villagers of the Thirteenth Century* (New York, 1941), pp. 329–30.   [4] *Select Cases in the Exchequer of Pleas*, pp. 194–5.
[5] M. Powicke, *op. cit.*, p. 124.   [6] E. 159/71, mm. 105–6.
[7] *Parl. Writs*, i, p. 369. M. Powicke's statement, *op. cit.*, p. 125, that in 1300 no payment to the infantry was recorded before they reached Carlisle is not in accordance with the facts. *Liber Quotidianus*, pp. 243–4, shows that they were paid on their way from the counties.

THE INFANTRY

The arrayers of infantry were usually given commissions that were equally valid for franchisal liberties as for the rest of the country. The second Welsh war saw local bailiffs appointed to raise troops from the Welsh Marcher lordships, but that was exceptional and indicative of the special treatment that was given them during the period of the Welsh wars.[1] The creation of separate commissions for the various liberties in the north of England in 1307, together with the evidence for the separate contingents from the lordships of the Welsh Marches also indicates a concession to local susceptibilities on the part of the government. It was probably also a more efficient way of collecting troops.[2] The one liberty that always received special treatment was that of Durham. When it was under Bishop Bek's rule no royal commissions were sent into the palatinate. For the winter campaign of 1299-1300 the king simply asked the bishop to provide 5,000 or 6,000 men, sending a royal clerk to assist the local administration in assembling them.[3] The demand for service from Durham was conspicuously unsuccessful on this occasion, the military tenants absolutely refusing to fight in Scotland.[4] Later, when the palatinate was in royal hands, Edward set up a normal commission, sensibly using local men, John FitzMarmaduke and Robert Hansard.[5] FitzMarmaduke had been a ringleader of the mutiny three years before.

The burden of supplying infantry for the wars was not equally distributed. It was obviously much easier to recruit men from the areas nearest to the point where the campaigns began. For the Welsh wars demands were made of Gloucestershire, Herefordshire, Shropshire, Staffordshire, Cheshire and Lancashire. The shift of the scene of fighting to Scotland moved the main burden of providing troops to Yorkshire, Cumberland, Northumberland and Westmorland. The men of Derbyshire and Nottinghamshire had been regularly called upon for the Welsh wars, and they attended the Scotch wars as consistently, their virtue being

---

[1] *Parl. Writs*, i, pp. 245-8; for a further discussion of franchises, see *infra*, pp. 225-35.
[2] *Parl. Writs*, i, pp. 379-80; *supra*, p. 99. [3] *Parl. Writs*, i, p. 326.
[4] *Infra*, p. 235. [5] *Parl. Writs*, i, p. 371.

THE INFANTRY

experience rather than proximity to the muster point.[1] The rest of England was hardly affected by Edward's need for manpower. Some infantry were raised in Lincolnshire to go to Wales in 1294,[2] and an undated portion of a pay roll, which probably refers to the army collected to go to Gascony in the following year, has payments to just over 1,400 men collected from the counties of Wiltshire, Kent, Oxford, Buckingham, Leicester, Warwick and Northampton.[3] In 1296 the coastal shires of the south-east were organized to provide infantry to meet the threat of a possible French invasion,[4] but during the rest of the reign there was hardly any recruiting in the south.

There was surprisingly little resistance to the commissioners of array. On one occasion the men of the Durham village of Pittington were each fined two shillings for refusing to do their service,[5] but the great majority of cases that came to court concerned abuses of the system, notably financial extortion, rather than refusal to accept its workings. The arrayers clearly did not arouse the same degree of resentment as the purveyors of foodstuffs.[6] It was not until the later years of Edward II that grievances about their activities became a political issue, and this was after unpopular innovations had been made in the system.[7]

One expedient for recruiting infantry adopted by the crown in 1294 indicates the lengths to which Edward was prepared to go in order to obtain the troops he needed. Claiming hypocritically to be moved by feelings of clemency, he announced that he was prepared to grant pardons to felons in return for service. Two justices, Brabazon and Bereford, were appointed to issue such pardons, and over three hundred were granted to men going to Gascony. The expedient was repeated in subsequent years: a commission was set up to recruit prisoners and outlaws for the Scotch

[1] Morris, *Welsh Wars*, p. 93.
[2] *A Lincolnshire Assize Roll for 1298*, ed. W. S. Thomson (Lincoln Record Soc., xxxvi, 1944), p. xxvi.
[3] E. 101/13/34/30.   [4] *Parl. Writs*, i, pp. 270-5.
[5] *Halmota Prioratus Dunelmensis*, ed. J. Booth and W. H. Longstaffe (Surtees Soc., lxxxii, 1889), p. 1.
[6] *Infra*, pp. 129-33.
[7] M. Powicke, *Military Obligation in Medieval England*, pp. 144-61.

campaign of 1296, and many pardons were issued in return for service in Flanders. The practice was continued in the later campaigns in Scotland. The accounts for the infantry in 1303 only specify nine men as outlaws, but from the fact that a special order was sent to the bailiff of Holderness to recruit criminals who had fled to sanctuary in the liberty of Beverley, it seems likely that many more were present on the campaign of that year. It is not possible to calculate with any accuracy the total number of criminals recruited by Edward I, for many of the pardons were probably not enrolled. However, recorded pardons for homicide alone total about 1,700. It is clear that this method of recruitment provided substantial numbers of men, and it is not surprising to find that protests about the practice were made early in the reign of Edward II.[1]

The crown did not greatly concern itself with the way in which the infantry were armed. The writs appointing the commissions of array did not go into more detail than asking for 'footsoldiers skilled in arms', save for rare occasions, as when archers or crossbowmen were specified in 1295.[2] The account roll for the first Welsh war shows that while the majority of the foot were bowmen, some were armed with pikes or lances.[3] But by the time of the Scotch wars the infantry are termed archers in virtually all the cases where their arms are specified. Though classed as archers, the infantry of Edward I's reign were not supplied with weapons in the same way that their successors were to be under Edward III. During the Hundred Years War huge quantities of bows, arrows and arrowheads were supplied to the government by sheriffs, and stored in the Tower of London.[4] In contrast, Edward I's soldiers rarely received weapons from the government, but had to remain content with those provided by their localities. An archer would have no more than one quiver of two dozen arrows with him, which helps to explain why the infantry hurled stones at the battle

---

[1] N. D. Hurnard, *The King's Pardon for Homicide before A.D. 1307* (Oxford, 1969), pp. 218–19, 248–50, 311–24; *Rôles Gascons*, iii, pp. 183–4.
[2] *Parl. Writs*, i, p. 270.   [3] Morris, *Welsh Wars*, p. 99; E. 101/3/11.
[4] H. J. Hewitt, *The Organisation of War under Edward III* (Manchester, 1966), pp. 63–71.

of Falkirk. Normally the only weapons that the government concerned itself with were the crossbows and heavy machines used for siege work and the defence of castles. The issue of 20s. on one occasion during the Welsh wars to enable Thomas Turberville to buy arrows for his infantry was highly exceptional.[1] The one incident that created a substantial need for bows and arrows, compelling the crown to take steps to provide them, was the siege of Stirling in 1304. This was partly because the infantry had been in Scotland a long time, and so had probably exhausted the ammunition they brought with them, and also because this was by far the longest drawn-out engagement the English were involved in during the reign, so creating an unprecedented need for arms. The sheriffs of London provided 130 bows and 200 quivers of arrows. From Lincolnshire came 286 bows and 1,200 arrows. Fifty-nine bows were sent from Newcastle, while Simon de Kyme, sheriff of Yorkshire, provided 320, along with other equipment. During June and July four men in the siege army were employed to make arrows.[2] On no other occasion did the crown make such efforts to see that the infantry were properly equipped, although obviously when the men mustered before the commissioners of array some form of inspection took place. The most surprisingly armed contingent of infantry to fight for Edward I was a select corps from Sherwood Forest, which appeared in 1303 equipped not with bows, but with slings.[3]

Once in the field the infantry were organized in units of twenty men, the ordinary soldiers being paid two pence a day, and their commander, the vintenar, twice as much. Five such sections of twenty men were combined under the command of a centenar, who was a fully-equipped cavalryman with a barded horse. In Wales in 1282 and 1294 a still larger unit of 1,000 men was used,[4] but later pay rolls give no indication that such arrangements were repeated. The men were usually grouped together according to the county they came from, while some infantrymen might serve together as they all came from a single estate. In 1300 the footsoldiers drawn from the earl of Lincoln's estates of Pontefract and

[1] E. 101/351/9. [2] B.M. Add. MS, 8835, ff. 8v, 9, 21v, 26v.
[3] Ibid., f. 73. [4] Morris, *Welsh Wars*, pp. 95–6.

THE INFANTRY

and Blackburnshire formed one body.[1] As desertion thinned the ranks, the units would be combined together and reformed.

Discipline in the field was the ultimate responsibility of the Marshal, who might of course exercise his rights by means of a deputy. The severity of Ralph Gorges' judgements when acting as marshal in Gascony in 1295 caused the mutiny of the infantry at Rioms, as a result of which several English knights, including the treacherous Thomas Turberville, were captured by the French.[2] One army plea roll survives, that of John Lovel, the deputy marshal, for 1296. Cases heard included one where six men were fined for insubordination toward their constable, and several fined for brawling.[3] The chain of command in the field is not clear, but it seems likely that the Marshal and Constable may have had much to do with the organization of the infantry in battle. Certainly in 1301 it was the Constable, Bohun, who was sent across to recall the infantry when they had engaged the enemy on the opposite side of an estuary in Galloway.[4]

The evidence of the numbers of infantry employed in the wars suggests that although it was possible to assemble substantial forces, the king and his advisers had by the end of the reign abandoned their belief in the value of very large armies. And the evidence of the methods of recruitment that were used does not suggest that the infantry that were assembled were of a high calibre. The persistent problem of desertion, never effectively solved, also demonstrates the poor quality of the troops. But it remains to be asked whether these indications of the inadequacy of the infantry are borne out by their performance on campaign.

Edward fought few battles in his wars, and those that were fought were not well reported by the chroniclers. One incident that has received a great deal of attention is the battle of Maes Moydog in 1295. Nicholas Trivet states that Warwick's army was composed of cavalry, crossbowmen and archers, and that in the battle the horse were combined in one line with the crossbowmen.[5]

---

[1] *Liber Quotidianus*, p. 245.   [2] *Chron. Guisborough*, p. 246.
[3] *Cal. Docs. Scot.*, ii, no. 822; E. 39/93/15, mm. 1, 5d.
[4] *Infra*, p. 110.
[5] *Nicholai Triveti Annales*, ed. T. Hog (London, 1845), p. 225.

However, the account for the army indicates that there were only thirteen crossbowmen and archers present,[1] and in order to make sense of Trivet's account it is necessary to assume that some of the other infantry, armed with longbows, were combined with the cavalry as well, and that the chronicler was mistaken in singling out the crossbowmen. A much more authoritative account of the battle makes no mention of unusual tactics. A newsletter reports the casualties as one squire of Robert FitzWalter's, and six infantrymen, adding that ten horses were lost. Far from the Welsh having taken up a defensive position throughout, the author noted that they 'attacked our men from the front, and they were the finest and quite the bravest Welsh that had ever been seen'.[2] What intermingling of infantry and cavalry did take place was more probably the result of the confusion of battle than of deliberate tactics. This is also true of the earlier battle of Orewin Bridge, when during the ascent of the English to the Welsh position the archers and cavalry were mixed up, although it was the latter who reached the top first.[3]

The most effective fighting force of infantry employed in Edward's Welsh wars was the contingent of Gascons who served in Wales in 1282. At one time their total strength was 210 horse and 1,313 foot. Armed with crossbows, they suffered considerable casualties. They were singled out for praise by the chronicler Langtoft, who likened them to lions. Perhaps because of the cost of this force, £7,618,[4] Gascons were not employed again in such numbers, although there was always a Gascon element among the household knights on all the campaigns.

In Gascony itself the infantry do not appear to have distinguished themselves. The disaster at Rioms was the result of the mutiny of the foot. In an engagement in 1296, when the English were ambushed, it was the infantry who suffered heavy casualties, while the more mobile cavalry escaped.[5] When the English suf-

[1] Edwards, 'The Battle of Maes Madog and the Welsh Campaign of 1294-5', E.H.R., xxxix (1924), p. 11.
[2] Hagnaby chronicle, B.M. Cotton. MS, Vesp. B. xi, f. 37.
[3] *Chron. Guisborough*, pp. 220-1.   [4] Morris, *Welsh Wars*, pp. 186-9.
[5] Hagnaby chronicle, B.M. Cotton. MS, Vesp. B. xi, f. 40.

THE INFANTRY

fered their second major defeat of the war early in 1297 at Bellegarde, the infantry took no part in the battle, but remained under cover of the woods.[1] In Flanders there was no fighting with the enemy, only skirmishes between the unruly Welsh and Edward's Flemish allies. The only occasion on which the footsoldiers proved worth the money spent on them was when they were sent forward carrying banners to deceive the French into thinking that the inadequate English army was an immense host;[2] a practical though unchivalrous trick reminiscent of Edward's use of the captured banners at Evesham. It does not seem likely that the 'French had learnt by experience a wholesome fear of the English and Welsh archers', as Tout thought.[3] That lesson was to be taught them by Edward III and the Black Prince.

In Scotland the only battle of the 1296 campaign, Dunbar, was won by Warenne's cavalry with swords and lances, not by infantry with arrows. And in the next year at Irvine a Scotch army under Stewart and Douglas surrendered to an English force with fewer infantry than their own, but stronger in cavalry, which suggests that it was the English knights that they feared, rather than the English bowmen.[4] Nevertheless, in his account of the battle of Falkirk in 1298, Walter of Guisborough gave the infantry the credit for breaking the strong Scotch defensive formations, the schiltroms. The Scotch cavalry had mostly fled at the approach of the English army, but the schiltroms remained, and the English horsemen were unable to scatter the rings of pikemen. It was the infantry with a hail of arrows and stones who achieved the breakthrough, which was then exploited to the full by the cavalry.[5] However, another, briefer version of the events of the battle does not suggest that the infantry played a prominent rôle, and instead credits the breaking of the schiltroms to a flanking movement, presumably executed by the cavalry.[6] Not all of the available

---

[1] *Chron. Guisborough*, p. 263.

[2] *The Chronicle of Bury St. Edmunds, 1212–1301*, ed. A. Gransden (London, 1964), pp. 143, 146.

[3] T. F. Tout, *The History of England from the Accession of Henry III to the Death of Edward III* (London, 1905), p. 211.   [4] *Chron. Guisborough*, pp. 278, 298.

[5] *Ibid.*, pp. 327–8.   [6] *Chron. Rishanger*, p. 415.

infantry were used in the battle, for a few days earlier the Welsh had been given wine on empty stomachs. In the inevitable brawl that followed, several men were killed before the cavalry drove the Welsh off. When it was pointed out to Edward that they might choose to join up with the Scots, the king declared his indifference: both were his enemies, and both could be defeated. But the Welsh did not desert. They remained at a discreet distance from the main army, and once it became clear that the English were victorious, joined in the rout.[1] The pay rolls suggest that the English foot suffered casualties of some 2,000, while Welsh losses were minimal.[2]

Falkirk was the one major engagement of the Scotch wars. The only occasion in the later campaigns when the infantry played a notable part was in 1300, early in August, when in Galloway the foot crossed an estuary and engaged the Scots on the other side, showing more courage than the king, who wished to avoid battle. Hereford was sent to order them to withdraw, whereupon the English knights thought that the earl was going to the assistance of the foot, and charged. Edward was forced to follow, and the Scots were driven back in confusion. But as there were no Welsh troops, experienced in guerilla warfare in rough country, Edward was unable to pursue the fleeing enemy.[3] For the later campaigns, those of 1301, 1303-4, and 1306-7, there is not enough evidence to show what use was made of the infantry in battle. However, the indications are that it was found more effective to employ smaller concentrations than had been the custom in the past.[4]

It was not only in battle that footsoldiers might be of value. Perhaps the most useful infantry in the Welsh wars were those equipped with axes, rather than those armed with pikes or bows. Edward's success depended on the maintenance of good communications, and much time and money was spent in cutting roads

---

[1] *Chron. Guisborough*, pp. 325-8; *Chron. Langtoft*, ii, p. 316; *Chron. Rishanger*, p. 386. [2] E. 101/12/17.

[3] *Chron. Rishanger*, pp. 441-2; H. Johnstone, *Edward of Caernarvon*, pp. 52-3. She is mistaken in thinking that the Welsh had deserted Edward: there were none on the campaign.

[4] *Supra*, pp. 97-9.

THE INFANTRY

through the dense forests of Wales. In 1277 household knights were used to supervise the workmen, and in August as many as 1,800 axemen were cutting a road through to Rhuddlan.[1] In 1287 over 600 such workmen, probably recruited in Shropshire and Staffordshire, were employed under Gloucester to cut a road from Morlais to Brecon. This crossed land claimed by Hereford, and appears to have led to the famous dispute between the earls.[2] No road-cutting operations took place on this scale in Scotland. Geographical conditions were different, and with the shortage of funds in the last years of the reign Edward had other priorities.

In addition to the great field armies that were used in Wales and Scotland, the English needed to deploy troops in the castles with which they held down conquered territory. These garrisons were the most regular of the troops employed by Edward I: the accounts reveal that some men served for very long stretches of time in them. There is no evidence to show how garrison troops were recruited. Presumably many of them initially came into royal service as members of the county levies, and were subsequently persuaded to remain in pay. It would be a tedious task to enumerate all the garrisons in detail: a few examples will suffice to give an impression of this very important section of the armed forces. In 1283, after the defeat of the Welsh, it was ordained that Conway, Criccieth and Harlech should have thirty men, while at Bere and Caernarvon there were to be forty. Roughly a third of these were to be crossbowmen.[3] In times of open hostilities numbers might well be much higher. In 1287 there was at Dryslwyn a force of two knights, twenty-two men-at-arms, twenty crossbowmen and eighty archers,[4] while in 1294 Reginald de Grey raised the number of men in Flint to twenty-four horse, twenty-four crossbowmen and 120 archers.[5]

Although the English did not build castles in Scotland on the majestic scale of those in Wales, they did hold an appreciable number of strongholds there, and many troops were engaged on garrison duty. In 1300 there were as many as 325 men in Edinburgh, of whom sixty-four were cavalry. Dirleton, a castle of

[1] Morris, *Welsh Wars*, p. 139. [2] *Ibid.*, pp. 212, 223–5.
[3] *Ibid.*, p. 200. [4] *Ibid.*, p. 214. [5] *Ibid.*, p. 244.

minor importance in comparison, was guarded by twenty men-at-arms and fifty footsoldiers.[1] A little earlier, in October 1298, the king and council ordained that there should be a permanent force of sixty men-at-arms and 1,000 foot at Berwick.[2] This level was almost reached in the next year when the foot in the town numbered 984.[3] Ordinances made in the winter of 1303–4 were much less lavish. In the four castles of Berwick, Roxburgh, Jedburgh and Edinburgh there were to be only thirty-four cavalrymen and 131 footsoldiers.[4] A list of garrisons made a little later, in May 1304, shows surprisingly large forces in Linlithgow and Kirkintilloch, with thirty-eight cavalry, the same number of archers, and sixty crossbowmen in the two castles. Roxburgh, Jedburgh and Edinburgh only mustered thirty-two cavalry, forty crossbowmen and nineteen archers between them.[5] The scale of the investment of English manpower in castles in Scotland at the end of the reign was considerable. In July 1306, a reasonably typical month, there were some 200 cavalry, twenty-two hobelars, or lightly-armed horsemen, 180 crossbowmen and 425 archers in royal pay serving in castles.[6]

The overall picture of the infantry forces in Edward I's armies is not particularly impressive. The evidence for the much-vaunted tactics of combining infantry and cavalry in one line of battle is unconvincing. Sophisticated tactics were not possible with large and ill-equipped levies, and after Falkirk they never succeeded in bringing the enemy to fight a decisive battle at close quarters. The Welsh were used extensively by Edward, who regretted their absence from the 1300 campaign, but they gave trouble at times, being as willing on occasion to fight their English comrades as the enemy. No effective solution was found to the problem of desertion, and for much of the reign the commissions of array were appointed to raise large numbers of men in such wide areas that proper supervision of recruitment was scarcely possible. Much remained to be done before the armies that were to win such great victories in the Hundred Years War could emerge. It was the

[1] E. 101/531/7. [2] *Cal. Docs. Scot.*, ii, no. 1022.
[3] E. 101/7/8. [4] E. 101/5/10. [5] E. 101/12/10.
[6] E. 101/13/11, ff. 11–15; E. 101/369/11, f. 89.

mounted archers who were to play the decisive rôle then, and the only precedent for such men in Edward I's armies was the Irish hobelar.[1] The tactics that were to win the battles of Crécy and Poitiers were worked out in the Scotch wars of the early years of Edward III's reign, not in the campaigns of Edward I.

But despite all this, the infantry did prove of value on several occasions, and the effect on enemy morale of the huge hosts that were assembled for some campaigns must have been considerable. It was a very remarkable administrative achievement to collect such large armies together. The 25,700 infantry and 3,000 or more cavalry present on the Falkirk campaign was probably the largest single army that had been raised up to that time by an English government. It was only exceeded during the middle ages by that assembled for the siege of Calais in 1347, which totalled about 32,000 men.[2] The second largest army of Edward III's reign was only about 15,000 strong.[3] In comparison with a still later period, 1585–1603, the size of Edward I's armies appears still more impressive, since the largest force that Elizabeth's government raised in those years was one of 12,620 sent to Ireland in 1601.[4] It was only in the middle of the seventeenth century that the size of armies greatly exceeded those of Edward I, with 60,000 or 70,000 men under parliamentary command in 1642, and with the army totalling some 42,000 men at the end of the Protectorate.[5] And although Edward I may not have been able to deal with the problem of desertion effectively, the Elizabethan government, despite greater severity of punishment, extending to execution, found the question equally insoluble.[6]

---

[1] J. E. Morris, 'Mounted Infantry in Medieval Warfare', *T.R.H.S.*, 3rd ser., viii (1914), p. 84.

[2] Morris, *op. cit.*, p. 97.

[3] A. E. Prince, 'The Strength of English Armies in the reign of Edward III', *E.H.R.*, xlvi (1931), p.356.

[4] C. G. Cruikshank, *Elizabeth's Army* (2nd ed., 1966), p. 290.

[5] C. H. Firth, *Cromwell's Army* (3rd ed., 1921), pp. 34–5.

[6] Cruikshank, *op. cit.*, pp. 165–8.

V

VICTUALLING

In theory there was no obligation on the crown to provide food for soldiers who were paid wages. Their pay was intended to be sufficient for their subsistence. Garrisons were often issued with food supplies in lieu of wages, the cost to the crown being the same in either case. In the *Articuli super Cartas* of 1300 it was firmly stated that purveyance of food supplies should not be made for the benefit of those who were in receipt of wages.[1] But in practice, if the wars were to be successful, the government had to ensure that the armies had enough to eat. The experiences of the Welsh wars of Henry III's reign had shown the levels of privation that might be suffered if victualling arrangements were not adequate. A letter from the English camp at Deganwy in 1245 told of a halfpenny loaf costing five pence, a load of corn twenty shillings, and a hen eight pence. To starvation was added the discomfort of living under canvas, with no warmth to be had.[2]

The simplest way for an army to feed itself was off the land. This technique was used with success by the English in their *chevauchées* during the Hundred Years War, and developed with great skill much later by the generals of the Thirty Years War. But the circumstances facing Edward I were such that he could not rely on local food supplies. In Wales, the country, with its backward agriculture, was too poor to support the English armies, although in 1277 the grain crop of Anglesey was harvested for the use of the English.[3] In Gascony, Flanders and Scotland Edward

[1] *Statutes of the Realm*, i, p. 137.
[2] J. E. Lloyd, *A History of Wales*, 3rd ed. (London, 1939), p. 704.
[3] Morris, *Welsh Wars*, p. 135.

was anxious not to alienate the local population. In Gascony the English were fighting a defensive war on land which was rightly theirs, in Flanders they were campaigning in the country of their allies, and in Scotland Edward was careful not to stir up more opposition than already faced him. In a letter written in 1303 two clerks wrote that the Irish troops had received no pay for nine weeks, and were extremely discontented to learn that funds had reached Berwick and were not being paid to them. There was a danger that they would start to rob those Scots who were loyal to Edward, something which was to be avoided.[1] It was only at the very end of his reign that the English, under the command of the prince of Wales, began to burn and pillage mercilessly. According to one chronicler, the king was furious when he heard of his son's activities. He was careful to order Valence to 'honour the loyal and spare them', an attitude which did not accord well with living off the land.[2]

It was of course impossible to prevent the ill-disciplined troops of the period from pillaging. In 1296 Hugh Torold, bailiff of the Earl Marshal, drove off 119 sheep that belonged to Robert of Bamburgh. Later in the same campaign Walter de Huntercombe was accused of seizing sixteen oxen and ten cows from a moor near Aberdeen. At about the turn of the century Sweetheart abbey put the cost of the war damage it had suffered at over £5,000, and Dundrennan abbey at £8,000, but these are hardly figures to be taken literally. In 1301 the bishop of Carlisle petitioned for a reduction in the farm of £10 a year that he paid for the parks and grazings of Carlisle castle, claiming that the crops and livestock had been eaten up and consumed by armies going to and returning from Scotland. One leader of Welsh troops sought a pardon for himself as a protection against prosecution on the grounds that his countrymen committed so many murders, robberies and arsons on their way to the war.[3] It is clear that theft, though contrary to royal policy, must have provided the army with substantial rations.

[1] E. 101/13/36/26.
[2] *Chron. Rishanger*, p. 320; *Cal. Docs. Scot.*, ii, no. 1782.
[3] *Ibid.*, nos. 822, 1123, 1187, 1410.

VICTUALLING

The demands of the armies for food offered openings to private entrepreneurs, who were encouraged by the crown. More was done during the Welsh wars than in the later campaigns in Scotland to persuade merchants to bring their goods for sale to the army. The techniques were familiar ones, used during Henry III's wars in Wales.[1] Safe-conducts and protections were granted in large numbers to merchants, and on occasion escorts provided for them. In 1277 and 1287, and probably on other occasions, the holding of markets was prohibited in the regions where the victuallers were expected to come from: for the first Welsh war these were Lancashire, Worcestershire, Shropshire, Staffordshire, Derbyshire, Gloucestershire, and Herefordshire.[2] For the Scotch wars, the crown did not use such drastic methods to force merchants to bring supplies, but in 1301 even men from Cornwall were asked to come north.[3] On occasion, the presence of merchants following the army saved a difficult situation. In 1298 when Edward arrived with his army at Stirling he found that his supplies of both food and cash had run out. Victuals were therefore bought on credit from the merchants present there, payment at the Exchequer being promised them. Twenty-eight bills survive, mostly dated between August and September, showing that Edward bought just over £380 worth of food and drink. Payment was reasonably prompt, most of the merchants receiving their money within a year.[4] Similarly, when the army arrived in Aberdeen in 1303 there were no royal stores to be found, so Edward had to rely on the willingness of the merchants to sell him goods on credit.[5] The royal household turned to the merchants only in an emergency, but the crown did not attempt to guarantee regular supplies for the whole army, so the infantry and cavalry not in the household were presumably compelled to obtain much from these private victuallers.

The ordinary footsoldiers must have brought supplies with them

---

[1] R. F. Walker, 'The Anglo-Welsh Wars, 1217–67', p. 502.
[2] *C.C.R., 1272–79*, p. 426; *C.V.C.R., 1277–1326*, p. 312.
[3] *C.C.R., 1296–1302*, pp. 487–90. [4] E. 404/1/2.
[5] This is stated in a receipt for flour worth £21, made out to John de Gore, 28 Aug. 1303, E. 101/371/21/96.

on campaign, as the infantryman who was obliged by his tenure to appear with a side of bacon did in 1277.[1] But more important were the arrangements that the magnates made to keep themselves and their men properly victualled. Unfortunately, owing to the dearth of private records, evidence is scanty on this subject, but the archives of the government contain sufficient material to indicate what was being done. In July 1277 a safe conduct was issued to the men of Gilbert de Clare carrying victuals through Lincolnshire, Northamptonshire, Shropshire and Staffordshire, which shows from how far afield the earl was drawing his supplies.[2] In 1282 Roger de Molis' men brought a ship from Bridgwater loaded with victuals for Roger and his men in Wales. Later that year Robert FitzWalter sent a yeoman of his to Ireland to buy supplies for him.[3] Magnates made similar arrangements for the wars in Scotland. In 1301 when the town of Poole was approached to provide ships for the crown the reply was that they had only two vessels, both of which had been taken by the earl of Lincoln to carry his victuals north to Scotland.[4] Two years later John Lovel of Titchmarsh was using a ship to have his supplies taken north. To his great annoyance it was arrested and held for eleven days in Scarborough.[5] Even royal officials took their own supplies on campaign. On one occasion Ralph Manton wrote to the sheriff of Lincoln asking him to have his own grain from Baddington sent north with the royal supplies.[6] Private victualling arrangements were made for the Flanders expedition of 1297. Henry de Bluntesdon, the king's almoner, took eighty-eight cheeses from God's House, Southampton, where he was warden.[7] The earl of Warwick sent goods across to Flanders, presumably intended for members of his family and retinue present on the campaign, since he himself did not take part in it.[8]

Reliance on local supplies, the activities of merchants, and the initiative of magnates and others in providing their own victuals

---

[1] *Supra*, p. 81.   [2] *C.P.R.*, *1272–81*, p. 223.
[3] *C.V.C.R.*, *1277–1326*, pp. 221, 241.   [4] E. 101/9/7/2.
[5] E. 13/26, m. 28.   [6] E. 101/10/18/97.
[7] *Sixth Report of the Royal Commission on Historical Manuscripts*, Appendix, p. 556.   [8] E. 101/6/18/27.

was hardly sufficient to meet the demands of Edward I's armies. The government had to take action itself to ensure adequate supplies. Machinery had to be set up to enable compulsory purchases to be made with the minimum of difficulty, at prices which were not inflated by the abnormal demands of war. Stores had to be set up in the main campaign centres, and clerks appointed to supervise them. The task was a considerable one, and of all the administrative problems which were involved in putting an army into the field, this bulks largest in contemporary records.

The royal household had always obtained much of its food supplies by exercising the right of prise, or compulsory purchase. This practice was liable to abuse, and attempts to restrict the activities of royal officials who seized goods without paying for them had been made in Magna Carta,[1] echoing a reforming ordinance of Henry I's.[2] In Henry III's reign the Petition of the Barons complained that Henry's officials were keeping back for their own use the greater part of the goods they purveyed, and that many merchants were impoverished because payment was inadequate.[3] As in many other respects, the early legislation of Edward I with regard to prises followed up the ideas of the baronial opposition to his father. In the Statute of Westminster I it was stated that prises should not be taken without the consent of the man whose goods were being removed. But Edward was careful to reserve his ancient rights, and the clause appears to have remained a dead letter.[4] Payment for goods taken for the household remained dilatory, and became more so in the difficult financial situation of the latter years of the reign. Robert Hood of London had ale taken from him in 1298 and in 1300: his son eventually received payment for it in the last year of Edward II's reign.[5]

It was possible to extend this unpopular system of prise, normally used to provide the household with its supplies, to obtain

[1] Stubbs, *Select Charters*, pp. 296-7.
[2] *Willelmi Malmesbiriensis Monachi, De Gestis Regum Anglorum*, ed. W. Stubbs, ii (Rolls Series, 1889), p. 487.
[3] Stubbs, *op. cit.*, p. 376.
[4] *Statutes of the Realm*, i, pp. 27-8.
[5] E. 404/481/1/4.

victuals for the army. Part of the army, after all, was the household in arms. This extension of the system was not novel in the reign of Edward I. For his Irish expedition Henry II purveyed supplies from many English counties. He took 6,424½ quarters of wheat, 2,000 of oats, and 584 of beans. In addition there were 4,106 carcases of salt pork, 160 quarters of salt and 840 weys of cheese. These supplies were all taken by the sheriffs, who answered for them in the pipe roll.[1] Similar prises were made during the Barons' Wars of Edward's youth: requisitions to feed the army besieging Kenilworth were so heavy as to exhaust the revenues of ten counties.[2] In taking prises for his Welsh wars, Edward I was simply following the example of his father.

For the first Welsh war the government appears to have neglected the question of victualling until a very late stage. Whereas the summonses to the cavalry were issued on 12 December 1276 for a muster on 1 July 1277,[3] it was not until 17 July that some royal clerks and sergeants were commissioned to buy up supplies of grain in nine counties. The prohibition on holding markets had been issued ten days earlier.[4] Unfortunately insufficient documents survive to give any reliable impression of the scale or effectiveness of the arrangements that were made. But since a much more elaborate machinery was set up for the war of 1282, it seems likely that the king and his advisers were not wholly content.

The attack on Roger Clifford in Hawarden castle that set off the second Welsh war took place on 21 March. A council was summoned to meet at Devizes on April 5 to make plans for the war,[5] and it was there that victualling arrangements were made. There was no question of waiting until the war had begun. Supplies were to be purveyed in Ponthieu, Gascony, Ireland and, of course, in England. The quantities required were specified in many cases: Ireland, for example, was to provide 4,000 quarters of oats and

---

[1] *Pipe Rolls, 17 and 18 Henry II* (Pipe Roll Society, xvi, xviii, 1893, 1894), *passim*. I owe this information to J. O. Prestwich.
[2] H. M. Cam, *The Hundred and the Hundred Rolls* (London, 1930), p. 101.
[3] *Parl. Writs*, i, p. 193.
[4] *C.C.R., 1272–79*, p. 426; *C.P.R., 1272–81*, p. 219.
[5] Morris, *Welsh Wars*, pp. 153–5.

VICTUALLING

2,000 of wheat. Orders were issued that all supplies from the counties near the Welsh borders were to be sold where the armies were. Whitchurch and Chester were singled out as victualling centres,[1] and at the latter a permanent supply centre was set up under John de Maidstone, a royal paymaster.[2] The accounts show the way in which royal clerks and sheriffs were used to buy up supplies which were then sent to the victualling centres, often on requisitioned carts. From there the goods were directed, frequently by water, to the garrisons and to the troops in the field. The wardrobe account for the year starting in November 1283 shows that over 6,600 tuns of wine were acquired by the government, and that it had at its disposal more than 12,000 quarters of wheat, and about 10,842 quarters of oats. 1,110 cattle and impressive quantities of dried fish were also purveyed. These figures do not represent the full totals, for in addition the special war account shows that £5,422 was spent on victualling, the purchase of war horses and miscellaneous items.[3] Similar methods of supplying the armies in Wales were used in 1294–5, and despite the loss of the commissariat train to a Welsh attack, and a difficult period when the king was at Conway and wine ran out, more than sufficient food was accumulated.[4]

The war with France imposed a heavy demand for food supplies, notably in 1296 when, with the Wardrobe taking responsibility for the campaign in Scotland, the Exchequer was given the task of organizing prises of foodstuffs for Gascony. In March and April the sheriffs of twelve southern counties were ordered to purvey a total of 13,500 quarters of wheat and 13,000 quarters of oats. The operation seems to have been carried out with excessive thoroughness, since after a complaint had been received orders were issued in May that no one should be left without enough corn to live on. In June further commissions to make prises were issued, directed to nine counties, four of which had been included in the previous order. Then on 17 September Richard of Louth arrived at the Exchequer with instructions from the king, the first

[1] *C.V.C.R., 1277–1326*, pp. 214, 216, 224, 248.
[2] E. 101/351/6.   [3] E. 372/130; *Chron. Oxenedes*, p. 334.
[4] Morris, *Welsh Wars*, p. 255; *Book of Prests*, ed. Fryde, pp. xxxiv–xxxvi.

of which was that 100,000 quarters of grain should be purveyed for Gascony. Complaints had been received earlier in the year from the army there, stating that it was in great distress for want of food and money.[1] But the Exchequer protested that the quantity demanded was unreasonable, and the king replied, showing a touch of humour, that he had certainly intended the quantity specified, and that even should he demand all the grain in England they should not question him, but that his real intention was that they should simply purvey all the grain that they could without excessively burdening the people of England. The result was that at the end of November orders went to most of the counties of England for the collection of a total of 33,800 quarters of wheat, 20,400 quarters of oats, 5,800 quarters of barley and 3,200 quarters of beans and peas.[2]

Such huge quantities of supplies were not collected in 1297, but even so the figures were substantial. Thirty-eight ships were used on the run to Gascony, leaving at different dates from ports in the south of England, carrying a total of 6,470 quarters of wheat, 10,542 quarters of oats, 952 quarters of beans, 2,500 stockfish and 571 tuns of flour. For the Flanders campaign 4,893 quarters of wheat was brought over from England, together with 3,831 quarters of other grains. This was more than was bought locally by royal officials.[3] A further indication of the burden placed on the country is provided by the accounts of individual sheriffs. From Lincolnshire 2,741 quarters of cereals was provided, an impressive total from a single county.[4] Yorkshire produced thirty-four tuns of flour, 1,194 quarters of wheat and 763 quarters of oats for Flanders.[5] 2,120 quarters of wheat, 500 quarters of barley, 1,724½ quarters of oats and 172 tuns of flour were sent to Gascony from Wiltshire and Hampshire. In 1296 and 1297 the sheriff of Kent collected together 2,221 quarters of wheat, 1,542 quarters of oats and 1,121 quarters of barley.[6]

[1] E. 159/69, mm. 19d, 76d, 80d, 85d.   [2] E. 159/70, mm. 5, 119–20.
[3] B.M. Add. MS, 7965, ff. 44–50, 89, 93, 96–7.
[4] *A Lincolnshire Assize Roll for 1298*, ed. W. S. Thomson (Lincoln Rec. Soc., 1944), p. lxi.   [5] B.M. Add. MS, 7965, f. 50.
[6] Liberate Roll, C. 62/74, 14 Dec., 28 Jan.

VICTUALLING

Large quantities of victuals were required by the English forces in Scotland during the last ten years of the reign. There were two main victualling bases where stores were collected before being sent on to the armies and the castle garrisons. One was at Berwick, where Peter of Dunwich was acting as receiver of victuals in 1297,[1] shortly to be replaced by Richard de Bromsgrove who held the office until the end of the reign. As far as supplies from England were concerned, this was the most important base. With the prevailing winds it was easier to take supplies up the east coast than the west, and the main grain-producing regions of England were in the east. Also, the majority of expeditions advanced north on the eastern route, through Newcastle and Berwick. The other supply centre was at Carlisle, with its port at Skinburness. In those years when the army did advance up the western route, the position of receiver of victuals there, held first by Richard of Abingdon and then by James Dalilegh, became extremely important, but otherwise it was mainly used as a convenient place for the collection of supplies from Ireland, and for the victualling of the castles of Dumfries and Lochmaben.

The simplest way of indicating the extent of the victualling operations for the wars in Scotland is to examine the figures of the supplies purveyed for two particular campaigns. In 1300 the government's task was simplified by the fact that appreciable quantities of victuals had been accumulated for the campaign that had never taken place in the previous year. In January additional and substantial quantities were ordered from eleven English counties and from Ireland. The table on the next page shows how much was provided for the army to eat.

The figures for receipts here include supplies left over from the previous year, so the table does not give an accurate picture of the response of the sheriffs to the orders sent them. Although the royal victuallers had almost 12,000 quarters of wheat and flour at their disposal during 1300, only about 6,000 were actually collected during the year, in response to a request for 10,000. The sheriff of Norfolk and Suffolk only sent north 753 quarters of wheat and 1,000 quarters of oats, not the 1,500 of the former and 1,200 of the

---

[1] Stevenson, *Documents*, ii, no. ccccxiii.

VICTUALLING

BERWICK[1]

	Ordered[2]	Receipts	Issues
Flour		291½ tuns (= c. 1,460 qu.)	250½ tuns (= c. 1,260 qu.)
Wheat	7,000 qu.	2,716 qu. 2½ bu.	2,140 qu. 2 bu.
Barley		99½ qu.	30½ qu.
Malt	4,300 qu.	2,668 qu. 7½ bu.	1,915 qu. 7½ bu.
Oats	8,000 qu.	4,739 qu.	3,114 qu. 2 bu.
Beans	1,000 qu.	973 qu. 6 bu.	856 qu. 2 bu.
Wine		734 tuns	316 tuns
Beef		50½ carcases	50½ carcases
Pork		14½ carcases	14½ carcases
Mutton		60 carcases	60 carcases
Herrings		28,500	28,500
Stockfish		14,336	6,568
Salt		418 qu. 6 bu.	31½ qu.

CARLISLE

	Ordered	Receipts	Issues
Flour		272½ qu. 657½ tuns (= c. 3,290 qu.)	272½ qu. 657½ tuns (= c. 3,290 qu.)
Wheat	3,000 qu.	4,508 qu. 7 bu.	3,555 qu. 2 bu.
Malt		1,129 qu. 7 bu.	1,052 qu. 1 bu.
Oats	2,300 qu.	7,769 qu. 5½ bu.	7,462 qu. 3½ bu.
Beans		52 qu. 5 bu.	41 qu. 2 bu.
Wine	300 tuns	623 tuns	611 tuns
Beef		101½ carcases	101½ carcases
Pork		521½ carcases	521½ carcases
Herrings		9,500	9,500
Stockfish	10,000	21 tuns, 23 fish	21 tuns, 263 fish[3]
Salt		22 qu. 5 bu.	22 qu. 5 bu.

latter that were demanded. On the other hand, he met the target exactly for malt, beans and peas. In providing 1,030 quarters, 7 bushels of wheat the sheriff of Lincolnshire exceeded the figure that he was asked for. The most incompetent was the sheriff of Nottinghamshire and Derbyshire, who in response to an order for 500 quarters of wheat, 300 quarters of oats and 300 quarters of

---

[1] Calculations from *Liber Quotidianus*, pp. 113–29. The original account for Berwick is B.M. Harleian MS, 626.

[2] *C.P.R., 1292–1301*, pp. 487–8.

[3] [*Sic*.]

VICTUALLING

malt only produced 133 quarters 7 bushels of wheat.[1] There were no complaints of any insufficiency of victuals, though there was anger with the quality of some of the grain sent from Ireland. A sample was sent back to Dublin, where a jury declared that it had come from the demesne lands of the vacant archbishopric of that city.[2]

The account for the Carlisle establishment during the 1301 campaign survives,[3] but that for Berwick does not. The expedition of 1303 was largely dependent on Berwick as a supply base, so the importance of Carlisle was greatly diminished. The next table shows the quantities of victuals ordered from the English counties, and the amounts actually available, including those left over from the previous year. The figures show that the sheriffs were on the

VICTUALLING, 1303

	Ordered[4]	Berwick[5]	Carlisle[6]	Total
Flour	1,250 qu.	290 tuns (= c. 1,450 qu.) 422 qu.		c. 1,872 qu.
Wheat	7,250 qu.	5,745 qu. 1 bu.	686 qu. 6 bu.	6,431 qu. 7 bu.
Rye, etc.		276 qu. 5 bu.		276 qu. 5 bu.
Barley		143 qu. 5 bu.		143 qu. 5 bu.
Malt	3,800 qu.	1,050 qu. 6 bu.	272 qu. 6 bu.	1,326 qu. 4 bu.
Oats	8,000 qu.	5,155 qu. 5½ bu.	818 qu. 3½ bu.	5,974 qu. 1 bu.
Beans	2,700 qu.	1,279 qu. ½ bu.	26 qu. 6 bu.	1,305 qu. 6½ bu.
Vetch		275 qu. 4 bu.		275 qu. 4 bu.
Wine		1,263½ tuns	102½ tuns	1,366 tuns
Salt	500 qu.	680 qu. 4 bu.		680 qu. 4 bu.
Cattle		44		44
Pork		447 carcases		447 carcases
Mutton		8 carcases		8 carcases
Venison		73 carcases		73 carcases
Stockfish		1,720	298, 21 qu.	2,018, 21 qu.
Salmon		380		380
Cod		45		45

[1] *Liber Quotidianus*, pp. 107–10; *C.P.R., 1292–1301*, p. 487.
[2] E. 101/547/14.
[3] In the main wardrobe book for the year, B.M. Add. MS, 7966a, ff. 58v–59.
[4] *C.P.R., 1301–7*, pp. 98–9, 126.   [5] B.M. Add. MS, 17360.
[6] E. 101/11/9.

VICTUALLING

whole efficient in providing supplies: it was only over malt and beans that their deliveries fell seriously short. With the campaign continuing over the winter into 1304, further supplies were needed. Orders were sent out in September and November,[1] and the next table compares the quantities requested, this being given in the top line of each entry, with the amounts actually supplied, given immediately below the first figure.

VICTUALLING, 1304[2]

County	Wheat	Malt	Oats	Beans	Barley
Yorks.	500 qu.	500 qu.	500 qu.	200 qu.	
	575 qu.	448 qu.	491 qu.	218 qu.	
Cambs. & Hunts.	500 qu.	400 qu.	400 qu.	100 qu.	
	562 qu.	180 qu.	275 qu.	63 qu.	
Essex & Herts.	300 qu.	300 qu.	300 qu.		
	518 qu.	–	309 qu.		
Norfolk & Suffolk	500 qu.	400 qu.	400 qu.	200 qu.	
	477 qu.	435 qu.	367 qu.	144 qu.	
Lincs.	500 qu.		400 qu.		
	451 qu.		496 qu.		
Northants.	500 qu.	500 qu.	500 qu.		
	300 qu.	–	293 qu.		
Northumbr.	300 qu.	300 qu.	400 qu.		
	89 qu.	–	139 qu.		5 qu.
Barton-on-Humber	100 qu.	200 qu.			
	105 qu.	210 qu.			
Lynn	500 qu.		1,000 qu.		500 qu.
	300 qu.		1,000 qu.		300 qu.

In some instances it seems probable that the initial orders were modified subsequently: in the case of Essex and Hertfordshire, for example, the demand for malt was abandoned, and an extra 200 quarters of wheat requested instead. Purveyances and purchases of victuals in addition to those noted on the table provided the army in Scotland with a further 3,680 quarters of wheat, 3,834 of oats, 1,038 of malt, 937 of barley and 354 of beans and peas. Much of this came from Hampshire, the Isle of Wight and Holder-

[1] *C.P.R., 1301–7*, pp. 159, 201.
[2] *Ibid.*, pp. 159, 201; *C.C.R., 1302–7*, pp. 120–1; E. 101/10/18/83; B.M. Add. MS. 8835, ff. 25–31.

ness and was collected by conventional methods. It is interesting to see how in the two latter cases Edward was profiting from the lands he had acquired so dubiously from Aveline de Forz and her mother. However, new expedients used in 1304 to collect supplies suggest that the usual methods had proved insufficient. The customs collectors at Hartepool were employed to buy up provisions, as were the collectors of tallage at Ravenser and Hull. Richard Dalton was required to collect substantial quantities that Walter Langton had negotiated as loans in kind to the crown. The supplies from Barton-on-Humber and Lynn noted in the table were obtained as loans in a similar way. Some supplies were bought from individuals. John Droxford's chaplain sold twenty quarters of wheat and sixty quarters of beans. But the inadequacy of normal purveyance was not due to any incompetence on the part of the local officials: as the table shows, they did remarkably well, in most cases collecting almost exactly the quantity ordered. The total victuals available to the army in 1304, according to the wardrobe book, were 7,057 quarters of wheat, 7,204 of oats, 2,311 of malt, 1,242 of barley and 953 of beans and peas.[1]

The first duty of the victualling officers was to keep the royal household properly supplied with food when in the field. An estimate of its needs survives, probably dating from 1304. Ten quarters of wheat were required each day, along with the same quantity of malt, amounting for the period from April to September to 1,830 quarters of each commodity. 1,500 cattle, 3,000 sheep, 1,200 pigs and 400 bacon carcases were wanted. For the horses 3,000 quarters of oats were needed.[2] These figures give a rough idea of how much was required for the household, and it can be seen that in the Scotch wars, if not in the Welsh, the crown was regularly exceeding this amount in grain supplies, though it was probably hard to obtain such large numbers of livestock. Much of the food that was collected was required by the castle garrisons,

[1] B.M. Add. MS, 8835, ff. 25–35.
[2] E. 101/13/36/220. This estimate cannot be earlier than 1302, as it mentions the countess of Hereford, and in that year the king's daughter Elizabeth married the earl. 1304 is suggested by the fact that the date from which the estimate runs is April.

and careful estimates were made of their needs. In the autumn of 1298 the Steward of the household, Walter Beauchamp, the Keeper of the Wardrobe, John Droxford, together with Robert Fitz-Walter, Hugh le Despenser and the constables of the castles, ordained both the size of the garrisons in Scotland and the quantities of victuals to be issued to them.[1] Some of the estimates survive. One set was worked out on the basis of twenty men needing one quarter of wheat a week and two of malt, for making ale. In another case, equal quantities of wheat and malt were specified, as in the household estimate, since wine was available. Substantial amounts of meat and fish were to be supplied. The horses were to have a peck of oats each night. Other documents show that supplies more or less matched these estimates, and that the men were provided with a generous if unhealthy diet containing over 5,000 calories a day.[2]

Some of the food collected by the sheriffs and sent to the victualling bases was used to pay the men their wages. Prests in kind were often made.[3] Gifts of food were made to soldiers of all classes. Very appreciable quantities were sold off to the army, both by the victuallers in Carlisle and Berwick and by the household officials, notably the pantler. The magnates may have had compunctions about accepting pay from the crown, but they had no reservations about taking full advantage of the government's victualling activities. In 1303 the earl of Gloucester, Ralph de Monthermer, bought £101 14s. 6d. worth of victuals, and in the following year £114 12s. 2d. worth.[4] Experience had shown that it was unsafe to rely too much on the activities of private victuallers, and to ensure that the troops were well supplied with food the crown itself had to perform the same task as the merchants. The victuallers apparently sold supplies off at the highest price they could obtain for them, which was of course profitable to the

[1] E. 101/7/10.
[2] M. C. Prestwich, 'Victualling Estimates for English Garrisons in Scotland during the Early Fourteenth Century', *E.H.R.*, lxxxii (1967), pp. 346-53.
[3] *Infra*, p. 159.
[4] E. 101/10/4. See also such victuallers accounts as E. 101/7/13 and E. 101/11/29.

crown. In 1300 wheat was purveyed at an average price of 4s. 5d. a quarter, but it was sold off in Scotland at prices between 5s. and 10s., the average being 7s. In that year receipts from sales of food supplies came to £7,290 13s. 4¾d.[1]

The victualling activities of the crown were extremely unpopular, involving as they did the compulsory purchase of staple food supplies. In the constitutional crisis of 1297 prises were a major issue. As already shown, the years immediately preceding the crisis saw exceptionally heavy demands imposed on the country. This was at a time when prices were at a very high level. They had been rising since the late 1280s, and reached a peak in 1295 when, according to the most reliable calculations, they reached a level of 9s. 2¾d. a quarter for wheat. They fell in the next year to 4s. 10d., but rose in the following to 6s. 4d.[2] The government was well aware of the burdens its demands were imposing, and of the abuses that were possible. In November 1296 an ordinance laid down the way in which the prise of grain should be conducted. There was concern lest the poorer classes, who could least afford to have their food taken without immediate payment, should suffer unduly, so the sheriff and the royal clerk assisting him were ordered to consult with the assessors of the twelfth levied that year, whose records of assessment would give a good idea of how much each man could afford to have taken from him. An indenture was to be drawn up between the assessors and the sheriff, showing the quantities to be purveyed. Additional safeguards were provided by further instructions stating that a record should be kept of all tallies issued as receipts for victuals, one copy to be kept in the hundred or wapentake, and the other to be presented by the sheriff to the Exchequer, where arrangements for payment were to be made. The government even went to the lengths of specifying the prices to be paid. These were astonishingly high: wheat at 12s., barley, beans and peas at 9s. a quarter.[3] These should perhaps be interpreted in the same way as the king claimed

---

[1] *Liber Quotidianus*, pp. 8–13, 104–34.
[2] D. L. Farmer, 'Some Grain Price Movements in Thirteenth-Century England', *Ec.H.R.*, 2nd ser., x (1957), p. 212.
[3] E. 159/70, mm. 119–20.

his demand for 100,000 quarters of grain should be: that generous payment was to be made, but that the instructions were not to be taken literally.

Despite the safeguards that were laid down, there were inevitably complaints against these prises, which were taken on an unprecedented scale. The opposition in 1297 could have put up a case against them on constitutional grounds, but in the *Monstraunces*, presented to Edward on 30 June, the argument was rather that the burden on the country was insupportable. It was pointed out that military service could not be performed, as the country was so impoverished by Edward's demands for supplies and his failure to pay for what was taken. Many were said to have been forced below subsistence level.[1] The *De Tallagio* suggested a solution to the problems presented by prises in terms which echoed Edward's own legislation in the Statute of Westminster I, stating that no goods should be taken without the consent of their owners. In the settlement of the crisis in the *Confirmatio Cartarum* the king conceded that in future the 'prises taken throughout our realm by our ministers in our name' would only be taken by 'the common assent of all the realm'. But the concession was rendered virtually valueless by the addition of a clause saving the king's ancient rights.[2]

It was clear that much had gone wrong with the conduct and administration of the prises, and in his attempt during 1298 to conciliate the opposition of the previous year Edward set up commissions in April to enquire into 'all grievances inflicted on the people in the king's name', in particular the seizure of goods for royal use. Pairs of justices were sent out to hold inquisitions by jury, and punish those found guilty of improper conduct. Sheriffs and other ministers were to answer for the misdeeds of their subordinates, if the latter should prove to have insufficient means to make amends.

The complaints revealed by the judicial enquiries were very much what would be expected. Bailiffs often took more grain from villagers than they handed on to the sheriffs. Tallies might

---

[1] *Chron. Guisborough*, p. 292.
[2] Stubbs, *Select Charters*, pp. 491–4.

not be given, and officials on occasion took goods for which they had no warrant. In Lincolnshire one man had been notably corrupt: the name of Thomas Easton, bailiff of Ness, appeared more often than any other in cases concerning prises. The intention that people should be left with enough supplies for their own livelihood was not always observed. In one case John Everard compelled Adam Besaunt to buy three quarters of malt, which he then took from him by way of prise. He also took a quarter of salt meat, turned Adam out of his house, and sealed up the doors.[1] In a Norfolk case the parson of Knavering complained that the local bailiff had unjustly taken seven quarters of wheat and two of barley, so that he had no food for his beasts and could not sow for six weeks. He also accused the bailiff of keeping back one quarter for his own use, and of taking £1 3s. unjustly. The official admitted taking the grain and the money, for which he had due warrant, but the jurors found that the parson had suffered no damage. Technically they were correct, but it seems clear that he had undergone some hardship.[2] There were also complaints about the way in which horses and carts were requisitioned by sheriffs in order to transport the supplies collected. One unfortunate man refused to let the sheriff of Yorkshire take his horse, since he had no other on his farm, and he needed it to get in his harvest. His recalcitrance involved him in a fine of one mark when the case was brought up in the Exchequer Court.[3]

Obviously, in spite of the many complaints, Edward I could not afford to abandon the system of prises. Not only did it provide him with supplies essential for war, but also with a means of anticipating his income. The crown sold the food to the armies long before it paid for the prises, which were thus forced loans in kind. The slowness of payment is illustrated by a general petition put forward in parliament in 1305, asking for payment of arrears of all sorts, including prises that had been taken before 1297.[4] After the constitutional crisis the system was changed in various

[1] *A Lincolnshire Assize Roll*, ed. Thomson, nos. 237, 240, 241, 305, 314, 317, 370, 371.
[2] Norfolk assize roll, J.I. 1/587, m. 3d.
[3] E. 13/22, m. 5.   [4] *Rot. Parl.*, i, p. 165.

ways, largely to pacify public opinion. The Exchequer was deprived of its rôle of administering prises. No longer did the king issue such vague orders as when he asked for 100,000 quarters of grain for Gascony. Now, specific instructions were sent under the privy seal to the Chancery, setting out precisely how much was required from each county. Of course, supplies were still collected by the sheriffs, with the assistance of royal clerks, but clearly the Exchequer had come under heavy criticism for its part in the prises, seizures and taxes in the years leading up to 1297, and it made good sense to make a minor administrative readjustment to satisfy public feeling.

The Chancery took much more trouble in the years after 1297 to explain the reasons for the royal need of victuals than had been taken before. Naturally the writs were extremely abusive of the Scots, and it was pointed out that as the great lords and men-at-arms were contributing directly to the war effort with their service, the lesser people had a moral obligation to assist by contributing food supplies. The use of the word prise became far less common: the writs tended to talk instead of purveyance.[1] But the opposition was not to be bought off by such obvious propaganda methods, and in the *Articuli super Cartas* of 1300 the system of prise was attacked. The crown was henceforth to exercise the right to keep only the household supplied with food, and the terms of the relevant passage make it clear that purveyance on the scale seen in recent years was excluded.[2] As a result writs for purveyance were not sent to the sheriffs in 1301, and instead the communities of the various counties were asked to aid the king by granting him a loan of victuals. Payment was promised out of the fifteenth provisionally granted at Lincoln earlier in the year, and commissioners were sent to conduct the negotiations with the counties.[3] It was only when agreement had been reached that orders were issued to the sheriffs instructing them to collect the supplies and send them north. The accounts specifically describe

---

[1] The originals show this use of propaganda better than the calendared versions of the writs: see for example E. 101/552/4/8, and E. 101/585/5.
[2] *Statutes of the Realm*, i, p. 137.
[3] *C.P.R.*, *1296–1301*, pp. 578–9.

this purveyance as a loan, and the voluntary nature of the proceedings is indicated by the way in which the counties of Nottingham and Derby selected their own representatives to collect the supplies together, rather than accept the services of the sheriff.[1] The government took greater pains than it had in the past to see that payment was actually made. In January 1303 firm letters were sent to the tax collectors,[2] and their accounts show that some money was paid over, though not necessarily all that was owed. In 1305 the men of Northumberland complained in parliament that they had received nothing from the tax collectors, who were at once ordered to make payment.[3]

Although these negotiations in 1301 were genuine, it is striking that in all cases it was agreed to provide the quantities suggested by the government. In later years this technique of direct negotiation was not repeated on such a scale: it was probably realized on both sides that it was a waste of time, though on occasion isolated loans of victuals were obtained. In 1304, for example, Walter Langton in person negotiated a loan of 100 quarters of wheat and 200 quarters of malt from Barton-on-Humber.[4] The government continued to try to ensure that payment was made, and in 1302 the aid due to be collected for the marriage of the king's eldest daughter was assigned to pay for the victuals needed for the campaign in Scotland in the following year.[5] But lack of cash meant that such good intentions could not be fulfilled.

Purveyance continued to be extremely unpopular in the closing years of Edward's reign. In 1303 grievances about the failure to make payment were running so high in Lincolnshire that it was agreed that no prises should be taken unless they were immediately paid for.[6] The men of Yorkshire complained that officials were failing to make out proper receipts and tallies for the victuals they took, so that if five quarters of wheat were taken, the receipt would only state that four had been received, leaving a profit of one quarter to the purveyor.[7] In 1303 the men of Beverley alleged

[1] E. 101/580/8/1; B.M. Add. MS, 7966a, f. 53.
[2] E. 101/10/18/39; E. 101/592/1/2.   [3] E. 179/91/1; *Rot. Parl.*, i, p. 164.
[4] E. 101/10/18/83.   [5] *C.C.R., 1302–7*, p. 68.
[6] S.C. 1/27/15.   [7] S.C. 1/31/62.

that, although John de Sheffield had obtained allowance at the Exchequer for goods worth £40 taken from them, he had never paid them the money. A common method of evasion was to move supplies into sanctuary, although the purveyors did not always show full respect to the church. In 1304 Nicholas Lovel was appointed by the sheriff of Yorkshire to collect corn in the village of Bulmer. A local jury decided how much each man should contribute, and it was decided that the parson should provide a quarter of wheat and one of oats. This was duly taken, and the following Sunday Lovel was publicly excommunicated by the parson. The crown, with Lovel, brought an action against him, and the defence put up was that Lovel was not actually named, but that all that was done was to issue a general condemnation of all who took goods from sanctuary. The result of the case, and of the counter-action brought by the parson, is regrettably, as so often happens, not recorded. To be a purveyor was certainly hazardous, and liable to worse threats than excommunication. In 1303 William of Wetwang was collecting victuals in Sledmere in Yorkshire when he was pursued with drawn sword by one Saer de Collum, and was only able to escape by hiding in the house of the prior of Kirkham.[1]

The burden of purveyance did not fall on all parts of the country with equal severity. In the Welsh wars it was naturally the counties nearest the campaigning area that were called on most. For the years from 1296 it is possible to show how often each county was requested to provide supplies:

Number of times	County
13	Yorks.
12	Lincoln, Cambs., Essex.
11	Hunts.
9	Norfolk, Suffolk, Notts.
8	Derby, Dorset, Somerset.
7	Herts., Sussex.
6	Surrey.
5	Hants, Glos., Northumb.

[1] E. 13/26, mm. 6, 22, 30, 32, 36.

Number of times	County
5	Berks.
3	Bedford, Bucks., Cornwall, Kent, Lancs., Leics., Northants., Rutland, Worcester, Devon.
2	Middlesex, Oxon., Warwicks., Westmorland, Wilts.
1	Cheshire, Cumberland, Salop., Staffs., Hereford.[1]

The reasons for these differences are not always immediately clear. It has been pointed out that there was no correlation between these demands for victuals and the amount of land in royal hands in the various counties.[2] One obvious criterion used was ease of transport to the place required, and in addition it made sense to draw supplies from the main grain-producing areas of England, such as East Anglia. But it was also politic to try to spread the burden: in asking for victuals from various southern counties in December 1301 the king pointed out that similar aid had been provided by the northern counties earlier in the year.[3] Considerations of cost and convenience, however, made it impossible to equalize demands for victuals over the whole country. Land transport was slow and expensive, while long sea journeys affected the condition of the cargoes. 1,125 quarters of wheat, together with appreciable quantities of other victuals, which arrived in Berwick in the early months of 1304 in seven ships all the way from the Isle of Wight and Southampton, were all rotten. One other ship was driven ashore long before it reached its destination.[4] In other years consignments from the Isle of Wight did reach Berwick safely,[5] but it clearly made more sense to take the bulk of supplies from Yorkshire, Lincolnshire and East Anglia.

[1] E. 159/69, mm. 76d, 80d; E. 159/70, mm. 119, 121; *C.P.R., 1292–1301*, pp. 224, 314, 344, 487–8, 578–9; *C.P.R., 1301–7*, pp. 3, 35, 98–9, 126, 159, 201, 238, 417–19, 423, 509.

[2] *A Lincolnshire Assize Roll for 1298*, ed. Thomson, pp. lxxvii–lxxix.

[3] *C.C.R., 1296–1302*, p. 574.

[4] E. 101/561/4/16; S. F. Hockey, 'The Transport of Isle of Wight corn to feed Edward I's army in Scotland', *E.H.R.*, lxxvii (1962), pp. 703–5.

[5] *Liber Quotidianus*, pp. 133–4.

Within the counties, the administration aimed at spreading the burden of purveyance as equitably as possible. It was normal for hundreds and wapentakes to be informed of exactly how much they were to supply, while local jurors might then decide how much should be taken from each man.[1] Demesne supplies were taken as well as those of the villagers,[2] and attempts made to ensure that the burden did not fall too heavily on those least able to bear it. With taxes on moveables only collected twice in the last ten years of the reign, the system of consultation with the assessors authorized in 1296 was impracticable, but in 1303 orders were issued that no corn was to be taken from anyone who did not possess at least £10 worth of goods.[3] In any case, it was obviously administratively simpler to take supplies from the relatively wealthy than from the poor.

It has been argued that one effect of purveyances was to raise prices, and that in this indirect way the poor would have been affected by royal demands for victuals,[4] but there were no contemporary complaints to this effect. Nor were there complaints that the government was forcing producers to sell at abnormally low prices, although a comparison of the prices offered by the purveyors with the national averages that have been calculated by Farmer reveals that the former were consistently lower. In 1304, for example, the figures were 4s. 10d. and 5s. 6d. respectively. A further indication that low prices were being paid by the crown is that royal officials obtained better prices for their own produce from the purveyors than other men. Simon de Kyme, sheriff of Yorkshire, paid 5s. a quarter for wheat in 1304 to everybody save John Sandale, who received 6s. Sandale obtained the same high price from the sheriffs of Essex and Hertfordshire, as did John Droxford from the sheriff of Hampshire.[5]

[1] E. 13/25, m. 49d; E. 13/26, m. 30.
[2] P. D. A. Harvey, *A Medieval Oxfordshire Village: Cuxham, 1240 to 1400* (Oxford, 1965), p. 111.   [3] *C.P.R., 1301–7*, p. 159.
[4] D. L. Farmer, 'An Examination of Price Fluctuations in Certain Articles in the Twelfth, Thirteenth and early Fourteenth Centuries' (Oxford D.Phil. thesis, 1958), p. 80.
[5] Farmer, 'Some Grain Price Movements in Thirteenth-Century England', *Ec.H.R.*, 2nd ser., x (1957), p. 212; B.M. Add. MS, 8835, ff. 23–35.

VICTUALLING

A comparison with the victualling arrangements of the sixteenth century shows quite clearly the superiority of Edward I's administration. Even during the most efficiently organized expedition of Henry VIII's reign, that of 1544, the council of Boulogne noted that 'we thinke surely that meny people have dide amongst us in their sikeines for lack of socour of freshe meates'. Men such as William Paulett and Stephen Gardiner, who hold a high place in the estimation of sixteenth-century historians, were less successful in dealing with the problem of keeping large armies adequately provisioned than the corrupt but extremely competent Walter Langton. With officials of the calibre of Bromsgrove and Dalilegh in charge of the victualling bases, Edward I never found that lack of victuals forced him to abandon a campaign after only six days on the Border, as happened in 1542.[1] There were occasional complaints: in 1303 a commission was set up to enquire into the reasons for the incompetence shown by the sheriff of Essex and Hertfordshire,[2] while on one occasion the Keeper of the Wardrobe wrote to the sheriff of Somerset and Dorset, complaining that he had not sent the supplies he had collected north, 'I marvel greatly at your immense folly'.[3] Commissariat arrangements broke down when the king was at Conway early in 1295, when there was no wine or beer, and food ran short.[4] There was a serious lack of victuals before the battle of Falkirk in 1298,[5] and in the winter of 1301–2 many horses died for want of fodder.[6] But such examples are not common. Though hardly spectacular, the achievement of Edward I's servants in building up so efficient a victualling service was very considerable. Without it, the king's military ventures could never have taken place.

---

[1] C. S. L. Davies, 'Provisions for Armies, 1509–50', *Ec.H.R.*, 2nd ser., xvii (1964), pp. 242, 245.
[2] *C.P.R., 1301–7*, p. 129.
[3] E. 101/585/5/12.
[4] Morris, *Welsh Wars*, p. 255.
[5] *Chron. Guisborough*, pp. 324–5.
[6] *Chron. Rishanger*, p. 210.

VI

THE NAVY

Transport of the huge quantities of supplies collected for Edward I's armies could best be achieved by sea. Ships were needed to carry troops to Gascony and to Flanders, and to form the bridges required for crossing the Menai straits and the Firth of Forth. In the war with Philip IV the navy assumed more than a mere logistical importance: control of the sea was essential if the enemy plans for invasion were to be thwarted. The sailors who served Edward I had a vital, if undramatic, rôle to play.

The fleet used in the first Welsh war was not large. Its core was provided by the Cinque Ports, which had an obligation to provide ships for fifteen days' unpaid service when called upon. The main squadron from the Ports was composed of eighteen ships, and a further seven joined later. There were also two ships from Bayonne and Southampton, and eight small vessels hired locally.[1] The fleet played an important part in keeping the army supplied, and in transporting men to Anglesey. More ships were used in the second Welsh war. Again the Cinque Ports produced the majority of the fleet: forty sailing vessels and two galleys. This amounted to roughly three-quarters of the full service of fifty-seven vessels the king was entitled to demand. In addition seven ships were acquired locally, and a bridge of boats constructed to take troops across to Anglesey. The cost of the fleet for this war came to £1,404.[2]

Valuable as the navy was in Wales, its services were obviously of much greater importance in the war with France. The immediate occasion of that war was the rivalry of the Cinque Ports with the sailors of Normandy, which erupted into hostilities in 1293.

[1] Morris, *Welsh Wars*, p. 128.   [2] *Ibid.*, pp. 173, 177.

Once war was officially declared in the following year both sides began to make naval preparations. Philip IV brought shipbuilders from Genoa to build galleys, some in Marseilles and some in Normandy. In April 1295 a squadron of thirty galleys sailed from the Mediterranean for service against the English. In addition the French had the use of some 220 merchant vessels requisitioned for the war, though in late November they received a severe setback when many vessels were destroyed in a storm. But Philip did not abandon hopes of launching an invasion fleet against England, and in 1297 he recruited the greatest naval expert of the time, the Genoese admiral Benedetto Zaccharia, to assist him. Fortunately for the English the truce was agreed before Zaccharia's plans could be carried out.[1]

Edward I began taking measures to combat the French naval threat in November 1294. Orders were sent out for the construction of thirty galleys, substantial vessels of 120 oars each, to be ready by Christmas. This date was of course grossly optimistic, but the ships were completed in the course of 1295. Unlike the French, the English do not seem to have made efforts to obtain the advice of shipbuilders from the Mediterranean although this types of vessel was comparatively rare in northern waters. The result was that the first of the two galleys built at London had to put back for repairs after its maiden voyage, while one built at Newcastle needed a refit after less than six months in service.[2] Little is known about the use and effectiveness of these galleys. In January 1297 the Southampton vessel, which two years earlier had a crew of four constables and 116 men, captured five French ships,[3] but such incidents were rare. Later in the same year, 1297, the Lyme Regis and Southampton galleys were used to escort ships

---

[1] C. Jourdain, 'Mémoire sur les commencements de la marine militaire sous Philippe le Bel', *Mémoires de l'académie des inscriptions et belles lettres*, xxx (1881), pp. 377–418; C. de la Roncière, *Histoire de la marine française*, i (Paris, 1889), pp. 333–63.

[2] R. J. Whitwell and C. Johnson, 'The "Newcastle" Galley, A.D. 1294', *Archaeologia Aeliana*, 4th ser., ii (1926), pp. 142–93; C. Johnson, 'London Shipbuilding, A.D. 1295', *Antiquaries Journal*, vii (1927), pp. 424–37; R. C. Anderson, 'English Galleys in 1295', *Mariner's Mirror*, xiv (1928), pp. 220–41.

[3] E. 163/2/4.

carrying money to Gascony, and the fleet taking the king's daughter Margaret, duchess of Brabant, across the North Sea was escorted by the galleys built in Ipswich and King's Lynn.[1] Once the war with France was over, no further use was made of the galleys.

The English government did not have to rely solely on specially-built ships to defend the coasts. Merchant ships could be requisitioned for war. The earliest indication that this was being done is a writ of protection of November 1294 for the sailors of Great Yarmouth who were serving with William Leyburn, captain of the fleet, and his subordinate, John Botetourt.[2] In 1295 efforts to defend England against the French were on a larger scale. News came in the spring of the steps being taken to bring together a large enemy fleet, and so in April the sheriffs of the coastal shires of the south, east and north-east were ordered to assemble ships at Portsmouth, Harwich, Orwell and Ravenser.[3] An account for only one of the squadrons that was collected survives; it was composed of eight ships, including the Grimsby and Newcastle galleys, which were guarding the coast from King's Lynn to Berwick in the late summer and autumn of the year.[4]

Arrangements were also made to defend the coasts with land forces against the threatened invasion. The Treasurer was ordered to see to this in December 1294, and William Leyburn and the constable of Dover were made responsible for organizing a guard system. Sheriffs were to make public proclamations asking for all to be ready and armed to repel the enemy.[5] At the end of August 1295, following an unsuccessful French attack on Dover at the beginning of the month, various magnates and knights were appointed to guard the coasts. A royal clerk, Peter of Dunwich, was made responsible for co-ordinating arrangements in eastern England. The cost of such arrangements was not born by the central government, but fell on the local communities.[6] The

---

[1] B.M. Add. MS, 7965, ff. 89, 90.
[2] C.P.R., 1292–1301, p. 126.
[3] E. 159/68, m. 80.
[4] E. 101/5/11.
[5] E. 159/68, m. 79.
[6] A. Z. Freeman, 'A Moat Defensive: the Coast Defense Scheme of 1295', *Speculum*, xlii (1967), pp. 446–8.

measures were hardly tested by the French: an attempt on Winchelsea was thwarted by a naval squadron from Yarmouth, and a raid on Hythe with seventeen ships and one galley resulted in the loss of the galley.[1] But the traitor Thomas Turberville considered that the defences were inadequate on the south coast, and pointed out in his letter to the French that the Isle of Wight was undefended.[2] Discovery of this letter in the autumn of 1295 may have spurred the government to make more elaborate arrangements in the following year. Evidence of musters of the defence forces suggests that the organization was being overhauled and made more efficient. Villages and hundreds were assessed to find out how many soldiers could be raised, and officers were put in charge of each group of ten men. The city of London provided a force of twenty men-at-arms for four weeks in Kent, each man being paid a lavish twenty marks. The numbers of men enrolled were quite considerable, though it seems doubtful that they would have been adequate to deal with a full-scale invasion. There were seventy-six fully-armed cavalrymen on the Isle of Wight in April 1296. The infantry forces in Hampshire totalled 504.[3]

Naval forces were larger in 1296 than in the previous year. In January Osbert de Spaldington was authorized to raise a fleet of 100 ships from the ports between King's Lynn and Berwick.[4] No account for this survives, but there is one for the next command to the south, that of John Botetourt, who had a fleet of ninety-four vessels drawn from ports between Harwich and King's Lynn, with a total complement of 3,578 men. No less than fifty-three of the ships came from Yarmouth.[5] The navy succeeded in preventing any French raids in 1296. In July the Master of the Templars in England reported that the enemy were preparing to descend on Yarmouth in ships disguised as fishing vessels.[6] However, no such attack took place. French activities were confined to the harassment of English merchant shipping at sea.[7]

In 1297, the last year of hostilities with France, the government

---

[1] *Ibid.*, p. 446; *Chron. Hagnaby*, B.M. Cotton. MS, Vesp. B. xi, f. 38.
[2] *Chron. Cotton*, p. 305.
[3] Freeman, *op. cit.*, pp. 447-58.
[4] *C.P.R., 1292–1301*, p. 180.
[5] C. 47/2/11.
[6] E. 159/69, m. 26.
[7] *Chron. Cotton*, p. 313.

could not afford to divert so much of its naval resources to the defence of the shores, as ships were needed for the transport of supplies to Gascony and men to Flanders. In March a commission was set up to provide ten well-armed ships to watch the French coast, and in July two squadrons were created to guard the English coasts, one of six ships to the north of the Thames, and one of twelve to the south of it. Clearly the panic over the invasion threat had largely subsided.[1]

Defence was only one part of the navy's rôle during these years of crisis. Of greater importance was the activity of English shipping in transporting men and supplies to Wales, Scotland, Gascony and Flanders. No details for 1295 survive, but the wardrobe account shows that the impressive sum of £12,852 6s. 1d. was spent on sailors' wages in the attack on Anglesey and in the fleets sent to Gascony. In the following year the account combines naval expenditure with the cost of maintaining the prisoners taken in Scotland, the two items coming to £18,278 11s. 6d.[2] According to the chroniclers the fleet used on the east coast of Scotland was only twenty-four strong, but in contrast, 134 ships were used to transport the Irish troops to Furness, and a squadron of thirty was then sent north to the Isles.[3] But the main expense that year must have been the fleet which carried Edmund of Lancaster and the earl of Lincoln to Gascony. Details survive of a part of this, fifty ships from the Cinque Ports whose wages from 7 March until 3 May came to £1,519 15s. 0d.[4]

In 1297 the bill for sailors' wages was much lower than it had been in the previous two years, amounting to only £5,586 19s. 3d. The main reason for the drop was that no large fleets were sent on the long and expensive run to Gascony. Thirty-eight ships took victuals there, and in addition a small convoy of six carried 11,000 marks to the paymasters of the army there. Early in the year a fleet of eighteen English and twelve Zeeland ships took the duchess of Brabant from England. In May seventeen ships were employed taking money to the count of Flanders and John de Bar. On their

---

[1] *C.P.R., 1292–1301*, pp. 245, 291.   [2] E. 372/144.
[3] *Chron. Rishanger*, p. 157; *Chron. Guisborough*, p. 274; E. 101/5/26, mm. 4, 5.   [4] E. 101/5/28.

return they sailed down the French coast as far as Normandy destroying enemy shipping.[1] The main naval enterprise in 1297, however, was the transport of the royal expedition to Flanders in August. Arrangements were made surprisingly late in the year. On 27 April writs were issued asking that all ships of over forty tons burthen should assemble at Winchelsea at Midsummer, and in addition, the Cinque Ports were asked to produce their full service. It was emphasized that no precedent was to be made of this expedient, and the king relied on his usual mixture of appeals to patriotism and threats to persuade the seaports to comply with the request. No very elaborate arrangements were made to collect the ships together, reliance being placed on the sheriffs and the town bailiffs, with the Warden of the Cinque Ports and the Captain of the king's sailors, William Leyburn, and his subordinate, John Botetourt, also playing their part.[2]

As the army that assembled was not as large as Edward had intended, the problem of raising sufficient ships was not so great as originally envisaged. The accounts show that there were thirty-two ships used simply for the transport of supplies and horses, while the main expedition was taken across to Flanders in 273 ships. Of these, seventy-three were provided by the Cinque Ports, and fifty-nine by their great rival Yarmouth. The king himself sailed in the *Cog St. Edward*, the largest of the Cinque Ports vessels, with a crew of forty-nine men. But this ship was not the largest of the fleet. That place was taken by the *Sainte Marie* of Bayonne, with a complement of 100 men. Another fleet, consisting of thirty-four ships, was needed to take Robert FitzPayn and those accompanying him to Flanders in October. The total number of sailors needed to transport all the forces and supplies to Flanders was about 5,800:[3] a large number in view of the fact that there were not many more than 9,000 men in the army. Presumably another substantial fleet was required to bring the expedition home in 1298, but apart from some writs ordering the collection of ships, little evidence of it survives.

[1] B.M. Add. MS, 7965, ff. 89v, 90v–92, 96–7, 105v.
[2] C.C.R., *1296–1302*, pp. 41, 99–102.
[3] B.M. Add. MS, 7965, ff. 91–3, 98–104v.

The one naval engagement that took place on the Flanders campaign was, ironically enough, between the sailors of the Cinque Ports and those of Yarmouth, in the port of Swyn. One Yarmouth source put the damages at thirty-seven ships, 171 men lost, and a financial cost of £15,356. The assize roll, probably more accurate, states that seventeen ships were burned, twelve more looted, and 165 men killed. Damages were put at £5,000.[1] The Wardrobe and all its equipment aboard the *Bayard* of Yarmouth were only saved from destruction in the fight by the quick-witted action of one Philip de Hales, who cut the mooring cable, enabling the ship to escape.[2]

Ships for the Scotch campaigns of the later years of the reign were collected in much the same way as they had been for Flanders and Gascony.[3] The only service the government could call on by established right was that of the Cinque Ports. The full total of fifty-seven ships was requested for the projected campaign of 1299 which never took place,[4] but for the following year the king stated that he would be content with half the usual number of ships, on condition that they were manned by the same number of sailors as the full quota, which came to 1,254 men. In fact they provided thirty ships, with a total complement of 1,106. Once they had completed their brief period of two weeks' unpaid service, these men were paid wages just like the men of the other ports, at the standard rate of 3*d*. a day for the ordinary sailors and 6*d*. for the shipmasters.[5] The next year, 1301, saw no demand made for service from the Cinque Ports, presumably because there was no feudal summons that year, and it was felt to be unreasonable to burden the Ports when no one else was similarly afflicted. However, they were asked to send twelve ships to Ireland at royal wages to assist in transporting men and supplies to Scotland.[6] As

[1] F. W. Brooks, 'The Cinque Ports Feud with Yarmouth', *Mariner's Mirror*, xix (1933), p. 44.   [2] B.M. Add. MS, 7965, f. 57.
[3] For the naval aspects of the Scotch wars see W. Stanford Reid, 'Sea Power in the Anglo-Scottish War, 1296–1328', *Mariner's Mirror*, lx (1960), pp. 7–23.
[4] *C.C.R., 1296–1302*, pp. 290, 307, 313.
[5] Powicke, *Thirteenth Century*, p. 655; *C.C.R., 1296–1302*, p. 348; *Liber Quotidianus*, pp. 275–7.
[6] *C.C.R., 1296–1302*, pp. 486–7.

no mention of these vessels appears in the accounts, it seems probable that the Ports did not comply with the royal request.

In these years relations between the crown and the Cinque Ports were not good. In one account they presented they claimed that they were owed a total of £2,476 6s. 8d., largely for the Gascon war, but a note at the foot of the document, written by a royal clerk, pointed out that they had not paid any of the taxes levied between 1294 and 1297, nor had they accounted for 600 marks received from the Treasurer of Ireland. In addition it was claimed that they had impeded the justices making enquiries about foreign coin circulating in England, and damages were put at £1,000. The barons of the Ports asserted that these debts were offset by the payment of 2,000 marks for the tax of a fifteenth levied in 1301. Eventually the crown appears to have agreed that it owed the Ports £500 in wages, and that the rest of the claims should be allowed to cancel each other out.[1]

In view of these disputes it is not surprising to find that in 1301 there were only three ships from the Cinque Ports on the wardrobe pay roll.[2] But in 1303, with a feudal summons, the Ports were asked for their service. As in 1300, the full number of ships was not demanded: twenty-five was suggested as a sufficient number. Although no account for the contingent survives, it is known that the king was not satisfied with their performance since a commission was set up in December 1303 to enquire into the desertion of men from the Cinque Ports and other Kentish seaports during the campaign.[3] The service of the Ports was again demanded in 1306, twenty-seven ships being requested. In fact, they only brought twenty-four, with a total complement of 990 men. The ships from Hythe arrived in Scotland on 3 July, and most of the others two days later. Instead of doing their unpaid service at once, they were at wages until 17 September, and then did fifteen days at their own cost. Most then returned south, but a squadron of twelve ships remained in the north at wages. The total cost to the crown of the fleet was £1,276 14s. 0d.[4]

To get the other ports to send ships to assist in the Scotch wars

[1] E. 101/5/30. [2] B.M. Add. MS, 7966a, ff. 130-1.
[3] C.C.R., 1296-1302, p. 612; C.P.R., 1301-7, p. 203. [4] E. 101/13/8.

the crown might either appoint commissioners to negotiate with the towns, or simply send writs to the mayors and bailiffs demanding that they send a specific number of vessels. It is not clear which method was employed in 1300, a year in which few ships from outside the Cinque Ports were engaged. In December 1299 and January 1300 Richard de Bromsgrove was using a small number of ships, never more than nine at any one time, on the task of taking food to the castles for which he was responsible.[1] During the summer some fifteen small ships were occupied in supplying the army in Galloway with victuals. There were also two substantial galleys, each with a crew of about fifty, provided by Simon de Montague. Eight Irish ships were also used.[2]

In 1301, since no service was requested from the Cinque Ports, Edward I had to make much more extensive demands on the naval capacity of the country to carry out his ambitious plan for a double campaign in Scotland. On 14 February orders were sent to various towns asking for a total of fifty-eight ships from England and ten from Ireland. In fact, more were provided. On the east coast over fifty were employed in carrying supplies, but these were small vessels, mostly with crews of ten men or less. There were only about ten ships equal in size to those that had been used to transport the royal expedition to Flanders. The fleet which assembled to support the operations of the prince's army in the west had one major task, to transport the Irish troops across to Skinburness. Forty-seven ships in all were needed for this, of which over twenty were Irish. No details are given in the wardrobe book of the number of sailors employed, but the tonnage of the various ships is given. The largest was the *Margaret* of Shoreham, of 195 tons, while there were ten other vessels over 100 tons burthen. Payment to the shipmasters was based on the unusual system of a negotiated sum, in most cases seven shillings, paid for each ton of the ship.[3]

Although more ships were used by the government in 1301 than had originally been ordered from the seaports, Edward I was not pleased with the performance of twelve towns in the south,

[1] B.M. Harl. MS, 626, ff. 12–13.   [2] *Liber Quotidianus*, pp. 271–9.
[3] B.M. Add. MS, 7966a, ff. 102–3, 130–1; *C.C.R., 1296–1302*, pp. 482–3.

including Southampton, Portsmouth and Bridgwater, which had not supplied the ships that had been promised. On 10 August commissioners were appointed to punish them, with additional appointments being made at the end of the month. It was discovered that there were ships in Bridgwater and Weymouth which could have been sent north, but the men of Poole stated that the only vessels they had were both taken to Scotland by the earl of Lincoln, the lord of the town. In Portsmouth harbour there were no suitable ships, while the two Seaford vessels were in Gascony.[1]

Similar difficulties in collecting ships for Scotland continued in the next years. On 10 November 1302 orders were issued for twenty-five ships from various ports to appear together with the Cinque Ports fleet at Ayr by 15 August of the following year. Peter of Dunwich was responsible for negotiating with some of the towns. In Bristol the burgesses agreed to send two ships, but Dunwich found it impossible to obtain crews, and Nicholas Fermbaud, constable of Bristol Castle, had to be asked to use all possible means, including distraint, to persuade men to serve. The responsibility for selecting fifty ships from the coastal towns from Essex to Northumberland was given to Walter Bacon. He was ordered to adopt the exceptional step of taking security from the towns that did agree to send ships to ensure that they fulfilled their promises. The men of the liberty of Durham refused to send the ships that were selected, and Bacon had to obtain the assistance of Robert Clifford, guardian of the Palatinate, to force the ports of Hartlepool, Wearmouth and Jarrow to co-operate. The towns of York, Beverley, Lincoln, Ely, Norwich and Cambridge did consent to provide ships, and then found the burden too great: they had to apply for royal assistance to compel the men of the surrounding areas to help them.[2]

In May 1303 there was a fleet of sixteen substantial ships at Berwick, while sixty-five small transport vessels were used to take supplies north. Thirty-one ships were needed to act first as transports and then as pontoons for the elaborate prefabricated bridges

[1] *C.P.R., 1301-7*, pp. 52-3; E. 101/9/7/2-6; E. 101/10/21/1, 5, 6.
[2] *C.C.R., 1296-1302*, p. 612; *C.C.R., 1302-7*, p. 76.

which Edward I had constructed for the crossing of the Forth. As in 1301 a large fleet was needed in the west to bring the Irish contingents to Scotland. Thirty-seven English and Welsh ships, and twenty-three Irish ones, were employed. An account of the cost of preparing the ships to carry horses shows that one ship might take from ten to thirty animals. Fifty vessels carried 820 horses between them. The total cost of the year's naval activities, including the transport of some Gascons who had served the king in England and Scotland back to their native land in six ships, came to £1,657. The contrast with the huge naval budgets of 1295 and 1296 is a striking one.[1] In 1304 naval activities were on a still smaller scale, with a fleet of some fifty small transport vessels being used to carry supplies and to perform such tasks as bringing the lead required for the counterweights of the great engines used in the siege of Stirling. Sailors' wages came to only £307 16s. 8d.[2]

The campaigns against Robert Bruce at the end of the reign saw, as far as can be determined from the incomplete accounts, a smaller transport fleet than ever. None of the usual commissions to collect ships from the ports was employed, and there were no large Irish contingents to be ferried across to Scotland. In 1306 the Cinque Ports' fleet was in Scotland, but otherwise only some twenty-five English ships appear to have been used in these final years of the reign. Early in 1307 Edward asked Hugh Bisset, lord of Antrim, to whom he had granted the Isle of Arran in 1298, to provide ships to pursue Bruce and his allies in the Isles, where they were thought to be hiding. Later, in June, Hugh Bisset's cousin John agreed to guard the coast near Kintyre with four barges manned by 100 men in return for fifty marks.[3]

The one exceptional feature of the naval efforts of Edward I's reign was the attempt during the period of the French war to build up a fleet of royal galleys. In contrast, there was nothing particularly impressive about the fleets created by requisitioning

---

[1] B.M. Add. MS, 17360, ff. 21-7; E. 101/11/2, ff. 2, 5v, 7-10; E. 101/10/29; E. 101/371/8/39; E. 101/364/14.

[2] B.M. Add. MS, 8835, ff. 99-112.

[3] E. 101/13/16, ff. 9-13; E. 101/368/27, f. 37; E. 101/369/11, ff. 139/40; E. 101/547/13; *Cal. Docs. Scot.*, ii, no. 1941.

merchant vessels. Richard I had formed a large navy to take him on crusade. In 1230 Henry III crossed to France with 288 ships, while 161 others were allowed to return from Portsmouth to their home ports as they were not required.[1] One of the largest fleets ever collected in the middle ages was that which took Edward III's army to France for the siege of Calais in 1347. The army was roughly 32,000 strong, and 738 ships were needed, with some 15,000 sailors to man them.[2]

Even though greater demands on the naval resources of England may have been made at other times, nevertheless Edward I's reign saw a considerable burden imposed on the seaports. Although the crews of the ships were paid reasonable wages, in the case of the Scotch campaigns the ports had to bear the cost of the voyage to the north and home again. While the crown would normally pay the cost of converting ships to carry horses, the rest of the expense of preparing them for the campaigns was the responsibility of the towns. Unfortunately no urban accounts giving details of such costs survive, but they were sufficient for the Cinque Ports and Yarmouth to need crown assistance to ensure that non-residents owning lands inside the towns made their contributions.[3] Seaports might also suffer from the loss of ships which had been commandeered to serve in the navy. But naval battles were rare, and such losses few, save in the internecine fight between the Cinque Ports and Yarmouth in 1297, which could hardly be blamed on the government. The only ships lost in action in Scotland were three vessels which entered the harbour of Berwick in 1296 during the initial attack on the town.[4] In 1305 the men of Dunwich petitioned in parliament for compensation for the loss in war of ten ships, whose value they put at £1,000.[5] But the accounts reveal few such losses, and the townsmen were probably exaggerating.

[1] F. W. Brooks, *The English Naval Forces, 1199–1272* (London, 1932), pp. 187–8.
[2] N. H. Nicolas, *A History of the Royal Navy*, ii (London, 1847), app. vii, pp. 507–10.
[3] *C.C.R., 1288–96*, p. 460.   [4] *Chron. Guisborough*, p. 274.
[5] *Memoranda de Parliamento, 1305*, ed. F. W. Maitland (Rolls series, 1893), no. 217.

The demands of war on the shipping of the nation must have affected trade and the fishing industry, though it is impossible to calculate the extent of dislocation. The effect of the great fleets that sailed for Gascony between 1294 and 1297 was probably not considerable. They were following a normal trade route, and the fact that they were transporting grain purveyed by the crown rather than grain purchased by merchants can have made little difference to the shipowners. In 1297 the sailors going to Gascony were not paid wages, but instead were paid freightage rates, in most cases a tun of flour costing 5s. 6d. and a quarter of wheat a shilling to transport.[1] This was presumably the normal commercial system of charging. The ships, having taken men and victuals to Gascony, were able, as usual, to carry wine on the return journey to England. The call for ships to take the army to Flanders must have disrupted normal shipping patterns far more than had the Gascon fleets. It is very doubtful, however, that such demands for ships can have done as much to limit trade in the Channel and the North Sea as did the embargo on Anglo-French trade and the high customs duties of the years from 1294 to 1297. There seem to have been few objections to Edward's commandeering of ships until 1301. By that time trade with the continent had revived after the French war, and the long voyage north to Scotland for which they were not paid was resented, especially by the men of the south coast ports. But the number of ships involved in the Scotch wars was not so large that their commandeering placed any considerable strain on the economy.

If the defence of the coasts during the period of the war with France was never tested severely, had it not been for the existence of the fleets Philip IV might well have made more of his plans to invade England. While it is hard to assess the effect of English naval activity in the war with Scotland, there can be little doubt that Scotch trade must have been adversely affected. The Scots would have found it far easier to obtain money, arms and assistance had it not been for English naval supremacy.[2] But the most

[1] B.M. Add. MS, 7965, ff. 96-7.
[2] W. Stanford Reid, 'Trade, Traders, and Scottish Independence', *Speculum*, xix (1954), pp. 210-22.

important function of the navy was to provide transport. It was by careful attention to the problems of supply that Edward's government was able to achieve its military successes, rather than by any brilliant feats of arms, and it was only by sea that the huge quantities of victuals could be carried to the armies. Much credit is due to the officials whose organizing ability ensured that sufficient vessels were available, though the last word of praise must go to the ships themselves, the *Blithes, Garlaundes, Godales* and *Marioles,* and even more to the men who sailed them, sometimes in the depths of winter, in support of the war effort.

VII

THE ADMINISTRATION AND COSTS OF WAR

The administrative problems posed by Edward I's wars in Wales, Gascony, Flanders and Scotland were immense. The military effort had to be co-ordinated, the men supplied with pay and victuals, records and accounts kept. The king's successes did not depend on brilliant strokes of generalship, but on efficient organization. England at this time was provided with an elaborate, efficient and well-tried civil service, and full use was made of the regular departments of Exchequer and Chancery. However, the scale of Edward's wars was such that a degree of flexibility was required which could not easily be provided by these departments. The rigorous, accurate but cumbersome accounting methods of the Exchequer were not suited to the inevitable confusion of a campaign.

It was through the Wardrobe that the Welsh wars were organized, and the system was continued in most of the later campaigns of the reign, with paymasters and victuallers acting under the direction of the wardrobe staff. The expansion of this branch of the royal household was first pointed out by Tout, but, understandably, administrative historians have been more concerned to unravel the office routines and the details of accounting practice than to examine the ways in which troops were actually paid and fed.[1]

---

[1] Tout, *Chapters*, ii, pp. 131–45; C. Johnson, 'The System of Account in the Wardrobe of Edward I', *T.R.H.S.*, 4th ser., vi (1923), pp. 50–72; J. H. Johnson, 'The System of Account in the Wardrobe of Edward II', *T.R.H.S.*, 4th ser., xii (1929), pp. 75–104; *Book of Prests*, ed. Fryde, pp. ix–xxvi.

The men who headed Edward's Wardrobe were among the most important civil servants in the whole royal service, and their part in the organization of war was absolutely vital. Unfortunately their activities were scarcely noticed by the chroniclers, and as a result little can be discovered about their personalities. If the voluminous records of the department contain a great deal of information which throws light on the day-to-day travels of these men, they are rarely of assistance in revealing the way in which decisions were made and political difficulties resolved.

The first Keeper of the Wardrobe in the reign was Antony Bek, later to gain great prominence and wealth as bishop of Durham. It was merely a temporary appointment, and from 1274 to 1280 the post was held by his brother Thomas, who appears to have run the department with efficiency but did not leave any mark of note. Although the Bek brothers were of aristocratic origin, the wardrobe staff during the rest of the reign were nearly all men of no great social standing. William of Louth, Thomas Bek's chief clerk, was initially employed by him personally rather than by the crown, but when Bek was appointed to the bishopric of St. Davids Louth became Keeper of the Wardrobe.[1] Well spoken of by the chroniclers,[2] it was very possibly due to his initiative that the department began to make up its records in the form of books rather than rolls: the earliest such document dates from 1286.[3] Louth was succeeded in 1290 by Walter Langton, who had served in the department since 1282 and was a former clerk of Robert Burnell's. He had been responsible for drawing up the special account for the Welsh war of 1282, and had served as cofferer when the Wardrobe accompanied the king to Gascony in 1286. Langton was later accused of strangling his mistress's husband with her assistance, and though this charge was not proved, his private conduct was certainly questionable. There is no doubt that he used his official position for his personal advancement, building up an impressive fortune in land by the techniques of

---

[1] Tout, *Chapters*, ii, pp. 14, 39.
[2] 'Annales de Oseneia', in *Annales Monastici*, iv, p. 325.
[3] Tout, *Chapters*, i, p. 47.

maintenance and champerty.[1] When he was arrested on the orders of Edward II in 1307, valuables worth almost £5,000 were found in his manors, and the value of his lands was estimated at some £1,300 a year.[2] But if not remarkable for his integrity, he was a man of ability and energy, and his five-year tenure of the Keepership of the Wardrobe was influential. During this period the arrangement of the account books was changed from a rather incoherent chronological form to a well-organized analytical system, in which the accounts of the various wardrobe offices were clearly distinguished.[3] Another side of Langton's activity is revealed by a letter written later by the king to Boniface VIII in defence of his minister in which Edward attributed his unpopularity in part to his action in reforming the royal household by dismissing useless personnel.[4]

When Langton was promoted from the Wardrobe in 1295 and as Treasurer came to play what was virtually the rôle of prime minister in the last ten years of Edward I's reign, the Keepership of the Wardrobe was entrusted to John Droxford. A man of importance, though not of Langton's calibre, surprisingly little is known of him personally. He first came into royal service when the king was in Gascony, and rose rapidly in the hierarchy to become Controller of the Wardrobe by 1290.[5] As Keeper, he was a regular member of the council, one of the small group of men playing an important part in the determination of royal policy, and on occasion replacing Langton when the Treasurer was abroad defending his dubious personal character. Although Droxford's activities were too multifarious for it to be possible to provide a comprehensive sketch, a good indication of his rôle is provided by the account of a journey he undertook in the summer of 1304. Leaving the court at Stirling on 17 June he went first to York, where the Exchequer was, to hasten the despatch of money for the army. Supplies were also needed, so he then rode to Boston in

---

[1] A. Beardwood, 'The Trial of Walter Langton, Bishop of Lichfield, 1307–1312', *Trans. American Phil. Soc.*, n.s., liv, part 3 (Philadelphia, 1964), pp. 6–7, and *passim*.
[2] E. 143/9/2.
[3] *Book of Prests*, ed. Fryde, p. xiv.
[4] *C.C.R., 1302–7*, p. 81.
[5] Tout, *Chapters*, ii, pp. 16–17.

Lincolnshire to hurry up the purveyors there. Next he toured southern England collecting funds from papal taxation, going to such monastic houses as Oseney, Reading and Hyde, ending up at Canterbury. Then he went to Amesbury to see the king's daughter Mary, who was a nun there, and escorted her to Windsor. Moving to London, Droxford met Langton and discussed affairs of state with him. By September he was back at court in the neighbourhood of Newcastle.[1] Such energy was typical of the man.

Though he was not as blatantly corrupt as Langton, Droxford was not above using his official position to try to obtain what he wanted, as the Cofferer of the Wardrobe, Walter Bedwin, discovered in 1307. His superior was trying 'par force de sa seigneurie' to obtain a prebend for his brother Roger which Bedwin claimed as an appurtenance of his office as treasurer of St. Peter's, York. However, Bedwin was assured by a correspondent that he was in the stronger position, as Langton supported him, and therefore he had nothing to fear from Droxford's intrigues.[2] The incident is a fascinating revelation of the private relationships between men who appear from the official records to be cogs meshing in perfect alignment.

Some of the other wardrobe officials were of great significance. One of the Controllers, William March, who held the office from 1283 to 1290, subsequently became Treasurer, and despite the unpopularity of the seizure of private treasure that had been deposited in churches which took place in 1294 and for which he was held responsible, was later, though unsuccessfully, put up as a candidate for canonization.[3] John Benstead, Controller from 1295 until 1305, was virtually the king's secretary, and was on one occasion termed by Edward 'our clerk who stays continually by our side'. His most important duty was custody of the privy seal, but he was also employed as a diplomat. Not long after the king's

[1] B.M. Add. MS, 8835, f. 13v.
[2] E. 101/368/18/61; *The Register of William Greenfield, Lord Archbishop of York, 1306–1315*, ed. W. Brown and A. H. Thompson, i (Surtees Soc., cxlv, 1931), p. 16.
[3] *Flores Historiarum*, iii, p. 274; Tout, *Chapters*, ii, p. 17 n. 5.

death Benstead resigned his clerical orders, married, and became a royal justice.[1]

The main concern of the Controllers of the Wardrobe was with the privy seal and the clerical business of the department. More important on the financial side was the office of Cofferer. Louth, March, Langton and Droxford all served a term as Cofferer.[2] The most important of the cofferers in the later years of the reign was Ralph Manton, who held the post from 1297 until 1303. It was he, if any one man can be singled out, who was the chief army paymaster. He also often acted as Droxford's deputy, in particular taking over the chore of accounting from the Keeper. Early in 1303 he was surprised by the enemy when in the company of John de Segrave at Roslin, south of Edinburgh. According to the chronicler Langtoft he tried to buy his safety from his captor, the former household knight Simon Fraser. But Fraser rebuked him, saying that he had betrayed the king who had appointed him paymaster, and had cheated Fraser and many others, giving them tallies and bills in lieu of cash, which they had still not succeeded in exchanging for coin. He also pointed out that Manton's military garb was hardly suitable for a cleric.[3] Fraser's accusation was not without point. As the administration frequently did not have the cash to pay wages, the Wardrobe had to issue creditors with bills or debentures, and Manton's seal appears very frequently on these. Fraser himself had been issued with one to a value of £20, which evidently he had had great difficulty in cashing, as a special mandate was issued ordering payment to be made to him.[4] And Manton certainly had a retinue more fitting for a knight than for a clerk, consisting in 1300 of five squires.[5] His successor in the Wardrobe was Walter Bedwin, one of his subordinates.

These men, Louth, Langton, Droxford and the others discussed, were the chief figures in the Wardrobe, and so played a major part in the administration of war. There was, however, no high degree of specialization in the Edwardian administration: officials

---

[1] C. L. Kingsford, 'John de Benstede and his missions for Edward I', *Essays in History presented to R. L. Poole*, ed. H. W. C. Davis (1927), pp. 332–59.
[2] Tout, *Chapters*, ii, p. 21.   [3] *Chron. Langtoft*, ii, pp. 344–6.
[4] S.C. 1/61/62a.   [5] *Liber Quotidianus*, p. 245.

were allocated as they became available to whatever tasks were of the greatest importance. A chamberlain of the Exchequer might find himself employed on wardrobe business, and a wardrobe clerk might find himself engaged on the task of assigning revenue to foreign merchants, normally a duty of exchequer officials.[1] It is dangerous to attempt to depict the bureaucracy in rigid departmental order.

The Wardrobe had to account to the Exchequer for the funds it received, for it was in theory a subordinate department. But in practice, on campaigns when the Wardrobe and its staff were present, it was they who took over the whole administrative burden. The independence of the Wardrobe in the first two Welsh wars was very striking, and is best illustrated by the financial arrangements for the war of 1282. A special account for the war was kept, and of the receipts totalling £102,621 barely £6,400 was handed over to the Wardrobe by the Exchequer. The majority of the receipts—mostly deriving from the customs, from a tax of a thirtieth on moveables, and from an allegedly voluntary aid, much of it levied from the towns—were collected directly by the wardrobe officials. The ordinary wardrobe account for the two years from November 1282 shows receipts of £101,754, and of this only about £23,700 was received from the Exchequer.[2] This situation of formal wardrobe independence was not enduring. Policy was changed with the appointment of William March as Treasurer and Walter Langton as Keeper of the Wardrobe. From 1290 the Exchequer took control of all the main sources of crown revenue and entered them on its records of receipts and issues.[3] Whereas in the early 1280s only two-fifths of the wardrobe income was derived from the Exchequer, now the proportion was far greater. Tout has calculated it to have been eighty-four per cent during Langton's keepership.[4] With this new policy,

[1] B.M. Add. MS, 7966a, ff. 42, 51v.

[2] Tout, *Chapters*, ii, pp. 113-15; E. 372/130.

[3] J. F. Willard, 'An Exchequer Reform under Edward I', *The Crusades and other Historical Essays presented to Dana C. Munro by his former students*, ed. L. J. Paetow (New York, 1928), pp. 225-43.

[4] Tout, *Chapters*, ii, p. 90.

the Welsh war of 1294–5 was largely financed by means of funds sent to the paymasters by the Exchequer, totalling at least £54,453, with a further £1,000 sent by the Irish treasury.[1]

The government succeeded in accumulating a huge quantity of cash in 1294–5, and this made it possible to finance the Welsh war by means of funds sent to Chester and other centres from Westminster.[2] But it was highly abnormal for the government to have such reserves available, and if it did not, then it was an unnecessarily slow and cumbersome process for the Exchequer to collect funds and transmit them to the Wardrobe. It was much more sensible to allow sheriffs and other collectors of revenue to pay funds directly to the Wardrobe, as long as some method could be found for the Exchequer to supervise the process. Tout saw the introduction of dated exchequer tallies in 1290 as the means of effecting this. Tallies were wooden sticks which were used as a form of receipt: the amount paid in would be entered on the tally by notching it, and it would then be split, half being retained by the Exchequer and the other half given to the man who paid in the money. He could then produce this before the barons of the Exchequer when he came to account for the revenues he had handled. Now Tout considered that these tallies were used after 1290 as a means of assigning revenue. The Exchequer would, in his opinion, hand a tally to the Wardrobe before the money had been paid in. The Wardrobe could then collect the funds specified on the tally from the sheriff or other official to whom it was made out, and give the tally over as a receipt. When accounting at the Exchequer, the sheriff could then produce it as evidence that payment had been made.[3] But Willard and Jenkinson have shown that this procedure was extremely rarely employed in Edward's reign, there being only one definite reference to its use.[4] The system that was used gave far more scope to the Wardrobe, and less to the Exchequer. Instead of using tallies, the principal instrument was

[1] *Book of Prests*, ed. Fryde, p. 227.
[2] *Ibid.*, pp. l–liii.   [3] Tout, *Chapters*, ii, pp. 100–1.
[4] H. Jenkinson, 'Medieval Tallies', *Archaeologia*, lxxiv (1925), pp. 289–351; Willard, *Parliamentary Taxes on Personal Property, 1290 to 1334* (Cambridge, Mass., 1934), pp. 233–9.

the written and sealed bill or receipt of the Wardrobe. The procedure was outlined in instructions issued to the collectors of the New Custom in 1304. The money they received was to be paid over to wardrobe officials in exchange for such receipts.[1] When the collectors went to the Exchequer, tallies were handed over in exchange for these documents, and they then proceeded to make their final account in the normal way.

A more detailed illustration of the working of the system may help to elucidate it further. In a book of wardrobe receipts it is noted that on 22 November 1303 Henry de Cobham, recently sheriff of Kent, paid £12 to Richard of Montpellier, who was receiving money for the Great Wardrobe. Cobham took the receipt he was given by Montpellier to the Exchequer and exchanged it for a tally, the normal form of exchequer receipt, on 16 January 1304. In the entry on the receipt roll it was noted that this sum of £12 was charged to the Wardrobe.[2] This method did not allow the Exchequer the same degree of control over determining who was to be paid that the later system of using tallies as a means of assignment provided. So although in the later years of the reign the greater part of wardrobe revenue appears in the accounts as being allocated to that department by the Exchequer, in practice the degree of exchequer control was negligible.

The allocation of funds to the Wardrobe by the Exchequer was in theory controlled by writs of liberate issued by the Chancery. But whereas the practice had been for such writs to be issued for quite small sums, it became usual under Edward I for block grants of huge sums to be made: in 1275-6 the whole of the exchequer contribution to the Wardrobe was authorized in a single writ for £3,000.[3] By the last years of the reign such writs were being issued long after the expenditure they were meant to cover had been incurred. Thus a writ of £11,405 dated 1 October 1304, and enrolled under that date, was in fact only made out after Walter Bedwin, a wardrobe official, brought a wardrobe bill requesting such a writ to the Chancery in 1307.[4] This situation illustrates very clearly the independence of the Wardrobe.

[1] E. 159/77, m. 61. [2] E. 101/365/6, f. 28v; E. 401/155; E. 403/117.
[3] Tout, *Chapters*, ii, p. 97. [4] C. 62/80.

The question of how revenue was raised, and the political effects of the Wardrobe's independence will be returned to later. For the present, the question is how the funds collected by the Wardrobe were then disbursed. The official mainly responsible for making payments was the cofferer, and he or his clerks normally paid the infantry troops of the main army in Wales or Scotland at intervals of a week or more. The infantry constables would receive 1s. a day, the vintenars, or men in charge of a platoon of twenty, 4d., and the ordinary footsoldiers 2d. When money was short, as was all too often the case, payment might well take place some time after the period of service to which it related. On 21 March 1304 wages were paid at St. Andrews for the period from 9 September until 23 September 1303. Payment for the next period, up to 20 October 1303, was made on 24 April 1304. Sometimes wages would be paid in kind, in the form of food, in which case responsibility for payment would devolve on a victualling officer. Issues of food in lieu of wages were made by Richard de Bromsgrove, receiver of victuals at Berwick, in June and August 1304.[1] Subsidiary paymasters were appointed to pay the wages of forces detached from the main armies. In 1294–5 the English troops were split up into several different forces. The Wardrobe remained with the king, while John Sandale paid out wages to Warwick's army. Roger de l'Isle paid some troops at Chester, as did Hugh de Cressingham. Nicholas de Ockham was allocated as paymaster to Valence's army in the south, and Hugh de Leominster performed the same function for the earl of Lincoln at Rhuddlan.[2] These paymasters were not ordinary wardrobe clerks, detached from headquarters to meet the needs of the campaign. Roger de l'Isle was Keeper of the Great Wardrobe,[3] and Sandale probably a subordinate of his at this time.[4] Cressingham, fat and unpopular, was a royal justice and had been steward of the queen's estates.[5] Nicholas de Ockham was a Treasurer's clerk, an

---

[1] E. 101/11/15/1, 2, 17, 18.   [2] *Book of Prests*, ed. Fryde, pp. 57, 60.
[3] Tout, *Chapters*, iv, pp. 392, n. 3, 394, n. 2.
[4] *The Registers of John de Sandale and Rigaud de Asserio, Bishops of Winchester, 1316–23*, ed. F. J. Baigent (Hants. Record Soc., 1897), p. xx.
[5] *Chron. Guisborough*, pp. 294, 303; Tout, *Chapters*, v, pp. 238–9.

exchequer official whose main responsibility was the writing of tallies.[1] Hugh de Leominster was certainly not a wardrobe clerk. After the end of the Welsh war he was appointed chamberlain of North Wales, where he already had connections, for he had earlier received a living at Caernarvon.[2] But all of these men were responsible to the Wardrobe, even though they were not permanent wardrobe clerks, and their accounts were incorporated in the general account for the department.

The system of paying cavalry their wages was rather different. The leader of each contingent was naturally responsible for the distribution of pay to his men. The standard rates were as follows: a banneret received 4s. a day, a knight 2s. and squires and sergeants 1s. Whereas the royal paymasters issued wages to the infantry at regular intervals, it was only in the first two Welsh wars that the cavalry, or at least much of it, was paid on a basis of forty-day periods of service.[3] Later it was usual for accounts with the cavalry to be drawn up at or after the end of their period of service with the army. But the men were not expected to finance themselves until then. Advances of money, known as prests, could be made and then subtracted from the total due to them as wages in the final reckoning. Any other sums due to them, notably payments in recompense for horses lost on campaign, were also taken into consideration. In 1300 John Botetourt served in the campaign in Scotland with a troop varying in number from six to eight. His knight Robert Bavent made account with the Wardrobe at Holme on 12 September for the period from 4 July. Wages due totalled £61 14s. 0d. Offsetting this was a letter assigning him £30 out of the farm of St. Briavels, and in addition he had been issued with wine and victuals to a value of £13 4s. 8d. He was therefore still owed £18 9s. 4d., which was carried over to the next account Botetourt made. This was for wages up to 3 November, totalling £26. In addition, he claimed £134 13s. 4d. outstanding to him for losses of horses on the Falkirk campaign, and £30 5s. 1d. for

---

[1] T. Madox, *The History and Antiquities of the Exchequer* (2nd edn., 1769), i, p. 270, n. b; ii, pp. 304–5.
[2] Tout, *Chapters*, vi, p. 61; *C.P.R., 1281–92*, p. 190.
[3] Morris, *Welsh Wars*, pp. 125, 163; E. 101/3/13; E. 101/4/1.

arrears of the fees he was owed as a banneret of the household. Against these debts were set prests he had received, totalling £98, so in all he was owed £111 7s. 9d. For this sum he was given a wardrobe bill, or acknowledgement of debt, which he could try to exchange for cash with any receiver of crown revenue.[1]

There were occasions when the Wardrobe was not available to perform the function of organizing the financial aspects of war. When Rhys ap Maredudd rose in revolt in 1287 the king was abroad in Gascony, and naturally the Wardrobe was with him. The regent, Edmund of Cornwall, had to use different means of organizing the campaign, and in July 1287 the Riccardi, who were the main Italian bankers used by the government in the first half of the reign, were ordered to pay all the king's money in their hands, and any future receipts, to Robert Tiptoft, Alan Plukenet, John de Mohaut and five paymasters.[2] The account of the Riccardi made subsequently with the Exchequer reveals that they did indeed perform the function that in more normal circumstances would have been the responsibility of the Wardrobe. The bankers were in a much better position than was the Exchequer to raise money quickly, and they possessed the same advantages of adaptability and elasticity as did the Wardrobe.[3]

The Wardrobe could not be present to organize and finance the war in Gascony between 1294 and 1298, for it was occupied with the campaigns in Wales, Scotland and Flanders. Special paymasters were appointed who, because of the problems of communication, were acting in virtual isolation. Peter of Aylesford, who had not previously held important office under the crown, was appointed paymaster, with Thomas of Cambridge as his controller. They were instructed not to make any payments without the advice of the veteran of the Welsh wars, Robert Tiptoft.[4] With Edmund of Lancaster in 1296 sailed John Sandale. Having proved his administrative ability in Wales, Sandale took the place of Aylesford who had died. Subsidiary officials were appointed to pay the men in the garrisons of Bourg and Blaye. These clerks in Gascony

[1] E. 101/7/11.   [2] *C.V.C.R., 1277-1326*, p. 309.
[3] The account of the Riccardi for this war is in E. 372/132.
[4] *Rôles Gascons*, iii, no. 2938.

received the great majority of their funds from the Exchequer: £120,000 as against nearly £8,000 from the Wardrobe.[1] Sandale and Cambridge accounted directly with the Exchequer for the money they spent, no supervision was exercised by the wardrobe staff. Of the clerks employed in Gascony, only Sandale appears to have had any form of wardrobe training.

The successful campaign in Scotland in 1296 was financed and organized by the Wardrobe, but on its completion a separate administration was set up there. Earl Warenne was made royal lieutenant, Hugh Cressingham Treasurer and Walter of Amersham,[2] a chancery clerk of considerable seniority and much judicial experience, Chancellor. However, this administration had little success. By the summer of 1297 Cressingham considered that only the shires of Roxburgh and Berwick were under proper control,[3] and on 12 July arrangements were made to strengthen the English position. Ralph FitzWilliam, Robert Clifford and Brian FitzAlan were given command of the border counties. The forces operating from Northumberland were to be financed by Walter of Amersham with Robert Heron as his controller, while in Cumberland equivalent positions were given to Richard of Abingdon and Robert de Barton.[4] Like the others, Abingdon had no wardrobe connection: he had been employed as chamberlain of Wales, and in 1299 was to become a baron of the Exchequer.[5] It was these men who shouldered the burden of organizing the English effort in the winter of 1297-8, when an attempt was made to revenge the disaster of Stirling Bridge. There was little activity in the west, so Abingdon had little to do. His receipts only totalled £909, whereas Amersham had £10,828 to dispose of.[6] As already shown, at its peak the army paid by Amersham numbered some 18,500 men, an immensely impressive number for a winter cam-

[1] E. 372/160.
[2] Barrow, *Robert Bruce*, p. 106; Amersham had been a king's clerk as early as 1279, *C.P.R., 1277-81*, p. 321.
[3] Stevenson, *Documents*, ii, no. ccclv.
[4] *Ibid.*, no. cccxlviii; *C.P.R., 1292-1301*, p. 315.
[5] A. B. Emden, *A Biographical Dictionary of the University of Oxford from A.D. 1176 to 1500*, i (Oxford, 1957), pp. 4-5.
[6] Gough, *Scotland in 1298*, pp. 265-8; E. 101/6/30.

paign. But despite this fine administrative achievement, little was accomplished. Warenne, the commander, arrived late and led the army no further than Roxburgh, while in the west Clifford only won a minor success with a raid into Annandale.[1]

Much has been made of these paymasters appointed in 1297 by A. Z. Freeman, who sees in them an important stage in the development of military administration, an advance on the *ad hoc* methods previously used. He considers that 'the Wardrobe expanded and split to accommodate the expanded nature of warfare in Scotland'.[2] In fact, the situation was quite different. The Wardrobe was fully occupied in 1297 with the preparations for the campaign in Flanders. The administration that had been set up in Scotland was incapable of dealing with the rapidly deteriorating situation, so, as a purely temporary expedient, military commands with appropriate pay departments were set up on the borders. Amersham and Abingdon had no connection with the Wardrobe, although the latter did eventually make his account with that department. Amersham, however, accounted directly with the Exchequer.[3]

Once the king had returned from Flanders a major attempt to avenge Stirling Bridge was possible. The Exchequer was moved to York, an act symbolizing the new seriousness with which Edward I was regarding the conquest of Scotland.[4] There was no need for the temporary administration that had been set up in the previous year, for the Wardrobe could now take on the burden of the war in Scotland. It was this, and not the difficulty of keeping Amersham and Abingdon supplied with cash, as Freeman suggests, which caused the abandonment of the system of local paymasters on the borders. Amersham retired from the scene, and Abingdon's rôle was changed into that of a receiver of victuals. From 1298 until 1304 the Wardrobe and its officials controlled the business of paying and feeding troops in Scotland.

[1] Barrow, *Robert Bruce*, p. 135.
[2] A. Z. Freeman, 'The King's Penny: the Headquarters Paymasters under Edward I, 1295–1307', *Journal of British Studies*, vi (1966), p. 19.
[3] Gough, *Scotland in 1298*, pp. 265–8; E. 101/6/30.
[4] Barrow, *op. cit.*, p. 139.

The main armies that were sent north were paid by the Wardrobe in the way already described. In 1301 when two armies took the field, the wardrobe of the prince of Wales under its keeper Walter Reynolds took on the task of paying the western army. A permanent administration was needed to deal with the difficulties of supplying the garrison forces throughout the year, and officials were appointed at Berwick and Carlisle. In 1298 John de Weston, a clerk who had not previously been in crown employment, was in charge of paying the Berwick garrison, and by 1301 he was also paying wages direct to the men in Edinburgh, Roxburgh and Jedburgh. In 1303 Kirkintilloch and Linlithgow were added to the list. Weston was responsible to the Wardrobe and accounted with that department, although he received hardly any funds directly from it. His income was largely derived from the sheriffs of the northern counties, and from the revenues that the English managed to collect in Scotland. In 1298-9 his receipts, all at this stage from England, came to £5,979, and payments out to only £4,711. Such a satisfactory balance was not long maintained, and by 1303 he was incurring expenditure of £10,368, with receipts of merely £2,040.[1] For the most part all Weston could do in 1303 and 1304 was to give the soldiers bills, stating the amount that they were owed, which, if they were lucky, they might be able to exchange for cash at some later date. It is hardly surprising to find the garrisons of Kirkintilloch and Linlithgow presenting petitions for the payment of arrears of wages in the parliament of 1305.[2] Weston was the only man employed purely as a paymaster in Scotland between 1298 and 1304.[3] The English military investment in the south-west of Scotland was not large enough to warrant such a man in Carlisle, and there the rôles of receiver of victuals and paymaster were combined by Abingdon until 1300,

---

[1] E. 101/7/8; E. 101/9/9; E. 101/11/11. To the receipts shown in this last mentioned account of Weston's should be added the sum shown to have been paid to him by the receiver of victuals at Berwick, in B.M. Add. MS, 17360, f. 54.
[2] *Memoranda de Parliamento*, pp. 169-70.
[3] A fact which makes A. Z. Freeman's failure to discuss him in 'The King's Penny', *Journal of British Studies*, vi (1966), rather strange.

when he was replaced by James de Dalilegh. Sales of victuals ensured an adequate supply of cash for these men, even though very little was raised from lands in Scotland.[1]

With the fall of Stirling and the surrender of the major Scotch nobles in 1304 Edward I was in a position to set up a puppet administration, as he had done in 1296. John of Brittany, the king's nephew, was appointed royal lieutenant, and William of Bevercotes Chancellor. Justices were nominated, and the financial administration put in the charge of John Sandale, who was made Chamberlain of Scotland.[2] One of the ablest of the officials who served Edward in his later years, Sandale was a Yorkshireman, like so many other clerks in the royal service.[3] After his experience as a paymaster in Wales and Gascony he was put in charge of the royal mints from 1298 until 1303. His success story did not end in 1307, for Edward II continued to favour him, and he ended his days as bishop of Winchester and Chancellor of England.[4] It was clearly intended that Sandale should finance the occupation of Scotland out of the revenues of that country, and be independent of the Wardrobe and Exchequer. But Bruce's revolt dashed any such plans, and in the last two years of the reign Sandale continued to hold the office of Chamberlain, while being in practice little more than the most important of the English paymasters. Although his accounts were never incorporated in the main wardrobe account books, effectively he was part of the wardrobe organization.

Lack of funds did not present an acute problem to the Wardrobe in the Welsh wars: in 1277, 1282 and 1287 the Riccardi were able to supply the money needed to supplement the ordinary resources of the crown. However, the constant succession of campaigns from 1294 onwards made matters much more difficult; a substantial

[1] E. 101/7/20; *Liber Quotidianus*, pp. 139-42; E. 101/11/19.
[2] Barrow, *Robert Bruce*, p. 190.
[3] J. L. Grassi, 'The Clerical Dynasties from Howdenshire, Nottinghamshire and Lindsey in the Royal Administration' (Oxford D.Phil. thesis, 1959). Others beside Sandale were William de Bevercotes, William Thorntoft, William Greenfield, Philip Willoughby, John Husthwayt, William Melton, Robert Woodhouse, Robert Cottingham and John Swanland.
[4] *The Registers of John de Sandale and Rigaud de Asserio, Bishops of Winchester, 1316-23*, pp. xvii-xlvii.

reserve of cash was built up in 1294, but was soon exhausted, and thereafter the government led a hand-to-mouth existence. A shortage of ready funds could have drastic consequences. At the end of August 1301 a sum of £200 was sent to Berwick for the payment of wages. This arrived late and was less than had been expected. Although the garrison was already a month in arrears, the £200 was not paid all to them, but was also split between the forces in Jedburgh and Roxburgh. The result was mutiny, mostly among the crossbowmen and archers supported by a few men-at-arms and even by a household knight, Walter de Teye. He claimed that the letters accompanying the money did not state that it was to be divided in this way, and seized £36 to pay to the discontented soldiers.[1] The outbreak of violence makes this incident exceptional, though delays in payment were common. In 1303 Alexander de Bikenore and Ralph Benton wrote that the Irish troops had received no pay for nine weeks, and were extremely discontented at hearing that funds had reached Berwick while they received none. There was a danger that they would start robbing those Scots who were loyal to Edward, or that they would simply desert.[2] In 1297 two troops of infantry who had been serving in Gascony came to Edward in person and protested that they had not been paid. They were only able to obtain enough money to pay for their journey home.[3] It was not simply the infantry who suffered from non-payment of wages: several leaders of cavalry troops thought it worth their while to petition in parliament for the arrears they were owed.[4]

The evidence suggests that the paymasters did their work efficiently and conscientiously. All the surviving pay rolls show the numbers of troops fluctuating from week to week, which suggests that proper checks were made to ensure that pay was only issued in respect of men who were actually present on the campaign. In contrast, the accounts for Edward III's army in Scotland in 1334 show no drop in the size of the contingents over three months'

[1] *Cal. Docs. Scot.*, ii, no. 1223.
[2] E. 101/13/36/26.
[3] B.M. Add. MS, 8835, ff. 52, 54.
[4] *Rot. Parl.*, i, pp. 162, 192, 199; *Memoranda de Parliamento*, nos. 58, 270, 358.

winter campaigning—a strong hint of considerable peculation.[1] In the sixteenth century when responsibility for paying wages was largely in the hands of the captains of contingents, corruption was virtually unchecked.[2] In 1294 one constable of infantry from Shropshire absconded with £4 13s. which he had received from the Wardrobe to pay to his men, but the money was recovered.[3] In 1296 a case arose in the Marshal's court concerning the misappropriation of wages, but the sum concerned was only £2 10s., and the matter was easily cleared up.[4] Such incidents were rare in Edward I's reign, however. It is striking that none of the complaints about non-payment of wages allege the corruption of officials as a cause.

How were Edward's officials rewarded for their service? Royal clerks received robes in the same way as the household knights: in 1300 Droxford had his at the same rate as the bannerets, and Benstead at that of the ordinary knights. They were also paid wages, although these were intended to cover expenses rather than as a reward. Manton was paid 10s. a day when he was sent to supervise the victualling and accounting in Berwick, Roxburgh and Edinburgh. Ralph Dalton was employed by the Wardrobe throughout most of 1300 in Yorkshire collecting victuals, investigating debts that were owed to the crown, and levying fines on infantrymen who had absconded from the army with their wages. He was paid at the rate of 2s. a day.[5] But the main form of reward for the royal clerks was of course presentation to benefices. St. Martin's le Grand in London had a long-standing connection with the royal administration, going back to the time when Roger of Salisbury was dean. That office was held by William of Louth and subsequently by William March,[6] while John Droxford was one of the canons. Droxford held in addition some seventeen prebends and canonries, and five churches, although he was only

[1] R. Nicholson, *Edward III and the Scots, the Formative Years of a Military Career, 1327–1335* (Oxford, 1965), p. 181.
[2] C. G. Cruikshank, *Elizabeth's Army*, pp. 143–58.
[3] *Book of Prests*, ed. Fryde, p. 214, n. 3.
[4] E. 39/93/115, m. 3. [5] *Liber Quotidianus*, pp. 73, 90, 313.
[6] *Victoria County History of London*, i, ed. W. Page (London, 1909), pp. 555, 564.

in deacon's orders.[1] John Sandale likewise was not ordained a priest, but he held by papal dispensation the office of chancellor of St. Patrick's, Dublin, and three churches in England.[2] As befitted such secular men, the royal clerks might receive the same type of reward as did the laymen who served the crown: Droxford was granted the wardship of the heir of Hugh of St. Philibert, and the custody of the lands of John Bisset together with the marriage of his heirs.[3] Also, the crown might exert its influence to obtain their election to bishoprics, though this honour never coincided with service in the Wardrobe. Louth, Langton and March all received sees.

The income of royal clerks naturally was not confined to sources bestowed by the crown. The bishop of Carlisle paid Droxford a pension of £40 a year.[4] Walter Langton attempted to force the abbey of St. Albans to pay £30 annually to one of his knights, but the monks resisted, supported by the prince of Wales. The demand ceased with the death of Edward I and the disgrace of Langton at the hands of Edward II. However, although he failed in this case, the Treasurer was successful in others. Langton's methods of building up an estate by purchase, exchange, maintenance and champerty have already been mentioned. When he was arrested an impressive number of people were found to owe him money as a result of letters of recognizance made out in his favour. It is often not clear why the sums mentioned in these documents were owed. In a few cases they were for payment of pensions, while many were given as security for the transfer of land. The total of the sums owed to him came to about £19,000.[5] Langton was almost certainly the most successful profiteer in the royal administration: earlier, Adam Stratton's wealth had been built up more in his capacity as steward of Isabella de Forz than as an exchequer official.[6] But the records reveal many recognizances made out in

---

[1] *Calendar of Papal Registers*, ii, p. 39. [2] *Ibid.*, p. 9.
[3] *Registrum Simonis de Gandavo, Diocesis Saresbiriensis, A.D. 1297–1315*, ed. C. T. Flower and M. C. B. Dawes (Cant. and York Soc., xli, 1934), ii, pp. 653, 683; *C.P.R., 1301–7*, p. 535. [4] *C.P.R., 1292–1301*, p. 573.
[5] A. Beardwood, 'The Trial of Walter Langton', pp. 29–31.
[6] Denholm-Young, *Seignorial Administration*, pp. 77–84.

favour of other royal servants. A large number of those due to John Droxford were made out by men from his home county of Hampshire, where he possessed property.¹ Interestingly, Droxford himself owed £120 to Langton in two recognizances, although there are no details of the nature of the transactions involved.²

Edward's clerks had extensive opportunities for private gain—though Langton's abuse of power was exceptional. But they worked hard for their opportunities, and showed remarkable efficiency in the conduct of the administration, even when in the later years of the reign they were struggling in the face of intolerable burdens of expenditure and lack of funds.

It is not possible to give a wholly accurate assessment of the extent of the war expenditure for which the clerks were responsible. Often it is not clear whether expenditure should be classified as military or not. For the Welsh war of 1282 a separate wardrobe account of war expenses was drawn up, but the ordinary account still contained some items obviously connected with the campaign. The state of the wardrobe accounts for the last years of the reign makes any calculation open to doubt. But with such qualifications, some estimates of expenditure can be made.

At the time of his father's death in 1272 Edward was on crusade. This was a very expensive enterprise, though unfortunately the precise costs cannot be calculated. To finance it Edward negotiated a loan from Louis IX of 70,000 *livres tournois*, or about £17,500, to be repaid out of the revenues of Gascony over seven years. A tax on moveables was negotiated in England, at the rate of a twentieth, and the receipts, which came to about £30,000, were allocated to pay for the crusade. A tenth on clerical incomes for two years was imposed by the papacy for the same purpose. This brought in some £22,000. In addition, Edward received at least 4,000 marks from the Jews, and in 1271 it was agreed that all revenues from wardships and escheats should go to meet the expenses of the crusade. Nevertheless, Edward still had to raise massive loans from Italian and Cahorsin merchants, and one reason

[1] As for example *C.C.R., 1288–96*, pp. 133, 188, 247, 314, 316.
[2] *Records of the Trial of Walter Langeton Bishop of Coventry and Lichfield, 1307–1312*, ed. A. Beardwood (Camden Soc., 4th ser., vi, 1969), pp. 156–7.

THE ADMINISTRATION AND COSTS OF WAR

for the grant of a tax of a fifteenth in 1275 was that it was needed to pay off his crusading debts.[1]

The first military enterprise that Edward embarked upon as king was the first Welsh war. This was not expensive, largely because it was short; little was done before January 1277, and by September the war was over. The wardrobe account separated normal expenditure in the year, amounting to only £15,534, from the military expenditure which came to £20,241. Costs not entered on these accounts brought the total spent on the war to just over £23,000.[2] The second Welsh war was much longer, lasting from the early summer of 1282 until the same time in the following year. The special wardrobe war account showed costs of over £90,000, but in addition the ordinary account, which in the early years of the reign showed expenditure averaging perhaps £23,000 a year, rose in 1283-4 to almost £80,000. This suggests that the total military expenditure was roughly £150,000.[3] In contrast, Rhys's rising of 1287 was cheaply put down: probably little more than £10,000 was spent.[4]

The conquest of Wales was achieved by the massive mobilization of men and resources, not by any brilliant strokes of generalship. The English success was consolidated by the construction of that splendid chain of castles in north Wales. Nothing very ambitious was attempted after the first war, but a huge building programme characterized the second war, the most notable castles being Conway, Caernarvon, Criccieth and Harlech. Following the revolt of 1294, one more castle was added, that of Beaumaris in Anglesey. Edward's castles in Wales have been the subject of

---

[1] R. Röhricht, 'Etudes sur les derniers temps du royaume de Jérusalem. A. La croisade du prince Edouard d'Angleterre', *Archives de l'orient latin*, i (Paris, 1881), pp. 618-20; *C.P.R., 1266-72*, pp. 442, 452, 463, 535, 545, 574, 617; Powicke, *Henry III and the Lord Edward*, ii, pp. 568-9; Powicke, *The Thirteenth Century*, pp. 223-4.

[2] Morris, *Welsh Wars*, p. 141; Tout, *Chapters*, ii, pp. 112-13.

[3] *Ibid.*, ii, pp. 113-15; vi, pp. 78-9. See also Morris's calculations in *Welsh Wars*, pp. 196-7. Strangely, Morris did not make use of the main enrolled wardrobe account.

[4] Morris, *Welsh Wars*, p. 219. See also R. A. Griffiths, 'The Revolt of Rhys ap Maredudd', *Welsh History Review*, 3 (1966-7), p. 134.

extensive study. Many accounts survive of these works undertaken under the general supervision of Edward's Savoyard expert, James of St. George, and although the series is not quite complete, it is clear that in the period up to the appointment of the king's eldest son as prince of Wales roughly £80,000 was spent. Not all the work was completed by then, of course: Beaumaris stands all too obviously unfinished today. By 1330, some £14,400 had been spent on that castle, while the cost of Caernarvon was in the region of £20,000.[1]

Expensive as the conquest of Wales was, far more was spent on the wars with France and Scotland in the second half of the reign. It was the needs of the French war that dominated the policies of the government between 1294 and 1297. Perhaps surprisingly, much the most expensive aspect of the war was the defensive struggle of the English troops in Gascony. In cash 40,000 marks was paid out to the first English paymaster there, Peter of Aylesford. As he died soon, he never made account with the Exchequer for this sum, but his successor, John Sandale, produced accounts in 1314. Expenditure in the period of wartime, reckoned as from 11 November 1294 when he took over, until 24 March 1298, and in the period of truce up to 14 August 1299, totalled £359,288 0s. 5d. Of this sum, wages paid to Gascon forces, horse and foot, amounted to £137,595 2s. 9d.[2] Of course, the sums mentioned in this account do not represent the total expended on the struggle in Gascony. In addition to Aylesford's costs which are not included, there was also considerable expenditure in England in support of the war. Soldiers had to be paid while awaiting embarkation, victuals purveyed had to be paid for, and sailors had to be paid their wages. Unfortunately the wardrobe accounts are not sufficiently detailed to allow any accurate calculations of the total spent in this way. For 1295, for example, it is stated that £12,852 6s. 1d. was spent on paying sailors both in going to Gascony and

[1] J. G. Edwards, 'Edward I's Castle-Building in Wales', *Proc. Brit. Ac.*, xxxii (1946), pp. 62–3; R. Allen Brown, H. M. Colvin, A. J. Taylor, *The History of the King's Works*, i (London, 1963), pp. 394, 406–7.
[2] Sandale's account is in E. 372/160. This is summarized and quoted in part by Bémont, *Rôles Gascons*, iii, pp. clxviii–clxix.

in transporting men and supplies to Anglesey. A rough estimate would be that in England the Wardrobe spent about £80,000 between 1294 and 1298 on the war in Gascony.[1] In addition, in October 1295 Edmund of Lancaster and several other magnates were advanced almost £2,000 directly by the Exchequer to assist them in their preparations for the expedition to Gascony.[2]

As was so often the case in Edward I's finances, income did not match expenditure in Gascony. Sandale's account showed expenses exceeding receipts by £59,139 1s. 3½d., but the Exchequer was not satisfied with the evidence produced, and after complex argument the deficit was calculated to be £97,989 13s. 8d. However, the real balance was probably closer to Sandale's statement than to the revision necessitated by the doubts and quibbles of the exchequer officials.[3] In all, the cost of saving Gascony, excluding the £30,690 12s. 6d. spent during the period of truce after the end of hostilities, was roughly £400,000.

Possibly taking inspiration from the plans which had failed King John at Bouvines, Edward I's strategy was to launch his main attack on Philip IV in northern France, with the aid of a coalition of continental rulers. According to one chronicler, it was Antony Bek, bishop of Durham, who put the plan for a grand alliance before the council, and this seems plausible, for it was he who was put in charge of the embassy sent abroad in June 1294.[4] Lavish promises of payment were made to the allies. The agreement with the German king, Adolph of Nassau, appears to have been that he should receive £40,000 by Christmas 1294, and a further £20,000 when Edward actually began his campaign in Flanders.[5] The archbishop of Cologne was initially promised 10,000 marks, with a further £2,000 as a gift.[6] Smaller sums were promised to other Germans. In the Low Countries, John, duke of

---

[1] E. 372/144. [2] C. 61/71; E. 403/99.
[3] E. 372/160. [4] *Chron. Langtoft*, ii, pp. 202–4.
[5] F. Trautz, *Die Könige von England und das Reich, 1272–1377* (Heidelberg, 1961), p. 147, nn. 225, 231.
[6] J. de Sturler, 'Deux comptes enrôlés de Robert de Segre, receveur et agent payeur d'Edouard Ier, roi d'Angleterre aux Pays-Bas (1294–1296)', *Bull. de la commission royale d'histoire*, cxxv (1959), p. 598.

Brabant, was due to receive 200,000 *livres tournois*, worth £50,000 at the rate of exchange current when the agreement was made in Anglesey in 1295. In addition he was promised £4,000 out of the new forty shilling customs duty, a grant intended to compensate the Brabantines for the damage that this tax would do to their economy.[1] Floris V, count of Holland, was owed 80,000 *livres tournois* in return for his support.[2] Early in 1297 the English achieved a very considerable diplomatic triumph in winning over the count of Flanders, but for the first year of the alliance 100,000 *livres tournois* was owed, with an additional 70,000 *livres* as a gift to the count.[3] There was another group of allies in eastern France. The count of Bar was owed 30,000 marks in return for service with 1,000 horse for six months.[4] A league of Burgundian nobles from the Franche-Comté was promised 60,000 *livres tournois* for the first year of the alliance, 1297, with 30,000 in each subsequent year.[5] These were merely the principal obligations incurred by Edward. In all, the English diplomatic offensive between 1294 and 1297 involved promises of subsidies totalling some £250,000. Of this impressive total, it can be shown that £165,784 was definitely paid. Evidence of some minor payments may not have survived, so the total may have been slightly higher.[6] It was often an expensive business to make the payments: it took seventeen ships, manned by 756 sailors, to take roughly £25,000 across the North Sea to Robert de Segre, the clerk entrusted in 1294 with the task of delivering the subsidies.[7]

[1] B. D. Lyon, 'Un compte de l'échiquier relatif aux relations d'Edouard Ier d'Angleterre avec le duc Jean II de Brabant', *Bull. de la commission royale d'histoire*, cxx (1955), p. 81; E. 159/68, m. 80d; *C.P.R., 1292-1301*, pp. 134-232.
[2] E. 405/1/5.   [3] C. 62/73; E. 405/1/11.   [4] C. 62/71.
[5] *Treaty Rolls, 1234-1325*, ed. P. Chaplais (London, 1955), pp. 132-3.
[6] I have given fuller details of these subsidies in my thesis, 'Edward I's Wars and their Financing, 1294-1307', pp. 445-54. E. B. Fryde, 'Financial Resources of Edward I in the Netherlands, 1294-1298', *Revue Belge*, xl (1962), pp. 1170-85, has calculated the total paid out as £142,026. But he has not included all the allies: the archbishop of Cologne being the most notable omission. Nor has he made use of the Jornalia Rolls, E. 405/1, which are invaluable in filling some of the gaps in the sadly deficient series of exchequer issue and receipt rolls.
[7] F. Bock, 'Englands Bezeihungen zum Reich unter Adolf von Nassau', *M.I.Ö.G.*, erg. bd xii (1932-3), p. 209; J. de Sturler, *op. cit.*, p. 601.

The eventual return on the money spent on the alliance was inconsiderable. A combined Flemish and German force did assemble in 1297, but was defeated at Veurne before Edward landed in Flanders, and although the Burgundians had some initial successes in eastern France, they were not strong enough to sustain a lengthy offensive. The most striking absentee of all those who had been paid subsidies was the king of Germany, Adolf of Nassau. There has been much controversy over the reason for this: was he unable to go on campaign because of the problems he faced in Germany, particularly the activities of Albrecht of Habsburg, or was he bribed to leave the alliance by the French? A French document which is so full of inaccuracies as to suggest that it must have been written many years later,[1] suggests the latter, but there is good reason to suppose that the author was confused between Adolf and Albrecht, who succeeded him as king. Albrecht certainly was subsidized by Philip IV, so whatever the truth of the matter, it is evident that French diplomatic activity had a part in preventing Adolf from assisting Edward.[2] But the English king too must share the blame for the failure of the grand alliance; had he not been forced to delay plans for a campaign until 1297, far more might have been achieved.

The final item of expenditure on the war with France was the campaign in Flanders. This was not very costly, as the army was small and transport costs far lower than for Gascony. The wardrobe book for 1297 shows that up to 19 November costs of just over £25,000 were incurred under the strictly military headings of wages and victualling, but there are items relevant to the cam-

[1] This has been published by F. Funck-Brentano, 'Document pour servir à l'histoire des relations de la France avec l'Angleterre et l'Allemagne sous le règne de Philippe le Bel', *Revue Historique*, xxxix (1889), pp. 328-34, and in *Monumenta Germaniae Historica, Constitutiones*, iii (Hanover, 1904), pp. 632-5.

[2] The alleged bribery of Adolf of Nassau has been a matter of bitter controversy. See in particular G. Barraclough, 'Edward I and Adolf of Nassau', *Cambridge Historical Journal*, vi (1940), pp. 225-62; F. Kern, 'Analekten zur Geschichte des 13. und 14. Jahrhunderts, ii, die Bestechung König Adolfs von Nassau', *M.I.Ö.G.*, xxx (1909), pp. 423-43; V. Samanek, 'Der Angebliche Verrat Adolfs von Nassau', *Historisches Vierteljahrschrift*, xxix (1935), pp. 302-41; F. Trautz, *Die Könige von England und das Reich, 1272-1377*, pp. 149-72.

paign in other sections of the account.[1] Regrettably, there is no similar account for the next year, merely the enrolled version which does not distinguish between the costs of the Flanders expedition and those of the Falkirk campaign. So although no accurate calculation of the expense of the expedition is possible, it seems unlikely that it was much in excess of £50,000. Such figures can only be very approximate, but the overall cost of the war with France in alliances and in direct military intervention probably amounted to the impressive figure of £615,000. In addition, in these years the crown had to meet the cost of putting down the Welsh revolt of 1294, and of financing the campaign of 1296 in Scotland and the subsequent military operations in the north, which culminated in the English triumph at Falkirk in 1298. The total military expenditure from 1294 until the king's return from Flanders early in 1298 was probably in the order of £750,000.

The format of the accounts for the years from 1298 until the end of the reign of Edward I makes it impossible to work out the precise costs of the wars in Scotland. Military accounts were not kept separately as they had been for the second Welsh war. The wardrobe account for 1300, the year of the Caerlaverock campaign, shows that the most expensive single item was the castle garrisons, on which £13,574 was spent. Victuals came to £5,063. The wages of the bannerets and knights amounted to £3,077, those of the crossbowmen and sergeants-at-arms to £1,038, while only £4,446 went to the infantry. Nearly £2,000 was spent in compensation for horses lost on the campaign. The total wardrobe expenditure for the year was £64,105, of which some two-thirds can be attributed to the needs of the war.[2] In 1301, with the ambitious double campaign, costs were naturally rather higher. The greatest increase was in infantry wages, totalling £15,746, but less was spent on castle garrisons and on victualling, these items totalling £8,915. The overall total of wardrobe expenditure was £77,291.[3] For the following year the only surviving account is a summary apparently made out for enrolment, although since it

[1] B.M. Add. MS, 7965.   [2] *Liber Quotidianus, passim.*
[3] B.M. Add. MS, 7966a, *passim.*

was never entered on the Pipe Roll, it seems likely that it failed to meet the exacting standards of the Exchequer. The total expenditure shown amounts to £61,949, even though there was no full-scale campaign in Scotland, as the king departed south after wintering at Linlithgow.[1] A similar document exists for the next year, the total expenditure being £64,026, and there is a complete wardrobe book for 1304. From these accounts it is possible to make a rough estimate of the cost of the campaigns of 1303 and 1304, which culminated with the capture of Stirling castle. Expenditure was probably in the order of £75,000 or £80,000.[2] Unfortunately the accounts for the last two years of the reign, which saw the struggle against Robert Bruce, are in such a confused state, and are so incomplete, that even such crude calculations are not possible.

In the period of the Welsh wars Edward I achieved great success at relatively low cost. There was no continual drain on resources, as the campaigns were fairly infrequent. From 1294 the situation changed completely. The government had expected heavy expenditure on the war with France, but the Welsh revolt and the need for a campaign in Scotland in 1296 had not been anticipated. The combined cost of these wars was unprecedented, and imposed exceptional burdens on the administration and on the country. After conclusion of the Flanders campaign early in 1298 Edward was still left with the problem of Scotland. Only in 1299, 1302 and 1305 was there no campaign, so there was a continuous demand for funds in a way that there had never been in Wales. Even though the crown did not engage in a lavish castle-building programme in Scotland as it had done in Wales, the burden of financing a substantial number of garrisons was considerable, while a campaign in the field cost at least £40,000. The problem of how to pay for the wars was immense.

[1] E. 101/360/25.   [2] E. 101/264/14; B.M. Add. MS, 8835.

VIII

THE CROWN REVENUE

The financial history of Edward I's reign has been described as 'a highly complicated and rather repellent subject'.[1] But complex subjects have their fascination, and it is necessary to probe beneath the stories of campaigns and sieges to the sordid realities of finance in order to discover how Edward I found the means to put his armies into the field. The case for financial and administrative history was put very clearly by Henry II's Treasurer, Richard FitzNeal:[2]

'We know indeed that chiefly by prudence, fortitude, temperance, justice and other virtues are kingdoms ruled and laws maintained; wherefore the rulers of the world must stand firm in these with all their strength. But it happens now and then that what is conceived with sound counsel and excellent intent may be the more expeditiously undertaken if funds are available, and what seemed difficult is easily carried out by adopting a particular routine of business.'

Edward I made it very clear to his exchequer officials that in his opinion his plans in 1301 were going awry for want of funds when he wrote to them in the following terms:[3]

'Be certain that if it had not been for a lack of cash we would have completed the bridge which was begun in order to cross the Firth of Forth, and understand clearly that if we had crossed this season, we would have dealt our enemies such a blow that our

---

[1] L. F. Salzman, *Edward I* (London, 1968), p. 212.
[2] *Dialogus de Scaccario*, translated in *English Historical Documents*, ii, *1042–1189*, ed. D. C. Douglas and G. W. Greenaway (London, 1953), pp. 491–2.
[3] E. 159/75, m. 7.

affairs in these parts would have been brought to a good and honourable end in a short time.'

While it was essential for success in war to have adequate supplies of money, the inevitable unpopularity of taxation and other methods of raising money was likely to provoke opposition and prove a threat to the political stability of the kingdom.

By this period what might be termed the traditional regular sources of revenue were hardly adequate to meet the crown's needs. The total revenue collected in their counties by the sheriffs, largely deriving from royal lands, perhaps reached £13,000 or £14,000.[1] There was little chance of increasing the royal revenue from land on the scale that was required for the financing of the wars, and Edward I's policy of land acquisition was not undertaken for financial reasons, but in order to provide an adequate endowment for his family.[2] It has been rightly pointed out by Wolffe that the real importance of the crown lands lay less in the income they provided than in the power of patronage they gave the crown.[3]

On occasion, large profits were made from justice, though the normal revenue from this source was estimated by the Exchequer in 1284 to be only approaching £1,200 a year. The same estimate of revenue calculated wardships to be worth a mere 500 marks, and escheats only 200 marks. The Chancery was thought to be worth 1,000 marks a year. From the Jewry £200 was expected, and from the mints and exchanges £500. Ecclesiastical vacancies were put at an annual value of 1,000 marks; again a surprisingly low figure.[4] The crown in fact received roughly £60,000 from episcopal vacancies in the course of the reign, or on average about £1,700 a year, though naturally far more came in some years than in others from this source.[5] The total estimated revenue in 1284 was £26,828 3s. 9¼d., and of this £8,000 was made up by the

---

[1] M. H. Mills, 'Exchequer Agenda and Estimate of Revenue, Easter Term 1284', *E.H.R.*, xl (1925), p. 231.   [2] *Supra*, pp 243–5.
[3] B. P. Wolffe, *The Crown Lands, 1461–1536* (London, 1970), p. 22.
[4] Mills, *op. cit.*, p. 233.
[5] My calculation from the figures provided by Margaret Howell, *Regalian Right in Medieval England* (London, 1962), pp. 212–33.

customs duties, which were not part of the traditional resources of the crown.[1]

Such an income was insufficient for Edward I's needs. What could be done? The king could revive his feudal rights to aids for such occasions as the marriage of his eldest daughter, and could levy tallage on his demesnes. English trade could be exploited by means of heavier customs duties. If necessary, loans could be negotiated. The French example of debasement of the coinage might be followed. But the most effective and most obvious method was to negotiate the grant of taxes from the laity and the clergy.

The collection of taxes on an assessment of the value of moveable property was not an innovation of Edward I's reign. This method of taxation had its origins in the twelfth century, and had been used by King John and Henry III. Nine such taxes were negotiated in Edward I's reign, and the following table lists them, giving the total assessment for each. In some cases the taxes were assessed at a double rate, the higher being paid by the towns and the ancient demesne.[2]

		£	s.	d.
1275	15th	81,054	2	8¼
1283	30th	42,765	10	1¼
1290	15th	116,346	12	11½
1294	10th and 6th	81,838	9	4¾
1295	11th and 7th	52,870	2	6¾
1296	12th and 8th	38,485	18	0½
1297	9th	34,419	2	2½
1301	15th	49,755	7	3½
1306	30th and 20th	34,777	13	8¾

The table shows that there were startling variations in the tax assessments. The levy made at the highest rate, the ninth of 1297, raised less than the lowest tax, the thirtieth and twentieth of 1306.

[1] Mills, *op. cit.*, p. 233.
[2] J. F. Willard, 'The Taxes upon Moveables in the Reign of Edward I', *E.H.R.*, xxviii (1913), pp. 519-21; Willard, *Parliamentary Taxes on Personal Property, 1290 to 1334* (Cambridge, Mass., 1934), p. 344.

The difficulty was that there was no permanent assessment: a new one had to be made each time, and the methods were not identical for each tax. In 1297 and 1301, for instance, the chief assessors of each county, appointed by the Exchequer, were ordered to have either four or two men elected in each vill or township to calculate the value of everyone's moveable goods, whereas in other years the task was done by a jury of twelve from each hundred, with the assistance of the reeve and four men from each vill.[1] In 1297 the sheriff and his officials were far more closely involved than usual in the process of assessment and collection.[2] Not all moveables were taxed, but the list of exempt goods was not always the same. It was not until 1296 that treasure in the form of coins was included as a taxable item.[3] In the last two taxes of the reign the clergy were treated more harshly than before, and were forced to pay on all their temporalities.[4]

But the differences in methods of assessment and in liability to tax are not sufficient to explain the wide variations between the totals of the various taxes. Nor does it seem probable that the wealth of the populace changed as startlingly as the figures suggest. A more plausible explanation is suggested by the records of the Oxfordshire village of Cuxham. The highest assessment of this village during the period 1290–1307 was that of 1294, amounting to £60 11s. 8d. The next year the villagers took care to have the valuation lowered. They spent lavishly on entertaining the assessors, with the result that the figure dropped to £12 18s. From 1297 direct bribery by the reeve in addition to entertainment became the rule, and in 1301 payment to the chief assessor was authorized by the sub-warden of Merton.[5] Cuxham provides a striking example of what must have been common in the whole country.

The government made some attempts to deal with the problem of under-assessment. Investigations were made into the failure of

---

[1] Willard, *Parliamentary Taxes*, pp. 55–6.
[2] A. T. Gaydon, *The Taxation of 1297* (Bedfordshire Historical Record Soc., xxxix, 1959), pp. x–xvii.
[3] J. A. C. Vincent, *Lancashire Lay Subsidies* (Lancashire and Cheshire Record Soc., xxvii, 1893), p. 192.   [4] Willard, *op. cit.*, pp. 96–101.
[5] Harvey, *A Medieval Oxfordshire Village, Cuxham 1240 to 1400*, pp. 105–8.

the sub-collectors of the 1290 fifteenth in Surrey, and it was found that under-valuation and other improprieties had occurred in fifteen places. The fines levied totalled £67 16s. 8d.[1] The enquiry into administrative malpractices in 1298 revealed much corruption,[2] and the memory of it may have spurred the taxers of 1301 and 1306 to greater rectitude. A more positive incentive was that in 1301 the collectors were given a much more lavish allowance for expenses than in former years: those for Berkshire obtained £30 as against £5 in 1297, those for Oxfordshire £27 as against £5. Such rises can be only partially explained in terms of the greater cost of the journey to York, where the Exchequer had moved in 1298, and of the increase in the number of collectors from two to three.[3]

The evidence shows that the yield of the taxes did not fall far short of the assessments, with the administration gaining in efficiency as it became more experienced. Arrears of the thirtieth collected between July 1284 and May 1289 totalled almost £8,500.[4] The first of the series of taxes in the years of war with France, the tenth and sixth, should have been fully paid by late May 1295, but by that date only about £45,000 had been received. Ten months later the total paid in to the Exchequer stood at £72,820.[5] One receipt roll survives for the twelfth and eighth negotiated in 1296, covering the period from late April until mid-September 1297. In this time £17,070 was paid to the Exchequer, all but £2,444 of it before 7 June. It had been decreed that half the tax was to be paid by 2 June, totalling some £19,000, and it is remarkable that the collectors should have come so close to achieving their target in a period of political turmoil.[6] What was happening in these

[1] *Surrey Taxation Returns. 15ths and 10ths. Part A—the 1332 assessment* (Surrey Record Soc., xviii, 1922), pp. xxx–xxxiv.
[2] *A Lincolnshire Assize Roll for 1298*, ed. Thomson, *passim*.
[3] Willard, *Parliamentary Taxes*, p. 202.
[4] Vincent, *op. cit.*, p. 169.
[5] *Ibid.*, pp. 184–5; E. 401/132; E. 401/1644. E. B. Fryde, in *Book of Prests*, p. li, has calculated arrears in the autumn of 1295 to have been about £7,000. This is based on the evidence of the final account, a document which, unlike the receipt rolls, gives no precise indication of the timetable of payment.
[6] Vincent, *op. cit.*, p. 195.

years from 1294 to 1298 was that the arrears on the earlier taxes in the series were left uncollected, while the attention of the officials was directed to the more recent levies. Thus by 1300 there were arrears of £100 due from Somerset on the tenth and sixth, £30 on the eleventh and seventh, but none on the twelfth and eighth, or the ninth.[1] The most efficiently collected tax of all was the last one of the reign. This was due to be paid in three instalments, of which the first yielded £10,364, almost exactly a third of the total assessment.[2]

The methods of collection were not identical for the various taxes. The first two saw separate assessors and collectors appointed. For the fifteenth of 1275 the Italian banking firm of the Riccardi were appointed along with the constable of the Tower of London to act as receivers of the tax, and for the thirtieth of 1283 the constables of the Tower, Nottingham and Bristol, acted as receivers, as did a royal clerk, William de Perton, at Chester. In addition, over £16,500 was raised by John Kirkby and various royal agents by direct negotiations with towns and religious houses in the summer of 1282, and the sums collected were accounted as a part of the subsidy.[3] The later taxes were controlled more directly by the Exchequer, and no separate receivers were appointed. In 1301 the crown was in considerable financial difficulties and a technique similar to that of 1282 was tried out. Officials equipped with details of the assessment of the last fifteenth approached fifty-seven towns to persuade them to compound for the tax by making a prompt payment of a lump sum.[4] At least fifteen agreed to this, though four were subsequently amerced for failing to pay in time.[5] In addition the Cinque Ports promised 2,000 marks, and the Templars and Hospitallers each compounded for the tax with 700 marks.[6]

On occasion the proceeds of taxation were assigned away in advance, so that the tax collectors made payment directly to royal creditors. The Riccardi received a sum approaching £60,000 from

[1] E. 159/73, m. 64d. [2] E. 159/80, m. 41.
[3] E. 372/123; E. 372/136; E. 359/4A. [4] C.C.R., 1296–1302, pp. 461–3.
[5] Willard, *Parliamentary Taxes*, p. 2; E. 159/75, m. 68.
[6] C.C.R., 1302–7, p. 278; C.P.R., 1292–1301, pp. 600, 606.

the fifteenth of 1275,[1] and it seems likely that the government had made them promises of payment before the tax was collected. Other Italian merchants had smaller debts repaid out of the proceeds of the tax.[2] But no large-scale assignments seem to have been made out of the thirtieth, and when, in 1290, the Exchequer took over full responsibility for the taxes on moveables the practice was temporarily abandoned.[3] The 1290s saw few instances of assignment, and these were on a small scale, as in 1295 when the cost of the royal galleys being built in Dartmouth, Lynn, Grimsby, Dunwich, Southampton and Lyme was partly met out of the receipts of the tenth and sixth.[4] But in 1301 the Exchequer was forced by an acute shortage of cash to make large-scale assignments. In October of that year the king wrote to the Exchequer stressing his need for money, and suggesting that with the receipts of the fifteenth, combined with those of the clerical taxes and the normal revenues brought in by the sheriffs at Michaelmas, there should be no lack of funds. In their reply the officials pointed out that the Treasurer had promised £6,000 out of the fifteenth to the Frescobaldi in repayment of loans, £2,000 to be paid from each instalment of the tax. £1,789 16s. 5d. was to be paid to certain Gascon merchants whose funds had been improperly seized by wardrobe officials in London that summer. Of the first instalment of the tax £4,000 was to be paid to the Welsh troops serving in Scotland, and out of the first two instalments a similar sum was assigned to some Gascons for wine taken from them. It was estimated that £9,789 16s. 5d. of the first instalment of the tax had been promised to these various creditors.[5] Nor were these the only assignments, for in March and April Edward had ordered payment for the victuals needed for the campaign to be made out of the fifteenth.[6] This system of assignment did not prove satisfactory. The Gascons,

[1] E. 101/126/1.
[2] E. A. Bond, 'Extracts from the Liberate Rolls, relative to Loans supplied by Italian Merchants to the Kings of England in the 13th and 14th centuries', *Archaeologia*, xxviii (1840), no. lxxxiii.
[3] Willard, *op. cit.*, p. 231.
[4] E. 159/68, m. 75.   [5] E. 159/75, mm. 5d, 7, 10.
[6] *C.P.R., 1292–1301*, p. 579; H. Hall, *Formula Book of Legal Records* (Cambridge, 1909), pp. 48–52.

for example, received little if any of what they were due, and the king had to order the Exchequer 'to cause issues to be assigned anew to the merchants in places where the Treasurer and Barons shall see fit'.[1] Orders that all the receipts from certain counties should be paid to the Welsh contradicted the earlier instructions for the payments for purveyance.[2] It was not surprising that for the final tax of the reign the practice was abandoned.

Despite the inconvenience of a form of taxation that required a new assessment for each grant, the taxes on moveables were the most efficient and profitable method of direct taxation available to the crown. The main drawback, however, was less administrative than political. Such taxes could only be levied with the consent of the community of the realm, and in the parliaments of 1300 and 1301 it became apparent that the granting of taxes might be used as a political weapon, a means of obtaining concessions from the crown. Accordingly, in the last years of the reign two prerogative taxes were imposed. The first of these was the feudal aid for the marriage of the king's eldest daughter. Collection of this at the rate of 40s. on each knight's fee was authorized in parliament as early as 1290, but as the fifteenth was granted shortly afterwards, Edward did not trouble to collect this antiquated tax. But in 1303, in a very different financial and political situation, this aid was remembered, and the machinery set in motion. Receipts were disappointing, however; £3,762 came in during 1303, £1,948 in the next year, and £1,122 in the rest of the reign.[3] Clearly, further sources of revenue were needed, and the Exchequer came up with the idea of reviving tallage. In July 1303 John Droxford reported to the council that the king was favourable to the scheme.[4] This royal right to tax crown demesnes and towns at will had been exercised fourteen times by Henry III, but never by Edward I, although the higher rate of taxation that was often applied to the

---

[1] *C.C.R., 1302–7*, p. 12.

[2] E. 159/75, mm. 72, 79. E. 179/91/1, a subsidy roll for Derbyshire, shows that although all receipts were ordered to go to the Welsh, some had been used to pay for purveyance. [3] E. 401/1667, 1670, 1676, 1678.

[4] J. F. Baldwin, *The King's Council in England during the Middle Ages* (Oxford. 1913), p. 466.

towns and demesnes was a reflection of the right that the king had to tallage. But this tax proved even less valuable than the feudal aid, yielding £2,862.[1] In 1305 another archaic method of raising money was revived. While fines from tenants-in-chief paid on the basis of the new quotas of military service yielded useful sums, though never worthy of comparison with the taxes on moveables, scutage assessed on the old knights' fees had at no time in Edward's reign produced any appreciable yield. Yet such a levy was now once again authorized in respect of the army summoned in 1300. So great was hostility to it that receipts came to less than £400.[2]

Far more important than these minor taxes, and second only to the lay subsidies in the amount they yielded, were the taxes paid by the clergy. There were two main ways in which the crown could tap the substantial wealth of the church. One was to take over part or all of the proceeds of the taxes imposed by Rome and intended for religious purposes, notably the crusades, while the other was to negotiate directly with the clergy in England for an aid.

These taxes on the clergy were assessed on a totally different basis from the lay taxes on moveables. They were income taxes, calculated on the rental value of estates rather than on actual revenues. For the first part of the reign the taxes granted by the clergy were collected on the basis of the assessment made under the direction of the bishop of Norwich in 1254, although the papal taxes were levied according to a new valuation made in 1276 for the sexennial tenth imposed in 1274. Then, in 1291, the imposition of a new crusading tenth was made the occasion for a new assessment. This provoked a loud outcry from the clergy, and Bartholomew Cotton complained that the assessors frequently doubled, trebled or even quadrupled the verdicts of juries.[3] But the complaints were clearly based on a comparison with earlier assessments, not with the actual revenues of clerical estates. Durham with an

[1] J. H. Ramsay, *A History of the Revenues of the Kings of England, 1066–1399* (Oxford, 1925), ii, p. 71.
[2] *Supra*, p. 82; Chew, 'Scutage under Edward I', *E.H.R.*, xxxvii (1922), pp. 321–36.
[3] *Chron. Cotton*, pp. 198–9.

annual income of over £3,500 had its temporalities assessed at £620, and its spiritualities at under £700.[1]

Edward first approached the clergy for a grant of taxation in 1275, but was refused on the grounds that they were already paying a tenth to the papacy. Four years later a request for a fifteenth to meet the expenses that had been incurred in Wales was successful, the southern convocation agreeing to pay at this rate for three years, while the York clergy granted a tenth for two years in 1280. In 1283 the clergy were asked for aid for the Welsh war at the twin assemblies at York and Northampton. But although the laymen granted a thirtieth, the clergy refused to co-operate, those at Northampton on the grounds that no representatives of the lower clergy were present. Eventually, after a full assembly had met at London, a triennial twentieth was granted by the southern convocation. It was not until 1286 that the northern clergy were ultimately prevailed upon to grant a triennial thirtieth. The last tax granted to the king on the old 1254 assessment was the clerical tenth of 1290, a grant made in return for the expulsion of the Jews from England.[2]

In 1294 the king demanded from the clergy the unprecedentedly high grant of a half, on the new and much heavier assessment of 1291. At an assembly of the clergy of both provinces summoned to meet in September, Edward was offered two tenths. Furious, he threatened to put them out of his protection unless his wishes were met. This was enough for the prelates, who capitulated promptly, while a few sharp words from John of Havering were enough to persuade those of the lower clergy who were thinking of holding out that this would be unwise. Payment was to be made in three instalments, the final one to come in early July 1295. The timetable was an exacting one for so large a tax—the Bury St. Edmunds chronicler estimated a yield of £101,000.[3]

[1] Rose Graham, *English Ecclesiastical Studies* (London, 1929), p. 259.
[2] H. S. Deighton, 'Clerical Taxation by Consent', *E.H.R.*, lxviii (1953), pp. 163–70.
[3] *The Chronicle of Bury St. Edmunds*, p. 124. This seems a reasonably accurate figure: a more recent estimate of the total value of the assessment is £210,644, Deighton, *op. cit.*, p. 175, in which case a half would yield £105,322.

Initially there was considerable difficulty in levying the tax. In Norfolk and Hereford there was trouble with parsons who hoped to avoid payment either by selling all their goods, or by taking them off their lands. Bishop Sutton of Lincoln sent no less than three lists of clergy to Edward with the request that they be arrested, as they had remained obdurate in their refusal to pay, despite excommunication. The Exchequer found collection difficult, as they possessed no copy of the assessment, and there was a muddle about the interpretation of the exemption allowed to those assessed at less than ten marks.[1] By Michaelmas 1295 roughly £66,000 had been received by the Exchequer from this moiety.[2]

The prelates assembled in parliament in November 1295 cannot have been sympathetic when Edward appeared in person to demand a new aid from them. Winchelsey offered a tenth, and the king, wanting more, employed the judges to threaten the clergy, but without success. The offer had to be accepted, although the archbishop promised a further tenth a year later if the war continued.[3] Part of the condition of the grant seems to have been that there should be no governmental interference in the collection of the tax: only the Abbot of Oseney received any help from the sheriffs. The effect of this can be easily seen. By the time set for the full payment, only about £5,000 had in fact been received, though by late September 1296, about two months after the payments were due, receipts totalled £11,243. But the total should have been some £20,000.[4]

The promised tenth in the following year did not materialize. The bull *Clericis Laicos* which prohibited the payment of taxes to lay authority enabled Winchelsey to resist Edward's demands, although the king was able to obtain £22,810 from the clergy by placing them out of his protection, and allowing them to buy back his favour with the sums that they would have paid had a tax been

---

[1] E. 159/68, mm. 68–70; *The Rolls and Registers of Bishop Oliver Sutton, 1280–1299*, ed. Rosalind M. T. Hill, v (Lincoln Record Soc., lx, 1965), pp. 149, 154.

[2] E. 401/1629, 1635, 1638. E. B. Fryde, *Book of Prests*, p. li, has calculated the ultimate yield of this tax, less arrears, as £68,900.

[3] 'Annales de Wigornia', in *Annales Monastici*, iv, p. 524.

[4] E. 401/1643, 1647.

granted.[1] With the settlement of the political crisis of 1297 marked by the issue of the *Confirmatio Cartarum*, and the military crisis of the English defeat at Stirling Bridge, combined with a relaxation of the papal position, grants were once more forthcoming from the clergy. The southern convocation granted a tenth; the northern, more threatened by the Scots, a fifth. Winchelsey insisted that there be no secular interference whatsoever in the collection of the money; the receipts were paid in to the New Temple. The archbishop was also firm that the tax was granted for the specific emergency only, and when, in 1305, he was summoned to the Exchequer to answer for 6,000 marks that had not been paid to the crown, he refused on the grounds that the emergency was over. But he did take his responsibilities over the tax very seriously, writing to the bishop of London in November 1297 to complain of the shortage of funds he was suffering, and explaining that he was borrowing money to meet his obligations. Later he complained that no bishops had followed his example in doing this.[2] The northern clergy were less affected by scruples than was Winchelsey; the fifth that they granted was collected with the aid of royal officials, and a final account drawn up with the Exchequer.[3]

Although Edward I's methods of extracting money from the clergy by direct grant between 1294 and 1298 almost proved politically disastrous in 1297, they were financially rewarding. There was a great problem in collecting the arrears: in 1296 the abbots of Burton, Glastonbury, Tavistock, Faversham and Colchester were singled out for their incompetence, and in May 1297 the lands of the abbot of Furness were taken into royal hands since he owed roughly £2,700 in arrears.[4] After the crisis year of 1297 there was no concerted effort to secure full payment, and by the time of Edward II's reign when those collectors who were not quit in their final accounts were brought before the Exchequer, most of the arrears were found to be irrecoverable.[5] Nevertheless,

---

[1] *Infra*, pp. 256–7.
[2] Deighton, *op. cit.*, p. 190; E. 159/78, m. 38d; Graham, *English Ecclesiastical Studies*, pp. 317–23.   [3] E. 372/155B.
[4] E. 159/69, m. 75; E. 159/70, m. 114.   [5] E. 372/155B; E. 363/1, 2.

it appears from the receipt rolls that during the period of hostilities with France these direct clerical taxes produced roughly £100,000, as against £150,000 from the lay taxes in the same period.[1]

The taxes granted in 1297 were the last subsidies that Edward I received as a result of direct negotiation with the English clergy. It seems likely that some attempts were made in 1300 and in 1301 to obtain further grants, but the bill presented in parliament by Henry Keighley firmly stated in its final clause that the prelates would not assent to any subsidy without papal consent.[2] Ironically, their flank was turned by the very man they hoped would protect them from taxation, since in a bull issued on 26 February Boniface VIII imposed a tenth on the English church for three years, half the proceeds of which were to go to the king.[3]

Edward had already profited considerably from papal taxation. By 1279 £8,000 had been granted to him by the papacy out of the crusading tenth imposed in 1275, and the money used to repay the Riccardi for their loans.[4] All the receipts of the tax were seized by the crown on the occasion of the second Welsh war, although Edward actually used only a little over £4,000 which was duly repaid out of the lay taxes. Negotiations on the subject of a crusade continued with Rome, and in 1287 the king took the cross. In 1289, after an embassy led by Otto de Grandson and William de Hotham had put the king's case to Nicholas IV, it was agreed that the proceeds of the tenth collected in England should be paid over to Edward, while a new tenth for six years was to be imposed. In fact, the king had already received some of the money in the form of a loan of £18,566 made in 1286, which was not repaid at all until some revenues were assigned for the purpose in 1302. In 1291, following the successful agreement with Nicholas he received a further 100,000 marks out of the tax.[5]

It seems that Edward's motives in obtaining payment of these

---

[1] E. 401/1629, 1635, 1638, 1643, 1647, 1653. This figure includes the fines for protection levied in 1297 in lieu of the fifth demanded by the crown.

[2] *Parl. Writs*, i, p. 105.

[3] W. E. Lunt, *Financial Relations of England with the Papacy to 1327* (Cambridge, Mass., 1939), p. 366.

[4] Riccardi account, E. 101/126/1.   [5] Lunt, *op. cit.*, pp. 336–46.

papal crusading tenths were perfectly honourable. He genuinely did plan to set out on crusade, and his promises to do so were not a means of obtaining funds by false pretences.[1] Edward wrote a letter to Florent of Hainault, Prince of Achaea, in June 1294, in which he stated his desire to visit Greece, but expressed his anger at the way in which in a short space of time circumstances had changed, making it impossible for him to go on crusade.[2] But before this the king had borrowed £10,000 from the papal collectors to cover expenditure in Gascony, and with the outbreak of war with France the king took control of the tax, seizing at least £32,480 which, like the loan, does not appear to have been repaid.[3] The needs of war took precedence over the king's desire to go once more to the East.

To those present at the Lincoln parliament of 1301 relations between the king and the papacy must have seemed at a low ebb. In 1300 Winchelsey had brought to Edward in Scotland a letter from Boniface VIII strongly criticizing the English claims and actions in Scotland, and in reply to this the famous Barons' Letter was drawn up in 1301, while Edward sent a detailed historical justification of his policies to Rome. But Boniface's attitude was transformed by his quarrel with Philip IV. Edward I became a favoured ally, and it is not surprising that when news of a papal grant to the king of half the proceeds of a new tenth reached France it was considered that Boniface had done this in order to enable Edward to reopen the war with France. There were some misunderstandings over the collection of the tax, and on Boniface's death the king claimed that he had been orally granted the entire proceeds of the tax, which was a view supported by the testimony of Otto de Grandson and Bartholomew de Ferentino, but not credited by Benedict IX and many of the English clergy. Nevertheless despite such arguments, the king did receive at least £41,690 from this tax during his reign.[4]

[1] Powicke, *Henry III and the Lord Edward*, ii, pp. 729-33.
[2] S.C. 1/13/66.
[3] Lunt, *op. cit.*, p. 363 shows that the collectors claimed that £33,033 was seized, but Fryde, *Book of Prests*, p. li, gives the figure of £32,480 from the receipt rolls of the Exchequer. [4] Lunt, *op. cit.*, p. 676.

The election of a Gascon in June 1305 as Pope Clement V was rapidly taken advantage of by Edward I. Shortly afterwards, a delegation from England set out for the Curia, and on 1 August a compliant Clement ordered the English church to pay an annual tenth for the next seven years. These receipts were intended to be used for the recovery of the Holy Land, those of the first year to go to Edward I, those of the second to the prince of Wales, and the rest to Edward again. The queen was to receive £2,000 a year from all but the second and last years of the tax. No attempt was made to persuade Edward to take a new pledge to go on crusade, and this time it does look as if the crusade was being used as an excuse to make the grant of the tenths to a lay power look more respectable. By the end of the Hilary term of 1307 £25,502 had been received by the Exchequer, with £2,996 more in the next term.[1]

During the last five years of the reign, Edward I obtained some £70,000 from the clergy by means of these tenths imposed by the papacy. At a time when the costs of the war in Scotland had to be met, and with the opposition likely to make the grant of taxation conditional upon the redress of grievances, it was extremely convenient that the king should have been in a position to receive the proceeds of taxes which he had not imposed. There was surprisingly little opposition to the papal taxes; not even at the Carlisle parliament in 1307, when there was bitter criticism of papal procurations and other exactions, did they come under much attack.[2] Only one chronicler indulged in a tirade against papal taxation.[3]

Over the whole reign Edward I probably received some £500,000 from direct taxes paid by the laity, and £300,000 from ecclesiastical taxes. For the period of crisis from 1294 until 1297 the equivalent figures are £150,000 and £130,000. Taxation on this scale had not been imposed at any earlier period, although the

[1] *Ibid.*, pp. 382–91.
[2] W. E. Lunt, 'William Testa and the Parliament of Carlisle', *E.H.R.*, xli (1926), pp. 332–57; H. G. Richardson and G. O. Sayles, 'The Parliament of Carlisle, 1307—Some New Documents', *E.H.R.*, liii (1938), pp. 425–37.
[3] *Flores Historiarum*, iii, p. 110.

tremendous efforts made to meet the demand for £100,000 to pay Richard I's ransom offer the closest parallel, when a fourth on moveables, the heaviest rate at which such a tax was ever levied, together with an aid of 20s. a fee, a carucage and a tallage were imposed. Following these measures of 1193 and 1194 were the taxes intended to pay for the defence and recovery of English possessions on the continent, notably the thirteenth of 1207, which yielded about £60,000.[1] The reign of Henry III did not see particularly heavy taxation: there were only four taxes on moveables, the fifteenth of 1225 producing almost £40,000.[2] The tallages, aids and carucages that were collected more frequently yielded very much less.[3]

How was the burden of taxation that Edward I's financial needs imposed on the country shared out? As the lay taxes were assessed and collected on the basis of the possessions of individuals rather than on land or income, there is little statistical evidence of the weight of incidence of these subsidies. Manorial accounts show only small payments, as there were not many moveables liable to taxation on most demesnes. In the year 1296–7 the earl of Cornwall's valuable manor of Berkhampstead was charged with only £2 6s. 9d. for the twelfth, a trivial sum in relation to receipts which totalled £160 7s. 4d.[4] The few detailed tax assessments that survive naturally give no indication of the incomes of the men whose moveables are listed, though they do make it clear that the burden of taxation fell not on the lay landlords, but on the villeins and free tenants. The very poor were always exempt, the principle usually adopted being that if, for example, a ninth was levied, those whose property was not worth 9s. would not be taxed. With the low rates of 1283 and 1306 this system could hardly apply, and the levels were set at half a mark and 10s. respectively.

It was not until 1297 that complaints about the weight of tax-

---

[1] A. L. Poole, *From Domesday Book to Magna Carta, 1087–1216* (2nd ed. Oxford, 1955), pp. 364–6, 420.

[2] Fred A. Cazel, Jr., 'The Fifteenth of 1225', *B.I.H.R.*, xxxiv (1961), p. 70.

[3] S. K. Mitchell, *Taxation in Medieval England* (New Haven, 1951), p. 358.

[4] *Ministers' Accounts of the Earldom of Cornwall, 1296–1297*, ed. L. Margaret Midgley, i (Camden Soc., 3rd ser., lxvi, 1942), pp. 17, 21.

ation were vociferously voiced in the political arena. Prior to that Edward's demands do not seem to have aroused the opposition that might have been expected. The chroniclers were of course far more interested in the question of clerical taxation, but the impression they give of a generally quiescent laity does not seem far from the truth. As Langtoft pointed out, it was better to pay harsh taxes than to be conquered,[1] and as a popular song, admittedly of slightly later date, stated, it was not the people who actually made the grant who had to pay heavily.[2] The magnates who campaigned in Edward's armies usually obtained exemption from the payment of the taxes.

The legal records reveal many examples of corrupt practice by tax collectors, notably levying money from those who should have been exempt by reason of their poverty, collecting expenses where these were not justified, and taking more money than was warranted by the assessment.[3] But they do not suggest that much resistance was offered to the collectors, whose task seems to have been much easier than that of the purveyors of victuals. Men did not feel so strongly about giving up cash to the king as they did about parting with goods, and it is interesting that in one case where violence was shown to a bailiff engaged in collecting arrears, he was making a seizure of cattle rather than collecting coin.[4]

There is more evidence of the burden of taxation from ecclesiastical estates than from lay, largely because the clerical taxes were assessed on the income of landlords, rather than on the property of individuals. In order to pay what was demanded for the moiety of 1294 the monks of Dunstable had to farm tithes and sell corrodies and property to a value of roughly a hundred marks.[5] The hospital of God's House, Southampton, failed to pay one instalment of the same tax which came to £25, and as a result eighteen

---

[1] *Chron. Langtoft*, ii, p. 214.
[2] *Anglo-Norman Political Songs*, ed. I. S. T. Aspin (Anglo-Norman Text Soc., 1953), p. 109.
[3] *A Lincolnshire Assize Roll for 1298*, ed. Thomson, p. xlix.
[4] *A Suffolk Hundred in the year 1283*, ed. E. Powell (Cambridge, 1910), pp. xvi–xviii.   [5] *Annales Monastici*, iii, pp. 387–8.

oxen were taken as pledges. Payment was eventually made, but the cost of obtaining the release of the beasts and of taking the money to London was almost a pound.[1] Ramsey abbey was in severe financial difficulties during the later years of Edward I's reign, and the letters of Abbot Sawtrey make it clear that the burden of taxation was one of the main reasons. He had to borrow money from friends to raise £1,000 for the papal tenths imposed in 1301, and in 1303 he was finding it difficult to obtain a mere twenty marks. His monks, who considered him financially incompetent, threatened strike action in 1300, saying that they would not sing services unless he made out a bond releasing them from liability for the debts he incurred.[2] In the north the difficulties of the clergy were aggravated by the damage done to their estates by the marauding Scots. A special proctor was appointed to plead in Rome for a reduction of the assessment in the diocese of Carlisle, and Bishop Halton firmly asserted the inability of the clergy to pay the sums demanded of them.[3] It is not surprising to find the canon of Barnwell writing in the bitterest terms of the extortions suffered by the church, the despoliation of the poor and the withdrawal of alms in the reign of Edward I.[4] A man of conventional piety, Edward never let this attribute interfere with political and financial realities.

One indication of the weight of taxation imposed by Edward I is provided by the mint accounts. In the first recoinage of the reign begun in 1279 it is likely that approximately £500,000 was produced by the mints. At the close of the reign the quantity of coin in circulation was increased by the import of much foreign silver: between 1300 and 1302 the accounts show that £262,000 worth of alien coin was minted into coin of the realm. Such figures give an impression of how much coin there was in

[1] Queen's College, Oxford, MSS, Rolls, 181 (Deposited in the Bodleian Library).
[2] *Chronicon Abbatiae Rameseiensis*, ed. W. D. Macray (Rolls Series, 1886), pp. 379, 380–1, 387, 393, 399–400.
[3] *Historical Papers and Letters from the Northern Registers*, ed J. Raine (Rolls Series, 1873), pp. 145, 151.
[4] *Liber Memorandorum Ecclesie de Bernewelle*, ed. J. W. Clark (Cambridge, 1907), p. 191.

circulation during this period. There were considerable fluctuations, and a shortage throughout the country during the period of greatest political and financial difficulty, 1294–7.[1] It seems unlikely that there was ever more than £1,000,000 current coin circulating at any time; the figure of £800,000 is probably nearer the mark. And that was roughly the amount that was raised in direct taxation in the course of the reign. In the year 1294–5 wardrobe receipts totalled over £124,000,[2] a figure almost certainly in excess of ten per cent of the total quantity of coin in circulation in England. The taxes needed to meet such demands must clearly have placed a massive imposition on the populace.

Direct taxation was by no means the only method by which a medieval monarch could effectively tap the wealth of his country. It was probably on the outbreak of the war with France that an anonymous foreigner presented Edward I with advice on the best way to raise money for war. Heavy customs duties were suggested, at the rate of 5 marks on each sack of wool exported, and at 1s. in the pound on all other merchandise taken in or out of the country. These measures were to be backed up by the more ambitious ones of a purchase tax of 2d. in the pound and elaborate sumptuary laws intended to reduce domestic expenditure and so free revenue for military purposes. The main item of the memorandum, the heavy export tax on wool, was adopted by the government, which was doubtless attracted by the author's calculation that this would yield 100,000 marks in six months.[3]

There was nothing new, in 1294, in the idea of an export tax on wool. In 1266 Edward had been granted the right to levy customs duties by his father, a measure which proved extremely unpopular, and collection was discontinued early in the new reign. In 1275 discussion between the crown and the merchants resulted in the grant in parliament of customs dues of 6s. 8d. on each sack of wool

---

[1] M. C. Prestwich, 'Edward I's Monetary Policies and their Consequences', *Ec.H.R.*, 2nd ser., xxii (1969), pp. 406–16.
[2] Tout, *Chapters*, vi, p. 80.
[3] W. H. Blaauw, *The Barons' War* (London, 1843), appendix, pp. 1–2; C. V. Langlois, 'Project for taxation presented to Edward I', *E.H.R.*, iv (1889), pp. 517–21.

exported. In return, the embargo on trade with Flanders—imposed in retaliation for the seizures of the goods of English merchants made by the orders of the countess of Flanders in 1270—was relaxed.[1] The revenue from this export duty naturally fluctuated with the fortunes of the wool trade, receipts varying from £8,100 in 1279-80 to £12,900 in 1291-2.[2]

Valuable as these receipts were, when the war with France broke out in 1294 the government sought further means of extracting money from the wool trade. The initial plan was to take a forced loan in wool, and on 12 July 1294 orders were issued for all wool, fells and hides to be taken into safe custody. The ostensible purpose of the exercise was to prevent any wool being exported to France, but it soon became clear that the crown's intention was to buy up all the wool on credit, export it, and take the profit that would normally have gone to the merchants. This plan had the approval of the magnates, on condition that adequate security was given to the owners of the wool. But the merchants were naturally bitterly opposed to a project which threatened their entire livelihood, and on receiving their complaints, almost certainly including the memorandum already mentioned, the king and his council agreed that instead of the forced loan, the merchants should pay heavily increased customs duties. In view of the wide variations in wool prices it was initially proposed that these should be five marks for the best wool, and three marks for the lower qualities, but the differential was soon abandoned, and the lower rate adopted. On 29 July officials were appointed to collect the new custom.[3]

The war naturally reduced the volume of trade considerably. The effects of the inevitable insecurity of wartime were magnified, not only by this new duty, known as the *maltolt*, but also by the English policy of using the wool trade as a diplomatic weapon, canalizing it first of all to Dordrecht and then to Malines. Although trade declined, revenues from the customs rose sharply with the increase in the duties. Unfortunately the accounts are not quite

[1] Powicke, *The Thirteenth Century*, pp. 619-30; E. Power, *The Wool Trade in English Medieval History* (Oxford, 1941), pp. 75-7.
[2] E. 372/124; E. 372/143.   [3] E. 159/68, m. 82.

complete—those from Southampton have not survived—but estimating on the basis of the proportion of trade from that port after 1298, the total customs revenue from 1294 until the end of September 1297 appears to have been about £116,000, or rather more than the yield of the lay subsidies in the same period.[1]

The government did not completely abandon its initial plan of profiting from English trade by itself acquiring wool in England and selling it abroad. Not all the wool arrested in 1294 was returned to its owners. That belonging to merchants suspected of trading with France was held by the crown, as was that belonging to the Italian firm of the Riccardi, which had failed to meet its obligations and gone bankrupt. In December 1294, 277 sacks of their wool were exported by the wool fleet sent to Dordrecht under the command of Laurence of Ludlow and Roger of Lincoln. But the fleet was wrecked, and Laurence drowned, though enough was salvaged for the royal agent in the Low Countries to be able to enter profits of over £1,000 in his accounts. In the next two years some 500 sacks of Riccardi wool were sold abroad.[2]

The policy of profiting from the wool trade by imposing heavy duties rather than by taking forced loans in wool was not reversed until 1297. In April a seizure was ordered, the original intention apparently being to take only the goods of foreign merchants, but the scope of the instructions was extended by the Exchequer, probably without the knowledge of the king. The measure was not effective. In the political climate of the time, the government was losing control at a local level. A new seizure was ordered at the end of July, with the stated purpose of producing revenue for the payment of the foreign allies: 30,000 marks for the king of Germany and 25,000 for the duke of Brabant. In addition, 20,000 marks was needed to cover the cost of taking the army to Flanders.

---

[1] E. 372/145, mm. 30–1; E. 372/146, m. 36; E. 372/149, mm. 38–41; E. 122/124/2, 3.

[2] J. de Sturler, *Les relations politiques et les échanges commerciaux entre le duché de Brabant et l'Angleterre au moyen âge* (Paris, 1936), pp. 184–5; 'Deux comptes "enrôlés" de Robert de Segre', *Bull de la Comm. Royale d'Hist.*, cxxv (1959), p. 593; E. B. Fryde, 'Financial Resources of Edward I in the Netherlands, 1294–1298', *Revue Belge*, xl (1962), p. 1182.

It was calculated that 8,000 sacks would provide enough in sales to meet this demand.[1] But nothing like this quantity was collected. Letters patent promising payment to those whose wool was taken show that only about 525 sacks were collected by nine of the fourteen commissions set up for the purpose.[2] The accounts of royal agents at Yarmouth, Hull, Boston and Southampton detail some 1,470 sacks received from the two prises of the year. There were some other agents, for example at Newcastle, so it is not possible to know exactly how much wool was taken, but clearly the measures did not come near to the expectations of the government in their execution.[3]

The government's attempt to profit directly from the wool trade did not prove very successful. Total receipts from the sales of wool in the Low Countries were probably about £25,000,[4] less than a quarter of the income from the heavy customs duties. Politically both policies proved extremely unpopular. Not only were important constitutional issues involved in the way in which they had been put into effect, but wool prices were also severely affected. The opposition in 1297 claimed that the duty raised by the *maltolt* amounted to one-fifth of the value of all the land in England. Though this was obviously an overstatement, it was clearly felt that the effect of the measure was not to pass the duty on to the consumers in Flanders to be paid by them in the form of higher prices, but that the merchants were forcing the producers to accept lower prices. Calculations to test this view are difficult, for the weights used to measure wool varied in different parts of the country, and the quality of the produce was not consistent. However, the examples collected by Thorold Rogers show that in the years 1294–6 prices were lower than in any previous period for which figures are available, and that this depression was not paralleled until the years after the Black Death.[5] Even though

[1] G. O. Sayles, 'The Seizure of Wool at Easter 1297', *E.H.R.*, lxvii (1952), pp. 543–7; E. 159/70, m. 42d, 115.

[2] *C.P.R., 1292–1301*, pp. 299–300, 310–11, 321–3, 332, 335.

[3] E. 372/152b; de Sturler's calculation in *op. cit.*, pp. 193–4, comes to twenty less sacks than mine.   [4] Fryde, *op. cit.*, p. 1185.

[5] J. E. Thorold Rogers, *A History of Agriculture and Prices in England*, i (Oxford, 1866), pp. 372, 386–94.

prices were recovering in 1297, the average of £5 a sack paid for the wool taken in the July prise was at least £1 less than it would have been in a normal year.[1] The leaders of the opposition were obviously right to stress the burden that Edward I's taxation of trade imposed on the country.

As a result of the constitutional crisis of 1297 the *maltolt* was lifted on 24 November, and replaced by the old scale of duties, each sack of wool being charged at half a mark. The immediate effect on the volume of exports was not startling, and in 1301–2 the war between Philip IV and the Flemings caused them to fall almost to the level of 1296. Though they later recovered to a point comparable with that of the years before 1294,[2] the rise in exports was by no means sufficient to bring the receipts from the customs anywhere near the amount that had been attained when the 40s. duty was in force. From Michaelmas 1297 until Michaelmas 1303 only about £53,000 was paid over to the officials at the ports.[3] It is hardly surprising that in 1303, with the need to pay for a new campaign in Scotland, the government should have held negotiations with the foreign merchants which resulted in the imposition of an extra duty of 3s. 4d. on each sack of wool they exported.[4] The introduction of this New Custom was the last change in the structure of the customs duties in Edward I's reign. From Michaelmas 1303 until the end of the reign, customs receipts totalled over £72,000, an average of about £18,000 a year, the rise being partly due to the new duty and partly to the increased volume of trade.[5]

The prosperity of the English wool trade in the final years of the reign assisted royal finances in another way. Much foreign silver was brought into the country by the merchants, and in accordance with the law was coined into sterling. The government naturally made a profit on such operations, receiving between May 1304 and the king's death £6,932. This was not the only period of the reign that saw the crown benefiting from coinage operations. In

---

[1] *C.P.R.*, *1292–1301*, pp. 310–11, 321–3, 332, 335.
[2] E. M. Carus-Wilson and Olive Coleman, *England's Export Trade, 1275–1547* (Oxford, 1963), pp. 38–41.
[3] E. 372/145, mm. 30–1; E. 372/146, m. 36; E. 372/149, mm. 38–41; E. 356/2.   [4] *Infra*, p. 268.   [5] E. 356/2.

1279 a full-scale recoinage was begun, a measure inspired by the poor state of the currency. In the first two years of the new coinage, receipts from the mints totalled £35,788, while the wardrobe accounts for the five years from 1279 show that £36,875 was paid to that department out of the profits of the recoinage. But during the years of greatest financial need, those of the war with France, receipts from this source were at a negligible level. In contrast, from 1295 Philip IV in France was making huge sums by the expedient of debasing the coinage, to such an extent that the *livre tournois* had halved in value on the exchange rate with sterling. There is no evidence to suggest that Edward ever contemplated following the French example: there was a strong tradition of maintaining the standard of the currency in England, and Philip attracted much adverse criticism for his action. But one motive for the English recoinage of 1279 must have been the pressing need for funds to pay for the Welsh war.[1]

The main source of profit from the monetary reform of 1279 was the mints. But as the activities of coin clippers were chiefly blamed for the poor state of the coinage, the recoinage was accompanied by a vigorous judicial campaign against those suspected of this offence, now threatened for the first time with capital punishment. The great majority of those accused were Jews, and the commission to the justices was amplified to take cognizance of other offences associated with the Jews, notably blasphemy. The proceedings appear to have been extremely biased, and it was not long before this became clear to the government and they were halted. Nevertheless some Jews were executed, and much property forfeited to the crown.[2] In 1279–80 the Wardrobe received £1,356 from this source.[3]

The Jews did not only suffer from judicial persecution: they were also liable to arbitrary taxation. The royal right to tallage the Jews had been extremely valuable in the past, and before his

---

[1] I have discussed these questions more fully in my article, 'Edward I's Monetary Policies and their Consequences', *Ec.H.R.*. 2nd ser., xxii (1969), pp. 406–16.

[2] H. G. Richardson, *The English Jewry under the Angevin Kings* (London, 1960), pp. 217–20.   [3] E. 372/124.

accession Edward had personally profited from it, as when his father had granted him a tallage of 6,000 marks, of which 4,000 was paid, for the financing of his crusade.[1] But by Edward's reign the extortions of the past had reduced Jewish resources to a fraction of what they had once been. The Exchequer hoped to raise 25,000 marks from a tallage imposed in 1273, but the figure proved grossly optimistic. More realistic were those of £1,000 in 1276 and 3,000 marks in 1278. Following the persecutions of 1279 the Jews had a respite from taxation until 1287, when a new tallage was imposed and the impossibly high figure of 20,000 marks was demanded. Not more than £4,000 seems actually to have been raised. Clearly, the continued presence of the Jews in England did not promise great financial advantage to the crown. That their expulsion might yield profits was suggested by the king's experience in Gascony. In 1289 the Gascon Jews were expelled, the motive being quite blatantly the acquisition of their assets by a king hard pressed to raise the funds needed to obtain the release of his cousin, Charles of Salerno, from captivity. In England in 1290 Edward justified his decision to treat the English Jews similarly by reference to their evasion of the Statute of the Jewry of 1275. However, the financial motive for the expulsion was quite clear. Not only did the crown acquire Jewish assets, but also the grants of taxation in 1290 were made in gratitude for the royal action, as the chroniclers stated at the time and the government admitted later.[2]

It would be wrong to view the expulsion of the Jews solely in financial terms. Edward's hostility to them was revealed as early as 1269 in the *Provisio Judaismi* which limited the way in which debts might be contracted with Jews.[3] It seems very probable that the decision to make blasphemy by Jews a capital offence was the king's own decision, a reflection of his Christian piety.[4] Not only

---

[1] *C.P.R., 1266–72*, p. 545.
[2] Richardson, *op. cit.*, pp. 214–16, 225–30; P. Elman, 'The Economic Causes of the Expulsion of the Jews in 1290', *Ec.H.R.*, vii (1936), p. 154; Vincent, *Lancashire Lay Subsidies*, i, p. 171.
[3] C. Roth, *A History of the Jews in England* (Oxford, 1941), p. 65; Denholm-Young, *Richard of Cornwall*, p. 143.   [4] Richardson, *op. cit.*, pp. 224–5.

did the Statute of 1275 prohibit usury, it also compelled Jews of either sex above the age of seven to wear a distinguishing badge, a more extreme measure than those in force on the continent.[1] But the king's attitude was probably less harsh than that of some of those influential with him. In 1275 all Jews were expelled from the lands of the queen mother,[2] and it is interesting that one chronicler attributed the action of 1290 to her influence.[3] When it was proposed in the council that Henry de Winton, a converted Jew, be given powers to investigate coin clipping, Thomas de Cantilupe, bishop of Hereford, protested hysterically that he would have power over Christians. Thomas threatened his resignation from the council, and the plan was accordingly dropped. On another occasion he dismissed a Jewish plea that he cease from persecuting them, demanding that they accept the Christian faith.[4] Such attitudes must have contributed to the decision to expel the Jews. In addition, of course, the expulsion would be popular with the landlords who were indebted to Jewish moneylenders.

The financial exigencies of the period immediately following Edward's return from Gascony were not, for once, the result of war, but of the obligations that the king had entered into to obtain the release of Charles of Salerno from captivity in Aragon. In October 1288 Edward paid 23,000 marks to Alfonso of Aragon, and entered into liabilities totalling 80,000 marks, which fortunately he was not called on to pay, as Charles and Alphonso made peace in 1271, and Edward's obligations were cancelled.[5] Edward's need for funds on his return to England was therefore considerable, and in addition to being a cause of the expulsion of the Jews and the official reason for the grant of the lay and clerical subsidies, his financial problems must also have been behind the decision to profit extensively from the trials of the justices instituted at this time.

---

[1] Roth, *op. cit.*, pp. 70–1.
[2] *Select Pleas, Starrs and other Records*, ed. J. M. Rigg (Selden Soc., xv, 1902), p. 85.
[3] 'Annales de Waverleia', in *Annales Monastici*, ii, p. 409.
[4] *Acta Sanctorum, Octobris*, ed. J. Bollandus, i (Paris, Rome, 1866), pp. 547–8, 560.
[5] Powicke, *The Thirteenth Century*, pp. 282–3.

When Edward landed in England in August 1289 he was greeted by the widespread complaints of his subjects directed against the corruption and injustice of the administration. An investigating commission was set up, and the result was a purge of the judicial bench. Some lesser men were also tried, but unlike the inquisitions of 1298, proceedings were largely directed against men of high standing in the legal hierarchy. The Chief Justice of Common Pleas, Thomas de Weyland, was forced into exile after he had attempted to flee from the king's wrath. But once the initial outburst had passed, Edward 'turned his attention rather to the monetary profits to be got from the business than to the demands of abstract justice'. Ralph Hengham, Chief Justice of the King's Bench, was fined 8,000 marks, of which he paid at least £4,303 6s. 8d. The total received in fines from the ten chief offenders came to £15,591 13s. 4d.,[1] and in addition the royal coffers received the substantial sum of £12,666 17s. 7d. found in Adam Stratton's house on his arrest.[2] The way in which the king allowed the guilty men to buy their freedom did not meet with the approval of the chroniclers,[3] and it seems probable that the long list given by the author of the *Mirror of Justices* of judges allegedly executed by King Alfred was a deliberate attempt to show up Edward's surprisingly lenient treatment.[4]

The administration had made great efforts under Edward to raise the money required by his policies. But although an impressive competence was displayed by the Exchequer and the subordinate officials such as tax collectors, the crown was never in a comfortable financial position. In particular, there were rarely adequate reserves of cash to meet the demands of the campaigns. Some means had to be found of providing funds when they were most needed, and the only solution was to develop a system of credit finance.

[1] *State Trials of the Reign of Edward the First, 1289–1293*, ed. T. F. Tout and H. Johnstone (Camden Soc., 3rd ser., ix, 1906), pp. xxix–xxx, xxxvi–xxxviii, and *passim*.   [2] Denholm-Young, *Seignorial Administration*, pp. 83–4.
[3] *Chron. Cotton*, p. 173; 'Annales de Oseneia', in *Annales Monastici*, iv, pp. 321–2.
[4] *The Mirror of Justices*, ed. W. J. Whittaker, introduction by F. W. Maitland (Selden Soc., vii, 1895), pp. 166–70.

IX

CREDIT FINANCE

There is no doubt that Edward I was very well aware of the importance of being adequately supplied with funds. No real budgeting was done, however, and without this it is inconceivable that any very careful consideration of the financial implications of policies could be made. There is no evidence of a proper balancing of probable expenditure against probable income. In 1284 the Exchequer did produce an estimate of revenue, but this was a result of the reorganization of the department consequent upon the Statute of Rhuddlan, and was not related to any likely costs that the government might incur.[1] In 1296 expenditure was estimated when the king demanded 60,000 infantry and 10,000 cavalry for his campaign in Scotland, and it was correctly calculated that £5,000 a week would be needed to pay such a force. No attempt was made to explain how so huge a sum was to be raised, however: the Exchequer was merely ordered to take no vacations, to cease crown building operations, and to see to collecting as much as they could from taxes, customs duties, and any other convenient sources.[2] A few years later, in 1301, a desperate plea to the Exchequer for funds was accompanied by a detailed estimate of expenditure, which was at the rate of £751 14s. 4d. a week. But in reply, the Exchequer was unable to match this precision with any estimate of future income. It knew how much of the tax of a fifteenth had been assigned away in advance, but could not state how much in all the tax was likely to raise. All it

---

[1] M. H. Mills, 'Exchequer Agenda and Estimate of Revenue, Easter Term 1284', *E.H.R.*, xl (1925), pp. 229–34.

[2] *Supra*, p. 94, n. 3; Stevenson, *Documents*, ii, pp. 20–1.

could do was to put a stop to any future assignment and direct all available funds to Scotland in the hope that they might prove sufficient.[1]

Even if realistic budgets had been produced, it is very unlikely that Edward would have allowed his plans to be altered substantially by such considerations: he was too obstinate a man. The best example of his determination to carry out his intentions in the face of extreme financial difficulties is that of the Flanders campaign of 1297. The king was resolute that this should take place, justifying it in his propaganda in terms of national necessity and of his obligations to his allies. The council expressed its alarm that he was setting out with totally inadequate funds,[2] but this did not deter him, any more than did the fact that the country was on the verge of civil war.

The obvious solution to the financial difficulties resulting from such situations was to borrow money. The normal machinery was simply not flexible enough to cope with the sudden increases in demand for cash that Edward's campaigns created. By the late thirteenth century the mechanisms of credit finance were familiar in England. In Henry III's reign loans to the crown were more and more dominated by Italian merchants. At least £54,000 was borrowed in Italy for the Sicilian adventure,[3] and on his crusade Edward became heavily indebted to the merchants of Lucca, who claimed to have advanced over £23,000. In addition, Robert Burnell in England received £7,687 from the same source.[4] It is hardly surprising to find that it was the firm of the Riccardi of Lucca who played the leading part in advancing money to the crown in the years up to 1294.

The reason for the prominence of the Italian merchants as a source of loans was simple: they had extensive resources, and had all the financial expertise of the highly developed Italian economy behind them. It was the prospects of the profits of the wool trade

[1] *Supra*, pp. 177–8; E. 159/75, m. 10.
[2] *Rôles Gascons*, iii, p. 357.
[3] *The Cambridge Economic History of Europe*, iii, ed. M. M. Postan, E. E. Rich, Edward Miller (Cambridge, 1963), p. 454.
[4] *C.P.R., 1272–81*, p. 132.

that first attracted them to England, and all the companies that advanced money to the crown were also fully engaged in trade. Documents drawn up by the Exchequer at the time of the wool seizure of 1294 provide ample indication of their activities.[1] Dealings in wool were often closely related to banking. A typical arrangement was that made in 1287 between the abbot of Meaux and the Riccardi, by which the merchants advanced 220 marks, and were to be repaid with sixty sacks of wool, to be handed over between 1290 and 1294.[2] In some instances the Italians appear as pure bankers. Roger Bigod owed the Riccardi over £1,000, and had to grant them two Irish manors in repayment.[3] Documents probably drawn up in 1294 show that one small firm, the Betti of Lucca, was owed £3,312, mostly by laymen. A note suggests that the Riccardi had debts due to them totalling £20,007, excluding the sums owed them by the crown.[4] The rich deposited their gains with the Italian bankers. The appropriation of Walter Langton's assets by the crown after his fall in 1307 revealed that the Ballardi owed him £2,120, and the Frescobaldi at least 1,000 marks and 2,000 florins.[5] In 1297 Edward seized 2,000 marks that the bishop of Winchester had deposited with the Spini.[6]

For the first part of the reign Edward I relied almost exclusively on the firm of the Riccardi of Lucca as crown bankers. In the first seven years of the reign this company had paid out over £200,000 on the king's behalf, and had been repaid all but £23,000.[7] The costs of the first Welsh war were almost exactly covered by a loan from the Riccardi.[8] The importance of the company is shown clearly by the fact that the head of the firm, Orlandino de Podio, was the one layman authorized in the Household Ordinance of

[1] G. Bigwood, 'Un marché de matières premières: laines d'Angleterre et marchands Italiens vers le fin du xiiie siècle', *Annales d'histoire économique et sociale*, 2e année, 6 (1930), p. 201; E. 159/68, mm. 86–9.
[2] Bigwood, *op. cit.*, p. 204.
[3] Denholm-Young, *Seignorial Administration*, p. 64.
[4] E. 101/126/12, 28.
[5] Beardwood, 'The Trial of Walter Langton', *Trans. American Phil. Soc.*, n.s., liv, part 3 (1964), p. 27.
[6] E. 159/71, m. 23.   [7] E. 101/126/1.
[8] Tout, *Chapters*, ii, pp. 112–13.

1279 to sleep in the Wardrobe.[1] The Riccardi did more than simply advance money to the crown. They played a prominent rôle in the collection of the fifteenth of 1275,[2] and acted as royal agents in obtaining loans from other Italian firms, being responsible in 1280 for the repayment of 17,250 marks to various merchants[3] and the negotiation of loans totalling almost £22,000 paid to the Wardrobe to finance the second Welsh war.[4] For the campaign of 1287 the Riccardi assumed the normal function of the Wardrobe, collecting funds and distributing them to paymasters in the field.[5] The crown's aggregate debt to the Riccardi for the years from 1272 until 1294 amounted to some £392,000. Not all this sum was advanced by the one firm, for it included the loans raised by the Riccardi on behalf of the crown from other companies, and an element of interest. Had Edward's credit with the Italian merchants in these years not been good, his successes in Wales would have been impossible.

The crown did not lose financially as a result of its dealings with the Riccardi. By 1276 repayments to the firm were in arrears by over £13,000, and in 1294 they were owed £18,924, which they never received. Of the repayments that were made, over £190,000 came out of the customs receipts. The fifteenth of 1275 provided some £57,000 for the merchants, and the crusading tenth £8,000. Miscellaneous sources, such as the fines on merchants who disobeyed the embargo on trade with Flanders at the outset of the reign, and the fine of Adam Stratton, made up the rest of the Riccardi's receipts.[6]

The Riccardi had played a part of the greatest significance in the financing of the Welsh wars, but Edward made no use of their resources on the outbreak of the war with Philip IV in 1294. The seizure of wool was not an act calculated to appeal to the

---

[1] *Ibid.*, p. 29. [2] *Supra*, p. 207.
[3] E. A. Bond, 'Extracts from the Liberate Rolls relative to loans supplied by Italian merchants in the thirteenth and fourteenth centuries', *Archaeologia*, xxviii (1840), pp. 280–1.
[4] E. 372/130. [5] *Supra*, p. 161.
[6] E. 101/126/1; E. 372/123, 124, 125, 133, 134, 143; *Cambridge Economic History of Europe*, iii, pp. 456–7. The figure given there of receipts of £97,000 from the fifteenth must be a misprint for £57,000.

merchants, and it looks as if the king may have decided to try to finance the war by collecting together sufficient reserves of cash, making it unnecessary to raise loans. Edward had little alternative, for Philip IV made the logical move of arresting all members of the company of the Riccardi in France and confiscating their assets. This naturally caused a catastrophic decline in confidence in the firm. Deposits were withdrawn, and bankruptcy ensued. Edward I showed no sympathy to them, but followed the example of his cousin and appropriated their assets, on the grounds that they were unable to fulfil their obligations to him. Not surprisingly no other Italian firm was to be found ready and willing to take up the position of royal bankers that the Riccardi had been forced to vacate.

Edward I's need of cash by the autumn of 1294, faced as he was by the unexpected Welsh revolt as well as the French war, was such that when the merchants proved reluctant to advance him money, he found it necessary to compel them to do so. Representatives of eight companies appeared at the Exchequer, and promised to lend a total of £12,000. Presumably they were threatened with expulsion and the confiscation of assets, while their co-operation was rewarded with the grant of export licences for their wool.[1] This loan was followed by others of the same type, described by the Chancery as being made 'for our most urgent affairs and for the advantage and defence of our realm'. Between 1294 and 1298 eleven companies yielded up £28,966 13s. 4d. in forced loans.[2] The precarious position of the companies in England was emphasized when in the autumn of 1295 arrangements were made for the seizure of the wool belonging to the Bardi, the Frescobaldi, and the companies of the Black and White Cerchi. In fact, it does not appear that their wool was appropriated by the crown.[3]

Acute as was Edward I's financial position in England between 1294 and 1298, it was much more severe abroad. Efforts had to be made to raise loans in the Low Countries and in Gascony. One obvious source was the English traders on the continent, but,

[1] *Book of Prests*, ed. Fryde, p. li; E. 159/68, mm. 64, 82d, 84.
[2] Bond, *op. cit.*, pp. 284-90. [3] E. 159/68, mm. 87-9.

faced as they were with having to pay the heavy customs duties, these men cannot have been very flush with funds. The accounts of Elias Russel, Gilbert Chesterton and the other English agents in the Low Countries suggest that at the outside perhaps £4,000 was raised from English merchants.[1] The documentation is even less complete for Gascony, although a few receipts do survive to show that English merchants did advance some small sums to the paymasters there.[2] Foreigners were a far more productive source of finance. In the Low Countries £1,200 came from Flemish traders, at least £510 from Germans, and from the Frescobaldi of Florence roughly £7,200. Other loans from Italians came to at least £1,100.[3] These loans were important, although modest in relation to the total expenditure on the war. Clearly Edward's credit worthiness had not yet recovered from the blow dealt it by the fall of the Riccardi, and it is interesting to note that the total of loans raised by him in the Low Countries was less than four per cent of those obtained there by his grandson Edward III in similar circumstances.[4] The English were more successful in Gascony. A consortium from Bayonne provided loans totalling £45,763, and there are references to at least £2,400 from other Gascon merchants, while almost £2,000 was borrowed by Henry Lacy from Spanish traders.[5] Loans probably made up about a quarter of the receipts in Gascony.

After Edward I's return to England from Flanders in 1298 the Italian firm of the Frescobaldi gradually assumed a similar position to that held by the Riccardi in the first half of the reign. It was in Flanders that this company first came to the rescue of the English king. They had not played a significant rôle in royal finance in the years of Riccardi dominance, although they were one of the major

---

[1] De Sturler, 'Deux comptes "enrôlés" de Robert de Segre', *Bull. de la comm. royale d'hist.*, cxxv (1959), pp. 594–7; Fryde, 'Financial Resources of Edward I in the Netherlands, 1294–1298', *Revue Belge*, xl (1962), p. 1176, n. 1; E. 372/146; E. 405/1/10; E. 101/684/22/7–16; E. 122/223/16; E. 122/224/15, 24, 279, 288; E. 159/70, m. 105.   [2] E. 163/2/9.

[3] E. 372/146; E. 122/55/5; E. 101/126/13/3; E. 101/126/11; E. 405/1/11. My figures differ in some particulars from those given by Fryde, *op. cit.*, p. 1176.

[4] Fryde, *op. cit.*, p. 1177.

[5] E. 101/353/21; E. 372/152b; E. 159/71 m. 49; E. 403/112.

firms operating in England: their contribution of £4,666 13s. 4d. to the forced loans was the largest from the companies involved.[1] It may have been in order to win royal favour and so obtain speedy repayment of this sum that they advanced £7,200 in Flanders, but the decision was certainly a strange one. They later regarded the decision to lend to Edward as a miscalculation, and claimed that when their connection with the English government became known in 1297 many of their depositors lost confidence and withdrew their funds. In 1302 such losses were put at 200,000 florins, roughly £30,000,[2] and in 1307 the estimate was £50,000.[3] After this, the Frescobaldi could hardly withdraw: their best chance of recouping the losses of 1297 was to make substantial profits out of lending to Edward, and to benefit from the royal favour.

How much did the Frescobaldi lend to Edward I? In 1302 they petitioned the king for payment of their debts, calculating that they had advanced a total of £32,886 9s. 4d. Most of this had been lent during the war years, for accounts show that between 1297 and 1302 they paid out roughly £13,250 on Edward I's behalf. Some repayments were made to them out of the customs, while they also had the custody of the mints of Newcastle, Hull, Exeter and Dublin. The crown debt to the firm in 1302 was probably about £20,000.[4] Unfortunately there are no fully detailed accounts for the years after 1302. Control over credit finance was gradually taken over from the Wardrobe by the Exchequer, and the best source for the later loans made by the Frescobaldi is provided by the final accounts made with the company at the Exchequer in 1310. These were not intended to provide a record of the total lent by the firm to the crown, but were primarily concerned with the money handed over to them in repayment. Not all of their

[1] Bond, op. cit., pp. 284–90.
[2] R. J. Whitwell, 'Italian Bankers and the English Crown', T.R.H.S., n.s. xvii (1903), p. 198.
[3] C. Johnson, 'A Financial House in the Fourteenth Century', Trans. St. Albans and Herts. Architectural and Archaeological Soc., i (1901), p. 332.
[4] Whitwell, op. cit., p. 198; E. 101/126/11; E. 101/126/13/3; E. 101/126/15, 21; E. 372/154.

receipts were included: they were not charged with their profits from the mints, nor with the money they received from the fifteenth of 1301. What the accounts do show is that the firm had lent at least £120,000 by 1310, and that at that date they were still owed £21,635, of which nearly £12,000 was money granted to them in recompense for the losses incurred in Edward's service. It seems probable, given the omissions in the accounts, that in all the Frescobaldi had lent some £150,000 over a period of sixteen years to Edward I and his son, of which they were repaid about £125,000.[1] But perhaps more important than discovering the totals lent and repaid is to ascertain at what level the debt to the Frescobaldi was running. As already shown, in 1302 it was roughly £20,000. In October 1305 it was estimated that the firm should be satisfied out of the customs receipts by Easter 1307,[2] which implies that Edward was in effect anticipating the customs revenue by about eighteen months. As full repayment was never achieved, since the Frescobaldi were expelled from England by the Ordainers, in purely financial terms the crown can only be considered to have benefited from its association with the firm.

Although the Frescobaldi did not receive a proper financial return for their investment in the English government, they did benefit in many ways from royal favour. It was customary for privileged merchants to be allowed to recover their debts through the Exchequer Court, just like the crown itself, and the exchequer plea rolls are full of actions brought by the Frescobaldi against monasteries who failed to meet their obligations. In Edward I's reign one of the heads of the firm, Coppuccio Cotenna, was described as a *valettus* of the Treasurer, a status whose precise implications are not clear, but which certainly allowed the firm to receive preferential treatment at the Exchequer.[3] In May 1306 the main companies in London, including the Frescobaldi, were summoned before the king's council and informed that if they left the

---

[1] E. 372/154. I have discussed these accounts in much more detail in my thesis, 'Edward I's Wars and their Financing, 1294-1307'.

[2] *C.P.R., 1301-7*, p. 395.

[3] E. 13/25, mm. 27, 47d; *Select Cases in the Exchequer of Pleas*, ed. Jenkinson and Formoy (Selden Soc., xlviii), pp. xcix, cxii–cxiii.

country, or exported any of their belongings, then all their assets would be confiscated. Security was demanded as a guarantee of their good behaviour. This was provided promptly for the Frescobaldi by William de Carleton, a baron of the Exchequer, but the other Italian firms refused to co-operate, and were only persuaded to comply with the request after a period of imprisonment in the Tower.[1]

It was under Edward II that the Frescobaldi received their most spectacular favours from the crown. In 1309 Amerigo dei Frescobaldi was granted six manors for the nominal rent of one penny, and in the next year an order was issued that all nominees of the firm to ecclesiastical offices were to be preferred to any others until they were provided with benefices to a value of £300 a year. Elaborate exemptions from tallages, aids, and burdens such as jury service were issued, and the culmination of royal favour came with the appointment of Bertus dei Frescobaldi to the king's council in 1310.[2] This generosity of Edward II's was ill-calculated. His father had been able to obtain loans without such favours being granted, and the effect of the grants was to provoke widespread resentment against the company. The opposition was anxious to remove any means that Edward II might have of achieving financial independence, and there were in addition obvious reasons for suspecting that the Italians were exercising an undue political influence. The consequent expulsion of the Frescobaldi from England by the Ordainers led to the rapid collapse of the company.

Some other Italian companies lent money to Edward I in the later years of the reign, though none on so substantial a scale as the Frescobaldi. Between 1294 and 1309 the Bardi lent £3,906 19s. 9d., of which £2,736 was taken by compulsion. By 1312 they had been repaid all but £431 5s. 4d.[3] An account of the Spini which survives in bad condition, and appears to date from the early years of Edward II, shows loans to Edward I and his son totalling almost £7,740.[4] The Ballardi of Lucca were the merchants regularly used by the Great Wardrobe, and they also lent money to the prince of Wales. Advances by this company between 1298 and 1307 totalled

[1] E. 159/79, m. 34d. [2] *C.P.R., 1307–13*, pp. 152, 294, 321, 305.
[3] E. 372/158. [4] E. 101/127/23.

£7,493 12s. 7d.; in repayment they received only £4,021 15s. 8d.[1]

As had been the case with the Riccardi, the customs receipts proved to be the most convenient source of revenue from which to repay the merchants who lent to the crown. During the years of the war with France the need for revenue was such that the government could not afford to pledge the customs to its creditors extensively, and most of the receipts were paid directly into the Exchequer: £11,183 out of a total of £14,088 in the case of Yarmouth, to give one example. But once the years of acute emergency were over, the pattern changed. Until Whitsun 1299 the customs revenues were used to repay the firms which had been forced to lend to the crown in the wartime period.[2] They were then handed over to the consortium of Bayonne merchants who had advanced so much in Gascony. They lent a further £4,333 6s. 8d. in England, and were granted £1,000 to cover their expenses while staying there. They were paid almost £51,700 in all, and ended with a deficit of only £56:[3] of all the merchants who lent to Edward I they did by far the best. Possibly the reason for this was political. The king would not wish to alienate his Gascon subjects, while it mattered far less if Italians went unpaid. Once the men of Bayonne were satisfied, the customs revenues, now enhanced by the introduction of the New Custom, were paid over to the Frescobaldi, who continued to receive by far the greater part of them until their expulsion from England. It should be stressed that in granting the customs to these various merchants the crown was not farming out an important source of revenue. Royal officials remained at the ports and the payment of receipts to the merchants was strictly supervised. In allocating resources in this way the government was not losing revenue as was all too possible when a system of farming such as that practised by the Tudors and Stuarts was adopted.

It was hard to raise loans outside the merchant community. Some magnates and officials advanced money on the Welsh campaign of 1282-3, Burnell producing 1,000 marks, John Kirkby £548, John de Bohun £980 and Robert Tiptoft 290 marks.[4] In

[1] E. 101/127/7. [2] E. 372/145, m. 30.
[3] E. 372/152B. [4] E. 372/130.

1284–5 Burnell lent Edward 2,300 marks.[1] But in the later years of the reign Edward's ministers and councillors, well aware of the financial situation, were too wary to lend in circumstances that, at best, meant that payment would be dilatory. In 1299 Edmund of Cornwall was promised repayment of a loan of 2,000 marks out of the proceeds of the first episcopal vacancy to come up.[2] Two years later his executors advanced 1,300 marks,[3] but otherwise no major loans from such sources appear on the records for this period. During campaigns it was common for small sums to be entered on the wardrobe accounts as loans, but these transactions appear to have been more in the nature of book-keeping formalities than true loans.

On one occasion the government resorted to a forced loan from its English subjects. At the very beginning of the war with France, early in July 1294,[4] royal commissioners were sent round the country to seize all the private deposits of money in churches: £10,795 was sent in to the Exchequer.[5] Powicke has attempted to justify this action on the grounds that it was intended to preserve the purity of the coinage, but no chronicle or official source contains anything to support this assertion.[6] The king denied responsibility for the measure, which was extremely unpopular, blaming William March, the Treasurer. This, together with complaints brought against him by the Londoners, led to his dismissal in the following year.[7] Demand for repayment of the money seized in 1294 was made in parliament in 1305,[8] and one issue roll of the

---

[1] E. 372/136.
[2] Howell, *Regalian Right in Medieval England*, p. 160. It is an interesting reflection on the state of the royal finances at the end of the reign that it was not until 1299 that revenue from episcopal vacancies was pledged in advance in this way.   [3] *C.P.R., 1292–1301*, p. 596; E. 159/80, m. 20.
[4] The chroniclers do not agree on the date. *Chron. Cotton*, p. 238, has 27 June, *Chron. Guisborough*, p. 248, has 4 July, while *Flores Historiarum*, iii, p. 274, gives 11 July.   [5] *Book of Prests*, ed. Fryde, p. li.
[6] Powicke, *The Thirteenth Century*, pp. 670–1; M. C. Prestwich, 'Edward I's Monetary Policies and their Consequences', *Ec.H.R.*, 2nd ser., xxii (1969), pp. 410–11.
[7] *Select Cases before the King's Council 1243–1482*, ed. I. S. Leadam and J. F. Balwin (Selden Soc., xxxv, 1918), pp. li–lvi.   [8] *Rot. Parl.*, i, p. 165.

Exchequer shows that at least £2,003 was restored.[1] Not surprisingly, the expedient was not repeated.

There is no doubt that the advances made by the Riccardi were of the very greatest value to Edward I. In a situation where heavy expenditure for a short period was envisaged, as was the case with the Welsh campaigns, it made very good sense to borrow money and then repay it over a longer period. But in the years after 1294 warfare was more or less continuous. Even though the prospects of a long war with France were perhaps remote, it must have been clear that the situation in Scotland was bound to absorb royal revenue for many years, either in the form of constant campaigns, or in the construction of castles and the upkeep of an occupation force. The prospect was not an attractive one for the potential lender, since future demands on revenue would inevitably diminish the chances of repayment. It is not surprising, therefore, to find that while the Riccardi were owed £392,000 for the loans they made before 1294, on a generous calculation Edward probably borrowed no more than £250,000 from all sources in England, Gascony and the Low Countries between 1294 and 1307, despite the fact that his financial needs were very much greater in these years.

It is clear that the surprisingly low level of borrowing in Edward I's later years was not the result of a government decision, but was rather the consequence of reluctance on the part of the merchants. In January 1297 Walter Langton and several others were authorized to raise a loan of £7,500,[2] but in fact less than £4,000 was collected.[3] In August 1301 letters of credence were issued for John Droxford to approach five Italian firms, presumably about loans.[4] None were forthcoming. In that year only the Bayonne merchants and the Frescobaldi were co-operative, the former with an advance of £2,000,[5] the latter with one of 400 marks.[6] The low state of royal credit at this time is demonstrated by the handing of jewels to the Bayonne merchants as security.

[1] E. 403/1322.   [2] *C.P.R., 1292–1301*, p. 226.
[3] Bond, 'Extracts from the Liberate Rolls', *Archaeologia*, xxviii (1840), pp. 286–90.
[4] *C.C.R., 1296–1302*, p. 463.   [5] E. 101/9/20.   [6] E. 101/126/21.

In Ireland the Justiciar and Treasurer were ordered to ask for loans to pay for the war in Scotland, but it was only possible to obtain money from the merchants there by seizing it.[1] Similar problems were encountered in 1303. Once again Droxford was sent south to negotiate a loan, with a credence directed to all foreign merchants, to the City authorities and to the collectors of the papal tenths.[2] Of all the merchants, the Frescobaldi alone responded to the appeal, and even they only paid out rather less than £2,000 in the period from August 1303 to January 1304.[3] The papal tax collectors produced £4,500, but this was hardly a loan, as it went to make up the king's share of the tax.[4] In Ireland royal envoys approached the company of the Spini. The merchants refused to lend any money until they had full authority from their London branch, together with guarantees of repayment, and they were clearly content when these delaying tactics proved successful.[5]

Despite such difficulties, and although the situation in the latter years of the reign with constant campaigns was not as favourable as that of the period of the Welsh wars, it is clear that the advantages of using the Italian bankers outweighed the disadvantages. As full payment was not made during Edward's reign to those who advanced money, with only a few exceptions, the crown did not lose in the strict financial sense. At times, notably in 1301, the crown was hampered because important sources of revenue had been pledged to repay loans. Edward I never, however, regarded such grants as those of the customs revenues as inviolable. Several mandates were issued to the Frescobaldi ordering them to make payments out of the customs that they alone were intended to receive, and when, in 1306, there was urgent need of money for Scotland, the Irish customs were simply removed from the hands of the merchants in order to pay for purveyance.[6]

The Italian bankers were more than mere suppliers of funds to

---

[1] *C.P.R., 1292–1301*, p. 595; *C.C.R., 1296–1302*, pp. 448–9. It is not known how much money was taken.

[2] *C.P.R., 1301–7*, p. 153.   [3] E. 101/126/23.

[4] *C.P.R., 1301–7*, pp. 158, 162–3; Lunt, *Financial Relations of the Papacy with England to 1327*, p. 676.   [5] E. 101/8/4, m. 3.

[6] *C.P.R., 1301–7*, pp. 399, 433, 459, 536; *C.C.R., 1302–7*, p. 379.

the crown. These companies were the exponents of the most advanced commercial techniques of the age, possessing facilities that the government could take advantage of, and methods from which it might learn. A comparison of the accounting practices of the Wardrobe with those of the merchants shows considerable similarities. Both wrote their accounts in books, not rolls, and the same organization of receipts in the first section and payments in the second is found.[1] It is very possible that Edward I's officials derived some of their ideas on this subject from the Riccardi and the Frescobaldi. Orlandino de Podio was particularly well placed to impart Italian ideas to the Wardrobe clerks.[2]

With their widespread international connections the Italian bankers could make payment in any country or currency by the use of bills of exchange, and these financial skills were taken advantage of by the government. So it was possible for Edward I to use the Frescobaldi to pay 1,500 marks in florins to the Burgundian nobles in Florence in 1298.[3] In 1301 when Otto de Grandson was in Rome as a royal envoy he was paid £100 by the Frescobaldi agents there on the strength of a letter of credit.[4] The Spini were used a little later to pay the expenses of Cardinal Walter Winterbourne, Edward's former confessor, at Rome.[5] Even at home it was extremely convenient for Edward I to have the services of the Italian firms. The highly significant part played by the Riccardi in the Welsh wars has already been pointed out, but the firm was also used for much smaller transactions, such as making payments to the papal nuncio Geoffrey de Vezzano,[6] or even paying four miners to go to Guernsey to look for silver mines.[7] The Ballardi were one of the main suppliers of goods to the Great Wardrobe, and in 1303 the same firm was used to carry money from London to Scotland.[8] The Frescobaldi paid out funds to and on behalf of the government all over the country. In 1300

---

[1] A good example of Italian accounting methods of this period is *Les livres des comptes des Gallerani*, ed. G. Bigwood and A. Grunzweig (Acad. Royale de Belgique, Comm. royale d'histoire, 1961–2).
[2] *Supra*, pp. 206–7.   [3] C. 47/13/1/28.   [4] E. 101/126/21.
[5] C. 47/4/4, f. 41; *C.P.R., 1301–7*, p. 366.
[6] E. 372/175, Riccardi account.   [7] E. 372/143.
[8] E. 101/127/7; E. 101/364/13, f. 34.

Ralph Manton borrowed 500 marks from them at Newcastle, and in 1303 they were advancing money at York.[1] The firm was used to pay off royal debtors, thus relieving royal officials who could devote themselves to more important matters. On occasion the Frescobaldi were even to be found supplying royal victualling officers in Scotland with grain.[2] Such examples could be multiplied almost indefinitely, but these few should make it clear that the agents of these Italian companies provided valuable assistance to the overworked royal administration.

Perhaps the main danger of relying to such an extent on the Italians was political. Aliens were never popular in England, and a group who were fulfilling some of the functions that had traditionally been performed by the Jews was likely to provoke considerable hostility. As the crisis of the Ordinances was to show, the Italians were an obvious target for attack. But at the time of the major crisis of Edward I's reign, in 1297, no clear replacement for the Riccardi had emerged. Most of the money that had been borrowed from the Italians since 1294 had been taken in forced loans, and there was obviously no sense accusing the merchants of exercising any sinister influence on the king. Later in the reign there were no protests against the Frescobaldi, but it seems probable that bitterness against them was building up, to come to a head in 1311. Although Edward I himself did not suffer the repercussions of his financial policy in this respect, the obligations to the Italians that he incurred were to prove a troublesome legacy to his son.

The absence of a proper budgeting system and the unwillingness of the king to limit his objectives to accord with the scale of his financial resources meant that the rôle of the merchant bankers was of the greatest importance. In the years up to 1294 it appears that the Riccardi were able to advance sufficient cash to enable the deficits to be met, but in the succeeding years the increase in expenditure, combined with the reluctance of the merchants to lend, meant that the financial situation was far more critical. One indication of the problem facing the government is the lack of

[1] E. 101/676/57/4; E. 101/126/23.
[2] E. 101/676/57/5; C. 47/35/10/10.

cash supplies in the later years of the reign revealed in the accounts. In the Welsh war of 1294–5 it had been possible to despatch sums of as much as £5,000 in single consignments to the paymasters.[1] In comparison, the largest sum sent to the army by the Exchequer between July and November 1301 was £1,000, and this was in response to a desperate plea for cash.[2] The wardrobe journal for the last year of Edward I's reign shows that the balance of cash in hand only once exceeded £1,000, at Christmas 1306, following the receipt of 2,000 marks. The amount was usually far lower.[3] Obviously the main reason for the lack of money was simply that resources were inadequate, and that lenders were unable or unwilling to make up the deficits fully. But there were in addition administrative reasons for the situation.

The practice of the Wardrobe of granting bills and debentures to its creditors, which could then be exchanged at a local level with sheriffs, tax collectors, or other receivers of royal revenue, meant that very little cash was collected by the Exchequer. The reforms of the early 1290s, which had been intended to reduce the independence of the Wardrobe and make it directly dependent on the Exchequer for funds, had been effectively circumvented by the device of these bills. Wardrobe officials and wardrobe creditors took charge of receipts before they ever reached the Exchequer, and all that department could do was to enter the payments on its records. It had no means of controlling the disbursement of revenue, and most serious of all, had no powers to limit the Wardrobe's issue of bills and debentures.[4] It was this situation that made any effective budgeting impossible.

Attempts were made to deal with the problem. In 1301 orders were issued to the sheriffs asking them to pay in their farms to the Exchequer at the end of June rather than at Michaelmas, and it was clearly government policy to have them make their payments in cash at York, where the Exchequer was then situated. But in fact only slightly over £3,000 was collected, and the expedient was

---

[1] *Book of Prests*, ed. Fryde, pp. 226–7.
[2] E. 101/9/20, p. 4.   [3] E. 101/370/16.
[4] M. C. Prestwich, 'Exchequer and Wardrobe in the later years of Edward I', *B.I.H.R.*, forthcoming.

not repeated.[1] Then, in 1304, all the sheriffs, bailiffs and others assembled for the Michaelmas profer in the Exchequer were told that in future no money was to be paid over to the Wardrobe unless specifically ordered in a royal writ.[2] When Walter Langton went abroad in 1305 and John Droxford took over his office of Treasurer on a temporary basis, rules were laid down for systematic regular payments to be made by the Exchequer to the royal household.[3] These reforms were all ineffective: the pressure of wartime needs was such that expenditure could not be kept in step with income. If there was no cash to pay creditors, then the only solution was to issue them with wardrobe bills or debentures. No administrative solutions could solve the basic problem that the crown's revenues were simply inadequate to meet its needs.

WARDROBE RECEIPTS AND EXPENSES[4]

Date	Receipt £ s. d.	Expenditure £ s. d.
1293–4	65,801 4 $1\frac{1}{2}$[5]	67,827 2 11
1294–5	124,792 9 $5\frac{1}{2}$	138,255 12 10
1295–6	105,324 4 1	83,648 0 $0\frac{1}{2}$
1296–7	106,356 12 $6\frac{1}{2}$	119,519 9 $4\frac{1}{2}$
1297–8	39,826 15 $0\frac{1}{2}$	78,549 4 6
1298–9	–	–
1299–1300	58,155 16 2	64,105 0 5[6]
1300–1	47,550 12 11	77,291 7 $7\frac{1}{2}$
1301–2	72,969 6 $1\frac{1}{4}$	61,949 6 $5\frac{1}{4}$[7]
1302–3	52,195 14 $0\frac{3}{4}$	64,036 11 1[8]
1303–4	–	68,958 5 3
1304–5	–	–
1305–6	64,128 3 $1\frac{1}{2}$	77,318 15 $10\frac{1}{4}$

[1] E. 159/75, m. 58d; M. H. Mills, 'Adventus Vicecomitum, 1272–1307', E.H.R., xxxviii (1923), p. 340.   [2] E. 159/78, m. 20.
[3] J. F. Willard, 'Ordinances for the guidance of a Deputy Treasurer, 22 October 1305', E.H.R., xlviii (1933), pp. 84–9.
[4] Unless otherwise stated, these figures are taken from Tout, Chapters, vi, pp. 80–3.
[5] Tout, ibid., has misread this figure from the account in E. 372/144.
[6] Liber Quotidianus, p. 360.   [7] E. 101/360/25.   [8] E. 101/364/14.

The inevitable consequence of this situation was that many of the Wardrobe's creditors went unpaid. A comparison of wardrobe receipts with the expenditure incurred by the department makes the position plain (see p. 220).

The accounts from which these figures are drawn are not totally reliable: some are drafts, and the infantry wages for 1303 are not found in the account for that year, but in the subsequent one. Accounts for the royal hunting establishment of the whole period from 1300 were all put together in the 1306 account. But the overall position is quite clear. The accounts showed a surplus of income over expenditure in only two years, 1296 and 1302. Over the whole period there was a substantial deficit. For the first three years of Droxford's keepership, from November 1295 until 1298, two sources show that the debt was in the region of £30,000.[1] The usual figure cited for the end of the reign is £60,000,[2] but this is taken from an account book made up in the late 1320s, and represents the sum still owing at that date. Early in Edward II's reign liberate writs were made out to John Droxford in his capacity as Keeper of Edward I's Wardrobe to a total of £118,000, of which £56,000 went to the Frescobaldi for the loans they had advanced. In addition, liberate writs were issued for £28,000 to pay the debts of the prince of Wales and £8,500 for money still owing to some Gascons for their service in the war. These debts were largely paid off in the course of Edward II's reign, so together with the £60,000 still owing in the late 1320s, it would seem that the total debt in 1307 must have been approximately £200,000.[3]

No particular group seems to have been treated worse than any other: all those who had dealings with the crown had reason to regret its insolvency. The judges petitioned in parliament in 1305 for payment of their wages. A general demand was made for the repayment of all those owed money for military service, for the seizure of private treasure from the churches in 1294, and the

[1] E. 372/144; E. 101/354/5.
[2] Tout, *Chapters*, ii, p. 125.
[3] Bond, *op. cit.*, pp. 247-9; E. 101/373/22. The date of the account showing debts of about £60,000, E. 101/357/15, is indicated by a reference to a Pipe Roll of 18 Edward II on f. 22.

prises of grain and wool. Even men of such lowly standing as the inhabitants of Roxburgh who had supplied Edward's soldiers with victuals presented petitions at this parliament.[1] The accounts of debts kept by the Wardrobe give a similar impression of payments owed to all and sundry. Such an important man as Aymer de Valence had to wait until 1322 to obtain part payment of wages due to him for the 1307 campaign.[2] The two Spanish household knights, Jaime, señor de Gerica, and Pascual of Valencia, petitioned vigorously for payment of what they were owed, but had to be content with grants of £200 and £100 respectively in 1305, made on condition that they ceased making any further demands.[3]

By the end of Edward I's reign the crown finances were in a chaotic state. No wardrobe accounts for the years since 1298 had been enrolled on the Pipe Rolls by the Exchequer; either they had not been presented or were found unsatisfactory. Attempts were still being made in the early years of Edward III's reign to put them in order.[4] No effective control was exercised over the level of expenditure, and debts were spiralling. The situation was not improved by the unfortunate incident of the robbery of plate and jewels from the treasury in Westminster in 1303.[5] But despite this gloomy picture much had been achieved in the course of the reign by Edward's financial advisers. The pattern of customs duties had been established with the Ancient Custom of 1275, the *maltolt* of 1294 and the New Custom of 1303, and was not to be changed fundamentally for the rest of the medieval period. Taxes on moveables had been developed into an essential fiscal expedient. The attempts to make use of tallage and a feudal aid in the last years of the reign had shown that there was little future in prerogative forms of taxation. It was clear that the consent and goodwill of the community of the realm was essential if adequate supplies of funds were to be forthcoming, and the importance of

[1] *Memoranda de Parliamento, 1305*, pp. 49–50, 103–4, 129–30, 169–71.
[2] E. 101/373/22.   [3] E. 175/1/17; E. 101/366/17.
[4] Tout, *Chapters*, ii, pp. 128–9; E. 159/103, mm. 185, 192d; E. 159/104, mm. 180d, 181, 239; E. 159/105, m. 183d.
[5] Tout, *Chapters*, ii, pp. 54–8. It does not seem that much was irrevocably lost as a result of the robbery.

Edward's financial expedients in promoting a system of parliamentary representation is self-evident. Considerable administrative reforms at the Exchequer had been carried out with the Statute of Rhuddlan of 1284 and with March's work in the early 1290s. The level of debt by the end of the reign bears witness to the failure of the government to match its aims to its resources, yet Edward's ministers were not irresponsible men. They did not resort to debasement of the coinage, and they did not aggravate the political situation by unpopular fiscal measures once the lesson of 1297 had been learnt. Although the administrative and financial achievement was in many ways remarkable, given the immense burden that Edward's wars placed on the machinery of government, it was inevitable that the king would find himself facing a considerable body of criticism and opposition.

X

THE CROWN AND THE MAGNATES

The reign of Edward I has been interpreted in terms of the transformation of England from a feudal into a national state. According to Powicke, 'Much can be said for the view that, as the common law had welded what is called the feudal system into the community, so under the stress of war and taxation, the community was enlarged to comprehend the people as a whole'.[1] But the pressure of demands for men, money and materials can divide nations as well as unite them. Edward had at his disposal a complex administrative machine, through which he could mobilize very considerable resources in support of his ambitious military policies. But in doing this he faced political as well as administrative problems. There was a major constitutional crisis in 1297, and the king bequeathed a troubled legacy of political discontent and financial insolvency to his son.

The group whose support was most essential to Edward in his military ventures was the magnates. The view that his reign saw the conversion of the incoherent feudal host into a national paid army has been shown to be based on a misreading of the evidence. An important element in his armies was that of the unpaid, non-feudal service of the magnates. What means did Edward have of cajoling, persuading and forcing them to join him in the great military enterprises of the reign?

It has been said, with considerable justification, that Edward I

---

[1] Powicke, *The Thirteenth Century*, p. 528.

'preferred masterfulness to the arts of political management'.[1] Some of his policies were certainly designed more with the intention of asserting his authority over the magnates than of winning their co-operation. Most notable was the series of *Quo Warranto* enquiries conducted in the years up to 1294. There was nothing novel in using this writ to call magnates to provide evidence in the courts of the rights by which they held their franchises. Henry III's government had investigated such liberties in a very similar way.[2] What was new was the systematic approach of Edward I and his advisers. On the king's return from his crusade in 1274 a remarkably comprehensive enquiry into the local administration of England was carried out. The object was to provide the government with the full possession of facts that was required if effective reforms were to be carried out. The enquiry covered a wide range of matters, and one result of the study of the returns, which were known as the Hundred Rolls, was the Statute of Westminster I, issued early in 1275. The Hundred Rolls suggested that further investigation of the franchises was needed, for in many cases the jurors had stated that they did not know by what right magnates were exercising rights of local jurisdiction.[3] The detailed story of the proceedings has been well and fully told by Professor Sutherland, and needs no repeating. The initial plan was over-ambitious. The scheme of having the cases heard in parliament was found quite impracticable, so massive was the amount of business, and at the Gloucester parliament of August 1278 the whole matter of enquiring into the franchises was transferred to the general eyres.

In the early stages of the *Quo Warranto* proceedings one man was singled out for special treatment. Gilbert de Clare, earl of Gloucester, was considered to have profited greatly by the usurpation of royal franchises in the confused situation of the Barons'

---

[1] K. B. McFarlane, 'Had Edward I a "Policy" towards the earls?', *History*, l (1965), p. 159.

[2] H. M. Cam, *Liberties and Communities in Medieval England* (2nd ed., 1963), p. 175.

[3] D. W. Sutherland, *Quo Warranto Proceedings in the reign of Edward I* (Oxford, 1963), p. 20.

Wars. Possibly Edward was attempting to revenge himself on the earl for the rôle that he had played in the late 1260s. The Exchequer drew up a special list from the evidence of the Hundred Rolls, detailing the earl's alleged usurpations, a measure not taken in any other case.[1] Gloucester was driven to protest in 1278, and petitioned in parliament that year to be allowed peaceful possession of his franchises,[2] but the king was not sympathetic. A vigorous attack continued, and a surprising amount was recovered from the earl. Five of the eight *Quo Warranto* actions brought in Kent in 1279 were against him. The famous story of resistance to the enquiry is generally told of Earl Warenne. It is said that when asked by the justices to state by what warrant he held his lands, he produced an old rusty sword and said 'Here, my lords, is my warrant', claiming that he held his lands by conquest as his ancestor had been a companion of William I. The story is a surprising one to be attributed to Warenne, who seems to have co-operated with the proceedings, and was not the type of man to threaten to defend his lands with the sword against anyone who tried to take them from him. But two versions attribute the incident to Gloucester, and although it bears the marks of being a popular legend, it seems very plausible in his case.[3]

The problem raised by the earl, whether Gloucester or Warenne, in claiming his franchises by right of conquest was a considerable one. For no hard and fast rules had been laid down by Edward or his council to determine which claims were to be accepted and which denied. Difficult cases were constantly postponed and referred to parliament, so a vast backlog of business built up. In 1279 the justices had stated that franchises could be claimed by tenure from time out of mind, but in 1280 William of Gislingham, representing the crown, contended that long tenure could not be claimed as a warrant for franchises. Judgement was reserved in such cases. Eventually, in 1290, Gilbert of Thornton and the other justices of the King's Bench ruled in favour of the arguments that had been set out earlier by Gislingham.[4] This naturally disturbed

---

[1] *Ibid.*, pp. 146–7.   [2] *Rot. Parl.*, i, p. 8.
[3] *Chron. Guisborough*, pp. 216, 259, note j; Cam, *op. cit.*, pp. 176–7.
[4] Sutherland, *op. cit.*, pp. 180–1.

the magnates, and at the Easter parliament the issue was settled, largely in their favour. In the Statute of *Quo Warranto* it was stated that the king was prepared to confirm in their tenure by letters patent all those who had held their franchises continuously from at least 1189. This preserved intact the Bractonian theory that all franchises were held of the king, and that their holders were merely exercising delegated authority. But, in a summary of the statute that was regarded as authoritative by the courts, prescriptive claims dating from before the accession of Richard I were accepted as valid without the need for any confirmation by Edward I. Plainly this was in practice more sensible than the procedure set out in the statute, even if it did mean a theoretical diminution of the crown's authority.[1] Cases of *Quo Warranto* continued to be heard in the eyres up to 1294, when on account of the war in Gascony all proceedings were halted, not to be resumed in the rest of the reign.[2]

The *Quo Warranto* proceedings were 'always slow, usually incomplete, and often futile'.[3] But they do illustrate the aggressive nature of Edward's government, even if they also demonstrate the way in which it was not always possible to translate intentions into effective action. Part of the object of the enquiry was obviously the recovery of a multitude of usurped franchises. But it also served the purpose of establishing royal authority over the exercise of franchisal justice, emphasizing the power of the crown. The recovery of franchises was a matter of political, rather than financial importance to Edward, since it reduced the authority of men such as the earl of Gloucester. The stress placed on Bractonian theories of kingship by the royal attorneys was a development of Henry III's autocratic ideas.[4] It may be that Gislingham and Thornton pressed their arguments further than the king intended, for there is certainly no indication that Edward was ever aiming at a general revocation of franchisal rights, but it is quite clear that in official circles the concept of kingship was one where the king ruled, rather than co-operated with, his magnates.

[1] *Ibid.*, pp. 91–9.   [2] *Ibid.*, p. 30.   [3] *Ibid.*, p. 188.
[4] M. T. Clanchy, 'Did Henry III have a Policy?' *History*, liii (1968), pp. 208–210.

A further indication of the government's attitude to franchises is provided by the treatment of urban liberties. London was taken into the king's hands in 1285, following the protest of the mayor at an apparent extension of royal judicial authority over the city. It was ruled through a warden appointed by Edward for the next thirteen years, and rights of self-government were only restored in return for 2,000 marks. Edward's hostility to London was of course of long standing, going back to the years of the Barons' War. Even the highly-favoured town of Hull, acquired from Meaux abbey, was not granted full self-government, but was ruled by royal officials. Bristol was fined £500 by the king in 1285, and in 1294 was taken into his hands. York was deprived of its rights of self-government between 1280 and 1282, and again in 1297. Other towns that received similar treatment in the course of the reign included Newcastle-upon-Tyne and Canterbury. In addition to such measures, smaller towns were losing their burghal status, as the crown gained new methods of defining their status with the introduction of a double rate of taxation, higher for towns and ancient demesnes than for the rest of the country, and as urban representation developed in parliament. The franchises of the towns were not destroyed by the government, but they were undoubtedly being eroded.[1]

It is striking that when Edward I most needed the support of the magnates, at the beginning of his struggle with Philip IV, a far more considerable opponent than Llywelyn of Wales had been, he should have abandoned the *Quo Warranto* enquiries. However the courts chose to treat these actions, they could never have been welcome to the possessors of franchises. Another change of policy took place in 1294 that was plainly the result of the alteration in the situation resulting from the French war. Part of the enquiry of 1274 was concerned with the question of whether tenants-in-chief had alienated any of the fees they held of the crown. In a royal ordinance of 1256 such alienations had been brought under crown control: they could only be made by special licence. The concern

[1] Williams, *Medieval London*, pp. 251–61; J. W. F. Hill, *Medieval Lincoln* (Cambridge, 1965), p. 213; *C.P.R., 1281–92*, pp. 41, 178; *C.F.R., 1272–1307*, pp. 45, 75, 130; E. 159/67, m. 31; E. 159/68, m. 41; E. 159/70, m. 62d.

of the crown was not with the military aspects of feudalism, for as has been shown, this was of no great importance in the later thirteenth century. Rather, the purpose of the ordinance was to protect the royal rights to the profitable feudal incidents of wardship and marriage. In the first part of his reign Edward I enforced this policy rigidly. Between 1272 and 1294 only fifty licences to alienate were issued to tenants-in-chief, and when it was discovered that an unlicensed alienation had taken place, the land in question was taken into the crown's hands until satisfaction had been made. From 1294 to 1307 no less than 294 licences were issued. Clearly Edward's attitude changed radically, and it seems that the reason was his need for support for his military policies. Of the thirty-one licences issued in 1294, no fewer than fifteen were granted to men who it was stated were going to Gascony on the king's service.[1]

The magnates felt justly aggrieved that while the crown rigidly controlled alienations made by tenants-in-chief, these latter had no power to control alienations made by their own mesne tenants. This grievance was partly met by the Statute of *Quia Emptores*, issued in the July parliament of 1290. This put an end to further sub-infeudation, permitting instead the practice of substitution should a mesne tenant wish to alienate some of his land. In this way the tenant-in-chief preserved his rights to the feudal incidents. But *Quia Emptores* did not apply to the relations between the crown and the tenants-in-chief, and it was only by the grant of licences to alienate that Edward could satisfy the demands of the great magnates.[2]

Attempts to categorize the legislation of Edward I in class terms, or as 'feudal' or 'anti-feudal' are doomed to failure. The intention was to clarify the law, and to remedy specific grievances, but no one group was consistently favoured. Although much of the legislation dealing with the vexed question of the relations between lords and tenants served to protect the latter from undue oppression, measures were also devised to put an end to various devious tricks by which tenants were able to evade their obligations

[1] J. M. W. Bean, *The Decline of English Feudalism* (Manchester, 1968), pp. 66–79. [2] *Ibid.*, pp. 79–103.

to do services. In one well-known case, that of *De Donis Conditionalibus*, the first clause of Westminster II, the intention was to protect the interest of donors by making entails of land more secure, but amendment of the initial draft thwarted this to a considerable extent. In neither draft nor amendment, however, can any direct political purpose be assumed.[1]

Edward himself was not the kind of man to concern himself with the inevitably technical aspects of legal reform. It may be that the guiding influence in the legal reforms was that of Robert Burnell. He had been in Edward's service since at least 1260, and on two occasions the king attempted to have him elected as archbishop of Canterbury: he was clearly of very great importance as a royal adviser until his death in 1292.[2] But the man who can be linked most closely with the process of legal reform is Ralph Hengham, Chief Justice of King's Bench, whose family was connected by marriage with Burnell's. Not only do Hengham's own writings betray a very close acquaintance with the new statutes, but his epitaph and statements attributed both to himself and to other justices in the Year Books also suggest he played a leading part.[3] The king's own attitude to the law is suggested by an incident when he was presiding in parliament over a case brought against Isabella de Redvers. Her attorney objected to the summons that she had been sent, on the grounds that it did not specify the charges being brought. Two justices were prepared to uphold the writ, but Hengham argued strongly against them. Edward, plainly impatient with their arguments, interrupted, saying 'I have nothing to do with your disputations, but, God's blood! you shall give me a good writ before you arise hence.'[4] The remark characterizes Edward's view of legal reform: the details were the

[1] T. F. T. Plucknett, *Legislation of Edward I* (Oxford, 1949), pp. 50-76, 131-5.
[2] Burnell's career has been studied by U. W. Hughes, 'A Biographical Sketch of Robert Burnell, with materials for his life' (Oxford University B.Litt. thesis, 1936).
[3] *Radulphi de Hengham Summae*, ed. W. H. Dunham jr. (Cambridge, 1932), pp. xlviii, lxiv-lxv.
[4] *Year Books, 3 Edward II, 1309-10*, ed. F. W. Maitland (Selden Soc., xx, 1905), pp. 196-7.

responsibility of his justices and clerks, while his concern was simply to get his own way.

A study of *Quo Warranto* and of the grants of licences to alienate suggests that the policies adopted towards the aristocracy were more aggressive in the years up to 1294 than in the later part of the reign. But although few new legal procedures were introduced in the latter years, Edward had quite sufficient weapons at his disposal to continue to challenge some of the great franchise holders. One target was the Welsh Marcher lords. The success of the Welsh wars had depended to a considerable extent on the co-operation of these men, but once success had been achieved in the wars, Edward could afford to adopt a much more rigorous attitude towards them.

The king had in his youth witnessed the vital rôle performed by the Marcher lords in the politics and campaigns of the Barons' Wars. Their military power was considerable, and in addition the liberties they enjoyed placed them in a very special position. The king's writ did not run in the Marcher lands; the only jurisdiction that the crown could claim was over advowsons, and in cases where there was a disputed claim to a lordship. The unique powers and privileges of the Marchers, inherited from the Welsh rulers whose lands the Normans had conquered,[1] were left largely unchallenged by Edward I in the *Quo Warranto* enquiries.[2] The king might challenge the greatest of the Marchers, Gilbert de Clare, over his English franchises, but he could not afford to face the united opposition of all the Marcher lords that an attack on the great Clare liberty of Glamorgan would probably have provoked.

Edward I made his attitude to the extensive liberties of the Welsh Marches plain early in the reign. In the Statute of Westminster I it was stated that 'in the marches of Wales, or in any other place where the king's writ runs not, then the king who is sovereign

---

[1] A. J. Otway-Ruthven, 'The Constitutional Position of the Great Lordships of South Wales', *T.R.H.S.*, 5th ser., viii (1958), pp. 1–20; J. G. Edwards, 'The Normans and the Welsh March', *Proc. Brit. Acad.*, xlii (1956).

[2] An exception was the Herefordshire eyre of 1292; Sutherland, *op. cit.*, p. 114, n. 3.

lord shall do right therein unto all such as will complain'. Clearly the king was not of a mind to accept limitations on his authority, even if they were justified by custom.[1] Two cases from the year 1281, however, do not suggest that in the period of the conquest of Wales the king was prepared to antagonize the Marchers by an enthusiastic application of this doctrine. In one, some citizens of Hereford complained that the earl of Hereford's officials had distrained upon their property in contravention of royal statute. The earl asserted that the king's statutes had no validity within his lands. Edward might have been expected to react vigorously to such a challenge, but although Hereford was summoned before the King's Bench, and his lands in Essex attached, the case seems to have been allowed to drop. The other case saw the earl of Gloucester summoned before the king to answer an accusation made by William de Braose, to the effect that his bailiffs had assaulted William on the king's highway. The earl claimed that he was not answerable for the case in the royal courts, as it had occurred within his liberty of Glamorgan. Once again there was no proper conclusion: the crown does not seem to have answered Gloucester's claim that he held his lands by conquest, and that he ought not to have to reply without the deliberation of the other Marcher lords.[2]

The defeat and death of Llywelyn at Orewin Bridge late in 1282 took the heart out of the Welsh resistance. In June 1283 his brother Dafydd was taken, and the conquest of Wales was achieved, though revolts necessitated further campaigns in 1287 and 1294–5. The issue of the Statute of Wales in 1284, which extended an English-style administration and legal system to Wales, marked the end of formal Welsh independence. No longer was there any strategic reason for the continued existence of the Marcher lordships, nor was it still necessary for the king to woo the support of the Marchers. Rather, their strength and independence represented a considerable potential threat to the aggressive monarchy of Edward I. At the close of the second

[1] T. F. T. Plucknett, *Legislation of Edward I*, p. 30.
[2] *Select Cases in the Court of King's Bench under Edward I*, vol. ii, ed. G. O. Sayles (Seldon Soc., lvii, 1938), pp. lvii–lviii.

Welsh war the earl of Gloucester had made great display of his position by paying the expenses of the king when Edward passed through Glamorgan. The monarch's ungrateful response was to adopt a very much tougher attitude towards the privileges of the Welsh Marchers during the rest of the reign.

The *cause célèbre* of Marcher privileges was of course that of the private war between the earls of Gloucester and Hereford, the result of a boundary dispute. The story is a well-known one, and need not be repeated at length. The right of the Marchers to wage such wars was well established, but in a strongly-worded proclamation the king ordered the earls in 1290 to desist. Until a final lapse, Hereford, the plaintiff, heeded this instruction, but Gloucester's men persisted in frequent raids. After lengthy hearings, and despite the clear hostility of many of the Marchers to the proceedings, the two earls were condemned to confiscation of their lands and imprisonment. After a relatively short period, Gloucester was allowed to redeem himself for 10,000 marks, and Hereford for 1,000 marks: the size of the sums reflecting the relative gravity of the two men's offences. Their lands were restored to them.[1] Another case also concerned Gloucester, who claimed the right to the custody of the bishopric of Llandaff during vacancies. The conclusion of this was that Gloucester surrendered his rights to Llandaff to the crown, but by the king's grace they were restored to him for his life only, to revert to the crown subsequently.[2] In a dispute between the prior of Goldcliff and Gloucester the king succeeded in establishing the royal right to hear cases concerning advowsons within the liberty of Glamorgan.[3]

It is plain that Gilbert earl of Gloucester was singled out for special treatment by Edward. He was of course the most notable of the Marchers, but in addition it must be remembered that he was Edward's antagonist in the 1260s, and that it was he who replaced the king's nominee Tiptoft in command in South Wales in 1282. There was a long record of hostility between the two men. But other Marcher lords suffered heavy-handed treatment from the

---

[1] Morris, *Welsh Wars*, pp. 220–39.
[2] Altschul, *A Baronial Family*, pp. 274–6; *Rot. Parl.*, i, pp. 42–3, 82–3.
[3] *Ibid.*, i, p. 80; Morris, *op. cit.*, pp. 238–9.

king. In 1292 Theobald de Verdun was sentenced to imprisonment for various offences and his liberty of Ewyas Lacy was confiscated. He was restored to his lands, like Gloucester and Hereford, and like them paid a fine to redeem his body. In his case, the sum was £500.[1] In 1299 the crown challenged the position of the Braose lordship of Gower, claiming that it was a part of the county of Carmarthen. During the lengthy legal proceedings the old Bractonian arguments about the inalienability of royal rights were once again cited. In the end, the king reconferred the liberty on William de Braose, but pressure was brought on him to grant his tenants a charter which severely limited his authority.[2] In his various dealings with the Marchers the king did not intend to destroy their liberties. He was quite willing to confirm Edmund Mortimer in the full enjoyment of his rights in Wigmore when these were challenged by Bogo de Clare in his capacity as royal bailiff of Montgomery.[3] But Edward was determined to impose some check on unlimited Marcher authority, and to establish the right of the tenants of the March to appeal to the crown. The custom of private war he was determined to eradicate.

The political effect of the king's determined policy toward the Marchers in the 1290s was plain to see. It seems highly probable that Humphrey de Bohun's part in the constitutional crisis of 1297 was prompted to some extent by the harsh treatment he had received in his great case against Gloucester. Unfortunately there are no full lists of all the men involved in the opposition in 1297, but strong Marcher participation is suggested by the fact that an opposition gathering, termed by the chronicler a parliament, took place in the forest of Wyre in the March.[4] It is also significant that no important Marcher accompanied the king to Flanders, and that in the *Monstraunces* presented to the king it was complained that men were being excluded from their franchises by the king's arbitrary will.[5]

[1] *Ibid.*, p. 238.
[2] Otway-Ruthven, *op. cit.*, p. 19; W. Rees, *South Wales and the March, 1284–1415*, pp. 49–50.
[3] *Rot. Parl.*, i, p. 45.
[4] *Flores Historiarum*, iii, p. 101.
[5] *Chron. Guisborough*, p. 292.

Edward's treatment of the privileges of the Marchers in the later years of the reign demonstrates that the abandonment of the *Quo Warranto* enquiries did not mean an end to attacks on franchises. A further illustration of this is provided by the complex story of the intervention in the palatinate of Durham, which was taken into the king's hands twice, from 1302 to 1303, and again from late in 1305 until the end of the reign. At the heart of the dispute was the question of the extent of royal jurisdictional authority, but many issues were intermingled. There was the *cause célèbre* of Antony Bek's quarrel with the prior of Durham, and also the dispute of the leading tenants of the palatinate with the bishop. Edward was provoked to intervene by such incidents as the imprisonment of one of the priory tenants for displaying royal letters of protection that had been issued on the prior's behalf, and the similar treatment accorded to royal messengers. He was further irritated by Bek's departure for Rome in 1302 to pursue his case against the prior at the Curia. It is very unlikely that the king would have taken such extreme measures as he did were it not for the obvious military importance of Durham in the Scotch wars. Bek's administration had been shown as incompetent by the mutiny of the Durham men in the winter campaign of 1299–1300. It was obviously more satisfactory to have the palatinate under the control of a trusted soldier, Robert Clifford. Interestingly, Edward used the same device as in Gower to weaken the power of a franchise holder: Bek had to grant a charter to his tenants. In Durham, as in the other cases, the king did not aim at the destruction of the liberty, but he was anxious to define and to limit it, ensuring that it was efficiently governed. So determined was Edward in this that he was prepared to break with as loyal and long-serving an adviser as Antony Bek.[1]

Edward I's treatment of the franchises is a good example of the attitude that he adopted toward his magnates, one of aggressiveness which might be modified if he needed support for his wars. There were other ways in which the king could bring pressure to bear on his magnates and compel them to co-operate with his

[1] C. M. Fraser, *A History of Antony Bek* (Oxford, 1957), pp. 176–210; *supra*, p. 103.

policies. In 1295 nineteen barons were ordered to go to Gascony at royal wages.[1] Several of them, headed by the earl of Arundel, proved unwilling, so Edward in a vicious letter ordered the Exchequer to collect the debts that they owed to the crown, to distrain their lands harshly, to offer them no manner of favour, but to oppress them with all available means. The debts that these men owed to the crown were impressive, the list being headed by Arundel with £5,232 and William de Vescy with £1,019. In the normal way, such debts were allowed to run on unpaid for years. Of Arundel's debt £4,496 was the residue of a relief of 10,000 marks that dated back to the reign of King John. The threat that such debts would be collected was sufficient to force the dissident barons to abandon their stand, and they dutifully, if resentfully, set off to Gascony.[2]

Most of the important men in England owed money to the Exchequer in this way, and so were potentially vulnerable to royal pressure. Even the wealthy Edmund of Cornwall had debts of £1,205.[3] An unusually large debt was that of Baldwin Wake, who early in the reign owed a total of £8,172 to the crown. Much of this dated back to a fine of 10,000 marks offered to John by Nicholas de Stuteville in 1205.[4] Humphrey de Bohun, the son of Edward's opponent in 1297, owed at least £4,000, but in 1304 was excused further payment.[5] On a smaller scale, Henry de Grey's debts at the end of the reign stood at £412,[6] while Reginald de Grey owed £351.[7] It was standard procedure at the beginning of every campaign for writs granting respite of debts to be issued to cover the period that the men were in the army. In November 1303 Edward sent a writ to the Exchequer informing the barons that some of those who had been thus favoured had left the army without permission. Writs were to be issued to the sheriffs asking

[1] *Parl. Writs*, i, p. 269.
[2] E. 159/68, mm. 65–6; *Book of Prests*, ed. Fryde, p. xlviii. The men involved were the earl of Arundel, Roger de Mohaut, Henry de Grey, John de Montfort, William Martin, Robert FitzRoger, Richard de Sutton, William de Vescy, Philip de Kyme, Walter de Huntercombe, Hugo Poinz, Peter Maulay, Edmund Mortimer and William Mortimer.
[3] S.C. 1/17/40.   [4] S.C. 1/17/16.   [5] E. 372/209.
[6] E. 159/79, m. 9d.   [7] E. 159/80, m. 8d.

them to collect the debts that these men owed, and all royal officials, including the justices, were reminded to regard those who were still in Scotland with as much favour as possible.[1]

This technique of threatening to collect such debts was naturally unpopular. In 1293 Roger Bigod owed £2,232, and at the Easter parliament at Westminster that year he petitioned to be excused payment. It was agreed that £1,432 be paid off at the rate of £100 a year.[2] Bigod had previously been heavily indebted to Italian merchants,[3] and two years before had handed some of his manors over to the king.[4] It seems very likely that the crown's intransigence with regard to his debts played a part in persuading him to oppose Edward in 1297. Arundel was also in financial difficulties at this period,[5] but in April 1297 he was granted respite of debts.[6] Bigod was not, and the fact is surely significant. It is also very probable that the demand made in 1295 that Archbishop Winchelsey pay off £3,568 in the space of three years contributed to his hostility towards Edward I.[7]

Edward was prepared to modify the natural rigour of his policies very considerably towards those who served him in his war. The opening of every campaign saw many respites of debts entered in the exchequer records. Similarly, men were granted writs of protection when they were in the field, so that their domestic interests were safeguarded. The king was even prepared to suspend actions of novel disseisin to ensure that no harm came to their estates.[8] A letter requesting protection for the earl of Warwick makes it clear that what he needed was relief from the claims of creditors, public and private, and this the king could provide.[9] So effective were these grants of protection that it became necessary in 1305 to legislate against those who pleaded them fraudulently.[10]

---

[1] E. 159/77, m. 4.   [2] E. 159/67, m. 19.
[3] Denholm-Young, *Seignorial Administration*, p. 64.
[4] *Ancient Kalendars and Inventories of the Treasury of the Exchequer*, ed. F. Palgrave, i (London, 1836), p. 43.
[5] S.C. 1/17/64, 65.   [6] E. 159/70, m. 23d.   [7] *Ibid.*, m. 8.
[8] E. 101/8/4, m. 2.   [9] C. 81/1699/102.
[10] H. M. Cam, *Law-finders and Law-makers* (London, 1962), pp. 134–5.

To obtain the co-operation of the nobility in his wars, Edward could not rely solely on the heavy-handed and harsh policies so far described. He had to make it worth while for men to serve him, as well as to make life hard for those who did not. The most obvious method was by giving grants of conquered lands to those who assisted in the campaigns. However, the king's policy in the first Welsh war was not conquest or the annexation of territory, but was rather the subjection of Llywelyn to English suzerainty. In territorial terms, therefore, the English did not make new gains. The crown recovered two of the four Cantrefs in the north, and also its former possessions in Carmarthen and Cardigan, while Marcher lords regained lands that had been seized by the Welsh. Edmund of Cornwall exchanged his rights to Carmarthen and Cardigan for lands in Derbyshire,[1] while the magnates received small reward for their part in the war.

The war of 1282 was a different matter. With Llywelyn killed and his brother captured, conquest was achieved, and Edward could set about rewarding his followers. Bigod was granted £1,000 for his services, and as recompense for his losses in the war.[2] Others received territorial grants. John Giffard, lord of Brimpsfield, received Llandovery, which he had held for a time previously by virtue of a claim through his wife. He also obtained the commote of Isgenen, and was made custodian of the royal castle of Builth. Morris plausibly suggests that these considerable favours were a reward for Giffard's rôle in commanding the army which defeated Llywelyn at Orewin Bridge. Roger Mortimer, who was with Giffard, also received a reward in the form of land. Important grants in Wales were made to John de Warenne, Henry de Lacy and Reginald de Grey.[3] In Scotland Edward succeeded in building up a vested interest in the war by means of grants of lands. On occasion he even allocated estates to his followers before they had been captured. Bothwell castle was granted to Aymer de Valence shortly before it was taken in 1301, while Lochmaben and Annandale were promised to Humphrey de Bohun on 10 April

---

[1] Morris, *Welsh Wars*, pp. 142–6.   [2] *C.P.R.*, *1281–92*, p. 149.

[3] Morris, *op. cit.* pp. 178, 182, 201; *C.V.C.R.*, *1277–1326*, pp. 222, 223, 240, 241, 243, 283; *Chron. Guisborough*, p. 220.

1306. In the following May John de Hastings was made earl of Menteith, even though the true possessor of the title had not at that time surrendered.[1]

Service in war was the surest way of winning the royal favour. John de Vescy, born in 1244, had been a ward of Peter of Savoy, a fact which may explain his firm adherence to the baronial cause in the civil wars. Early in 1267 he led a rising, but was besieged at Alnwick and forced to surrender. He accompanied Edward on his crusade, and became the king's devoted friend, serving him loyally in Wales. In 1290 his heart was buried at Blackfriars, together with those of Queen Eleanor of Castile and the king's son Alfonso.[2] On a very different level was Roger le Peytevin, a disreputable poverty-stricken knight, who had been a Montfortian and had fought staunchly at Ely in 1267. Forcible seizure of some property he claimed led to his imprisonment early in the reign of Edward I, but he was released in order to fight for the king in Wales in the first Welsh war, and probably recovered some of his lands in return for his service.[3]

Robert FitzRoger was one of the men who appeared at the Exchequer in 1297 to protest against the levying of the tax of an eighth for which proper consent had not been obtained. By good service in Scotland he soon undid the harm that this must have done his standing with the king. In 1300 he was appointed royal lieutenant in Northumberland,[4] and two years later was pardoned his debts at the Exchequer in recognition of his services.[5] In 1306 he was formally thanked for his rôle in protecting the marches against Robert Bruce.[6] Royal favour was extended to FitzRoger's bloodthirsty family. As a result of his part in the Scotch wars one of his sons was pardoned for murdering his own brother, and a little later the victim's wife was herself pardoned, at Robert's instance, for committing a murder.[7]

---

[1] *Cal. Docs. Scot.*, ii, nos. 1214, 1757, 1771.
[2] *Complete Peerage*, ed. V. Gibbs *et al.*, xii, pt. ii (1959), pp. 278–9.
[3] D. W. Sutherland, 'Peytevin v. La Lynde', *Law Quarterly Review*, lxxxiii (1967), pp. 527–31.
[4] *C.P.R., 1292–1301*, p. 491.
[5] E. 368/73, m. 10d.
[6] *C.C.R., 1302–7*, pp. 432–3.
[7] *C.P.R., 1301–7*, pp. 430, 469.

THE CROWN AND THE MAGNATES

Obviously, the king was most likely to obtain the support of his magnates in his campaigns if the wars he fought were popular. The royal writs show that the administration was well aware of the need to explain the reasons for the demands for men and materials necessitated by the wars. In the early stages of the Welsh wars the language employed was straightforward, with statements about the murders committed by the Welsh and the contempt of the crown displayed by Llywelyn.[1] By 1283 the phraseology had become more extreme. The summons to the Shrewsbury parliament stated that 'The tongue of man can scarcely recount the evil deeds committed by the Welsh upon the king's progenitors'. The unfortunate Dafydd was 'the last survivor of the family of traitors'.[2] The writs concerning Scotland laid a constant stress on the fact that the king's enemies were also traitors. The grief and damage caused by their activities were frequently mentioned, and it was emphasized that the war was in the interests of the nation as a whole, not solely of the king.[3] The crisis year of 1297 naturally saw much propaganda produced: the king issuing a lengthy justification of his position.[4] It is interesting to find that in a writ to the Exchequer the king asked the barons to appoint men skilled in addressing the people to see about the collection of the tax of an eighth.[5]

Edward I won general support for his wars in Wales and Scotland, although there was little enthusiasm for the conflict with Philip IV. A tract probably written by a clerk in the entourage of Archbishop Pecham was an elaborate tirade against the Welsh, condemning especially their objectionable sexual habits.[6] The Welsh princely family in particular came under attack from English writers. Royal propaganda against the Welsh was in accord with popular opinion, although with many Welshmen fighting on the English side in the wars, and the Marcher lords having many ties and sympathies with the Welsh, the literature

---

[1] For example, *Parl. Writs*, i, p. 193. [2] *Ibid.*, p. 15.
[3] A good example is in E. 101/552/4/8. The calendared version, *C.P.R., 1292–1301*, p. 578, gives no impression of the tone of the original writ demanding victuals for the war. [4] *Chron. Cotton*, pp. 330–4.
[5] E. 159/70, m. 36. [6] Powicke, *Thirteenth Century*, pp. 383–4.

does not display the savage hatred that was to be directed later in the reign against the Scots. Many popular songs testify to this hatred. One quoted by Langtoft puts English feelings very succinctly:

> 'For Scottes
> Telle I for sottes
> And wrecches unwar.'[1]

That the enemy were 'an inconstant and treacherous people, prepared to commit all manner of crimes'[2] was so familiar a fact as to be hardly worth repeating. William Wallace and the traitor Simon Fraser were the objects of an hysterical detestation. Atrocity stories such as that of the burning of two hundred schoolboys in Corbridge, and the report that after the battle of Stirling Bridge the body of Hugh Cressingham was skinned assisted in the creation of an atmosphere of enthusiasm for the war.[3] There can have been little need to fan hatred among the inhabitants of the north of England who suffered from Scotch raids. The accounts of the lands confiscated from John Balliol are, for the years 1298 and 1299, full of references to the devastation wrought in Northumberland by enemy raids. Several manors are reported to have been entirely deserted as a result of the war.[4]

There was a conscious romanticization of the wars in Wales and Scotland which must have helped to popularize them. Both countries had their Arthurian legends, and it appears to have been a conscious policy of Edward I to set himself up as a new Arthur.[5] There is little evidence to suggest that the king himself was a great reader of grail romances, but his interest in the subject was clearly indicated in 1278, when he had the tomb of Arthur and Guinevere at Glastonbury opened, and the bodies reburied. Round Tables were held on several occasions, notably at Nefyn in 1284 and at Falkirk in 1302. The knighting of the king's eldest son, Edward, in 1306 was the occasion of great festivities, said by Langtoft to

[1] *Chron. Langtoft*, ii, p. 252.   [2] *Chron. Rishanger*, p. 445.
[3] Barrow, *Robert Bruce*, p. 100, n. 2; *Chron. Langtoft*, ii, p. 300.
[4] E. 372/146, m. 23.
[5] R. S. Loomis, 'Edward I, Arthurian Enthusiast', *Speculum*, xxviii (1953), pp. 114–27.

have been unequalled since the coronation of King Arthur at Caerleon: the comparison seems significant.[1] Almost three hundred young men were knighted along with the prince. At the great feast which concluded the celebrations, two swans were brought in, and all present swore oaths on them. The prince vowed that he would never spend two nights in the same bed until the murder of John Comyn had been revenged, and Scotland conquered.[2] This oath was akin to that sworn by Percival in Chrétien de Troyes' *Conte de Graal*.[3]

The chief material symbol of the conquest of Wales was the splendid castle built at Caernarvon. The site was traditionally linked with the Roman past, and in 1283 a body alleged to be that of Magnus Maximus, father of Constantine, was reburied there. In the tale of Maximus' dream, contained in the *Mabinogion*, the place is identified with the castle of which the emperor dreamed, and where he found his princess. Now the castle built by Edward at Caernarvon differs strikingly from the other castles in Wales constructed during his reign, for it has polygonal towers, and bands of coloured stone in the masonry. The similarity to the walls of Constantinople is striking, and it is plain that the castle was built in this way in a conscious desire to recall the legendary past.[4]

During this period war was a normal occupation of the upper classes, and this was one reason why Edward had no very great difficulty in raising sufficient cavalry forces for popular wars. When war was not available, men turned to tournaments as the nearest substitute, though on one occasion, in 1306, the substitute proved more attractive than the real thing, when the tedium of the occupation of Scotland overcame several important members of the prince of Wales' entourage, and they departed to take part in tournaments abroad. There must have been many men in Edward's armies who fought simply because it was their way of

---

[1] *Chron. Langtoft*, ii, p. 368.
[2] Hilda Johnstone, *Edward of Caernarvon, 1284–1307*, pp. 107–8.
[3] Loomis, *op. cit.*, p. 123.
[4] R. Allen Brown, H. M. Colvin, A. J. Taylor, *The History of the King's Works*, i, pp. 369–71.

life and they enjoyed it. But it is interesting to find that Brian FitzAlan, a north country knight, owned a copy of the grail romance *Perlesvaus*,[1] and plainly the idealism of the Arthurian revival contributed to the Edwardian war effort.

The needs of war were not the only determinant of Edward I's policies toward the aristocracy. One of the aims of the king in his dealings with the landed aristocracy was to try to provide substantial estates for his own family. In doing so he must have hoped to gain political advantages. If he succeeded in linking the major comital families of England to the crown by marriage alliances, then this would surely increase his own authority. And if he succeeded in acquiring new estates for the crown, then this might increase its wealth and reduce the degree of dependence on grants of taxation.

The methods employed by Edward and his officials to achieve these ends were not notable for their impartiality and integrity. On the death of Aveline de Forz, countess of Aumale, the young wife of Edmund of Lancaster, in 1274, the considerable Aumale estates should have gone to Aveline's heirs. In the absence of any close relations the king supported a bogus claimant, who was rewarded with a paltry £100 in land, while the crown obtained the Aumale lands. There is considerable doubt about the propriety of the king's dealings with Aveline's mother, Isabel de Redvers, countess of Devon and Lady of Wight. On her deathbed in 1293 she was persuaded to disinherit her rightful heir, Hugh de Courtenay, in return for 6,000 marks. The proceedings were later challenged, and it seems highly probable that the charter by which the reversions of three manors and the Isle of Wight were granted to the crown was forged.[2] The unfortunate Hugh de Courtenay was a minor at the time of the transaction, and it looks as if the king initially pretended that he was merely taking over the lands until Hugh came of age.[3]

---

[1] Denholm-Young, *History and Heraldry*, pp. 23, n. 4, 127, n. 2.

[2] K. B. McFarlane, 'Had Edward I a "Policy" towards the earls?', *History*, l (1965), pp. 151–3.

[3] This is what was thought to be the situation by the writer of an anonymous letter in S.C. 1/48/165.

Edward I married two of his daughters to English earls. In 1283 it was agreed that Joan of Acre should marry Gilbert de Clare, earl of Gloucester, but owing to delays in obtaining an annulment of his earlier marriage, and a papal dispensation for the new one, the ceremony did not take place until 1290. It seems at first sight surprising that the king should ally himself by marriage to the magnate who was most opposed to him, but examination of the terms of the match reveals his motives. Gloucester's children by his earlier marriage were disinherited, and his estates entailed on the heirs born to the second marriage. Should no children be born, twenty-five manors were to go to Joan and her heirs, while she was to have a jointure of the Clare lands. So if children were born, this would mean that the next earl of Gloucester would be a nephew of the king, and if there was no issue, then the royal family would benefit in territorial terms. A similar entail was created when in 1302 Elizabeth was married to Humphrey de Bohun, earl of Hereford, son of the man who opposed Edward in 1297. By these arrangements Edward provided very well for his daughters, while also ensuring that, should the direct line of Clare or Bohun die out, the crown would benefit, rather than any collateral heirs. Similar arrangements were made in 1294 when the king's nephew, Thomas of Lancaster, married Alice, sole surviving offspring of Henry de Lacy, earl of Lincoln. Again the collateral heirs were cut off from their expectations, but this time it was the house of Lancaster rather than the crown that was to benefit.

The other major example of the king's manipulation of the rules of inheritance was the agreement he made in 1302 with Roger Bigod, earl of Norfolk. Bigod surrendered his lands to the crown, and received them back entailed upon the heirs of his body, with reversion to the crown. According to Walter of Guisborough the earl did this in order to disinherit his brother, who was pressing him for the repayment of debts. The king eased the earl's financial difficulties by granting him £1,000 a year in land, for his lifetime. Since Bigod at this time was sixty, and without heirs, it was virtually certain that by this settlement the crown would gain the Norfolk earldom and lands, as indeed happened.[1] While Guis-

[1] McFarlane, *op. cit.*, pp. 153–6.

borough may be correct in stating that Bigod agreed to the king's offer in order to spite his brother, there may well also be truth in the view expressed by another writer, who considered that the king forced the entail on the earl in retaliation for the part that Bigod had played in the opposition movement of 1297.[1]

An ordinance issued in 1306 revealed the extent to which the king was concerned to provide a special status for the members of his family. This laid down that in future no grants of the franchise of return of writ were to be issued, save to his own children. In fact he did not adhere to this strictly, for such a grant was made to Thomas of Lancaster, his nephew, but the ordinance is nevertheless very revealing, both of his attitude to franchises and of his determination to ensure the position of the royal family.[2]

In his personal dealings with the comital families Edward I displayed attitudes that had not changed at all since 1269 when he had effectively disinherited Robert Ferrers in the interests of his own brother Edmund of Lancaster. It may be that the king hoped that by creating ties of marriage and blood with the great families of England he would find it easier to obtain their co-operation in his military enterprises, but it does not appear that this was the effect of his actions. The royal family did of course benefit very considerably, and the crown acquired some important estates, notably Holderness and the Isle of Wight. But as one chronicler, Langtoft, pointed out, not a single earl accompanied the king on his futile expedition to Flanders. This he attributed to Edward's lack of generosity,[3] and it was a fair criticism of the king's policy, even though some grants of lands conquered in Wales and Scotland were made to those who served in the wars.

Edward I did not possess the sympathy with his aristocracy that was to be displayed by his grandson Edward III, whose reign witnessed a striking co-operation between crown and magnates. It is significant that Edward I raised no new families to comital rank, despite the considerable services rendered to him by such as the

---

[1] *Chron. Rishanger*, p. 227.
[2] *Rot. Parl.*, i, p. 211; M. T. Clanchy, 'The Franchise of Return of Writs', *T.R.H.S.*, 5th ser., xvii (1967), p. 78.
[3] *Chron. Langtoft*, ii, p. 296.

Percies and Cliffords. Yet despite the aggressive attitude of the king toward the magnates, characterized by the *Quo Warranto* enquiries and his treatment of the Marcher lords in the later years of the reign, Edward was able by means of propaganda and a system of financial rewards and penalties, promises and threats to obtain the support that he needed for his wars in Wales and Scotland.

XI

THE CRISIS OF 1297 AND ITS ORIGINS

There is a striking contrast between the later years of Edward I, which witnessed constant political and constitutional argument, and the years of his greatest successes, before the outbreak of the war with France. But even in the earlier period Edward did not go uncriticized. Archbishop Pecham at the council of Reading in 1279 ordered the publication of Magna Carta in a way which implied that he considered that the king was not observing it. The earl of Gloucester barely concealed his opposition to the king. Edward was forced to abandon his plan to conduct the war in Wales in 1282 with an army entirely at royal wages. Yet there were no major crises which yielded documents criticizing the conduct of the government before 1297, and there were no proposals for novel schemes of reform.

For an elaborate indictment of Edward I and his government in the first part of the reign it is necessary to turn to a curious book, the *Mirror of Justices*, probably written about 1290. This is a work about the law, and most of the impressively long list of complaints relate to legal matters. Many amount to little more than petty quibbles, but some of the author's complaints were important. The first was that the king was not subject to the law, as he should be, but was above it. Secondly, parliament was held infrequently and only for the purpose of obtaining aids, not for dispensing of justice. Ordinances were not enacted by common assent of the king and his earls, but were made by the king, his clerks, aliens and councillors who did not dare oppose him. Another serious complaint was that corrupt justices and officials were not punished as they should have been. Magna Carta, according to this work, was 'damnably disregarded by the governors of the law and by subsequent statutes'. The introduction of imprisonment as a penalty for debt in the Statute of Merchants was, claimed the author, a contravention of the famous clause 39 of the 1215 Magna Carta.[1]

The *Mirror of Justices* did not achieve widespread popularity, but for all its quirks and eccentricities, it accurately reflected many criticisms of the government. Were the crises of the later years, in particular that of 1297, the result of such grievances, which were not directly the result of war, or were they rather simply the consequence of the insupportable demands of the king's military policies? Was the crisis of 1297, like that of 1340-1, the product of an abnormal situation, or was it, like that of 1258, the result of a long build-up of discontent?

The opposition to Edward in 1297 was two-fold: the clerical and the lay, and the two are best dealt with separately. Although the rôle of the two earls, Roger Bigod of Norfolk and Humphrey de Bohun of Hereford, is well known, the composition of the secular opposition is not easy to ascertain. The only other person named in the royal pardon issued in November 1297 was John Ferrers.[2] The document known as *De Tallagio non Concedendo*, about which there has been some controversy, but which appears to be a baronial draft for a settlement,[3] names the same three individuals. Ferrers' grievance was of long standing. His consistent hostility to the king is easily explained in terms of Edward's treatment of his father, the earl of Derby, in 1269. Ferrers was hardly a man of the same stature as Bigod and Bohun, and the chronicles do not suggest that he played a rôle of great significance in the events of 1297. It seems very likely that he was put in the same

---

[1] *Mirror of Justices*, pp. 155-6, 166, 175, 179 and *passim*.

[2] *Statutes of the Realm*, i, pp. 61-2.

[3] Stubbs, *Select Charters*, pp. 493-4. The chief critic of the document's authenticity is Edwards, 'Confirmatio Cartarum and Baronial Grievances in 1297', *E.H.R.*, lviii (1943), pp. 147-71, 273-300. It is defended by Rothwell, 'The Confirmation of the Charters, 1297', *E.H.R.*, lx (1945), pp. 300-15.

category as Bohun and Bigod in *De Tallagio* in recognition of the justice of his claim to the earldom his father had once held.

Bigod and Bohun also had private grievances against the king. Bigod was being hard pressed to pay the debts he owed to the crown,[1] and Bohun must have felt aggrieved at the way he had been treated in the case of his dispute with the earl of Gloucester. In addition, they felt that their hereditary offices of Marshal and Constable were threatened by the king. This matter first came to a crisis in 1282, when Edward's intention of making the army a force wholly paid by the crown had been opposed. Bohun demanded from the king the emoluments of his office of Constable, and this was presumably a part of the general insistence that the army be organized on traditional feudal lines.[2] The next row concerning the hereditary offices came in 1294, when Bigod, the Marshal, was appointed to command the army in South Wales, and Roger de Molis was appointed marshal of the force. The wardrobe accounts reveal that the king was himself receiving the fees due to the Marshal. After protests, Bigod was promised that no precedents would be made of his being ordered away from his rightful place at the king's side. The officials were ordered to cease levying the Marshal's fees, on the excuse of scarcities in the army, though it seems more likely that this was intended to pacify Bigod.[3] The issue of the rights and duties of the Marshal and Constable was to be revived in 1297.[4]

One of the most celebrated incidents of the 1297 crisis was the arrival of Bigod, Bohun and their followers at the Exchequer on 22 August. They effectively protested at the levy of a tax of an eighth which had not been duly and constitutionally granted. The letter from the Exchequer to the king describing this incident names Robert FitzRoger, Alan la Zouche, John de Segrave, John Lovel and Henry le Tyes as accompanying the earls.[5] All but the

---

[1] *Supra*, p. 237. [2] Morris, *Welsh Wars*, p. 155.
[3] *Ibid.*, pp. 250–1; Wardrobe account for 23 Edward I, E. 372/144.
[4] *Infra*, p. 251.
[5] 'Extracts from the Memoranda Rolls (L.T.R.) of the Exchequer: 1. The Negotiations preceding the *Confirmatio Cartarum* (1297 a.d.)', *T.R.H.S.*, n.s. iii (1886), p. 284.

last named appear as bannerets of Bigod's household in a list which probably dates from this year.[1] John de Segrave was bound by indenture to serve Bigod for life.[2] John Lovel, lord of Titchmarsh in Northamptonshire, held the manor of Minster Lovell in Oxfordshire from Alan la Zouche,[3] and was given land in Yorkshire by Bigod. Robert FitzRoger held land in Northumberland and East Anglia, and appears with Lovel as a witness to a charter issued by Bigod.[4] Though these men do not form a clear territorial interest, they were linked by the ties of personal loyalty and the network of tenurial connections that would be expected in a political grouping of this period.

Beyond this, evidence of the composition of the opposition to the crown in 1297 is slight. In the autumn various writs of summons were issued by the government in England at a time when the situation seemed to be deteriorating into a state of civil war, and one of these, sent out on 9 September, appears to be a demand that the opposition should present themselves for negotiations. From this the names of Nicholas Segrave, Fulk FitzWarin, Robert de Tateshall and Edmund Mortimer can be added to the list of opposition leaders, although Tateshall's inclusion was probably based on misinformation, for his son was serving the king in Flanders, and he was an old associate of Reginald de Grey, who was a leading member of the council advising the young prince Edward. By 16 September his loyalty, together with that of FitzWarin, was recognized by the government.[5] It seems likely that there was considerable Marcher participation in the opposition,[6] but the composition of the movement cannot be analysed in the way that has been possible for the baronial opposition to King John. The party was swiftly formed, and swiftly disintegrated in the course of the year. FitzRoger was employed by the crown early in March, and by October was appointed to the custody of the Northumberland march.[7]

[1] C. 81/1698/130.
[2] Denholm-Young, *Seignorial Administration*, pp. 167–8.
[3] *C.I.P.M.*, v, p. 141. [4] *C.Ch.R.*, *1300–27*, p. 31.
[5] Morris, *Welsh Wars*, pp. 280–2; *Parl. Writs*, i, p. 56.
[6] *Supra*, p. 234. [7] *C.P.R.*, *1292–1301*, pp. 40, 312.

Important as individual grievances were in arousing the hostility of Bigod, Bohun and Ferrers, the other leaders who can be identified do not seem to have had strong personal reasons for opposing the king, although it is worth noting that Robert FitzRoger was one of those forced to go to Gascony in 1295 by the threat that the Exchequer would collect all the debts he owed to the crown by means of distraint.[1] What were the issues over which the opposition disagreed with the crown? Firstly there was the question of military service, which has already been discussed. Bigod objected to the king's plan of sending a feudal army to Gascony while a royal expedition went to Flanders. That plan was substituted for a summons of novel type, making no mention of homage or fealty. But a muster at London proved no more acceptable, while the inclusion in the summons of all landowners with at least twenty librates of land broadened the basis of the opposition. The king's offer of pay to those who served abroad does not seem to have mollified many. Some did, however, appear at London on the specified date, 7 July. Edward then ordered the Marshal and Constable to draw up lists of how many horses they had, and how many were prepared to serve in Flanders. It looks as if the king, furious at the recalcitrance shown by the earls, decided to burden them with all the tasks that could conceivably be considered part of their offices. Naturally, Bigod and Bohun refused, sending Robert Turmy to inform the king that this was the job of a household official, as the men had not assembled in response to a formal feudal summons. Edward informed them that no precedent would be made of the task of drawing up these lists, but the earls were adamant in their refusal, and accordingly the king dismissed them from their offices. Thomas de Berkeley and Geoffrey de Geneville were appointed in their place, as Constable and Marshal respectively.[2]

Suspicion of Edward's intentions with regard to military service in 1297 must have been heightened by memories of earlier attempts to extend the system of military obligation, going back to that of 1282. There appears to have been hostility to his plans for a feudal summons for service in Gascony in 1294, although

[1] *Supra*, p. 236, n. 2   [2] *Chron. Cotton*, p. 331; *supra*, pp. 84-5.

THE CRISIS OF 1297 AND ITS ORIGINS

the campaign was abandoned because of the Welsh revolt. An important group of magnates had opposed paid service against the French in 1295. So it was very predictable that the question of service should be an important element in the 1297 crisis.

Another important element in the crisis was the question of consent to taxation. By 1297 the reserves of cash that had been built up in the early stages of the war with France had long been exhausted, and the Flanders expedition made the king's need of money more acute than ever. He could hardly approach the Salisbury parliament for a tax on moveables, for it was less than three months since the grant of the twelfth and eighth. But by July the financial situation was such that a new tax was clearly needed. As parliament could not be summoned in a short time, and as such an assembly would almost certainly have been disclined to make grants, Edward obtained agreement to the collection of a tax of an eighth 'from the people standing around in his chamber', as one chronicler put it.[1] The Exchequer promptly prepared the administrative machinery for levying the tax, and by 14 August the officials were claiming that all was ready.[2] These plans, however, were thwarted by Bigod and Bohun, with their supporters, who appeared at the Exchequer on 22 August. Bohun acted as spokesman, and the main point he made was that the tax had not been properly negotiated, but was being arbitrarily imposed. He emphasized that to pay such a levy to which due assent had not been given was to admit to being in a condition of servitude.[3]

This was a straightforward constitutional argument. In the Magna Carta of John's reign it was stated that no scutages or aids save for the three traditional aids should be levied without the common counsel of the realm.[4] Although this clause was omitted from the reissues of the charter, the principle of consent for taxes on moveables was maintained. The problem was, how should the consenting body be constituted? In the early thirteenth century the idea of a representative assembly, with powers to bind the whole

[1] *Flores Historiarum*, iii, p. 296.   [2] E. 159/70, m. 36.
[3] 'Extracts from the Memoranda Rolls (L.T.R.) of the Exchequer', *T.R.H.S.*, n.s. iii (1886), p. 284.   [4] Stubbs, *Select Charters*, p. 294.

nation to what was agreed, was not fully accepted. A fortieth was granted in a great council in 1232 after considerable argument, but three years later Richard Percy, William, count of Aumale, and John, earl of Lincoln, were opposing collection of the tax on their lands on the grounds that they had not personally consented to it.[1] In 1254 the magnates refused a general aid. The government accordingly made a direct appeal to the men who would have paid the aid had it been granted in the great council. Two knights from each shire were summoned to appear before the council, and they were to be empowered by the county courts to grant a tax.[2]

Such precedents led to the practice by which grants of taxes on moveables were made by an assembly of magnates and shire representatives. Although the principle was generally accepted in Edward's reign, the formula for the summons of the shire representatives, emphasizing the powers that they were to have to bind the community of the county to the decision made in parliament, was not established until the 1290s.[3] Consent by the burgesses to taxation was more often obtained by individual negotiations with the towns than by the attendance of representatives in parliament. That taxes need not be granted in full parliament was shown by the unusual arrangements made for the financing of the second Welsh war. In the summer and autumn of 1283 various towns and counties were approached for financial aid by royal officials under the direction of John Kirkby. This was only moderately successful, realizing receipts of £16,533 6s. 6d.[4] Accordingly, two assemblies were summoned to meet in January 1283, one at York and one at Northampton. This division was made so that the clergy of the two provinces could be approached separately, and it was obviously convenient to summon the shire and borough representatives at the same time. No magnates were summoned, for they could be consulted in the armies in Wales. The assemblies granted a tax, on condition that the magnates agreed. According to one account, the rate initially agreed on was a fifteenth, but

---

[1] Mitchell, *Taxation in Medieval England*, pp. 200–1.   [2] *Ibid.*, pp. 213–18.
[3] J. G. Edwards, 'The *Plena Potestas* of English Parliamentary Representatives', *Oxford Essays in Medieval History presented to H. E. Salter* (Oxford, 1934), pp. 141–54.   [4] Wardrobe account, in E. 372/136.

ultimately the rate was fixed at a thirtieth. The sums paid to Kirkby in 1282 were counted as a part of the tax.[1] It seems very likely that the legislation of September 1283, the Statute of Acton Burnell, intended to ease and simplify the process of debt collection, was the result of pressure put on the king and his officials in the course of these negotiations for financial aid from the burgesses. It may also reflect the concern of the Riccardi, who contributed so much to the financing of the war of 1282–3, about the recovery of debts due to them.

Although the type of assembly that should grant taxes was not formally laid down by 1297, there was a tradition of consulting the shire representatives as well as the magnates, and in 1290, 1294, 1295 and 1296 taxes on moveables had been granted in parliament. It was clearly appreciated by the government that they were on weak ground in that no representatives had been involved in the grant of the eighth, and no formal gathering of magnates had been summoned. Detailed orders were issued to the assessors instructing them how to justify the tax. The people were to be approached in the most courteous way possible, and were to be told that the earls and barons had consented to the tax on their behalf. But, hardly surprisingly, no elaborate constitutional arguments were put forward. Emphasis was placed instead on an emotional plea that the king was risking his life on their behalf, and that the least his subjects could do was to pray for him and pay their taxes.[2] The opposition's case as expressed in *De Tallagio* was that taxes should not be imposed without the consent of all the magnates, lay and ecclesiastical, knights, burgesses and free men of the realm. Edward was not prepared to accept this view, even though it did represent the normal method of granting taxes. In the *Confirmatio Cartarum* he simply promised that he would take no aids and prises save the customary ones without the 'common assent of the whole realm', a carefully imprecise phrase which did not commit him to consulting shire and borough representatives.[3]

The crown was also on weak ground over the *maltolt*, the 40s.

[1] Mitchell, *op. cit.*, pp. 225–6; 'Annales de Waverleia', in *Annales Monastici*, ii, p. 399; Stubbs, *Select Charters*, p. 462.
[2] E. 159/70, m. 124.   [3] Stubbs, *Select Charters*, pp. 295, 491, 493.

export tax on wool. The merchants had consented to this, as a substitute for a seizure of wool, and the government presumably argued that as it was they who were to pay the tax, no one else need be consulted about it. But in the April parliament of 1275 the customs duties on wool, woolfells and leather had been granted at the request of the merchants by the magnates and others in the assembly.[1] And although it was the merchants who paid the *maltolt*, the burden of the tax was in part passed on to the farmers. Prices were severely depressed during the years of the war with France.[2] So both in terms of precedent and interest the magnates were entitled to feel that they should have been consulted over the *maltolt*. The 40s. duty was therefore formally given up in the *Confirmatio Cartarum*, and a promise made that no such levies would be imposed in future without the consent of the community of the realm.[3]

The many prises that were taken by the government to provide victuals for the armies provided another grievance. As already shown, the crown was traditionally entitled to such prises for the royal household, but Edward I's extension of the system constituted an unwarranted use of a prerogative right. In the *Confirmatio* the king promised that no precedent was to be established by these prises, and further, he promised that they would not be taken in the future without the consent of the community.[4]

The crisis of 1297 was not simply a matter of argument over the constitutional forms that grants of taxes and customs duties should take. In the first statement of the opposition that survives, the so-called *Monstraunces*, the constitutional arguments take second place to a forceful statement of the hardships that the king's exactions have caused. It is stated that even if service was owed in Flanders, it could not be performed, as the community of the realm was so impoverished as a result of the various aids and prises.[5] The succession of annual taxes, the series of prises coinciding with a period of high prices, imposed a heavy burden on the country. By 1298 the

---

[1] Stubbs, *Select Charters*, p. 443.   [2] *Supra*, p. 128.
[3] Stubbs, *op. cit.* p. 491.
[4] *Supra*, pp. 118–9; Stubbs, *op. cit.* p. 491.
[5] *Chron. Guisborough*, pp. 292–3.

northern clergy were so short of cash that they were permitted to pay their taxes in kind, rather than in coin.[1] A popular song of Edward's reign expressed the opinion that the burden of royal exactions was reducing farmers to a state of misery, 'For ever the furthe peni mot to the kynge'. Seed corn had to be sold to meet the demand for silver, and as a result land had to lie fallow. Even if the song exaggerates, and few peasants were in fact reduced to beggary, it is significant that economic woes should be blamed on royal taxation, and not on the activities of landlords.[2] The *Monstraunces* pointed out that many were reduced to subsistence level or below by the king's demands.

Edward's quarrel with the clergy in 1297 was over the issue of taxation. There was nothing new in the king requesting aid from the clergy in that year. When they granted a tenth in 1295 Archbishop Winchelsey promised a further tenth in the following year if the war should still be in progress.[3] This was accordingly demanded at the Bury St. Edmunds parliament in November 1296. But Winchelsey made four points in a speech replying to the request. Two were in the king's favour: the promise of the previous year, and the danger from France. Against these, however, he was able to refer to the recent papal prohibition of such grants, made in the bull *Clericis Laicos*, and to the poverty of the church.[4] A further argument was that since the assembly was summoned by the king, rather than by the ecclesiastical authorities, it was constitutionally improper to make a grant.[5] The outcome was that the clergy delayed their answer until next Hilary, when a synod of the whole English clergy met at St. Paul's. Winchelsey on that occasion came out strongly against the royal demand, reading out the papal bull in the presence of the royal emissaries, Hugh Despenser and John of Berwick. They repeated a threat that had

---

[1] *Councils and Synods with other Documents relating to the English Church*, ed. F. M. Powicke and C. R. Cheney (Oxford, 1964), p. 1186.
[2] *Political Songs*, ed. Wright, pp. 149–52.
[3] 'Annales de Wigornia', in *Annales Monastici*, iv, p. 524.
[4] *Chron. Cotton*, p. 314.
[5] *Historical Works of Gervase of Canterbury*, ed. W. Stubbs, ii (Rolls Series, 1880), p. 315.

been made before, particularly in 1294, that if no grant was forthcoming the king would place the clergy out of his protection, and this time the threat was carried out.[1]

The royal demand had been for a fifth, and Edward made it known that payment of the equivalent sum would buy back his protection. The archbishop pronounced sentence of excommunication on all those who obeyed the king in this,[2] but was ignored by those clerks in royal service, and by those of the northern province.[3] Severe pressure was put on the clergy by the crown. Cotton complained in particular of the seizure of horses,[4] while the archbishop's lands and valuables were taken by the crown.[5] In Lent Winchelsey summoned a convocation of the southern province, and conceded that individuals should be allowed to follow their own consciences, with the inevitable result that almost all paid up and obtained protections.[6] The total raised in this way was £22,810,[7] just over double the proceeds of the tenth of the previous year.

In July the king achieved a great political triumph with his formal reconciliation with Winchelsey. Part of the understanding between the two men was that if the clergy who had been summoned for a convocation in the summer made a grant, then Edward would confirm the Charters. Winchelsey was to negotiate a settlement between the king and the earls. But the latter refused any overtures from Edward, who decided to carry out his plans for a Flemish campaign without their support.[8] For this, further financial support was needed from the clergy, and so he approached convocation for an aid, hoping for a moiety.[9] Although the clergy were reasonably sympathetic, they insisted on getting permission from Rome before making a grant. This was similar

---

[1] *Chron. Cotton*, pp. 314–18; *Chron. Guisborough*, pp. 286–8.
[2] *Chron. Cotton*, p. 320.
[3] *Chron. Langtoft*, ii, p. 278; *Annales Monastici*, iii, p. 466; *C.P.R., 1292–1301*, pp. 235–7.   [4] *Chron. Cotton*, p. 322.   [5] *Chron. Guisborough*, p. 288.
[6] *C.P.R., 1292–1301*, pp. 261–6. C. 47/2/1 is a bundle of original receipts for these fines.   [7] E. 401/1653.
[8] Rothwell, 'The Confirmation of the Charters, 1297', *E.H.R.*, lx (1945), pp. 24–35, has the fullest account of these events.
[9] *Chronicle of Bury St. Edmunds*, p. 140.

to the situation in France, and the awareness of the English clergy of events across the Channel is shown by the inclusion of correspondence between the French bishops and the papacy in the registers of Winchelsey[1] and the bishop of Carlisle.[2] The king's reaction to this reasonable demand was typical. He at once imposed a tax of a third on all the temporalities of the church, with the option of paying a fifth on all ecclesiastical property. It was stated in a royal proclamation that as the clergy were forbidden to defend the country by force of arms, they should do it by paying money.[3] There is no evidence of the collection of substantial sums from this tax; it seems to have suffered the same fate as the eighth on moveables.

This was not just a question of the clergy being prohibited by papal bull from paying the taxes which the king demanded. Winchelsey's attitude of extreme legalism was not generally shared. His failure to carry his own Convocation with him over his refusal to pay the fines demanded by the king shows the isolation of his position, as does the reaction of the northern clergy. Winchelsey did nothing to prepare the way for Boniface VIII's withdrawal, in the bull *Etsi de Statu*, from the extreme view he had set out in *Clericis Laicos*. It is plain that the personal attitude of the archbishop was in large part responsible for the gravity of the crisis between church and state in 1297.

Winchelsey had not been archbishop long. Elected in 1293 and enthroned in 1295, he refused to take the oath of fealty in the terms demanded by the king, but confined his obligation to his temporalities.[4] Shortly afterwards Edward demanded that Winchelsey pay off debts totalling £3,568 in the course of three years, a very harsh request.[5] So even before 1297 relations between king and primate were not congenial. The archbishop was an inflexible man, lacking the kind of political skill that was to be displayed by Stratford in the 1340-1 crisis. He never combined

[1] Powicke, *The Thirteenth Century*, p. 676, n. 2.
[2] *Historical Letters and Papers from the Northern Registers*, pp. 124-30.
[3] *Parl. Writs*, i, p. 396; Deighton, 'Clerical Taxation by Consent', *E.H.R.*, lxviii, pp. 185-6.
[4] Powicke, *op. cit.* pp. 672-3, n. 1. [5] *Supra*, p. 237.

his forces with those of the lay opposition, and at a crucial point in the development of the crisis the king achieved a form of reconciliation with him. Winchelsey seems to have erroneously imagined that he could play the part of a peacemaker at a time when it should have been evident that no agreement between the king and the earls was possible. It is striking that of all the leaders of the opposition of 1297, it was only against Winchelsey that the king held a deep and bitter grudge for the rest of his life.

Relations between the crown and the church had not been smooth during the earlier years of the reign, and the crisis can be seen as the culmination of previous difficulties. There had been arguments over taxation, but the main issue had been that of jurisdiction. This dispute was largely settled in 1286 when the writ *Circumspecte Agatis*, which later came to have the force of a statute, was issued. Edward was a conventionally religious man, a lavish patron of the abbey of Vale Royal, but he had never been willing to show subservience to the church. Pecham on one occasion wrote to him, suggesting that he might do well to display in his actions the faith in God and the church to which he was constantly making reference.[1] The dispute of 1297 arose out of the special circumstances of war, and was aggravated by the intransigence of an obstinate and inexperienced archbishop, but in view of Edward's general attitude, it was hardly surprising that the church should play a significant rôle in the opposition.

The opposition in 1297 did not set out an elaborate programme. They proposed no new schemes of government after the pattern of the 1258 reforms, and they demanded no purges of the administrative personnel. Their attitude was essentially a conservative one, with the request for the confirmation of the Charters, the maintenance of the customary laws and liberties of the land, and the abandonment of the novel and arbitrary exactions to which the king had been forced to resort in the past few years. The documents expressing the views of Bigod, Bohun and their allies, the *Monstraunces* and *De Tallagio non Concedendo*, did not make any radical claims. The first of these laid more stress on the burden

---

[1] *Registrum Epistolarum Fratris Johannis Peckham, Archiepiscopi Cantuariensis*, ed. C. T. Martin, ii (Rolls series, 1884), pp. 523–4.

imposed on the country by Edward's policy than on the legal and constitutional technicalities of the right of the king to prises and taxation: it was a splendid piece of propaganda, but was not a carefully argued case. The *De Tallagio*, a draft settlement of the crisis probably drawn up after the king had sailed for Flanders, did not set out any new principles. The document stressed that the consent of all men down to the rank of freeman was required for taxation. Although this was found unacceptable by the crown, and was modified in the *Confirmatio* to the less specific 'common assent of the realm', the *De Tallagio* did not go very far. In 1295 the king had proclaimed in a summons to the clergy the principle that 'what touches all should be approved by all', and the writ for the collection of the tax of an eleventh and seventh in that year stated that consent had been given by earls, barons, knights, citizens, burgesses and others of the realm.[1] The solution offered by the *De Tallagio* to the problem of prises, that no goods should be taken without consent, merely echoed Edward's own legislation in the First Statute of Westminster.[2]

The only sanction the opposition proposed to place on Edward in the *De Tallagio* was the excommunication of all who acted contrary to the Charters and the additions made to them in the document. But Edward was not prepared to add new clauses to the Charters, and although in the *Confirmatio Cartarum*, the official settlement of the crisis, he was willing to allow that Magna Carta and the Charter of the Forest should be enforced by means of threats of excommunication made twice a year, this provision does not seem to have been applied to the new concessions made in the document. In these he promised not to make a precedent of the 'aids, mises and prises' taken by him. In future such aids were to be taken with the consent of the realm, and the *maltolt* was abolished.[3] From this settlement, it might seem that the differences between the king and the opposition were not considerable, and that once the immediate circumstances of the French war and the Flemish campaign were over, the constitutional struggle would end. But the personal grievances of Bigod, Bohun and Winchelsey

[1] *Chron. Guisborough*, pp. 292–3; Stubbs, *Select Charters*, pp. 480–2, 493–4.
[2] *Supra*, p. 118.   [3] See also *infra*, pp. 265–6.

were not satisfied by the outcome of the crisis of 1297. The arguments about military service had not been resolved: no mention was made of the matter in the *Confirmatio Cartarum*. And, of course, the war in Scotland meant that the king could not abandon all the expedients to which he resorted between 1294 and 1297. Troops still had to be recruited. Purveyance was as necessary as ever. Money still had to be collected for the financing of war, even if the level of expenditure was not to be quite so high as it was in the years of the French war. And the events of the last ten years of Edward I's reign reveal that there was a general suspicion of the king's intentions and methods which went beyond the particular conditions of 1297 that had caused the crisis of that year.

XII

POLITICS AND THE KING, 1298–1307

Edward I was presented with considerable problems in the last years of his reign. His financial difficulties were acute, he faced continuing arguments over the issue of military service, and he failed to conquer Scotland. But in spite of all this, no major crisis occurred after 1297. It was not until Edward II's reign that the government and its methods came under severe criticism and attack once more. It has even been argued, by Professor Rothwell, that Edward triumphed over his opponents in his later years, successfully preserving his prerogative rights, and forcing them to abandon the demand for the confirmation of the Charters which had been the main plank of their programme.[1] In view of the crisis that followed the king's death, the extent of this triumph seems rather questionable, and it is necessary to see to what extent the problems confronting Edward II were the result of the legacy his father left him, as well as to analyse the nature of the political situation in the old king's later years.

The inadequate nature of the settlement made in the autumn of 1297 was demonstrated soon after the king's return from Flanders in 1298. Bigod and Bohun suspected that Edward might argue that the promises he had made were invalid, since they had been made abroad. They therefore requested a new confirmation at the opening of the campaign that was to see the great victory of Falkirk. The king was unwilling to swear in person, but the deadlock was resolved by the earl of Lincoln, Earl Warenne, the bishop

[1] H. Rothwell, 'Edward I and the Struggle for the Charters, 1297–1305', *Studies in Medieval History presented to F. M. Powicke*, pp. 319–32.

of Durham and Ralph de Monthermer who pledged that if victory was achieved the king would implement his promises.[1] The connection between war and politics is made very clear by this: Edward was essentially offering a concession in return for military assistance. The particular issue that concerned Bigod and Bohun at this time was that of the Forest. The harshness of Forest administration had been one of the complaints in the *Monstraunces*,[2] and what they wanted was a commission to enquire into the proper boundaries of the Forest. It was suspected that the crown was exercising Forest jurisdiction in areas where it had no rights to do so. This was a direct attack on a financially valuable aspect of the royal prerogative, and was much resented by Edward.

After the battle of Falkirk the English army retired to Carlisle, where Bigod and Bohun refused to countenance further operations in Scotland, asserting that they had not been consulted as was their right. Edward wrote in October to the Exchequer asking them to look up the rights and duties of the two earls in their capacities as Marshal and Constable so it seems that this question was once more in dispute, as it had been in 1297. The reply was hardly satisfactory, for it did no more than summarize the fees of the two officers as set out in the twelfth-century *Constitutio Domus Regis*. The Constable was to receive 5s. a day when out of court, along with some provisions, and 3s. 6d. if he dined in the household. Archaic and irrelevant though these fees were, the young Humphrey de Bohun was paid on this basis on the 1300 campaign, receiving the meagre total of £17 5s. 9d.[3] But in 1298 his father and Bigod were not to be satisfied so easily, and following their departure from the army,

---

[1] *Chron. Guisborough*, p. 324.   [2] *Ibid.*, p. 293.
[3] E. 368/70, m. 22d; *Liber Quotidianus*, p. 201. There is no contemporary account of the claims made by the Constable, but in *Select Cases in the Court of King's Bench*, ed. G. O. Sayles, i (Selden Soc., lv, 1936), pp. cxlix-cl, there is a statement of the rights of the Marshal which was probably drawn up shortly after Bigod's death. He was entitled to payments on a graduated scale from all who did homage to the king, and from those incarcerated in his custody. In wartime he was to receive the fines levied in his court on all save those in receipt of royal robes. He was also entitled to all particoloured beasts taken as booty. An undated note of this period, C. 47/3/21/23, suggests that he should receive the armour and money of the commander of any garrison that surrendered, and

the king decided against further operations in Scotland that autumn and winter.

At the Lent parliament in 1299 arguments between the king and the earls continued. Humphrey de Bohun had died late in the previous year, but his place was taken by his son and namesake, who with Bigod demanded the reissue of the charters that had been promised before Falkirk. The king prevaricated, and then confirmed the suspicions of the opposition by issuing the statute known as *De Finibus Levatis* in April. Although a perambulation of the bounds of the Forest was promised, there was a saving clause protecting the rights of the crown, and it was made clear that the findings of the commissioners were not to be automatically implemented, but would be referred to the king. Edward's attitude was made abundantly clear by the reissue of the Forest Charter that went with the statute, which omitted the first five clauses dealing with the boundaries of the Forest. There was great anger when this was read out in the cemetery of St. Paul's, and the extent of the king's evasiveness and trickery became apparent. A new assembly was held, at which the king was forced to agree to the perambulation. This was in May 1299, too late in the year for the plans for a campaign in Scotland that year to be revived. The political quarrels were influencing the conduct of the war in the most unwelcome way for the king.[1]

---

two tuns of wine, a length of the best cloth and a quantity of wax from all captured towns. A later statement of the rights of the Marshal, probably dating from the time of Richard II's coronation, is in B.M. Cotton. MS, Vesp. B. vii, ff. 105v-107. B.M. Cotton. MS, Nero D. vi, f. 85, has another treatise of similar date on the offices of Marshal and Constable. It confirms many of the details of the earlier documents, and provides additional ones. The Constable was entitled to all beasts without horns, pigs, and unshod horses. He was to receive 4d. from all merchants and whores following the army. The two men claimed important military duties. They were to arrange billeting, the setting up of camp, and sentry duty. The Marshal, with a wardrobe clerk, was to receive the proffers of feudal service, and he had a right to attend councils of war. The task of maintaining order in the army was his. The problem of the rôle of the Marshal and Constable under Edward I is further discussed *supra*, pp. 72, 80, 85 and *infra*, p. 267.

[1] *Chron. Guisborough*, pp. 329-30; *Statutes of the Realm*, i, pp. 127-8.

Following the failure of the winter campaign of 1299–1300, when the magnates refused to co-operate because of the inclement conditions and because they alleged that the terms of the Confirmation were not being adhered to,[1] the king was forced to take a conciliatory line towards the opposition. At the parliament held in March 1300 in London the charters were yet again confirmed, and a series of articles known as the *Articuli super Cartas* granted by the king. These dealt at length with abuses of the royal right of prises, prohibited the use of the privy seal in common law cases, limited the jurisdiction of the steward and marshal of the household, and stated that sheriffs were henceforth to be elected in the county courts. The clauses of the *Confirmatio Cartarum* of 1297 were not repeated, but where they had proved inadequate, in the matter of prises, the new *Articuli* provided a remedy. It was now made clear that the right of prise could only be used to supply the royal household, and not the entire army.[2] The result was that in 1301 the king negotiated the purveyance he took for the campaign in Scotland with the county communities, something he had not felt obliged to do as a result of the *Confirmatio*.[3] The prerogative right of prise itself was not challenged, but it was now defined in a way that severely limited it.

Perversely, Rothwell saw in the parliament of 1300 a victory for the king. He made the valid point that the concessions of the *Articuli* were qualified by a clause saving the king's prerogative, but continued by arguing that whereas in 1297 the *Confirmatio* was added to the Charters, and that 'prises were treated as a matter to which the Charters were applicable', in 1300 the concessions were separated from the matter of the Charters. Accordingly prise offences were treated as 'maladministration of the prerogative'.[4] Although the opposition in 1297 may well have intended to have additional articles inserted in Magna Carta, as Guisborough erroneously supposed was done, the *Confirmatio* was a quite separate document from the Charters, written in French not Latin, and issued in the form of letters patent. The clauses in it relating to aids, mises, prises and the *maltolt* were not given the same force as

[1] *Chron. Guisborough*, p. 332.   [2] *Statutes of the Realm*, i, pp. 136–41.
[3] *Supra*, pp. 131–2.   [4] Rothwell, *op. cit.*, pp. 327–9.

the Charters, which were backed by the sanction of excommunication. Just as in 1300, the concessions of 1297 were separate from the Charters, and the *Articuli* did not represent a retreat from the position gained in the *Confirmatio*.[1]

Although the king was prepared to grant the *Articuli* he remained stubborn over the question of the perambulation. Arrangements were in hand for the commissions to start work, but he refused to accept that their findings should be accepted without question. The opposition made the grant of a twentieth conditional upon this, and the king therefore declined to levy the tax. But in the following year, after the expense of the Caerlaverock campaign, he had to swallow his pride. At the Lincoln parliament in 1301 the opposition expressed their demands in a bill presented by Henry Keighley, who was to suffer imprisonment five years later for his action.[2] The confirmation of the Charters was requested, together with the cancellation of statutes that contravened them. Purveyance was to be abolished and, along with other reforms, the findings of the perambulation were to be put into effect in return for a grant of a fifteenth. Edward agreed to this last demand, and the fifteenth was granted with the insulting proviso that it was not to be collected before Michaelmas, by which time it would be possible to see if the government was meeting the conditions imposed. Early in October the grant was officially confirmed by the magnates in the royal army at Glasgow and those in the prince of Wales' company at Ayr.[3]

The perambulations of the Forest that were the price of the fifteenth caused much land to be put out of the Forest jurisdiction. There was no question of Edward I having extended the boundaries: the jurors alleged illegal afforestation under Henry II, Richard and John, stating that they knew this from the tales of their ancestors and the common talk of the county. The evidence was inadequate, and the results of the perambulations clearly unjust. But Edward could do little, for in letters patent he had

[1] *Chron. Guisborough*, p. 311; *supra*, p. 260.
[2] W. Stubbs, *Constitutional History*, ii, pp. 157-8.
[3] E. 159/75, m. 59d. Willard, *Parliamentary Taxes on Personal Property*, p. 24, has mistaken Newcastle-on-Ayr for Newcastle-on-Tyne.

agreed that districts which lay outside the boundaries agreed by the commissioners should be disafforested.[1] All he could do was to prohibit those now put out of the Forest from exercising rights of common within its boundaries, unless they chose to return to their original state.[2]

The other major issue over which the king conceded victory to the opposition in the early years of the fourteenth century was that of military service. His attempt to summon all those holding forty librates of land in 1300 was criticized, and was not repeated. Neither was the novel expedient of sending individual requests for service at pay to about 935 men, adopted in lieu of such a summons in 1301, repeated. No official documents set out the king's concessions on this issue, but the extent of the opposition's victory can be seen from the fact that after 1301 all major summonses for cavalry service used the traditional strict feudal formula.[3]

There was also argument in 1301 over the old question of the rôle of the Marshal. In May John Benstead, Controller of the Wardrobe, was sent to discuss the matter with Bigod. The outcome of the negotiations was an agreement that John Segrave, who acted as Marshal's deputy on the campaign, should receive £100 in lieu of the booty to which he was entitled. Bigod only agreed to this on condition that the king promised to make no allegations that the Marshal or his deputy were not doing their duty in the army, and that no precedent was to be made of the arrangement. Bohun, the Constable, was more accommodating, and made over to the king his rights to the fees pertaining to his office; this was, however, to be only for the one campaign, and was not to prejudice any future claims. Edward was unable to remove the Marshal and Constable from their hereditary positions which gave them important powers over the army.[4]

One victory, however, Edward did win in 1301. It was agreed in parliament to set up a committee of twenty-six to adjudicate on the matters in dispute between the king and community of the

---

[1] *Select Pleas of the Forest*, ed. G. J. Turner (Selden Soc., xiii, 1901), pp. civ–cv.
[2] *Statutes of the Realm*, i, p. 144.   [3] *Supra*, pp. 89–90.
[4] E. 101/20/17; *Cal. Docs. Scot*, ii, nos. 1209, 1323.

realm. However, presumably as a result of royal pressure, the members refused to act as judges over their monarch.[1] According to one account, a similar commission was set up in the next year, but nothing is known of the outcome.[2]

The great weakness of the crown in face of the opposition was its dependence on grants of taxation for the financing of the war in Scotland. Without the war, Edward would not have had to be so conciliatory. Attempts were made to find other sources of supply, and in 1303 a partial success was achieved, when negotiations with the representatives of the foreign merchants resulted in their agreeing to the imposition of additional customs duties. These amounted to an extra 3s. 4d. on each sack of wool and a similar increase of half the original duty on the other commodities on which duty was paid. An *ad valorem* duty of 3d. in the pound was also imposed. In return, various privileges were granted to the foreign merchants in the *Carta Mercatoria*, intended to give them freedom of movement, and to provide them with protection against undue interference. A special court was set up in London to hear cases in which they were involved, and it was conceded that henceforth they were to be free from prises.[3] These new duties put foreign merchants at a financial disadvantage as compared with their English rivals who did not have to pay them. But this was not the result of a far-sighted government policy of favouring English traders. The original intention had been that the New Customs should be paid by all, and soundings had been taken by exchequer officials, who reported that the English merchants were quite willing to pay the increased duties.[4] Representatives of the towns were accordingly summoned to a council at York in June 1303. When they met, the initial discussions were shown to have been misleading, for the assembly unanimously refused to make any grant.[5] Such negotiations for aid were of course a contravention of the *Confirmatio* of 1297, and it seems likely that pressure was brought to bear on the merchants by the opposition,

---

[1] *Chron. Langtoft*, ii, pp. 330–2.   [2] *Supra*, p. 90.
[3] Powicke, *Thirteenth Century*, pp. 630–1, gives a good summary of the *Carta Mercatoria*.
[4] S.C. 1/31/99.   [5] *Parl. Writs*, i, pp. 134–5.

for in view of their earlier attitude it seems improbable that their decision to refuse the grant was unaided.

In 1305 Edward's problems in Scotland appeared to be over. His position was further strengthened by the election of Bertrand de Got, a Gascon and a former royal clerk, as Pope Clement V. With his aid Edward was able to take the political initiative. He received a papal bull absolving him from the concessions he had made, and he brought charges against Winchelsey at the Curia, in which the archbishop's political rôle figured largely. As a result, Edward's most hated opponent was suspended from office in February 1306, and did not return to England during the king's lifetime.[1] But Edward's victory was a very limited one. Even with the pressure of the renewal of war in Scotland he did not revert to the practices of arbitrary exactions that had been so bitterly resented between 1294 and 1297, with the sole exception of the purveyance of foodstuffs that was essential for the military campaigns of 1306 and 1307.[2] No novel forms of military summons were issued, and even the tax of a twentieth and thirtieth was granted in lieu of the feudal aid to which the king was entitled on the occasion of the knighting of his eldest son.[3]

Political disputes in the years after the king's return from Flanders never reached the degree of bitterness that was felt in 1297. There was no propaganda war between crown and opposition and no threat of civil war. One reason for this was the weakness of the opposition's leadership. Bohun died in 1298, and Bigod was in financial difficulties. He could not afford to continue in the rôle he had taken on in 1297, and the bargain that Edward made with him in 1302 is indicative of his insecure position.[4] The fact that in 1301 protests against the crown were made in a bill produced by Henry Keighley, a knight of the shire, suggests that powerful aristocratic support for the opposition was lacking. The man Edward regarded as his chief opponent was, of course,

---

[1] J. H. Denton, 'Pope Clement V's career as a royal clerk', *E.H.R.*, lxxxiii (1968), pp. 303–14; *Foedera*, I, ii, p. 978; Powicke, *Thirteenth Century*, p. 718.

[2] For purveyance in 1306, see *C.P.R., 1301–7*, pp. 417–19, and E. 101/369/11, ff. 71–6.

[3] Vincent, *Lancashire Lay Subsidies*, p. 254.   [4] *Supra*, p. 244.

Archbishop Winchelsey. In particular, the king held him responsible for his humiliation at the Lincoln parliament of 1301. He was even suspected of plotting the deposition of Edward on that occasion and, according to one account, the king had documentary evidence of his treachery.[1] The archbishop does not appear to have had wide support. His action in bringing the papal bull *Scimus Fili*, in which Boniface VIII condemned the English actions in Scotland, to the king in Galloway in 1300 cannot have commended itself to the magnates, who were sympathetic to Edward's war aims, and were prepared to append their seals to an elaborate letter denying the papal claims.[2]

Edward adopted a more conciliatory attitude towards the opposition in these later years of the reign than he had done in 1297. With the great enquiry into the misdeeds of royal officials that took place in 1298 he demonstrated his willingness to deal with the local abuses, particularly in the administration of prises, which had done so much to aggravate the situation during the period of the war with France.[3] Again, in the Ordinance of the Forest of 1306, the king took measures to prevent the repetition of practices which had contributed greatly to popular discontent with the government.[4] The financial situation was still critical, because of the continuing struggle in Scotland. But after concessions had been exacted from Edward in 1301 in return for a fifteenth, the crown virtually abandoned the attempt to pay its way. Rather than resort to unpopular exactions, the king turned to the inadequate prerogative rights to tallage and feudal aids, and accepted a massive and rising level of indebtedness. Despite the pressure for repayment at the parliament of 1305, it seems clear that it was politically safer to incur heavy debts than to levy oppressive taxes and to seize private property.[5] And while the war in Scotland remained popular, Edward could rely on the military support of

---

[1] R. Twysden, *Historiae Anglicanae Scriptores Decem* (1652), pp. 1990, 2004-5 (William Thorn's chronicle).

[2] Powicke, *The Thirteenth Century*, pp. 702, 705.

[3] *A Lincolnshire Assize Roll for 1298*, ed. Thomson, pp. cxxiii-cxxvii and *passim*; *supra*, p. 129.

[4] *Statutes of the Realm*, i, pp. 147-9.   [5] *Supra*, pp. 221-2.

many of the magnates even though he could not offer prompt and satisfactory financial recompense for their services.

On one matter Edward was not prepared to compromise with his opponents. He would not dismiss or discipline his chief minister, Walter Langton. This man was an obvious target for attack. Charges brought against him by John de Lovetot at Rome did not relate to his conduct in office, but to his private life and his alleged ecclesiastical misdemeanours: simony, plurality and even doing homage to the devil. But at the Lincoln parliament, according to Langtoft, he was accused of overthrowing ancient customs and laws in the Exchequer, and his dismissal was requested. Edward I gave Langton his fullest support, even going so far as to exile his own son from court when the prince quarrelled with the Treasurer in 1305. In parliament in 1307 charges of champerty were brought against Langton by John Ferrers, and these were sufficiently well-founded for him to find it necessary to have royal letters of pardon made out.[1]

Earlier in the reign Edward had shown no reluctance to dismiss ministers. There had been the state trials following his return from Gascony in 1289, and in 1295 William March, the man held responsible for the seizure of private treasure in 1294, had been removed from office. Edward was not a man to take responsibility for unpopular actions if there was a convenient ministerial scapegoat. In one instance, the appointment of Isabella de Vescy to the custody of Bamburgh castle in 1304, the king certainly tried to ensure that he should not be held responsible. The letters were to be issued under the exchequer seal, and the king wrote to the Treasurer to emphasize that, although he was willing that Isabella should have the castle, it was not to be done at his command.[2] Langton was too valuable to Edward, and the opposition in the final years of the reign too weak, for him to be dismissed. And it does not appear that Edward himself suffered as much from Langton's unpopularity as might be expected. In the contemporary

---

[1] Beardwood, 'The Trial of Walter Langton', pp. 5-8; Johnstone, *Edward of Caernarvon*, pp. 97-8.

[2] M. C. Prestwich, 'Isabella de Vescy and the Custody of Bamburgh Castle', *B.I.H.R.*, xliv (1971), p. 149.

Song of Trailbaston, for example, the king was excepted from a curse on those responsible for the peace-keeping measures taken in 1304.[1]

Probably one reason why the opposition lacked real effectiveness in the last years of the reign was that the king was an old man. Unlike Edward III in his later years, Edward I was an imposing and frightening figure in his sixties. It obviously made good sense for potential opposition leaders to hold their fire until the old king died, and wait until his young, inexperienced and incompetent son was on the throne, before attempting to remedy the grievances that were building up in Edward I's later years.

It was an extremely difficult legacy that Edward I left to his son. There was an immense burden of debt, an unfinished war, and the constitutional arguments had hardly been satisfactorily concluded by the papal bull absolving the king from his oaths. But it has recently been argued by J. R. Maddicott that, 'there is no evidence that Edward II inherited the bitter feelings against the Crown which his father had so often aroused; and certainly there was very little continuity between the opposition parties of the two reigns.'[2] To test this view it will be necessary to examine the composition and policies of both administration and opposition in the early years of Edward II.

Changes in the personnel of the government made shortly after his accession declared Edward II's independence of his father. Walter Langton was dismissed and arrested. The men who had headed Edward's household as prince were given high office, with Walter Reynolds becoming Treasurer and William Melton, an enemy of Langton, Controller of the Wardrobe. John Droxford was transferred to the post of Chancellor of the Exchequer, while his office of Keeper of the Wardrobe went to the only one of Edward I's top officials who had the confidence of Edward II, John Benstead.[3] Ralph Baldock, the Chancellor, was replaced by

---

[1] *Anglo-Norman Political Songs*, ed. Aspin, p. 69. For these measures, see *infra*, p. 289.

[2] J. R. Maddicott, *Thomas of Lancaster, 1307–1322* (Oxford, 1970), p. 67.

[3] Tout, *Chapters*, ii, pp. 191–2; *The Place of Edward II in English History* (2nd ed., Manchester, 1936), pp. 70–2; *The Liber Epistolaris of Richard de Bury*, ed. N. Denholm-Young (Roxburgh Club, 1950), p. 503.

a former holder of the office, John Langton, who had been dismissed by Edward I in 1302.[1]

These new appointments, however, did not mean radical changes in policy, and instead of placating the opposition, the changes merely increased the numbers of the discontented. The new officials had been trained under the same system as the old, and the financial administration continued to be run on the same lines as under Edward I, with the Wardrobe playing a dominant rôle, and the Italian bankers much in evidence. There were no further attempts by the Exchequer to curb the Wardrobe, and the one new administrative development of the early years of Edward II was that the Chamber began to increase in importance, with some revenues from land reserved for its use.[2] This was hardly likely to be welcomed by the opposition, whose aim was to ensure that the revenues of the country were all paid directly into the Exchequer. Although he had no enthusiasm for it, Edward II could not abandon the war in Scotland, where successive failures did little to increase the credibility of the new government. And added to all the problems inherited from Edward I was one new one, that of the king's relationship with Piers Gaveston.

It did not take long for signs of discontent to appear once the old king was dead. The first indication of trouble is contained in a curious document issued at Boulogne shortly after the king's marriage there in January 1308. This was in the form of letters patent in the name of Antony Bek and eight others including Henry Lacy, John Botetourt and John of Berwick, all three councillors of Edward I. They stressed their loyalty to the crown, agreeing to amend those things that had been done contrary to the royal dignity, and significantly also promising to redress 'the oppressions which have been committed and are still daily being committed against the people'. This is taken by Maddicott as being directed solely against Gaveston,[3] but it seems a curiously

---

[1] Tout, *Chapters*, ii, p. 192, points to this appointment as indicating continuity with the old regime. But E. 101/368/18/63 makes it clear that Langton was removed from office rather than voluntarily resigning, and S.C. 1/27/213 indicates that he was very unsure of his standing with the king after 1302.

[2] Tout, *Chapters*, ii, pp. 314–20. [3] Maddicott, *Thomas of Lancaster*, p. 73.

oblique way of attacking the royal favourite. Taken in conjunction with the additional clause inserted in the oath sworn by the king at his coronation, in which he promised to observe 'the just laws and customs that the community of the realm shall have chosen', it looks as if political argument was ranging far beyond the immediate issue of the lavish grants that had been made to Gaveston, and his objectionable behaviour. It seems quite probable that the addition to the coronation oath was prompted by memories of the way in which Edward I had gone back on his concessions in 1305.[1]

The events of 1309 show that in some quarters redress of the familiar grievances against the crown—the failure to govern the country in accordance with the Great Charter, the abuse of purveyance, the jurisdiction of the steward and marshal of the household and the misuse of the privy seal—were more important than the Gaveston question. The Statute of Stamford, largely consisting of a reissue of the *Articuli Super Cartas* of 1300, dealt with these questions, and was the price that Edward II had to pay for the return of Gaveston to England after he had been exiled in the previous year.[2]

The full extent to which the thinking of the opposition was still dominated by the events of the later years of Edward I's reign can best be seen in the Ordinances of 1311. The old arguments were repeated and amplified. The baronage now claimed the right to interpret the Charters, with the assistance of the justices. Clauses relating to the Forest provided for a thorough purge of the Forest administration. A prohibition was placed on all prises, except those regarded as ancient and rightful. Letters under the privy seal were not to be used to delay or alter the course of common law actions. The steward and marshal of the household were to confine their jurisdiction to trespasses within the verge.

The Ordainers went much further than the opposition had done previously, and produced a very wide-ranging criticism of the government. The financial administration came under attack. It was stated that all the revenues of the country should be paid into

[1] M. McKisack, *The Fourteenth Century, 1307–1399* (Oxford, 1959), p. 6.
[2] *Statutes of the Realm*, i, pp. 154–6.

the Exchequer, which was an attack on the independence of the Wardrobe. Customs dues were not to be paid to the alien merchants, and the Frescobaldi were to be arrested and made to account for the money they had received in this way. The New Customs were abolished, and it was declared that the *Carta Mercatoria* issued in 1303 was contrary to Magna Carta and the franchise of London.

The attack on the jurisdiction of the marshal and steward of the household, first made in the *Articuli* of 1300, was almost certainly prompted by the way in which this household court had been used since about 1290 for the recording and enforcement of recognizances of debt. The Ordinances extended the attack on the way in which Edward I had made it easier for merchants to collect debts they were owed. No longer could they make use of the Exchequer Court, for only actions concerning the king and his ministers could be heard there. The workings of the Statute of Merchants were confined to cases between merchants. Not only did this prevent merchants from using this statute to collect debts owed to them by landowners, but it also prohibited one of the methods used by Walter Langton to build up his estates.

The clause in the Ordinances forbidding the king to leave the country or make war without the consent of the baronage was relevant to Edward II's campaign of 1310 in Scotland, but it seems likely that the events of 1297 were also in the minds of the Ordainers. One of the recruiting methods introduced by Edward I was criticized: the lavish grant of pardons and writs of protection. Changes in the monetary system were not to be made arbitrarily, but only after consultation. Presumably it was felt that insufficient consultation had taken place in 1299 and 1300 on this matter. Between 1302 and 1305 Edward I had held no full parliaments, probably because he wished to avoid the political arguments that such gatherings would have entailed. The Ordinances now stated that parliaments should be held once or twice a year.[1]

It is abundantly clear from this that the programme of the Ordainers looked back to the events and grievances of Edward I's

---

[1] *Select Cases in the Court of King's Bench under Edward I*, ed. G. O. Sayles, ii (Selden Soc., lvii, 1938), p. lxxxvii; *Statutes of the Realm*, i, pp. 157–67.

later years. Was this continuity of programme matched by a continuity of personnel, or is Maddicott correct in assuming that the only man who was deeply involved in both the crisis of 1297 and that of 1310–11 was Archbishop Winchelsey?[1]

Only a few of those involved in the crisis of 1297 can be clearly identified, while the composition of the opposition in 1300 and 1301 is virtually unknown. Equally, only the leaders of the movement against Edward II in his early years are specified by the sources. Despite the inadequacies of the evidence, it is clear that some of those active against Edward I also played a part in the opposition to his son. Robert FitzRoger was one of those who protested at the Exchequer in 1297 against the levy of the eighth, and he was one of the Ordainers elected in 1310.[2] John Lovel, a man closely associated with Roger Bigod, was another of the protesters of 1297, and he was one of the opposition leaders who in 1310 issued letters patent promising that the king's concessions to them would not be turned to his prejudice or disadvantage.[3] But Lovel and FitzRoger died in 1310. A further link is suggested by the fact that William Martin, one of those who refused to go to Gascony in 1295 until severely threatened with distraint, was one of the Ordainers.[4] Interestingly, another Ordainer was Hugh de Courtenay, who had been deprived of his rightful inheritance by Edward I in 1293.[5]

It seems, therefore, that there was some continuity of personnel as well as policy between the oppositions facing Edward I and Edward II. It should, however, be added that the hostility of the earls to Edward II was probably due in large part to their resentment of the position of Piers Gaveston, and the personal folly of the new king meant that the serious situation he inherited from Edward I was turned into a critical one. But it is abundantly evident that the crisis of 1310–11 was not simply the result of

[1] Maddicott, *Thomas of Lancaster*, pp. 68–9.
[2] *Supra*, p. 249; J. Conway Davies, *The Baronial Opposition to Edward II* (Cambridge, 1918), p. 361.
[3] *Ibid.*, p. 360; *C.C.R., 1302–7*, p. 480; *C.Ch.R., 1300–26*, pp. 31, 34; *C.C.R., 1307–13*, pp. 253, 291.
[4] *Supra*, p. 236, n. 2.   [5] *Supra*, p. 243.

Edward II's misgovernment, as the barons had initially indicated in their petition for the appointment of the Ordainers.[1] It is a considerable tribute to the power of the old king's personality that it was not until his son's reign that the most effective movement of political opposition since that of 1297 took place. And whereas the 1297 crisis was largely concerned with the expedients to which the crown had resorted in wartime, the crisis of the Ordinances produced a far fuller indictment of the system of government. Not all the aspects that came under attack were related to war. The way in which debt collection had been facilitated by Edward I had harmed the landowning classes. If parliament did not meet regularly they were deprived of one of the best opportunities they had of expressing their views. Such clauses in the Ordinances reflected the views of the author of the *Mirror of Justices* some twenty years earlier. But most of the criticisms against the administration, particularly the financial ones, were attacks on the way in which the government had responded to the pressures of wartime, and there is no doubt that the incessant demands for men, money and materials were the prime cause of the political problems of the last years of the reign of Edward I.

No discussion of the politics of this period would be complete without an examination of the character of the king himself. What sort of ruler was Edward I? Had he changed since the days when his lack of political wisdom and indifference to all save his own interests had imperilled the position of the crown in the crises of the late 1250s and 1260s? Had he learnt his political lessons and become a sound and sagacious statesman? The fickle young ruffian described by Matthew Paris and the author of the *Song of Lewes*[2] was described in *Fleta* as a ruler who, 'a friend of peace, a patron of charity, a maker of law, a son of power, does govern the people subject to his rule with never failing righteousness'.[3] On his death lavish eulogies of Edward were written, notably by John of London, who even praised him for the mercy and justice

---

[1] Conway Davies, *The Baronial Opposition to Edward II*, pp. 358–9.
[2] *Supra*, pp. 18–19.
[3] *Fleta*, ed. H. G. Richardson and G. O. Sayles, ii (Selden Soc., lxxii, 1955), p. 2.

he displayed towards the Welsh and Scots.[1] The dominant view of English historians, epitomized in the writings of Powicke, has been of Edward as a great organizer and law-maker, concerned above all to ascertain, define and enforce his legal rights. His unattractive traits are often explained in terms of a deterioration of character in his later years, when he was saddened by the death of his wife Eleanor, deprived of the advice of Robert Burnell, and frustrated by failure in Scotland.

Certainly Edward learnt much from his experiences in the late 1250s and 1260s. A conventional and conservative man, he came to understand the political value of instituting reforms and ensuring that government was efficiently conducted. He was aware of the value of propaganda and of making as wide an appeal as possible to his subjects, notably by summoning representatives to parliaments. He learnt that former opponents could turn into loyal supporters, as in the case of John d'Eyville, and so he displayed a wise moderation toward the lay magnates who opposed him in 1297.

The king, however, had not undergone a complete transformation since his youth. One of the more outstanding characteristics of his behaviour in the course of the crises of Heny III's reign had been his lack of regard for any promises that he made. His untrustworthiness had been shown by his initial refusal to swear to the Provisions of Oxford after he had agreed to accept the decisions of the twenty-four, his escape after his surrender at Gloucester in 1264, and his flight to join the Marchers in 1265 following the solemn assurances given on his release from close custody.[2] Edward revealed similar, though even less excusable, bad faith in his dealings with Llywelyn, as one minor incident clearly reveals. An English merchant, Robert of Leicester, complained that Llywelyn's men had seized his goods before the war of 1277. In defence the Welsh said that they had been taken as right of wreck. When complaint was made before the justice of Chester, goods belonging to Llywelyn in Chester were seized. Llywelyn

[1] *Chronicles of the Reigns of Edward I and II*, ed. Stubbs (Rolls Series, 1883), ii, pp. 3–21.
[2] *Supra*, pp. 20–4.

complained to Edward on several occasions, and the king denied knowledge or responsibility, although a letter from the justice makes it clear that the distraint was made on the king's express orders.[1] Edward was consistently determined to extend his rights and powers in Wales by all possible means, misinterpreting the Treaty of Aberconway and ignoring past precedents.

Edward can be accused of bad faith towards his Flemish allies when he abandoned them in 1297, but that was perhaps excusable in view of the weakness of his forces. In his relations with other countries, it was his treatment of the Scots that showed his unreliability most clearly. The way in which he went back on the promises he made during the negotiations that preceded the hearing of the Great Cause, insisting in particular on his right to hear appeals against judgements made by John Balliol, was criticized by Boniface VIII in *Scimus Fili*.[2] It is hardly surprising that in the Declaration of Arbroath of 1320 the Scots were to declare, with much justification, that Edward 'came in the guise of a friend and ally to invade them as an enemy'.[3] In his dealings with the Welsh and Scots Edward developed a technique of applying pressure so that he could ultimately intervene with some justification, and he was prepared to delay the use of force until he had compelled his opponents to make a move. His firm determination to have his own way despite all setbacks and obstacles, and his lack of sympathy and understanding for his opponents, are very clear. In the case of the French war, his determination was revealed as unthinking obstinacy, for despite his problems in Wales and Scotland he refused to change his plans, and even when faced by imminent civil war at home, set out on his Flemish campaign with totally inadequate forces.

The picture revealed by a study of Edward's external policies is of an obstinate, proud man, so confident in the rectitude of his own cause as to be prepared to use the most dubious methods to obtain his own ends, and capable on occasion of surprising folly.

---

[1] *The Welsh Assize Roll, 1277–1284*, ed. Conway Davies, pp. 55–6, 76–7.

[2] *Anglo-Scottish Relations, 1174–1328: Some Selected Documents*, ed. E. L. G. Stones (London, 1965), p. 84.

[3] Duncan, *The Nation of Scots and the Declaration of Arbroath (1320)*, p. 35.

Does this match with other evidence about Edward's character? It certainly accords with the methods he used to control the English nobility, the way in which he tried to have his way by putting pressure on them, attacking their franchises and threatening to collect debts, rather than by using a system of grants and rewards for services. His manipulation of the normal rules of inheritance, notably in the cases of Aveline de Forz and Isabella de Redvers, provide examples of the way in which he was prepared to use highly dubious forms of legal chicanery which can be set beside his cavalier attitude towards the agreements made at various times with the Welsh and Scots.[1] Another illustration of his bullying techniques is provided by the means he employed to obtain taxes from the clergy by threatening to place them out of his protection.[2]

On a more personal level, the unattractive aspects of the king's character are shown by the childish petulance he displayed at the siege of Stirling, when he refused to allow the garrison to surrender until his latest siege engine had been tried out on the castle. There was the savagery towards Bruce's sister Mary and the countess of Buchan, placed in cages hung from the walls of Roxburgh and Berwick.[3] An entry in a wardrobe book refers to the repair of a coronet belonging to his daughter Elizabeth which Edward had thrown into the fire, so testifying to the evil temper he could display on occasion. He is said to have torn out as much of his son's hair as he could, when understandably infuriated by the young man's infatuation with Piers Gaveston.[4]

Edward in maturity continued to display many of the characteristics of his youth. Alongside his clemency to John d'Eyville and his moderation towards Bigod and Bohun must be placed the way in which he never forgave the Londoners for their rôle in the Barons' Wars, and his lasting hostility towards the Ferrers family. It is not surprising that he carried through a bitter vendetta against William Wallace, and that he was never prepared to forgive Winchelsey. The king's interest in legal reform and sound govern-

---

[1] *Supra*, p. 243. [2] *Supra*, pp. 186–8.
[3] Barrow, *Robert Bruce*, pp. 181, 230.
[4] H. Johnstone, *Edward of Caernarvon*, pp. 123–4.

ment was not based on any intellectual foundations: the household accounts and inventories mention no books he is likely to have read, although the use of Arthurian legend in royal propaganda may reflect his personal interests. While he paid for the education of two nephews of one of his Gascon clerks at Oxford in 1290,[1] Edward was no patron of learning. The legal records do not suggest that he took any technical interest in the reforms instituted by such men as Hengham: Edward was no Henry II. He was capable of displaying a remarkable ignorance of the realities of administration. The two most notable examples of this both date from 1296, when he requested 60,000 infantry for the campaign in Scotland, and 100,000 quarters of grain for Gascony.[2] It is therefore perhaps not so surprising to find that in the last fifteen years of reign the reforming drive that had characterized the earlier years disappeared. Edward had instigated reform for reasons of policy rather than from personal conviction. His policies—and particularly the *Quo Warranto* enquiries—had perhaps not achieved all that he had hoped, and from the 1290s he was surrounded by different ministers and advisers.

Edward was not a brilliant, inspired ruler. But he had a strong personality, sometimes displayed in fits of temper, great determination and immense confidence. He made massive demands on his ministers and on his subjects as a result of his very considerable acquisitiveness. He aimed to achieve his conquests prudently, by means of a massive mobilization of all available resources, rather than by brilliant feats of generalship. Politically, Edward had undoubted ability, though here also he tended to rely on subduing his opponents with a show of force rather than the use of skill. Much was achieved in his reign, but at the same time he posed new problems for his successor: he left an uncompleted war in Scotland, a huge financial deficit, and an unresolved political and constitutional dispute.

[1] C. 47/4/4, ff. 41, 43. [2] *Supra*, pp. 94, 121.

XIII

THE SOCIAL CONSEQUENCES OF WAR

The effects of war upon government and politics in the reign of Edward I were very considerable. The need to organize the supply of men, money and materials prompted a development of administrative techniques. The costs of the campaigns made the crown increasingly dependent on the grant of taxation by its subjects represented in parliamentary assemblies. With the grant of the Ancient Custom in 1275, and the imposition of the *maltolt* in 1294, a pattern was set for the taxation of English trade in the rest of the middle ages. The demands made for military service, for money and for goods inevitably prompted political opposition, and as resources were not fully capable of meeting the immense requirements, the situation inherited by Edward II on his father's death was an uncomfortable one.

It would be wrong to express the changes that took place between 1272 and 1307 in terms of the replacement of a feudal by a national state; such generalizations obfuscate rather than illuminate the realities of the position. But the period was marked by aggressive government, both at home and externally, while at the same time the necessity for a measure of popular support was becoming increasingly evident in the later years of the reign. A clear contrast can be made between this period and the first twenty years of Edward's rule. In the age of Burnell and Hengham the government was in control of events, with much valuable work of legal reform being carried out, as well as the conquest of Wales and the reorganization of the Gascon administration. With

Burnell's death and Hengham's dismissal, and the unexpected combination of a war with Philip IV and revolts in Wales and Scotland, the period of crisis began, and the crown was unable to do more than react to events and circumstances dominated by war and its needs.

What were the wider effects of the wars of Edward I's reign, the impact upon society and the economy? During the Hundred Years War men like Hugh Calveley, Robert Knollys and John Chandos, having started from relatively obscure origins, gained wealth and reputation. Did they have counterparts under Edward I? In the late thirteenth and early fourteenth centuries war does not seem to have been a very important instrument in providing an impetus to social mobility. There were no great ransoms to be won in Wales and Scotland, while the English were not successful enough on the continent. Unlike their successors in the Hundred Years War, Edward I's captains had no opportunities of taking and holding castles on their own, and of ravaging a rich countryside. There is no evidence to suggest that men like John Kingston, constable of Edinburgh from 1298 until the end of the reign, or William de Felton, commander first at Beaumaris and then at Linlithgow, made great profits out of war. Of course there were some men, like Eustace de l'Hacche,[1] who rose in social status through their loyal service in the royal household. But Edward was not a king who believed in ruling by means of extensive patronage. He was an unfailing champion of the interests of his own family, and was in addition far more generous to foreigners than to his own English subjects. Amadeus of Savoy was granted 1,000 marks a year for ten years in 1299, when such a grant could least be afforded.[2] John of Brittany was also highly favoured, as was Otto de Grandson. It is interesting to see how much more the latter received than did Robert Tiptoft, even though they held equivalent posts as justiciars of North and West Wales respectively. No grants of lands to Tiptoft are recorded after 1272, though he did acquire estates from men such as John de Lovetot and Adam of Newmarket. Grandson received lavish estates from

[1] *Supra*, p. 45.
[2] C.P.R., 1292–1301, p. 425.

the king in Ireland, custody of the Channel Isles for life, and was given two manors and houses in London by the Queen Mother.[1]

The territorial gains that Edward's conquests yielded were not sufficient to enable new men to build up substantial estates. No new Marchers were established in Wales, and in the north it was representatives of established baronial families who profited from the opportunities of war. Robert Clifford moved his family seat from South Wales to Westmorland, Henry Percy from Hampshire to Alnwick, and the earl of Warwick bought Barnard Castle from the crown.[2] This was not a period of social stagnation, but it would be incorrect to argue that war was instrumental in bringing substantial wealth to new families. Indeed, it was more likely to serve as a cause of impoverishment, as Brian FitzAlan appreciated when he refused an important command in Scotland on the grounds that he could not afford it.[3] It was not the military leaders, but the officials and justices who were in the best position to build up fortunes in the service of Edward I, as is demonstrated by the startling ability of those judges found guilty in the state trials of the early 1290s to pay their fines, and also by the evidence of Walter Langton's riches.

The way in which the magnates were summoned to perform military service had important social implications. There was at this time no clearly defined peerage in England. No particular title was used to distinguish a baron from a knight; both were entitled *dominus* in the records, just like important royal clerks without a university education. There was a technical meaning to the word *baro*: a baron paid a relief of £100 up to 1297, 100 marks thereafter. In practice, however, the term was loosely used, and comprised such a range of individuals as to be ineffective as a method of defining a distinct social group. But Edward's methods of summoning the magnates for service in war and for attendance in parliament did contribute substantially to the development of a

---

[1] Kingsford, 'Sir Otho de Grandison', *T.R.H.S.*, 3rd ser., iii (1909), pp. 129–30; W. H. Waters, *The Edwardian Settlement of North Wales* (Cardiff, 1935), p. 10; *C.I.P.M.*, iii, pp. 368–72; *C.Ch.R., 1267–1300*, p. 147.

[2] Denholm-Young, *History and Heraldry*, pp. 101–2.

[3] Stevenson, *Documents*, ii, pp. 222–4.

real peerage in the fourteenth century. No single principle of selection can be identified. An analysis of the summonses to parliament between 1295 and 1297 shows a predominance of men from the Welsh and Scotch borders, but there was no consistency in the number or status of those summoned. Later, the list of men individually summoned for service in Scotland in 1299 was used as a basis for subsequent parliamentary writs of summons. The process has with some justification been described as 'slap-dash': one man who died in 1300 was summoned to parliament in 1304. Despite the undeniably haphazard element in selection, there is no doubt that the king wished to be advised in parliament by those who served him best in war. By the closing years of the reign a standard list had evolved of those entitled to individual summonses. The stage was set for the emergence of the parliamentary peerage of the fourteenth century.[1]

The methods of summoning the rest of the cavalry for war, and of consulting the shire and borough representatives in parliament, did not have so clear an effect on the process of social stratification. The use of distraint of knighthood, combined with the conscious glorification of knightly status in such ceremonies as the Round Tables and the Feast of the Swans doubtless helped to slow the decline in the number of knights in the country. But Edward's attempts to impose an obligation to perform military service on all possessing land of a specific value, irrespective of whether they were knights or not, marked a stage in the process by which the squires came to play an increasingly important rôle in society and in government. However, resistance to his plans meant that the class of forty-librate men did not come to form a clearly-defined, distinct social group. The increasingly regular attendance of representatives in parliament was not so much a means of increasing the prominence of the class of 'country gentry' as a recognition of their standing and importance in local administration. It was also a reflection of the king's need for money, as substantial direct taxes could only be obtained by consent.

It is hard to estimate what impact the mobilization of infantry

[1] *Supra*, p. 88; Jolliffe, *Constitutional History*, p. 348; J. E. Powell and K. Wallis, *The House of Lords in the Middle Ages* (London, 1968), pp. 223-31, 251-7.

forces had on the country. In a year such as 1298, it seems that some five per cent of the adult male population was probably called to arms, and in view of the policy of recruiting in certain areas only, the drain on manpower in the northern counties and in Wales must have been much greater than this figure. But England at this time was not an underpopulated country, and by harvest time, when all available labour was needed on the land, the majority of soldiers had normally returned from campaign. It has been suggested that serving in war provided an alternative to 'starving in the village',[1] but in view of the abundant evidence that men were prepared to pay substantial bribes to avoid service, and given their propensity to desert once recruited, this seems unlikely. The financial burden on a village of buying equipment and paying the expenses of the recruits going to the muster must have outweighed any possible benefits from wages brought back by soldiers returning from capaign.

Did royal financial policy have any significant social and economic results? It appears that the great ecclesiastical foundations were harder hit by taxation than lay landlords. This was only to be expected, as they did not contribute directly to the war effort in the way that the secular magnates did. Although the level of taxation was remarkably high, particularly in the later years of the reign, there is no evidence to suggest that through taxes any general redistribution of national wealth took place. It was, of course, a principle of the taxation on moveables that men should not be taxed on those goods which they needed for the maintenance of their position in society. The system of heavy export duties on wool, with light ones on cloth, was ultimately to be of great importance in transforming the pattern of English trade, but that this would happen was hardly evident in the reign of Edward I. Nor did the heavier customs dues paid by the alien merchants after 1303 have any results as yet. The government's reliance on the Italian merchants as providers of credit facilities did no more than recognize the rôle that these merchants had come to take in English mercantile finance, but it did also of course preclude the emergence of native-born government

[1] R. H. Hilton, *A Medieval Society* (London, 1966), p. 166.

financiers like Richard Lyons and the de la Pole family who came to prominence in the reign of Edward III.

In economic terms it would be impossible to argue that Edward I's wars benefited the country in the way that it has been suggested it profited from the Hundred Years War.[1] There were no appreciable gains from ransoms or from captured territory, and both in subsidies paid to the foreign allies and in wages paid to English troops in Flanders and Gascony, the war with Philip IV witnessed a substantial drain on English monetary resources. Trade suffered from the requisitioning of ships for the campaigns, and between 1294 and 1298 was very adversely affected by the French war and the seizures and taxation of wool. The methods used to provide the armies with food must have had their effect, the harshness and unpredictability of purveyance upsetting many calculations and so disturbing the running of many estates. The recruitment of men for the army may have had similar effects on occasion, but probably more serious was the call for skilled workmen to build the great Welsh castles, which must have had its effect on the building industry. The economic effects of taxation cannot be calculated precisely, though an increased burden must have made it more difficult for landlords, especially ecclesiastics, to raise the funds needed for the improvement of their estates. And it cannot be argued that the government spent the money it collected in taxes in such a way as to promote economic activity.

The later years of Edward I's reign witnessed an increasing breakdown in the maintenance of law and order, and while this can be partially explained in terms of the purge of the judicial bench on Edward's return from Gascony and of Burnell's death, it is apparent that the government's single-minded concentration on war after 1294 took all the impetus out of the drive to overhaul the legal system. The halting of the *Quo Warranto* enquiries was a direct result of the outbreak of war, and it is striking that after 1294 only two general eyres were held in the rest of the reign.[2] The neglect of legal matters was not because earlier achievements

---

[1] K. B. McFarlane, 'England and the Hundred Years' War', *Past and Present*, 22 (1962), pp. 3–13.
[2] Sutherland, *Quo Warranto Proceedings in the Reign of Edward I*, p. 30.

had left little more to be done, as the evidence makes very clear.

The situation in the first half of the reign had been far from perfect. The Statute of Winchester of 1285 had, according to the preamble, been prompted by the prevalence of violent crime and the difficulty of obtaining indictments.[1] The workings of justice were wide open to the use of bribery, corruption and influence, as the trials of the justices that began in 1289 showed. A particular problem was maintenance and champerty, or the support of a claimant in the courts by an influential man in return for a share in the profits of litigation. In 1293 a writ of conspiracy was introduced to provide a remedy for those who suffered from the power that sworn confederacies could exercise in the courts. In the following year the justices at York were told that 'there were so many and so influential maintainers of false plaints and champertors and conspirators leagued together to maintain any business whatsoever that justice and truth were completely choked'. In 1305 another set of justices in York wrote to say that no serious indictments had been brought before them, although they had private information to show that the truth was being deliberately concealed from them. Investigations revealed that a sworn confederacy had come to exercise a complete stranglehold over the city.[2]

Many scandalous stories are revealed by the records. In 1303 a group of men besieged and entered the town of Shrewsbury, assaulted the bailiffs and broke their staffs of office, installed men of their own choosing in their place, and intimidated the men of the town from trading. Two years later a private war was taking place between the Berkeleys and the burgesses of Bristol. The argument was over the question whether some of the burgesses owed suit of court to the Berkeleys, and in the course of the struggle it was alleged that the manor of Bedminster was sacked by the burgesses, that some of the burgesses were beaten up and thrown into a cesspit, and that the mayor of Bristol had had his legs broken by the Berkeleys' men. There was another private war between Thomas of Lancaster and the prior of Tutbury at

---

[1] Stubbs, *Select Charters*, p. 464.
[2] G. O. Sayles, 'The Dissolution of a Gild at York in 1306', *E.H.R.*, lv (1940), pp. 83-98.

about the same time. In another incident one of Winchelsey's houses was broken into, and the dean of Ospringe put on a horse, facing backwards and grasping its tail. He was paraded in this way through the township of Selling in Kent, and then cast into a filthy place. Many of the archbishop's muniments were destroyed.[1] Such evidence of disorder is not quantifiable, but the clear impression given by the records of a situation deteriorating rapidly in the years after the outbreak of war with France is confirmed by a royal ordinance of 1306 which spoke prophetically of the 'riots and outrages which are like the beginning of civil war'.[2]

One way in which the king's wars caused a worsening in the domestic situation is suggested by the frequency with which malcontents took advantage of the absence of lords on campaign to break down enclosures, trample crops, and drive off livestock. Earl Warenne, Humphrey de Bohun, William la Zouche and Walter Huntercombe, to name only a few, all suffered in this way in 1304.[3] But the main effect of the wars was that they diverted the government's attention from this problem. Under pressure from the opposition the *Articuli* provided that actions for conspiracy could be initiated by direct plaint before the justices as well as by writ, and the same document also contained a clause directed against maintenance by royal ministers. However, it was not until the war in Scotland appeared to be over that the crown really began to try to deal with the problem of law and order. In November 1304 special commissions were set up to restore order. They were known as Trailbaston enquiries, after the popular name for the gangs of men armed with staves who terrorized the countryside. The records of these commissioners are a sorry tale of murders and robbery, intimidation and violence.[4]

A popular song of the time tells of an ex-soldier, who had served the king loyally in Flanders, Gascony and Scotland;

[1] *C.P.R., 1301–7*, pp. 197, 271, 274–5, 347–8, 352–3, 356, 405–6.
[2] E. 159/79, m. 41d.
[3] *C.P.R., 1301–7*, pp. 278, 285.
[4] *Select Cases in the Court of King's Bench under Edward II*, ed. G. O. Sayles, iv (Selden Soc., lxxiv, 1957), pp. liii–lvii. The problem of law and order is also discussed by Denholm-Young, *History and Heraldry*, pp. 125–7.

persecuted by justices of Trailbaston, he was compelled to take refuge from the law in the greenwood.[1] It is very likely that returned soldiers did try to better themselves by the use of arms, and that in this way, too, Edward's wars encouraged domestic disorder. In addition, the technique adopted after 1294 of recruiting for the army by pardoning criminals assisted in the breakdown of law and order.[2]

In the early 1290s Edward I was in a position of great strength. He appeared to be controlling the internal tensions of the country skilfully, and to be confidently directing the expansive energies of a vigorous society. The great series of legislative statutes, the methods by which the aristocracy was manipulated, the victories in Wales and the king's triumph as the arbiter between the rival claimants to the throne of Scotland are impressive testimony. Governments better equipped than Edward's to calculate the costs and consequences of war have made worse mistakes, but in the later years of the reign the country suffered considerably as a result of the king's military involvements. In 1297 Edward's subjects represented themselves as oppressed, and the country as impoverished as a result of the way in which men, money and supplies had been raised for war. Ten years later, at the time of his death, Edward I left to the son he distrusted a government weakened by debt and a country threatened by disorder, with the problem of Scotland unresolved. Though it would be foolish to attribute all the gains and losses of Edward's reign to the consequences of war, they played a very large part in shaping the precarious fortunes of English society and government in a particularly formative period.

[1] *Anglo-Norman Political Songs*, ed. Aspin, pp. 69–73.
[2] *Supra*, pp. 104–5.

LIST OF SOURCES

A. MANUSCRIPT SOURCES

(i) *Public Record Office*

Chancery
C. 47 (Chancery Miscellanea)
C. 62 (Liberate Rolls)
C. 67 (Supplementary Patent Rolls)
C. 81 (Chancery Warrants)

Duchy of Lancaster
D.L. 29/1/2 (Account of the estates and household of Henry Lacy, earl of Lincoln, 1305)

Exchequer of Pleas
E. 13 (Plea Rolls)

Exchequer, King's Remembrancer
E. 101 (Accounts Various)
E. 122 (Customs Accounts)
E. 143 (Extents and Inquisitions)
E. 159 (Memoranda Rolls)
E. 163 (Miscellanea)
E. 179 (Subsidy Rolls)

Exchequer, Lord Treasurer's Remembrancer
E. 356 (Enrolled Customs Accounts)
E. 359 (Accounts of subsidies, aids, etc.)
E. 363 (Exannual Rolls)
E. 368 (Memoranda Rolls)
E. 372 (Pipe Rolls)

LIST OF SOURCES

Exchequer of Receipt
    E. 401 (Receipt Rolls)
    E. 403 (Issue Rolls)
    E. 404 (Warrants for Issue)
    E. 405/1 (Jornalia Rolls)
Justices Itinerant
    J.I. 1 (Assize Rolls)
Special Collections
    S.C. 1 (Ancient Correspondence)

(ii) *British Museum*
    Additional MSS
        7965 (Wardrobe account, 1297)
        7966a (Wardrobe account, 1301)
        8835 (Wardrobe account, 1304)
        17360 (Victualler's account at Berwick, 1303)
        35292 (Wardrobe journal, 1303–5)
        35292 (Wardrobe prests, 1304)
    Cottonian MSS
        Vesp. B. vii
        Vesp. B. xi (The Hagnaby chronicle)
        Nero D. vi
    Harleian MSS
        152 (Wardrobe prests, 1306)
        626 (Victualler's account at Berwick, 1303)

(iii) *Bodleian Library, Oxford*
    Dodsworth M.S, 70
    Queen's College MSS, Rolls, 181 (Account of the manor of Heckley, Hants, 1296)

B. PRINTED SOURCES

(i) *Chronicles*
    Annales Monastici, ed. H. R. Luard, i–iv (Rolls Series, 1864–9)
    Bartholomaei de Cotton, Historia Anglicana, ed. H. R. Luard (Rolls Series, 1859)

LIST OF SOURCES

Chronica Johannis de Oxenedes, ed. H. Ellis (Rolls Series, 1859)

The Chronicle of Bury St. Edmunds, 1212–1301, ed. A. Gransden (London, 1964)

The Chronicle of Pierre de Langtoft, ed. T. Wright, ii (Rolls Series, 1868)

The Chronicle of Walter of Guisborough, ed. H. Rothwell (Camden Society, 3rd series, lxxxix, 1957)

Chronicles of the Reigns of Edward I and Edward II, ed. W. Stubbs, i (Rolls Series, 1882)

Chronicon Abbatiae Rameseiensis, ed. W. D. Macray (Rolls Series, 1886)

Chronicon de Lanercost, ed. J. Stevenson (Maitland Club, Edinburgh, 1839)

Flores Historiarum, ed. H. R. Luard, iii (Rolls Series, 1890)

Historiae Anglicanae Scriptores Decem, ed. R. Twysden (London, 1652)

Matthaei Parisiensis, Chronica Majora, ed. H. R. Luard, v (Rolls Series, 1880)

Nicholai Triveti Annales, ed. T. Hog (London, 1845)

The Siege of Carlaverock, ed. N. H. Nicolas (London, 1828)

The Song of Lewes, ed. C. L. Kingsford (Oxford, 1890)

Willelmi Rishanger, Chronica et Annales, ed. H. T. Riley (Rolls Series, 1865)

(ii) *Published and Calendared Documents*

Acta Sanctorum, Octobris, ed. J. Bollandus, i (Paris, Rome, 1866)

Ancient Kalendars and Inventories of the Treasury of the Exchequer, ed. F. Palgrave (London, 1836)

Anglo-Norman Political Songs, ed. I. S. T. Aspin (Anglo-Norman Text Soc., 1953)

Anglo-Scottish Relations, 1174–1328: Some Selected Documents, ed. E. L. G. Stones (London, 1965)

LIST OF SOURCES

E. A. Bond, 'Extracts from the Liberate Rolls relative to Loans supplied by Italian Merchants in the thirteenth and fourteenth centuries', *Archaeologia*, xxviii (1840), pp. 207-326

Book of Prests of the King's Wardrobe for 1294-5, ed. E. B. Fryde (Oxford, 1962)

Calendar of Ancient Correspondence Concerning Wales, ed. J. G. Edwards (Cardiff, 1936)

Calendar of Chancery Warrants, 1244-1326

Calendar of Charter Rolls

Calendar of Close Rolls

Calendar of Documents relating to Scotland, ed. J. Bain, ii (Edinburgh, 1884)

Calendar of Fine Rolls

Calendar of Inquisitions Post Mortem

Calendar of Patent Rolls

Calendar of Various Chancery Rolls

Close Rolls, 1259-61

Councils and Synods with other Documents relating to the English Church, ii, ed. F. M. Powicke and C. R. Cheney (Oxford, 1964)

Documents illustrative of the History of Scotland, 1286-1306, ed. J. Stevenson (Edinburgh, 1870)

'Extracts from the Memoranda Rolls (L.T.R.) of the Exchequer:— 1. The Negotiations preceding the Confirmatio Cartarum (1297 a.d.)', *T.R.H.S.*, new series, iii (1886)

Fleta, ed. H. G. Richardson and G. O. Sayles, ii (Selden Soc., lxxii, 1955)

Formula Book of Legal Records, ed. H. Hall (Cambridge, 1909)

F. Funck-Brentano, 'Document pour servir à l'histoire des relations de la France avec l'Angleterre et l'Allemagne sous le règne de Philippe le Bel', *Revue Historique*, xxxix (1889)

Halmota Prioratus Dunelmensis, ed. W. H. Longstaffe and J. Booth (Surtees Society, lxxxii, 1889)

LIST OF SOURCES

Historical Manuscripts Commission, Sixth Report (London, 1877)

Historical Papers and Letters from the Northern Registers, ed. J. Raine (Rolls Series, 1873)

Liber Quotidianus Contrarotulatoris Garderobiae, ed. J. Nichols, introduction by J. Topham (Society of Antiquaries, 1787)

A Lincolnshire Assize Roll for 1298, ed. W. S. Thomson (Lincoln Record Society, xxxvi, 1944)

Les livres des comptes des Gallerani, ed. G. Bigwood and A. Grunzweig (Academie Royale de Belgique, Commission royale d'histoire, 1961–2).

B. D. Lyon, 'Un compte de l'échiquier relatif aux relations d'Edouard Ier d'Angleterre avec le duc Jean II de Brabant', *Bulletin de la commission royale d'histoire*, cxx (1955), pp. 67–93

Memoranda de Parliamento, 1305, ed. F. W. Maitland (Rolls Series, 1893)

Ministers' Accounts of the Earldom of Cornwall, 1296–1297, ed. L. Margaret Midgley (Camden Society, 3rd series, lxvi, 1942; lxvii, 1945)

The Mirror of Justices, ed. W. J. Whittaker, introduction by F. W. Maitland (Selden Society, vii, 1895)

Monumenta Germaniae Historica—Legum sectio iv. Constitutiones et Acta Publica Imperatorum et Regum, iii, 1273–1298, ed. J. Schwalm (Hanover, 1904)

Parliamentary Writs and Writs of Military Summons, ed. F. Palgrave, i (London, 1827)

Political Songs of England, from the reign of John to that of Edward II, ed. T. Wright (Camden Society, 1839)

Records of the Trial of Walter Langeton, Bishop of Coventry and Lichfield, 1307–1312, ed. A. Beardwood (Camden Society, 4th series, vi, 1969)

The Register of William Greenfield, Lord Archbishop of York, 1306–1315, ed. A. H. Thompson and W. Brown (Surtees Society, cxlv, 1931)

The Registers of John de Sandale and Rigaud de Asserio,

LIST OF SOURCES

Bishops of Winchester, 1316–1323, ed. F. J. Baigent (Hants Record Society, 1897)

Registrum Epistolarum Fratris Johannis Peckham, Archiepiscopi Cantuariensis, ed. C. T. Martin, ii (Rolls Series, 1884)

Registrum Ricardi de Swinfield, Episcopi Herefordensis, 1283–1317, ed. W. W. Capes (Canterbury and York Society, 1909)

Registrum Roberti de Winchelsey, Archiepiscopi Cantuariensis, 1294–1308, ed. R. Graham (Canterbury and York Society, 1952–56)

Registrum Simonis de Gandavo, Diocesis Saresbiriensis, A.D. 1297-1315, ed. C. T. Flower and M. C. B. Dawes (Canterbury and York Society, 1934)

Rôles Gascons, iii, ed. C. Bémont (Paris, 1906)

The Rolls and Registers of Bishop Oliver Sutton, 1280–1299, ed. Rosalind M. T. Hill (Lincoln Record Society, 1965)

Rotuli Parliamentorum, i (London, 1783)

T. Rymer, *Foedera*, I, ii (Rec. Comm. edn., 1816)

Scotland in 1298, ed. H. Gough (Paisley, 1888)

Select Cases before the King's Council 1243–1482, ed. I. S. Leadam and J. F. Baldwin (Selden Society, xxxv, 1918)

Select Cases in the Court of King's Bench under Edward I, ed. G. O. Sayles (Selden Society, lv, 1936; lvii, 1938; lviii, 1939)

Select Cases in the Exchequer of Pleas, ed. H. Jenkinson and Beryl E. R. Formoy (Selden Society, xlviii, 1932)

Select Charters, ed. W. Stubbs (9th ed., Oxford, 1913, reprinted 1962)

Select Pleas, Starrs and other Records, ed. J. M. Rigg (Selden Society, xv, 1902)

State Trials of the Reign of Edward the First, 1289–1293, ed. T. F. Tout and H. Johnstone (Camden Society, 3rd series, ix, 1906)

Statutes of the Realm, i (London, 1810)

LIST OF SOURCES

Treaty Rolls, i, ed. P. Chaplais (London, 1955)

J. de Sturler, 'Deux comptes enrôlés de Robert de Segre, receveur et agent payeur d'Edouard Ier, roi d'Angleterre, aux Pays-Bas (1294-1296)', *Bulletin de la commission royale d'histoire*, cxxv (1959)

Two 'Compoti' of the Lancashire and Cheshire manors of Henry de Lacy, Earl of Lincoln, ed. P. A. Lyons (Chetham Society, cxii, 1884)

The Welsh Assize Roll, 1277-1284, ed. J. Conway Davies (Cardiff, 1940)

Year Books, 3 Edward II, 1309-10, ed. F. W. Maitland (Selden Society, xx, 1905)

INDEX

Aberconway, Treaty of, 28, 279; see also Conway
Aberdeen, 54, 115–16
Abingdon (Berks.)
  abbot of, 79
  Richard of, 122, 162–4
Accrington (Lancs.), 63
Adolf of Nassau, king of Germany, 32, 172, 174, 197
Albrecht of Habsburg, king of Germany, 174
Alfonso III, king of Aragon, 202
Alfonso, son of Edward I, 239
Alnwick (Northumb.), 239, 284
Amersham, Walter of, 162–3
Amesbury priory (Wilts.), 65, 154
Amiens, Mise of, 23
Anglesey, 28–30, 114, 137, 141, 170, 172
Annandale (Dumfries), 36, 57, 62, 163, 238
Aquitaine, 30
Arbroath, Declaration of, 279
Archers, 74, 81, 105–9, 112
Arcy, Philip d', 58
Arran, Isle of, 147
Arthur, king of Britain: crowned, 242; exhumed, 241; revival, 241–3, 281

Articuli super Cartas (1300), 89, 114, 131, 265–6, 274–5, 289
Arundel,
  earls of, see FitzAlan
  Richard of, 63
Arwystli, cantref of, 28
Athol, John of Strathbogie, earl of (1284–1306), 77
Atrocities, 18, 53–4, 115, 241, 280
Aylesford, Peter of, 161, 171
Ayr, 146, 266

Bachelors, 20
Bacon, Walter, 146
Badlesmere, Bartholomew, 44, 60, 65, 77
Baldock, Ralph, bishop of London (1304–13), Chancellor (1307), 272
Ballardi, 206, 212, 217
Balliol, John, king of Scots, 33–4, 75, 241, 279
Bamburgh (Northumb.)
  castle, 271
  Robert of, 115
Bannockburn, battle of (1314), 35
Bar, count of, see John
Bardi, 208, 212
Bardolf, Hugh, 71

299

INDEX

Barnard Castle (Durham), 284
Barnwell (Cambs.), canon of, 194
Barons' Letter (1301), 190, 270
Barton, Robert de, 162
Barton-on-Humber (Lincs.), 125–126, 132
Bassetlaw, hundred of (Notts.), 101
Bath and Wells, bishops of, *see* Burnell, March
Bavent, Robert, 160
Bayonne (dép. Basses-Pyrenèes), 30, 142, 209, 213, 215
Beauchamp
    Walter, Steward of the Household (1289–1303), 44, 56, 60, 127
    Walter, junior, 44
    William, earl of Warwick (1268–98), 66, 117, 237, 284; in Wales, 30, 51, 71–3, 107, 159; in Scotland, 64, 73
Beaumaris castle (Anglesey), 13, 170–1, 283
Bedfordshire, 134
Bedminster (Som.), 288
Bedwin, Walter, 155, 158
Bek
    Antony, Keeper of Wardrobe (1274), bishop of Durham (1283–1311), 152, 262–3, 273; advice in 1294, 172; recruiting troops, 84; in Flanders, 77; administration of palatinate, 103, 235
    Thomas, Keeper of Wardrobe (1274–80), 152
Bellegarde, battle of (1297), 31, 109
Benedict IX, pope, 190

Benstead, John, Controller of Wardrobe (1295-1305), 154–155, 167, 267, 272
Benton, Ralph, 166
Bere castle (Merioneth), 29, 49, 111
Bereford, William, 104
Berkeley
    Maurice de, 64, 288
    Thomas de, 62, 64, 85, 251, 288
Berkhamsted (Herts.), 192
Berkshire, 134, 181
Berwick, John of, 59, 100, 256, 273
Berwick-on-Tweed, 36, 52, 58, 96, 115, 139–40, 280; capture (1296), 34, 148; garrison, 112, 164, 166; victualling, 122–4, 127, 134, 146, 159, 267
Besaunt, Adam, 130
Bevercotes, William of, 165
Beverley (Yorks.), 105, 132, 146
Bigod, Roger, earl of Norfolk (1270-1306), 115, 267, 276, 280; in Wales, 64, 72, 238; in Scotland, 64, 73, 263; debts, 206, 237, 269; entail of lands, 244-5, 269; opposition to Edward I, 39, 74–5, 77, 84–85, 248–52, 259–60, 262–4; retinue, 61–2, 64; *see also* Marshal
Bikenore
    Alexander de, 166
    Thomas de, 45, 58
Birmingham, Thomas de, 81
Bisset
    Hugh, lord of Antrim, 147
    John, 147, 168
Blackburnshire (Lancs.), 107

INDEX

Blanche, sister of Philip IV, 31
Blaye (dép. Gironde), 161
Bluntesdon, Henry de, 117
Bohun
    Humphrey de, earl of Hereford (1275–98), 23, 232, 264, 269, 280; in Wales, 30, 71–3; in Scotland, 73; opposition to Edward I, 39, 74–5, 77, 85, 248–52, 259–60, 262–3; quarrel with Gloucester, 111, 233–4, 249; *see also* Constable
    Humphrey de, earl of Hereford (1298–1322), 244, 264, 267, 289; in Scotland, 55, 99, 107, 110, 238; debts, 236; retinue, 62; *see also* Constable
    John de, 213
Bois, Richard du, 58
Bokland, John de, 59
Boniface VIII, pope, 153, 189–90, 270, 279
Boston (Lincs.), 153, 198
Botetourt, John, 57–8, 60, 273; in Scotland, 55, 57, naval commands, 57, 139–40, 142; retinue, 65, 160; wages, 160–161
Bothwell castle (Lanark), 36, 75, 238
Boulogne (dép. Pas-de-Calais), 273
Boulton, Adam of, 102
Bourg (dép. Gironde), 161
Brabant, duke of, *see* John
Brabazon, Roger, 100, 104
Braose, William de, 232, 234
Brecon, 15, 111
Briddeshale, Gilbert de, 58
Bridges, of boats, 29, 146–7, 177

Bridgwater (Som.), 117, 146
Bristol, 22–3, 26, 146, 182, 228, 288
Brittany, John of, earl of Richmond (1306–1334), 31, 37, 165, 283
Bromsgrove, Richard de, 122, 136, 145, 159
Bruce
    Mary, 280
    Robert, the Competitor, 33
    Robert, king of Scots, 239; deserts Scots (1302), 36; rising against Edward I (1306–1307), 37, 53–4, 56, 98–9, 147, 165
Brun, Richard le, 45, 100
Buchan, Isabel, countess of, 280
Buckinghamshire, 104, 134
Builth (Radnor), 29
    castle, 238
Bulmer (Yorks.), 133
Bures, Robert de, 45
Burgh, Richard de, earl of Ulster (1280–1325), 71, 74
Burgh-by-Sands (Cumb.), 37
Burnell, Robert, Chancellor (1274–1292), bishop of Bath and Wells (1275–92), 152, 282–3; influence, 230, 278, 287; loans, 213–14
Burton (Staffs.), abbot of, 188
Bury St. Edmunds (Suff.), chronicler of, 186

Caerlaverock castle (Dumfries), 36, 55, 74, 95; *see also* Song
Caernarvon, 160
    castle, 13, 29, 111, 170–1, 242
    county, 29

301

INDEX

Cambridge, 146
 Thomas of, 161-2
Cambridgeshire, 125, 133
Canterbury, 154, 228; see also St. Augustine's
 archbishops of, see Pecham, Winchelsey
 convocation of, 186, 188, 257-8
Cantilupe
 Thomas de, bishop of Hereford (1275-82), 202
 Walter, bishop of Worcester (1236-66), 23
 William de, 45, 56, 80
Cantrefs, the Four (Rhos, Rhufoniog, Dyffryn Clwyd, Tegeingl), 15, 28, 238
Cardigan, 26, 28, 49, 238
Carleton, William de, 212
Carlisle, 35-6, 52, 96; victualling, 122-4, 127, 164
 bishop of, see Halton
Carmarthen
 castle, 49
 county, 26, 28, 234, 238
Carta Mercatoria (1303), 268, 275
Castle-building, 13, 29, 111, 170-71, 242
 garrisons, 74, 111-2, 127, 164, 166
Casualties, 108, 110
Cavapenna, Arnold de, 46, 59
Centenars, 101-2, 106
Chamber, king's, 56, 252, 273
Chancery, 131, 151, 158, 178, 208
Chandos, Robert, 81
Charles
 Edward, 57
 William, Steward of the Household (1270-1), 44

Chaucecombe, Thomas, 60
Chaworth, Payn de, 50, 71
Cheshire, 71, 134
Chester, 24, 28-30, 50, 58, 94, 120, 157, 182, 278
Chesterton, Gilbert, 209
Chew, H. M., 67, 76
Chichester, bishop of, see Langton
Chroniclers, see Barnwell, Bury St. Edmunds, Cotton, Guisborough, Hagnaby, Langtoft, London, Paris
Cinque Ports, 182; dispute with Normans, 30, 137; naval service, 137, 141-8
Clare
 Bogo de, 234
 Gilbert de, earl of Gloucester (1262-95), 24, 117; in Wales, 29, 60, 72-3, 111, 232; entail of lands, 244; franchises, 225-7, 231; opposition to Edward I, 26-7, 274; quarrel with Hereford, 111, 233-4, 249
 Richard de, earl of Gloucester (1243-62), 20-1
 Thomas de, 44
Clement V, pope, 191, 269
Clericis Laicos (1296), 187, 256, 258
Clifford
 Robert, 49, 146, 162, 235, 284; in Scotland, 54, 57, 74, 163; retinue, 65
 Roger, 23, 42-3, 49, 119
Coastal defence, 139-41
Cobham, Henry de, 81, 158
Colchester, abbot of, 188
Collum, Saer de, 133

302

INDEX

Cologne, Siegfried, archbishop of, 172
Commiltones, 46–7
Commissions of array, 58, 99–101, 103–6
Comyn, John, 37, 53, 242
Confirmatio Cartarum (1297), 86, 129, 254–5, 260–1, 265–6, 268
Constable, office of, 70–2, 80, 249, 251, 263, 267; *see also* Bohun
Conway castle (Caernarvon), 13, 29–30, 111, 120, 136, 170
Corbridge (Northumb.), 241
Cornwall, 116, 134
  earls of, *see* Edmund, Gaveston, Richard
Corruption, 23, 59, 152–4, 167–9, 180–1, 193, 248, 284, 288
Cotenna, Coppuccio, 211
Cotton, Bartholomew, 101, 185, 257
Council, royal, 43, 60, 153, 202, 205, 211–12, 247, 253
Courtenay, Hugh, 79, 243, 276
Courtrai, battle of (1302), 32
Coventry and Lichfield, bishop of, *see* Langton
Cressingham, Hugh, 65, 100–1, 159, 163, 241
Criccieth castle (Caernarvon), 29, 111, 170
Crusade, 25–6, 42–4, 61, 169, 189–91
Cumberland, 103, 134, 162
Currency, 144, 194–5, 199–200, 202; *see also* Mints
Customs, *see* Taxation

Dafydd ap Gruffydd, brother of Llywelyn, 27–9, 43, 232, 240

Dalilegh, James, 122, 136, 165
Dalton
  Ralph, 167
  Richard, 126
Dartmouth (Devon), 183
Daubeny, Ralph, 50
Debts: royal, 205, 207, 210–13, 221–3, 270, 281; magnate, 76, 206, 236–7, 275, 277, 280; *see also* Loans, Subsidies
Deganwy (Denbigh), 15, 17, 19, 28, 114
Denholm-Young, N., 46, 68
Derby, earl of, *see* Ferrers
Derbyshire, 103, 116, 123, 132–3, 238
Desertion, 95–9, 107, 112–13, 144, 167, 242
Despenser, Hugh le, 64, 70, 77, 127, 256
De Tallagio non Concedendo (1297), 86, 129, 248–9, 254, 259–60
Devizes (Wilts.), 51, 72, 119
Devon, 134
Dirleton castle (E. Lothian), 36, 111
Dordrecht (Holland), 196–7
Dorset, 133, 136
Douglas, William, lord of, 109
Dover, 139
Droxford
  John, Keeper of Wardrobe (1295–1307), bishop of Bath and Wells (1309–1329), 95, 126–7, 135–6, 153–5, 220–1, 272; negotiates loans, 215–16; relations with colleagues, 154, 169; rewards, 167–8
  Roger, 154
Dryslwyn castle (Carms.), 111

Dublin, 124, 210
  archbishop of, *see* Hotham
Dumfries, 37
  castle, 36, 54, 122
Dunbar
  battle of (1296), 35, 109
  earl of, *see* Patrick
Dundrennan abbey (Kirkcudbright), 115
Dunfermline abbey (Fife), 70, 98
Dunstable (Beds.), 193
Dunwich (Suff.), 183
  Peter of, 122, 139, 146, 148
Durham
  bishop of, *see* Bek
  bishopric of, 185–6
  palatinate of, 103, 146, 235
  prior of, 235
Dyserth (Flint), 19

Easton, Thomas, 130
Edinburgh castle, 36, 111–12, 164, 167
Edmund, earl of Cornwall (1272–1300), 25, 65, 192, 214, 236; in Wales, 161; in Gascony, 76
Edmund, earl of Lancaster (1267–96), 17, 30–1, 73, 76, 141, 172, 245
Edward I: birth, 25–6; early career, 15 ff., 278; character, 26–7, 53, 272, 277 ff.; family policy, 244–5; queens, *see* Eleanor of Castile, Margaret; children, *see* Alfonso, Edward II, Elizabeth, Joan, Margaret, Mary, Botetourt; death, 37; policy toward church, 186–7, 190–1, 194, 256–9, 269; legislation, 229–231, 280–1, *see also* Statutes; policy toward magnates, 25, 225 ff., 243 ff., 280; attitude toward ministers, 153, 177–8, 203, 271; administration, *see* Chancery, Council, Exchequer, Taxation, Wardrobe; policy in Wales, 15, 19, 27 ff., 278–9, *see also* Wales; Gascony, *see* Gascony; relations with Philip IV, 30–2, 75, 138, 172–3; in Flanders, 35, 52, 77, 174, 279, *see also* Flanders; policy in Scotland, 32 ff., 53, 93–4, 96, 165, 279, *see also* Scotland; *see also* Crusade, Strategy, Tactics
Edward II: birth, 29; early career, 32, 86, 191, 250, 280; in Scotland, 53–4, 65, 99, 115, 164, 242, 266; dispute with Walter Langton, 168, 271–2; as king, 40, 61, 91, 118, 153, 165, 212, 221, 262, 272–7, 282
Edward III, 91, 113, 148, 166, 209, 245, 272, 287
Eleanor of Castile, first wife of Edward I, 30, 43, 239, 278
  of Provence, wife of Henry III, 22, 202, 284
Elizabeth, countess of Holland, subsequently countess of Hereford, daughter of Edward I, 46, 244, 280
Ely (Cambs.), 146, 239
  bishop of, *see* Kirkby
Enfield, Bartholomew de, 62
Eskdale (Cumb.), 100

INDEX

Essex, 125, 133, 136
Esti de Statu (1297), 258
Etton (Yorks.), 102
Everard, John, 130
Evesham, battle of (1265), 15, 17, 24–5, 109
Ewyas Lacy, liberty of, 234
Exchequer, 65, 70, 133, 161–3, 165, 172, 188, 197, 203, 213–215, 223, 239, 249, 251, 271; accounting methods, 151, 172, see also Tallies; administration of prises, 120–1, 128, 131; administration of taxes, 180–3, 187, 191, 252; Court, 130, 211, 275; estimates, 178–9, 201, 204; instructions to, 94, 120–1, 177–8, 183–4, 204, 220, 236, 240, 263; officials of, see Abingdon, Carleton, Langton, March, Ockham; relations with Italians, 206, 208, 210–212; relations with Wardrobe, 156–8, 210, 219–20, 222, 275; at York, 153, 181, 219
Exeter, 210
Eyville, John d', 24–5, 49, 278, 280

Falkirk (Stirling), 241
  battle of (1298), 35, 42, 55, 68–9, 94–5, 106, 109–10, 112
Falkirk Roll of Arms, 68–9, 83, 87
Farmer, D. L., 135
Faversham (Kent), abbot of, 188
Feast of the Swans (1306), 54, 285
Fees and robes, 42, 44–5, 47, 62–3
Felton, William, 45, 100, 283

Ferentino, Bartholomew de, 190
Fermbaud, Nicholas, 146
Ferre
  Guy, senior and junior, 44
  Reginald, 44
Ferrers
  John, 248, 251, 271, 280
  Robert, earl of Derby (1260–6), 25, 245, 248, 280
Feudal service, see Military service
Firth of Forth, 37, 137, 147, 177
FitzAlan
  Brian, 162, 243, 284
  Edmund, earl of Arundel (1306–26), 99
  Richard, earl of Arundel (1291–1302), 73, 76, 84, 236–7
FitzMarmaduke, John, 103
FitzOtto, Hugh, 44
FitzPayn, Robert, 71, 100, 142
FitzRoger, Robert, 100, 239, 249–251, 276
FitzWalter, Robert, 108, 117, 127
FitzWarin, Fulk, 250
FitzWilliam, Ralph, 162
Flanders, 196, 198, 207, 210; campaign in (1297), 32, 35, 52, 69, 77, 85–7, 93, 109, 115, 143, 174–5, 205, 245, 251–2; transport to, 142, 149, 197; victualling for, 117, 121
  count of, 32, 141, 173
Fleta, 277
Flint, 58, 111
  county of, 29
Florent of Hainault, prince of Achaea, 190
Floris V, count of Holland, 173

305

INDEX

Forest: administration, 19, 270, 274; boundaries, 264, 266–7; Charter, 39, 260, 264; Ordinance (1306), 270

Forz
    Aveline de, countess of Aumale, 126, 243, 280
    Isabella de, *see* Redvers

France, 20, 30–2, 75–7, 137–9, 141, 148–9, 171–2, 200, 208; *see also* Gascony, Philip IV, Ponthieu

Franche-Comté, league of nobles in, 173–4, 217

Franchises, 225–8, 231–5, 245, 280

Fraser, Simon, 59, 155, 241

Freeman, A. Z., 163

Frescobaldi, 183, 206, 209–12, 215–18, 221, 275
    Amerigo dei, 212
    Bertus dei, 212

Freville, Alexander, 45

Furness (Lancs.), 141
    abbot of, 188

Galleys, 138–9, 147

Galloway, 35–6, 107, 110, 145, 270

Gascons: debts to, 166, 221; in household, 45–6, 48; service in Britain, 108, 147; *see also* Merchants

Gascony: Edward I in, 29, 47, 51, 152–3, 161, 201–2; war in (1294–8), 31–2, 74–6, 93, 107–9, 115, 161–2, 171–2, 227; loans raised in, 208–9, 213, 215; recruiting for, 100–1, 104, 236, 251; revenues, 169; transport to, 137, 139, 141, 149; victualling for, 120–1, 131, 281

Gaveston
    Arnold de, 45
    Piers, earl of Cornwall (1307–1312), 45, 58, 274, 276, 280

Geneville, Geoffrey de, 44, 85, 251

Giffard, Godfrey, bishop of Worcester (1268–1302), 65

Giffard, John, 29, 238

Gillesland (Cumb.), 100

Gislingham, William of, 226–7

Glamorgan, 231–3

Glasgow, 36, 266

Glastonbury (Som.), 241
    abbot of, 188

Glentrool (Kirkcudbright), 55–6

Gloucester, 23, 278
    earls of, *see* Clare, Monthermer

Gloucestershire, 116, 133

Goldcliff (Mon.), prior of, 233

Gorges
    family, 44
    Ralph, 107

Got, Bertrand de, *see* Clement V

Gower (Glam.), 234–5

Grandson
    Otto de, 43–4, 49–50, 59, 189–190, 217, 283
    William de, 81

Gravesend, Richard, bishop of London (1280–1303), 188

Grey
    family, 44, 99
    Henry de, 236
    Reginald de, 100, 111, 236, 238, 250
    Simon de, 48

Grimsby (Lincs.), 139, 183

INDEX

Gruffydd ap Gwenwynwyn, 28
Guernsey, 217
Guisborough, Walter of, 93, 109, 244–5, 265

Hacche, Eustace de l', 45, 60, 283
Hagnaby (Lincs.), chronicle of, 90
Hales, Philip de, 143
Halesowen (Worcs.), 102
Halton (Ches.), 63
    John, bishop of Carlisle (1292–1324), 115, 168, 194, 258
Hampshire, 121, 125, 133, 135, 140, 169
Hansard, Robert, 103
Harlech castle (Merioneth), 13, 29, 111, 170
Hartlepool (Durham), 126, 146
Harwich (Essex), 139–40
Hastang, Robert, 74
Hastings, John, 70, 77, 239
Hausted, family, 45
Hauville, Elias de, 59
Havering, John de, 100, 186
Hawarden castle (Flint), 15, 43, 119
Hengham, Ralph, 203, 230, 281–3
Henry I, 41–2, 118
Henry II, 78, 83, 119, 177, 266, 281
Henry III, 16, 20–2, 26, 118, 225; relations with France, 14, 20–1, 148; relations with Wales, 15, 17, see also Wales; finances, 18, 179, 192, 205; household, 42, 44
Hereford, 232
    bishops of, see Cantilupe, Swinfield
    earls of, see Bohun

Herefordshire, 71, 116, 134, 187
Heron, Robert, 162
Hertfordshire, 125, 133, 136
Hobelars, 55, 74, 80, 112
Holderness (Yorks.), 105, 125–6, 245
Holland, counts of, see Floris, John
Holme (Cumb.), 160
Hood, Robert, 118
Horses, 41, 50, 52, 63, 69, 78, 81, 126–7, 136, 147, 257
Hospitallers, 182
Hotham, William de, archbishop of Dublin (1296–8), 77, 189
Houschold, royal: aliens, 43, 45–6, 48; bannerets, 42–3, 47, 50–2, 54; jurisdiction, 265, 274–5; knights, 38, 41 ff.; sergeants, 42, 45, 48, 56; squires, 44–8, 51, 56; stewards, see Beauchamp, Charles; see also Chamber, Wardrobe
Hudlestone, John de, 100
Hull, see Kingston-upon-Hull
Hundred Rolls, 225–6
Huntercombe, Walter, 100, 115, 289
Huntingdonshire, 125, 133
Hyde abbey (Hants), 154
Hythe (Kent), 140, 144

Indentures, 61–2, 74, 250
Inkpen, Roger, 64–5
Inverkip castle (Renfrew), 75
Ipswich (Suff.), 139
Ireland, 206, 284; revenues, 144, 216; ships from, 145, 147; supplies from, 119, 122, **124**,

INDEX

Ireland—*cont.*
  143; troops from, 74, 94–5, 113, 141, 143, 147, 166
Irvine (Ayr), 109
Isgenen, commote of, 238

Jaime, señor de Gerica, 46, 222
Jarrow (Durham), 146
Jedburgh castle, 36, 112, 164, 166
Jenkinson, H., 157
Jesmond, Adam of, 61
Jews, 169, 178, 186, 200–2
Joan of Acre, countess of Gloucester, daughter of Edward I, 244
John
  King, 14, 75, 172, 179, 236
  count of Bar, 141, 173
  count of Holland, 45
  II, duke of Brabant, 46, 172–3, 197

Keighley, Henry, 189, 266, 269
Kenilworth (Warws.), 24–5, 119
  Dictum of, 24–5
Kent, 104, 121, 134, 140
King's Lynn (Norf.), 125–6, 139–140, 183
Kingston, John de, 74, 283
Kingston-upon-Hull (Yorks.), 126, 198, 210, 228
Kintyre, 147
Kirkby, John, bishop of Ely (1286–90), 182, 213, 253–4
Kirkham (Yorks.), prior of, 133
Kirkintilloch castle (Dunbarton), 112, 164
Knavering (Norf.), 130
Knoville, Bogo de, 45, 58
Kyme, Simon de, 106, 135

Lacy
  Alice de, 244
  Henry de, earl of Lincoln (1272–1311), 72, 99, 117, 146, 262, 273; in Wales, 50, 64, 71–2, 238; in Gascony, 31, 76, 141, 209; in Scotland, 69, 75; entail of lands, 244; retinue, 62–5
Lancashire, 95, 99, 116, 134
Lancaster, earls of, *see* Edmund, Thomas
Lanercost priory (Cumb.), 37
Langford, John de, 81
Langley, Geoffrey of, 19
Langtoft, Peter, 85, 108, 155, 193, 241, 245, 271
Langton
  John, Chancellor (1292–1302), bishop of Chichester (1305–1337), 273
  Walter, Keeper of Wardrobe (1290–5), Treasurer (1295–1307), bishop of Coventry and Lichfield (1296–1321), 99, 136, 152–6, 220; character, 271; dismissal (1307), 168, 272; negotiates with localities, 89, 102, 126, 132; negotiates loan, 215; retinue, 77, 81; wealth, 168–9, 206, 284
Latimer
  William, 43–4, 57, 59
  William, junior, 43, 71
Launditch, hundred of (Norf.), 101
Leicester
  earl of, *see* Montfort
  Robert of, 278

INDEX

Leicestershire, 104, 134
Leominster, Hugh, 159–60
L'Estrange
   John, 44–5, 51
   Roger, 29, 44, 48–9, 58
Lewes, battle of (1264), 17, 24, 49, 277; *see also* Song
Leyburn
   Nicholas, 45, 62–3
   Robert, 63
   Roger, 23–4, 45, 50
   William, 45, 51, 57, 139, 142
Lincoln, 146
   bishop of, *see* Sutton
   earl of, *see* Lacy
   Roger of, 197
Lincolnshire, 106, 117, 121, 123, 125, 130, 132–3
Linlithgow castle (W. Lothian), 36, 74, 112, 164, 176, 283
L'Isle, Roger de, 159
Livingstone, Archibald, 74
Llandaff (Glam.), 233
Llandovery (Carms.), 238
Llywelyn
   the Great, prince of Gwynedd, 14
   ap Gruffydd, prince of Wales, 15, 22–3, 26–9, 228, 232, 238, 240, 278
Loans: forced, 154, 208; from Italians, 39, 205 ff.; from Louis IX, 169; from magnates and officials, 213–14; of victuals, 126, 132; *see also* Droxford, Gascony, Langton, Merchants
Lochmaben castle (Dumfries), 36, 122, 238
Lodden (Norf.), 62

London, 106, 138, 140, 186, 194, 211, 216, 268, 275, 285; Edward I's attitude toward, 25, 228; musters at (1297), 85–7, 251; Tower of, 22, 182; *see also* Parliament, St. Martin's le Grand, St. Paul's
   bishops of, *see* Baldock, Gravesend
   John of, 277
Londoners, 24–5, 214, 280
Loudoun Hill, battle of (1307), 37, 56
Louis IX, king of France, 21, 23, 169
Louth
   Richard of, 120
   William of, Keeper of Wardrobe (1280–90), 152, 155, 167–8
Lovel
   John, 60, 107, 117, 249–50, 276
   Nicholas, 133
Lovetot, John de, 271, 283
Ludlow, Laurence of, 197
Lusignan, Geoffrey de, 20
Lyme Regis (Dors.), 138, 183
Lynn, *see* King's Lynn

Mabinogion, 242
Maddicott, J.R., 272–3, 276
Maes Moydog, battle of (1295), 30, 51, 73, 107–8
Magna Carta, 118, 247–8, 252, 260, 274–5; reissues, 39, 262, 265; *see also* Confirmatio Cartarum
Maidstone, John de, 120
Malines (Mechelen, Belgium), 196

INDEX

Malory, Peter, 100
Maltolt, see Taxation
Manners, Baldwin, 65
Manton, Ralph, 36, 117, 155, 167, 218
March
 earls of, see Mortimer, Patrick
 William, Treasurer (1290-95), bishop of Bath and Wells (1293-1302), 75, 84, 139, 154-5, 167-8; reform of Exchequer under, 156, 223; dismissal, 214, 271
Marcher lords, Welsh, 15, 23, 28, 49-50, 231-5, 246, 250
Margaret
 second wife of Edward I, 31, 191
 duchess of Brabant, daughter of Edward I, 46, 139, 141
 of Norway, queen of Scots, 33
Marshal
 Court of, 167
 office of, 71, 79-80, 107, 249-251, 263, 267
 Richard, earl of Pembroke (1231-4), 17
Martin, William, 276
Mary, daughter of Edward I, 154
Maulay
 family, 45
 Peter, 61
Meaux abbey (Yorks.), 206, 228
Meirionydd (Merioneth), 17, 29
Melton, William, 272
Menai Straits, 137
Mendlesham (Suff.), 58
Merchants: grant of customs, 255, 268, see also Taxation; victualling, 116-17; Cahorsin, 169; Flemish, 209; Gascon, 183-4, 209, 213 215; German, 209; Italian, 39, 169, 183, 205 ff., 237, 273, 286; Spanish, 209; *see also* Ballardi, Bardi, Frescobaldi, Riccardi, Spini, Trade
Merton College, Oxford, 180
Methven, battle of (1306), 37, 54, 99
Military service: feudal, 67-70, 72, 74-6, 78 ff., 88-9, 251, 255, 267; paid, 50 ff., 67 ff., 159-61, 252; unpaid, 68 ff.; twenty- and forty-librate men, 83 ff., 252
Minster Lovell (Oxon.), 250
Mints, 194-5, 200, 210-11; *see also* Currency
Mirror of Justices, 203, 247-8, 277
Mohaut
 John de, 51, 161
 Robert de, 15, 77
Molis
 Nicholas de, 17
 Roger de, 117, 249
Monstraunces (1297), 85, 129, 234, 256, 259
Montague, Simon de, 57, 135
Montfort
 Eleanor de, 27-8
 Peter de, 23
 Simon de, earl of Leicester (1231-65), 16-24, 27
 Simon de, junior, 23-4
Montgomery, 26, 29-30, 234
 Peace of (1247), 26-7
Monthermer, Ralph de, earl of Gloucester *jure uxoris* (1297-1307), 37, 55-6, 73, 127, 263

INDEX

Mont Martin, Matthew de, 54
Montpellier, Richard of, 158
Moor, C., 48
Morham, family, 45
Morlais (Glam.), 111
Morris, J. E., 50, 62, 67–8, 75, 238
Mortimer
    Edmund, 234, 250
    Roger, earl of March (1328–1330), 44, 47
    Roger, 23, 29, 238
    William, 100–1
Murray, Andrew, 35

Nefyn (Caernarvon), 241
Newcastle-upon-Tyne, 94, 106, 122, 138–9, 154, 198, 210, 218, 228
Newmarket (Suff.), 101
    Adam of, 282
Nicholas IV, pope, 189
Nithsdale (Dumfries), 36, 55, 57
Norfolk, 122, 125, 133, 187
    earl of, *see* Bigod
Norham (Northumb.), 33
Northampton, 23, 83, 186, 253
Northamptonshire, 104, 117, 125, 134
Northumberland, 89, 102–3, 125, 132–3, 162, 239, 241, 250
Norwich, 146
Nottingham castle, 43, 182
Nottinghamshire, 103, 123, 132–133

Ockham, Nicholas de, 159
Oddingseles, family, 44
Ordainers, 211–12, 275–7
Orewin Bridge, battle of (1282), 29, 108, 232, 238

Orwell (Cambs.), 139
Oseney abbey (Oxon.), 154, 187
Ospringe (Kent), 289
Oswestry (Salop.), 73
Ottobuono, papal legate, 26
Oxford, 23, 281
    Provisions of, 20, 22, 278
Oxfordshire, 104, 134, 181

Pardons, 104–5, 239, 248, 290
Paris
    Matthew, 18–19, 42, 53, 277
    parlement of, 30–1
Parliament, 13, 60, 62, 247, 252–253, 275, 277, 284–5
    Oxford (1258), 19–20
    Westminster (1259), 21
    London (1260), 21
    London (1275), 255
    Gloucester (1278), 225
    Shrewsbury (1283), 240
    Westminster (1290), 227, 229
    Bury St. Edmunds (1296), 256
    Salisbury (1297), 77, 84, 252
    London (1299), 264
    London (1300), 184, 265
    Lincoln (1301), 90, 184, 190, 266, 267–8, 271
    Westminster (1302), 90
    Westminster (1305), 130, 132, 214, 221–2, 270
    Carlisle (1307), 60, 191
Pascual of Valencia, 46, 222
Patrick, earl of Dunbar and March (1290–1308), 74
Pauncefoot, Grimbald, 58
Paymasters, 102, 151, 157, 159 ff., 171, 173, 207

311

INDEX

Pecham, John, archbishop of Canterbury (1279–92), 240, 247, 259
Pembroke, earls of, see Marshal, Valence
Percy, Henry, 66, 68, 284; in Scotland, 60, 64–5, 70, 73; retinue, 65
Perth, 37, 54
Perton, William de, 182
Peverel, Robert, 81
Peytevin, Roger le, 239
Philip IV, king of France, 30–2, 34–5, 59, 75, 84, 137–8, 149, 172, 174, 199–200, 207–8, 240, 283, 287
Pittington (Durham), 104
Plukenet, Alan, 50, 161
Podio, Orlandino de, 206, 217
Pontefract (Yorks.), 107
Ponthieu, 119
Pontoise, John of, bishop of Winchester (1282–1304), 206
Poole (Dors.), 117, 146
Portsmouth, 63, 139, 146
Powicke, F. M., 33, 67, 214, 224, 278
M. R., 67
Prests, 54, 72, 76, 160–1
Prices: foodstuffs, 128, 135; wool, 198–9, 255
Prise, see Purveyance; Trade, wool
Propaganda, 32, 131, 240–2, 278
Protections, 62–5, 86, 237, 275
Purveyance, 114, 118 ff.; conflict over, 128–32, 255, 260, 265–266, 268, 274; cost, 120, 175
Pychard, Miles, 86

Quo Warranto, 225–8, 231, 235, 246, 281, 287; see also Statutes
Quotas of service, 67, 78 ff.

Ramsey (Hunts.), abbot of, 75, 194
Ravenser (Yorks.), 126, 139
Reading (Berks.), 247
abbey, 154
Redvers, Isabella de, countess of Aumale, 168, 230, 243, 280
Reynolds, Walter, archbishop of Canterbury (1313–27), 54, 164, 272
Rhuddlan castle (Flint), 58, 111
Rhys ap Maredudd, 29, 51, 161, 170
Riccardi, 161, 189, 205–9, 213, 215, 217–18, 254; in Wales, 165; receivers of taxes, 182; bankruptcy, 197
Richard, earl of Cornwall (1227–1272), 18, 21, 26
Richmond, earl of, see Brittany
Rioms, battle of (1295), 31, 107, 108
Rithre, William de, 71
Rivers, family, 44
Rogers, J. E. Thorold, 198
Roslin, battle of (1303), 36, 155
Rothwell, H., 90, 262, 265
Round Tables, 241, 285
Roxburgh, 162, 222
castle, 36, 74, 112, 163–4, 166–7, 280
Rue, William de, 55
Russel
Elias, 209
John, 45
William, 45
Rutland, 134

INDEX

St. Albans (Herts.), abbey, 168
St. Andrews (Fife), 159
St. Augustine's, Canterbury, abbot of, 81
St. Briavels (Gloucs.), 160
St. George, James of, 171
St. John, John, 55, 59, 99
St. Martin's le Grand, London, 167
St. Patrick's, Dublin, 168
St. Paul's, London, 21, 256, 264
St. Philibert, Hugh de, 82, 168
Salerno, Charles of, 201–2
Sandale, John, 135, 168; in Wales, 159; in Gascony, 161–2, 171–172; in Scotland, 54, 165
Savoy
    Amadeus of, 59, 283
    Peter of, 239
Scarborough (Yorks.), 117
Scimus Fili (1299), 270, 279
Scone, Stone of, 13, 35
Scotland, 13, 32 ff., 51 ff., 93 ff., 175–6; campaign of 1296, 34–5, 51, 74, 84, 92, 94, 105, 120, 204, 281; winter campaign of 1297–8, 64, 69–70, 73, 94; campaign of 1298, 35, 52, 66, 68–71, 87, 91, 94–5, 100, 113, 136, 160, 175, 262–3; winter campaign of 1299–1300, 95, 103, 235; campaign of 1300, 35–6, 52, 66, 69–70, 79–80, 88, 95–6, 110, 122, 143, 160, 175, 266; campaign of 1301, 36, 52–3, 89, 96–7, 164, 175, 266–7; campaign of 1303–4, 36–7, 52–3, 70–1, 80, 89, 97–8, 124–6, 146–7; campaigns of 1306–7, 37, 53–6, 62, 80, 89, 99, 147; revenues, 164–5; English policy toward, *see* Edward I; English officials in, *see* Amersham, Cressingham, John of Britanny, Sandale, Warenne
Scots
    raid England, 241
    kings of, *see* Balliol, Bruce
    queen of, *see* Margaret
Scutage, *see* Taxation
Seaford (Suss.), 146
Segrave
    John de, 45, 57, 61–2, 155, 249–250, 267
    Nicholas de, 45, 250
Segre, Robert de, 173
Selkirk
    castle, 36
    Forest, 57
Selling (Kent), 289
Sheffield, John de, 133
Sheriffs: recruiting cavalry, 84–86; recruiting infantry, 96, 99; purveyancing, 119 ff., 135–6; revenues collected by, 178, 180, 183, 219–20
Sherwood Forest, 106
Shrewsbury, 71, 84, 111, 116–17, 134, 167
Skinburness (Cumb.), 122, 145
Sledmere (Yorks.), 133
Somerset, 133, 136, 182
Song
    of Caerlaverock, 52, 65, 69–70, 83, 88
    of Lewes, 19, 177
    of Trailbaston, 272, 289–90
South Cave (Yorks.), 101

313

INDEX

Southampton, 134, 138, 146, 183, 197–8
God's House, 117, 193
Southwark, 19
Spaldington, Osbert de, 140
Spini, 206, 212, 216
Stafford, Edmund, 61
Staffordshire, 84, 111, 116–17, 134
Stapleton, John, 63
Statutes: Acton Burnell (1283), 254; *Circumspecte Agatis* (1286), 259; *De Finibus Levatis* (1299), 264; Jewry (1275) 202; Merchants (1285), 248, 275; *Quia Emptores* (1290), 229; *Quo Warranto* (1290), 227; Rhuddlan (1284), 204, 223; Stamford (1309), 274; Wales (1284), 29, 232; Westminster I (1275), 118, 225, 231, 260; Westminster II (1285), 230; Winchester (1285), 83, 288
Stewart, James the, 109
Stillingfleet, Nicholas de, 102
Stirling, 116, 153
  Bridge, battle of (1297), 35, 69, 163, 188, 241
  castle, 35–7, 53, 98, 106, 147, 165, 176, 180
Stopham, William, 62
Strategy: in Wales, 31, 170; against Philip IV, 31, 172; in Scotland, 52–3, 93, 98, 177–178; *see also* Castle-building, Flanders, Gascony, Scotland, Wales
Stratton, Adam, 65, 168, 203, 207
Stuteville, Nicholas de, 236

Subsidies, to foreign allies, 131, 172–4, 197, 202, 217
Suffolk, 122, 125, 133
Sulleye, family, 45
Summonses: cavalry, *see* Military service; infantry, 94 ff., *see also* Commissions of array; parliamentary, 60, 284–5
Surrey, 133, 181
  earls of, *see* Warenne
Sussex, 133
Sutherland, D. W., 225
Sutton, Oliver, bishop of Lincoln (1280–99), 187
Sweetheart abbey (Kirkcudbright), 115
Swinfield, Richard, bishop of Hereford (1283–1317), 81
Swyn (Belgium), 143

Tactics, 17, 36, 92, 107–13
Tallage, *see* Taxation
Tallies, Exchequer, 157–8, 160
Tany, Luke de, 29, 44
Tateshall, Robert de, 250
Tavistock (Devon), abbot of, 188
Taxation, 39, 228; arrears, 181–2, 188; assessment, 179–81, 185, 187, 192–3; assignment, 79–81, 185, 187; burden, 192–5, 286; clerical, 185 ff., 256–8, 280; collection, 180–2, 184, 187–8; customs, 178–9, 195–196, 213, 216, 222; *maltolt*, 196–9, 254–5; New Custom, 158, 199, 268, 254–5; exemptions, 180, 192–3, 212; feudal (aids, scutages), 80, 82, 132, 179, 184–5, 222, 269–70; of moveables, 18, 131, 179 ff.,

207, 239, 249, 252–4, 266, 269–70; negotiation, 184, 186–9, 195–6, 199, 252 ff.; papal, 169, 185, 189–91, 207; proposals (1294), 195; tallage, 18, 184–5, 222, 270

Temple
 the New (London), 22, 188
 knights of the, 182
 Master of the, 140
Teye, Walter de, 166
Thomas, earl of Lancaster (1298–1322), 99, 244–5, 288
Thornton, Gilbert of, 226–7
Three Castles (Grosmont, Skenfrith, White Castle), 23
Tiptoft, Robert, 42–3, 283; in Wales, 60, 72, 161, 213
Torold, Hugh, 115
Tournaments, 22, 242
Tout, T. F., 41, 151, 156–7
Towns, 145–6, 179, 228, 268
Trade, 149, 179, 196, 268, 286–7; wool, 196 ff., 205–6, 282, 286–7
Trailbaston, commissions of, 58, 289–90; *see also* Song
Transport, by sea, 117, 121–2, 134, 137, 141 ff., 173
Tregoz, family, 44
Trivet, Nicholas, 107–8
Turberville
 Hugh, 44, 49, 58
 Thomas, 44, 49, 59, 106, 140
Turmy, Robert, 251
Tutbury (Staffs.), prior of, 288
Tyes, Henry le, 249

Ulster, earl of, *see* Burgh

Vale Royal (Ches.), 259
Valence
 Aymer de, earl of Pembroke (1307–24), in Scotland, 37, 54, 56, 75, 99, 115, 222, 238; retinue, 55, 62, 64–5
 William de, earl of Pembroke (1247–96), 65
Veer, John de, 101
Verdun, Theobald de, 234
Vescy
 Isabella de, 271
 John de, 239
 William de, 76, 236
Veurne, battle of (1297), 31, 174
Vezzano, Geoffrey de, 217
Victuallers, 38, 122, 126, 151, 164–5
Vintenars, 106, 159

Wages: cavalry, 41, 69 ff., 160–1, 175; infantry, 41, 94, 97, 99, 102, 159, 175; in Gascony, 76, 93, 171; sailors', 141, 143, 147; in kind, 114, 127, 159; *see also* Paymasters
Wake, Baldwin, 236
Wales, 76, 240–2, 284, 286; Henry III's wars, 15, 17, 26, 114; campaign of 1277, 28, 48, 71, 79, 92, 111, 119, 170, 200, 238; campaign of 1282–1283, 28–9, 48, 51, 58, 60, 71, 79, 93, 103, 106, 108, 119–20, 156, 169–70, 238, 253; campaign of 1287, 29–30, 51, 61, 92–3, 111, 161, 170; campaign of 1294–5, 30, 51, 73, 93, 101, 106–8, 120, 157, 159, 170, 208, 219;

INDEX

Wales—*cont.*
  English policy in, *see* Henry III, Edward I; English officials in, *see* Abingdon, Grandson, Langley, Leominster, Tiptoft; *see also* Castle-building, Marcher lords
Wallace, William, 35, 37, 53, 241, 280
Wallingford (Berks.), 18, 49
Wardrobe, 151 ff.; bills and debentures, 158; as dormitory, 207; expenditure and receipts, 39, 156–8, 219–22; in Flanders, 69, 143; military administration, 39, 120, 155 ff.; officials, 152, *see also* Bedwin, Bek, Benstead, Droxford, Langton, Louth, Manton; records, 70, 73, 217, 221–2; relations with Exchequer, *see* Exchequer
  Great, 158–9, 212, 217
Warenne
  John de, earl of Surrey (1240–1304), 84, 226, 238, 262, 289; in Scotland, 35, 72–3, 94, 109, 162–3
  John de, earl of Surrey (1306–1347), 44, 47, 99
Warwick, earl of, *see* Beauchamp
Warwickshire, 104, 134
Weapons, 41, 101, 105–6, 109
  siege, 36, 53, 98, 147
Wearmouth (Durham), 146
Welles, Adam de, 45, 80
Welsh: infantry, 92–5, 97, 99–100, 109–10, 112, 183–4; bravery, 108; sexual habits, 240

Westminster, 26, 157; *see also* Parliament
  Abbey, 13, 222
Westmorland, 103, 134, 284
Weston, John de, 164
Wetwang, William of, 133
Weyland, Thomas de, 59, 203
Weymouth (Dors.), 146
Whitchurch (Heref.), 120
Wight, Isle of, 125, 134, 140, 245
Wigmore (Heref.), 234
Willard, J. F., 157
Wiltshire, 104, 121, 134
Winchelsea (Suss.), 77, 86, 140, 142
Winchelsey, Robert, archbishop of Canterbury (1294–1313), 190, 289; debts to crown, 237, 258; opposition to Edward I, 256–60, 269–70, 276, 280; attitude toward taxation, 187–8, 256–7
Winchester, bishop of, *see* Pontoise
Windsor (Berks.), 23, 154
Winterbourne, Walter, 217
Winton, Henry de, 202
Wolffe, B. P., 178
Worcester, bishops of, *see* Cantilupe, Giffard
Worcestershire, 116, 134
Workmen, 98, 110–111, 287
Wyre, Forest of (Worcs., Salop.), 234

Yarmouth (Norf.), 139–40, 142–143, 148, 198, 213
York, 84, 146, 153, 181, 186, 218–19, 228, 253, 268, 288
  convocation of, 186, 188